Las Tejanas

300 Years

T E R E S A   P A L O M O   A C O S T A

NUMBER TEN

Jack and Doris Smothers Series in Texas History, Life, and Culture

las
Tejanas
of History

AND RUTHE WINEGARTEN

University of Texas Press, Austin

LIBRARY OF CONGRESS CATALOGING-IN-PUBLICATION DATA

Acosta, Teresa Palomo.
    Las Tejanas : 300 years of history / Teresa Palomo Acosta and Ruthe Winegarten.— 1st ed.
        p.   cm.
Includes bibliographical references (p.   ) and index.
    ISBN 0-292-74710-1 (cloth : alk. paper)
    ISBN 0-292-70527-1 (pbk. : alk. paper)
    1. Mexican American women—Texas—History.   2. Mexican American women—Texas—Social conditions.   3. Texas—History.   4. Texas—Ethnic relations.   I. Winegarten, Ruthe.   II. Title.
    F395.M5 A75   2003
    976.4004'6872—dc21

                                                            2002009360

**WITH RESPECT FOR AND IN MEMORY OF
THE THREE JOVITAS**

Jovita Idar (1885–1946)
FEMINIST, JOURNALIST, TEACHER

Jovita Pérez (1897–1970)
PIONEER BUSINESSWOMAN, COMMUNITY LEADER

Jovita González de Mireles (1904–1983)
FOLKLORIST, HISTORIAN, WRITER

AND FOR THE FUTURE TEJANAS

Contents

BY CYNTHIA E. OROZCO

Foreword

When the famous Mexican American singer-star Selena Quintanilla Pérez died in 1995, she had achieved widespread national and international fame and several books were written about her. Yet no other Tejana has received such interest and attention. Despite the rich history of Selena and other Tejanas, both famous and ordinary, scholars have ignored the history of Mexican American women in Texas. Indeed, the Tejanos, people of mixed Spanish/Mexican/Indian/African descent, were largely unknown to non-Texans until Selena died. Even less is known about Tejanas.

This book, by authors Teresa Palomo Acosta and Ruthe Winegarten, is the first history of Mexican descent women in Texas. Several generations of Mexican American women historians, both professional and untrained, wrote histories before this book, but only now in the new millennium has a book-length survey been written. "Generations" here refers to a specific period or era in history in which social, economic, and political conditions created a cohort experience.

Perhaps one of the first Tejanas to write Tejano history was Adina Emilia De Zavala, the granddaughter of statesman Lorenzo de Zavala. In the late nineteenth century, it was clear to De Zavala that Texas historians were already ignoring and erasing the Spanish record. It is significant that she was a founding member of the Texas State Historical Association in 1897, though only in recent years has her historical work been recovered. Because of her class privilege and her mother's European American heritage, she had access to an education that few other Tejanas had. Few women historians existed in the United States in the nineteenth century. Still, like most women of her time, she was not conscious of women's history.

A second generation of Tejana historians appeared in the 1930s, with Jovita González (later Jovita González de Mireles) as the most significant member of this group. Not only was González the first Mexican American in Texas to write essays in English, she was perhaps the first Tejana to obtain a master's degree in history before the 1970s. Like De Zavala, González used her middle-class privilege to assert racial/ethnic interests—the need to claim a Tejano and Tejana past. Another member of this generation was María Elena Zamora O'Shea of the Rio Grande Valley.

All of these women were unique. Mexican American women who were high school and college graduates were few. Among them was middle-class Emma Tenayuca, who asserted her voice as a historian in the 1930s. Scholars have largely cast her as a labor leader, but personal visits with Tenayuca, correspondence with her, and a reading of her co-authored essay "The Mexican Question," written during the Depression, reveal that she was an intellectual with a command of international history and politics. A communist who left Texas in fear for her life, she attended college in California.

Chicano Studies, which emerged in the late 1960s, and even Chicana Studies, which was emerging in the 1980s and came to fruition in the 1990s, failed Tenayuca. In 1984, when Chicana feminists demanded the first conference on Chicana Studies, she was finally recognized by the National Association for Chicano Studies. From 1984 to Tenayuca's death in 2000, Chicano/Chicana Studies intellectuals used Tenayuca as a symbol of a Chicana radical past. However, we failed her in not getting her story out before her death.

A third generation of Tejana historians appeared in the 1970s. This generation included historians molded by the burgeoning field of women's history. It included Martha P. Cotera and Evey Chapa. Cotera authored the first Chicana history book, *Diosa y Hembra: The History and Heritage of Chicanas in the U.S.,* which constituted the first survey of Chicana history. Cotera's pioneering work inspired the few Tejanas at Texas colleges and universities with the awareness that we had a past specific to our ethnicity, race, region, and gender. Her work taught my generation and later generations that women like Jovita González existed. Likewise, Chicana writers and poets Carmen Tafolla, Inés Hernández, and Teresa Palomo Acosta had also begun to write about women's past.

In the 1980s a fourth generation began to emerge and included the first generation of professionally trained historians. These included Tejanas Irene Ledesma, Yolanda Romero, Cynthia Orozco, and Emma Pérez, all of whom finished their doctorates in the early 1990s. Three of these Tejanas left Texas to find a more supportive environment for graduate study, making Romero the first Tejana to obtain a Ph.D. in U.S. history in Texas. At this writing, no other Tejana has earned a doctorate in U.S. history from a Texas college. These historians differed from earlier generations in that they had professional training and their training was in the new fields of Chicano history and women's history, both of which had become available to Tejanas in the late 1960s and early 1970s. Unfortunately, our colleague Ledesma died early in her career.

The *New Handbook of Texas*, published in 1996, included this generation's work. Mainstream Texas historians began to accept Tejano history's legitimacy in the late 1980s. In 1988 the Texas State Historical Association (TSHA) decided to hire several research associates to write encyclopedic entries for the *Handbook*. Cuban American María-Cristina García, Orozco, and Palomo Acosta were hired to conduct research and write entries. While they were not instructed to write about women, each decided to write Tejanas into history. Of particular note, García contributed to our knowledge of Houston Hispanas, Acosta enriched our knowledge of women and the arts, and Orozco wrote the survey of the Tejana past. Ironically, the inclusion of Tejanas as women was more of an accident than planned inclusion on the part of TSHA.

Throughout the 1980s and 1990s, Chicana history in the United States remained undervalued and underrecognized, though some significant advances were made.

Yolanda Chávez Leyva of El Paso received her doctorate from Arizona in the late 1990s. In the late 1990s, European American women historians at the University of Texas at San Antonio (UTSA) came to realize the need for more Tejana history. I taught at UTSA and helped to train then graduate student Gabriela González of Laredo. UTSA also provided initial support to Ruthe Winegarten, an established European American woman historian and expert on Texas women, and Leyva to develop a book about Tejanas. Leyva, who worked at UTSA later, left the project to attend other responsibilities. Then Acosta, fiercely dedicated to women and their work, joined Winegarten.

Winegarten has also been a tenacious woman warrior historian. She is a pioneer in Texas women's history, having authored the most books on the topic. She emerged during Cotera's generation and has dedicated her life to writing Texas women's history. Her work on African American women in Texas was path-breaking. Finally, she committed herself to balancing the focus of Texas women's history by writing about women of Mexican descent.

Likewise, Acosta has contributed to writing about history and culture. She has worked as a journalist, educator, poet, teacher, researcher, university administrator, literacy advocate, and historian. A first-rate poet, her book *Nile & Other Poems* shows her reading of Tejana history through the discipline of poetry. She is perhaps the most inspiring promoter of Tejanas.

Most Tejana history has been written in spite of Texas institutions, history departments, Chicano studies, and women's studies. All the major historical institutions have neglected Tejanas, despite the fact that women are the majority and Hispanics are the major ethnic group/race in Texas. Historical societies, museums, and universities need to provide funds to advance Tejana history. Moreover, schools also need to foster serious integration of Tejanas into the curriculum.

This book gives voice to both individual Tejanas and Tejanas as a group—women about whom only a few historians have known. Interestingly enough, both Acosta and Winegarten have continued the work of Martha P. Cotera, their peer. In doing so, they have completed a circle of life.

CYNTHIA E. OROZCO

Acknowledgments

We wish to acknowledge the numerous individuals who have assisted us in the completion of this book.

We sincerely thank four gracious and rare women in McGregor, Texas, who kindly consented to be interviewed about their lives in the cotton belt during the 1930s: Sabina Palomo Acosta, Lucía Alderete Anaya, Juanita Palomo Campos, and María Quiroz de León. Their stories made the experiences of Mexican origin women in rural Texas during the Great Depression come alive. Señora de León died as this book was being completed. We are saddened by her loss. May she rest in peace.

Many individuals read chapter drafts of this book. We are grateful for their time and talent. They include Adán Benavides Jr., Lucy Cárdenas, Carolina Castillo Crimm, Arnoldo De León, Gabriela González, Nancy Baker Jones, Juanita Luna Lawhn, Cynthia E. Orozco, Bárbara J. Robles, Marc Sanders, and Rebecca Sharpless. We thank Lucy Cárdenas and Gabriela González for sharing their materials on women in Laredo business and politics. We are greatly indebted to Cynthia E. Orozco, whose vast knowledge about Tejana history helped guide our efforts.

We are grateful to the following individuals, who provided financial support for our work. Nancy Baker Jones, in gratitude for the women's history research staff at the *New Handbook of Texas* revision project; David Richards; Sherry A. Smith; Ellen C. Temple; and Genevieve Vaughan. We received grants and institutional support from the Austin

Writers League in cooperation with the Texas Commission on the Arts; the Center for the Study of Women and Gender at the University of Texas at San Antonio; the Dougherty Foundation; the Nettie Lee Benson Latin American Collection at the University of Texas at Austin; the Summerlee Foundation; the Texas Federation of Women's Clubs; the Texas State Historical Association; the University of Texas Press; and the Woman's Collection, Texas Woman's University.

We express our deepest gratitude and appreciation for the very valuable assistance provided to us by librarians and archivists across the state.

Other individuals who provided important research and computer assistance and moral support include Vivian Castleberry, Henry J. Hauschild, Cindy Huyser, Sharon Kahn, Yolanda Chávez Leyva, Pauline López, Janice McIver, Virginia Raymond, Delmer Rogers, Marc Sanders, Linda Schott, Charles Spurlin, Frieda Werden, Martha Wilson, Debbie Winegarten, and Carmen Zacarías. We especially offer our appreciation to Theresa J. May, assistant director and editor-in-chief of the University of Texas Press, for her support and her keen interest in publishing this book.

Introduction

OVERVIEW

This book is the first general history of Tejanas, women of Spanish-Mexican origin in Texas. Our account covers their history in the state from 1700 to 2000.

We believe that this book is important and timely for two major reasons. First, the population of Mexican Americans in Texas has grown dramatically in the last decade, generating the need for such a publication. Second, a number of Tejana and other scholars have added greatly to our understanding of Mexican American women's history in the state through their work on the *New Handbook of Texas* (Texas State Historical Association, 1996). Their efforts resulted in significant *Handbook* articles on Tejanas in the arts, business, civil rights, community building, education, feminism, labor, politics, religion, and other areas. These researchers' contributions to the *New Handbook of Texas* provided the first substantial coverage of Mexican American women's history in any publication on Texas history published to that date.

A SURVEY OF TEJANAS OVER THREE HUNDRED YEARS

In writing this book, our first concern was to create a broad outline of Tejanas rather than to develop a theoretical analysis or to discuss their relationship with others in the state—women of other ethnic or racial groups, for instance. We have thus provided the reader a general survey of Mexican origin women, placing them within the framework of Tejano history. We have also included a time line that provides a general context for understanding Tejana history.

In our account we lay out the rich tapestry of Tejana history across three centuries. We show that Mexican origin women have played central roles as pioneers in the settlement of the land that became Texas. We describe their work as community builders and leaders; as founders of organizations; and as innovative educators, astute businesswomen, experienced professionals, committed trade unionists, and groundbreaking artists.

Our book is thus partly a celebration of Tejanas' notable contributions from 1700 to 2000, partly an account of their economic, human, and political struggles and triumphs in the state.

TERMINOLOGY

In general we use the term "Tejana" to define the woman who is our subject, but we have also used related terms, including "Chicana," "mestiza," "Mexican," "Mexicana," "Mexican origin (or Mexican descent) woman," "Mexican American," and "Texas Mexican." We believe that these terms reflect more fully the cultural, ethnic, and racial heritage of the women.

We recognize that some in the Mexican origin community in the state have more recently adopted the term "Hispanic" to identify themselves, and we acknowledge that the government and mass media have also adopted the term to refer generally to Spanish-speaking people in the United States. The terms "Latina" and "Latino" have also gained wider usage recently. We have used the terms "Hispanic," "Latina," and "Latino" whenever they are part of an organization's name, when they are self-determined identifiers, or when public records depict Mexican Americans as Hispanics, Latinas, and Latinos.

FUTURE RESEARCH AND PUBLICATIONS

We anticipate that our book will encourage others to write new interpretations of Mexican American women's history, books and articles that will add in-depth insights to the numerous topics that we cover in a general manner. For instance, accounts that discuss women in the colonial era and the nineteenth century can fill in gaps in Tejana history from those periods. Likewise, accounts that cover Texas Mexican women's roles in the Mexican Revolution are also greatly needed. The area of labor history can benefit from new ideas, and women's roles as business and professional leaders offer a fertile terrain for scholars. Moreover, Mexican American female politicians, including those involved in the Raza Unida Party from the late 1960s to the mid-1970s, deserve both an oral history project and a book. In addition, much-needed scholarship on native women in the state will bring a greater understanding of the indigenous roots of Mexican American women.

The extraordinary output of Tejana musicians, stage performers, writers, and visual artists must also be excavated. Numerous publications from various periods can provide the researcher valuable materials on the artistic endeavors of Mexican American women in Texas. For example, literary anthologies and journals from the 1970s await scholars willing to investigate Tejanas' literary output during the Chicano literary renaissance. Moreover, we urge scholars to write biographies about Tejanas in Austin, Dallas, El Paso, Houston, Laredo, the Rio Grande Valley, San Antonio, and other locations. There is virtually no region of the state where a wellspring of materials cannot be plumbed.

We look forward to future scholars' work in expanding and challenging what we have written, for the more that is written about Tejanas, the better our understanding of our entire state's history. Some of these future scholars are still students in our public schools and universities as this book is completed. We support their entry into university teaching, archival research, and public service in the interest of women's history.

THE ROLE OF EDUCATORS AND TEJANA HISTORY

We likewise envision that this book will foster the study of Mexican American women's history in the state's public schools, where Mexican origin students will shortly become the majority. We believe that young Mexican American female students in particular should be given the opportunity to learn about their predecessors' legacy to them. We therefore urge educators to support the study of Tejana history and to reward it academically. We likewise call on public institutions to create programs that prize Tejana history and bring it before the general public.

Finally, we invite our readers to learn about Tejanas, women whose past and future history is firmly rooted in the place known as Texas.

TERESA PALOMO ACOSTA
RUTHE WINEGARTEN

Las Tejanas

CHAPTER ONE

Native Women, Mestizas, and Colonists

Native American parents and Spanish godparents participate in the baptism of a baby in San Fernando Church, San Antonio, in 1740. Drawing by José Cisneros. Courtesy University of Texas Institute of Texan Cultures.

"Our ancestors were here long before the Anglo-Americans. It is they who are the newcomers."[1] With these words, María L. de Hernández, a Tejana leader, claimed for her people their long history in the land that became Texas.

In the keynote speech at a state convention of the Raza Unida Party, delivered more than 250 years after Spanish-Mexican women entered the recorded history of present-day Texas, Hernández called on Mexican Americans to recover their indigenous and mestizo (Spanish / Mexican / Indian / African) heritages. When Hernández uttered these words on July 12, 1970, she declared to her fellow delegates that Tejanas' history is linked to people whose ancestral homes lay in the American Southwest: Native American women residing in the northern frontier of New Spain who intermarried with Spanish and mestizo explorers and soldiers, and women of indigenous, Spanish-Mexican, and African heritage. Beginning in the 1700s, many of these women "undertook the arduous journey north from Mexico to colonize the area" that became Texas.[2] With their entry into this region in the eighteenth century, all of these women contributed to the institutions that Spain used to settle present-day Texas: expeditions, missions, presidios, and *ranchos*. Through their participation in the colonizing efforts, women helped establish the first major Tejano settlements of San Antonio, Goliad, Nacogdoches, Laredo, and Victoria.[3]

Native women in the northern frontier contributed to the *mestizaje* (the mixing of racial ancestry) of Texas Mexicans by marrying with Spanish and mestizo soldiers or colonists and giving birth to children of native, European, and black ancestry. Most Texas Mexicans spring from a mixture of indigenous, European, and African heritages.

Some early Tejanas who arrived in the northern provinces of New Spain received land grants as widows or as single women. They became quite wealthy and influential in their communities. However, most of the early Tejanas were poor women who were part of the mestiza population who lived and worked in the missions, presidios, and *ranchos*.[4]

ANGELINA: GUIDE AND TRANSLATOR

A learned Indian woman who . . . served as an interpreter.[5]

FATHER ISIDRO FELIX DE ESPINOSA

Angelina, probably a member of the Caddo nation, is the only woman for whom a Texas county and river are named. She is one of the first known indigenous women to whom Tejanas are bound historically and culturally. The Spanish established a mission among her people in 1690 in present-day East Texas. The mission marked the beginning of a friendship between the two peoples. In 1690 Father Damian Massanet described Angelina as an "Indian maiden with a bright intellect and possessing striking personal appearance," who "expressed a desire to learn the Father's language." She received the baptismal name Angelina from the Spanish missionaries. A later account describes her as "learned" and "sagacious." In the 1690s she traveled to study at San Juan Bautista

Angelina, a member of the Caddo Nation, was a guide and translator for the
Spanish and French from around 1716 to 1721. She is the only woman for
whom a Texas county and river are named. Painting by Ancel Nunn. Courtesy
Claude Smithhart, Lufkin.

Mission in Guerrero, Coahuila, Mexico, thirty-five miles south of
present-day Eagle Pass. She later returned to her people. From 1716 to
1721, Angelina served as a guide, translator, and interpreter between
native peoples and the Spanish and French.[6]

Caddo, Tejas, and Hasinai are all names for one tribal grouping. Angelina's people were the Hainai, the leading tribe in the Hasinai confederacy. The Hasinai tribes were matrilineal, tracing descent through
their mothers.[7] Because none of these native women left a diary or
memoir behind, our knowledge of Angelina and her people have come
to us only through records that the Europeans kept. They wrote that
the Tejas were peaceful, friendly people who traded with the Spanish

and initially welcomed the establishment of missions. Female leaders among the Hasinai were not uncommon. Henry de Tonti wrote on March 30, 1690, of a woman who may have been Angelina:

"A woman, who governed this nation, came to visit me with the principal persons of the village." He described her people's fields as beautiful, noting that their economy included fishing and hunting.[8]

The Caddos apparently limited their involvement with the Spanish in East Texas to trading. They provided corn and meat to the missionaries and soldiers in exchange for Spanish-manufactured goods. However, they never abandoned their villages in favor of mission life, because they did not need the protection that these outposts offered. In addition, they did not convert to Christianity, "being fully satisfied with their own religion."[9]

The Caddos were the most advanced, numerous, and productive of the hundreds of indigenous nations who occupied the region. They had "achieved a level of cultural development unsurpassed" by other Indian nations. They also possessed advanced techniques and tools, and were highly successful agriculturists with an abundant food supply. The Caddos, who are best known for the women's "fascinating and varied pottery," had lived in the area for approximately a thousand years when they first met Europeans.[10] Caddo women were described as being "fair and pretty" and wearing "deerskin dresses, bordered with colored beads, and bone earrings." The Caddos lived in grass houses, slept in hammocks made from buffalo hides, and enjoyed an abundance of food and domesticated animals, including chickens and turkeys. They had large granaries and cultivated corn, beans, squash, melons, nuts, peaches, plums, and figs. When Angelina was an interpreter for Domingo Ramón in 1716, she and her companions reportedly served the Spanish a delicious meal of corn, melons, tamales, and cooked beans with corn and nuts.[11]

The land north of the Rio Grande was still largely unknown in the eighteenth century, but the Spanish gradually tried to subdue it, spurred to greater efforts when they saw the French starting to edge in from the east. Besides translating for the Spanish, Angelina worked with French Canadian guide, hunter, and explorer Louis Juchereau de St. Denis, whom she may have met in 1712 in East Texas. A member of his party noted that a Spanish-speaking woman named Angelique

had helped St. Denis hire guides from among her tribe. In 1713 St. Denis was placed under house arrest at San Juan Bautista under a Spanish
regulation forbidding foreign traders on Texas soil. He then married
Manuela Sánchez, the step-granddaughter of Diego Ramón, who was
commandant of Presidio San Juan Bautista, and switched allegiance to
Spain. By 1716 Angelina and St. Denis, now a commissary officer, traveled with Domingo Ramón to found Spanish missions and presidios in
East Texas. (Manuela, who was pregnant, could not travel.) These new
institutions ultimately had an extraordinary impact on the indigenous
people, spreading a new religion, new customs, and, regrettably, new
diseases and new forms of greed that would nearly destroy them.[12]

In 1718 Angelina helped found San Antonio de Valero Mission (the
Alamo) as part of an expedition led by Martín de Alarcón, the Spanish
governor of Texas. St. Denis also participated in the expedition, which
included delivering supplies to the missions in East Texas, where the
Caddos lived.[13]

The last written record of Angelina comes from 1721. That year
Governor José de Azlor, Marqués de San Miguel de Aguayo, led an
entrada (invasion) to reassert Spanish dominion over present-day East
Texas and reoccupy missions and presidios that had been abandoned
when the French invaded in 1719. A delegation of friendly Caddos
(eight captains and four women) received the group. The Caddos were
reportedly "delighted at the prospect of the Spaniards returning to East
Texas and reestablishing their presidios and missions." One of the
women who greeted the governor was called Angelina. She functioned
as interpreter, "being fluent in Spanish and the language of the Tejas."
The rest of Angelina's life is clouded in mystery, and no one knows her
ultimate fate. After St. Denis was accused of being a French loyalist, he
retreated with Manuela to French territory. They lived the rest of their
lives in Natchitoches, Louisiana.[14]

*Around 1719 Angelina may have participated in an expedition to save
Francois Simars de Bellisle, a slave to a Gulf Coast Indian widow who had
reportedly obtained him by rescuing him from the stake. She forced de Bellisle to do menial work and to consume flesh from a captured enemy [a
practice attributed to the Karankawas]. He managed to send a letter, calling for help. De Bellisle reported falling into the hands of the Assinais [an-
other name for the Caddos], especially a Spanish-speaking woman named
"Angelica," who had lived with the Spanish since her childhood. She offered*

to send two of her children as guides to take him to the French, and she
"served me all the best she had, and she had as much love for me as if I
had been her child." [15]

WHERE ARE THE CADDOS NOW?

During the first 170 years of contact between the Caddos and Europeans, from about 1520 to 1690, the numbers of Caddos reportedly decreased dramatically from around 200,000 to only 12,675.[16] As was the case among other tribes, they died from smallpox and measles, unfamiliar European diseases for which native peoples had not yet developed antibodies. Warfare with the Spanish and other indigenous nations, as well as their affiliation with the missions, also contributed to their demise. One 1767 diary reported that conditions in Texas were so deplorable that the women became sterile.[17]

Yet another way that tribal people disappeared was by their assimilation into the Tejano community, thereby becoming part of the *mestizaje* (group having mixed racial ancestry). For instance, by 1716 most members of the Hasinai Caddo confederacy had either been absorbed by other groups or become extinct. As late as 1859 a few hundred Caddos were still in Texas, where they were threatened with "massacre by white people." The Caddos were forced to abandon their homes, crops, cattle, and horses in Texas and take up reservation life in Indian Territory.[18] Nevertheless, their genetic heritage and many cultural contributions, including ways of cooking and gardening, extending hospitality, and rearing children, have continued, having been passed down and incorporated into Tejanas' culture.

OTHER INDIGENOUS NATIONS

The Caddos were only one of hundreds of indigenous nations occupying present-day Texas at the time of the Spanish explorations. Other significant groups included the Karankawas, whose land extended from Galveston Bay to Corpus Christi. In 1528 they were the first to have contact with a Spanish expedition. Both the French and Spanish tried repeatedly and unsuccessfully to bring the Karankawas into mission life.[19] From the Nueces River south, along part of what is now the Texas–Mexico border, lived tribes known collectively as Coahuiltecans. Under attack by both the Spanish and the Apaches, many of them either fled the area or moved into the missions established nearby, where

María de Jesús de Agreda (1602–1665), also known as the Lady in Blue, was a Spanish nun who claimed that, from 1620 to 1631 while in a trance, she made five hundred trips to Texas and preached to the native peoples. Copied from *Our Catholic Heritage in Texas,* by Carlos Castañeda. Courtesy University of Texas Institute of Texan Cultures.

they married people of other tribes.[20] In addition, the Comanches, a Plains people, fought against European settlers and other indigenous groups in Texas for more than one hundred years. Although the men were dominant, Comanche women exercised power, owned horses, and constructed tepees. They practiced herbalism and midwifery, and had a rich tradition of ornamental crafts.[21]

People referred to as Jumanos, who lived along what is now the western part of the Texas-Mexico border, played a major role in trade between Spanish Mexico and other native peoples to the north and east. They may have spread the legend of the "Lady in Blue," who reportedly appeared to them in the 1600s and instructed them in the Christian faith, some time before they encountered Europeans. Father

Alonso de Benavides, who began to Christianize the Jumanos in 1627, believed the Lady in Blue to be Mother María de Jesús de Agreda, a Spanish nun and mystic said to have the gift of bilocation. From the age of eighteen, de Agreda periodically fell into a trance. While her body was in the convent, she claimed, it was also transported to an unknown land, later identified as present-day New Mexico and West Texas. She reportedly appeared to the natives through bilocation on some five hundred occasions between 1620 and 1631. This story was widely repeated both in Europe and among various native peoples, including the Tejas. De Agreda later repudiated her bilocation experiences and declared that Benavides had browbeaten her into making the claims.[22]

INTERMARRIAGE AND MISSION LIFE

Many Christians might marry native women and many Christian women might marry native men, because the two groups could communicate and learn from each other.[23]

CATHOLIC CHURCH DECREE, 1503

From the early days of contact, the Catholic Church supported the idea of intermarriage between Spanish soldiers and colonists and the native women. Church records also document a few marriages between Spanish women and Native American men. For example, Juana Rodríguez, "a Spaniard," wed Melchor de Medina of the Muruam tribe, and Felipa Sara was married to Francisco Parrilla of the Sana tribe. Despite the church's official sanction of these marriages, some families disapproved of such unions. In 1781 the uncles and brothers of Ana María de la Trinidad Garnes, a *mulata,* forbade her marriage to an Indian. Most mixed marriages involved Tejanos and Indian women. Juan País, a Spanish soldier, married a young Indian woman named Margarita, a servant in the household of Captain Nicolás Flores y Valdez.[24]

Besides marrying Spanish-Mexican men, a number of Indian women at the missions also married men from other Indian nations. As early as 1703, baptisms and marriages between Native American individuals were carefully recorded. That year María de la Cruz, whose parents were described as "pagans," was baptized at San Antonio de Valero Mission.[25]

Year 1703
On June 24, 1703, after having fulfilled the prescriptions of our holy Mother the Church and the sacred canons, I witnessed the

marriage of the Indian Nicolás, belonging to the Jarame tribe, with Isabel, an Indian woman of the Sana tribe. Witnesses to the preparation of the contracting party were Sergeant Domingo Ramos, a Spaniard, and Lorenzo García, a Spanish soldier; on the woman's side were Lorenzo, a Mescalero Indian, and José, an Indian of the Yorica tribe, all from the pueblo of San Juan Bautista. The marriage banns were announced on the three feast days prior to the date.[26]   FRAY ANTONIO DE SAN BUENAVENTURA

Year 1716
Entry 28: Carlos Salinas, child, and Santiago Abila, child, died. On August 26, 1716, I solemnly baptized 2 children and anointed them with holy oils. One of them was named Carlos Salinas, 5 or 6 years of age, whose sponsor was Lorenzo Longoria; the other Santiago de Abila, 3 years of age, whose godmother was Francisca, a bilingual Indian of this mission.[27]   FRAY FRANCISCO RUIZ

In 1755 a mission priest instructed a native woman in the "mysteries of our holy faith," and since she was gravely ill, "baptized her and named her Petra." In 1772 a priest at the San Bernardo Mission baptized "an infant girl, María Antonia Casimira, the legitimate daughter of Luis Rodas and his wife, María Dolores," both of the Lipan tribe.[28]

Catholic officials compiled other detailed documents of Native Americans who were affiliated with missions, making it possible for future scholars to assemble the names of many tribes that have now disappeared. In 1994 the Inter-Tribal Council of American Indians in San Antonio disclosed records documenting the burial of more than a thousand native people at Alamo Plaza East and demanded that the location be permanently closed to vehicular traffic. The city council agreed to the request.[29]

Around the missions and presidios, women who were mestizas, Christianized Indians, *mulatas,* and Spanish-Mexicans lived side by side. At one of the larger missions, 237 women reportedly dried meats, prepared food, and made soap, candles, and clothing.[30] The women's networks, based on ties of blood, friendship, and skill sharing, were vital to the settlement of the Spanish-Mexican frontier.[31]

Tejanas were midwives to mission Indians, and they baptized babies who were stillborn or at risk of imminent death. Women also performed this important sacrament when no priest was at hand. In addition, they served as baptism sponsors for Indian babies. Fray Francisco Aparicio noted that when he baptized an infant girl, Anna Josefa of the Mayeye tribe, "her sponsor was Antonia Cortinas whom I informed about her obligation."[32]

Starting in 1804, a Spanish royal cedula decreed that Caesarian operations should be performed on all women who died in childbirth, to ensure Christian baptism.[33] When María de la Candelaria of the Coco tribe died during labor, "she was opened" and a priest poured the waters of baptism on the child and named him Juan.[34]

THE FIRST SPANISH-MEXICAN WOMEN TO ENTER TEXAS

Expeditions to explore and build presidios, missions, colonies, and ranches left from San Juan Bautista, the gateway to Spanish Texas, near present-day Eagle Pass. Women were part of the first two expeditions to establish permanent settlements in Texas (for which Angelina translated) in 1716 and 1718. They departed from south of the Rio Grande, traveling north with husbands who were artisans, farmers, and ranchers. Many of the frontier soldiers in the expeditions were of mixed ancestry.[35]

Seven or eight wives accompanied approximately twenty soldiers in 1716 to reestablish a mission in East Texas, which became the town of Nacogdoches. Ana Guerra, a young mestiza, married Lorenzo Mercado, a soldier, en route.[36] These women are the first recorded Spanish-Mexican women to enter Texas. In the years that followed, women from Mexico founded and colonized many other locations in what is now Texas, including San Antonio (San Antonio de Béxar Presidio, 1718), Goliad (La Bahía, 1749), Laredo (1755), and Victoria (1824).

THE FOUNDING OF SAN FERNANDO DE BÉXAR (SAN ANTONIO)

The city of San Antonio grew out of several original settlements: San Antonio de Béxar Presidio and five missions founded between 1718 and 1731, and the villa of San Fernando de Béxar, chartered by Canary Islanders in 1731. The first settlers in 1718 included six married soldiers and their families. The young women of marriageable age often wedded local soldiers. Military wives tilled the land, scrubbed, washed, and bore children without a doctor. The plaza of the presidio was off-limits to "women, citizens, mulattoes, Negroes, and *mestizos*."[37]

Men sometimes took on the cooking chores for the San Antonio missions in order to stop the "disorder" the bachelors reportedly caused when women were present in the kitchen. The wives of male servants

Descendants of the Canary Islanders who settled in San Antonio in 1731 bring flowers to an outdoor altar in honor of Our Lady of Sorrows, in front of the Spanish Governor's Palace in San Antonio in 1933. *San Antonio Light* Collection, University of Texas Institute of Texan Cultures.

made hardtack and bread for the priests, washed fleeces in the river, and wove blankets and cloth on looms. Two mission Indian women were appointed to clean the church and sacristy every Saturday. They were also issued a supply of soap, depending upon the amount of clothes they had to wash. Each week one woman was appointed to make tortillas for the priest's table.[38]

THE CANARY ISLANDERS

On March 9, 1731, fifteen families consisting of fifty-six exhausted immigrants from the Canary Islands arrived at San Antonio de Béxar Presidio. They formed the nucleus of the villa San Fernando de Béxar, the military community that had been in the area since 1718. The colonists had landed first in Veracruz, Mexico. The journey was so arduous that one of the voyagers, Lucía Hernández, a mother of five, became ill and died.[39]

Two wealthy widows—Doña María Robaina Betancour, mother of five, and María Rodríguez—were among the group. After settling in San Antonio de Béxar, María Betancour remarried, gave birth to five more children, and built a home on Plaza de la Islas, the main square. By the time of her death, she had accumulated a considerable amount of property. Her will, which was filed in 1779, attested to her origins, religious faith, financial status, marriages, and children. It also noted that she owned one day's irrigation water in the lower labor, a *suerte* (about 26 acres), a stone house, and all the cattle bearing her brand. In addition, she owned a ranch near Cibolo Creek, a chest from the Canary Islands, fifteen images of saints, a mattress, a quilt, a woolen skirt, and a branding iron.[40]

María Provana was also a woman of property, whose possessions included those she brought from the Canary Islands and those acquired in Texas—petticoats, handkerchiefs, silk stockings, two horses, a saddle and saddlebags, a bridle, sheepskins, mattresses, and "a copper pot and its lid which may also be used as a skillet."[41] Provana was described in the list of Canary Islanders taken at Quautitlán, Mexico, on November 8, 1730, as a woman "about 27 years old, [who possessed a] good figure, slender, long face, fair complexion, black hair & eyebrows, [and a] thin nose."[42]

Women often assumed responsibility for political and business affairs when the men were away from the presidio. María Pérez Cassiano, a descendant of Canary Islanders, was Texas's first First Lady. In 1804 her father, Juan Ignacio Pérez, a lieutenant colonel in the Spanish army, bought the Spanish Governor's Palace and turned it into the family home. In 1808 María Pérez married Colonel Manuel Antonio Cordero y Bustamante, the Spanish governor of Texas, and ran the affairs of state in his absence. In 1814 she began reviewing the troops while riding sidesaddle on her spirited horse. She cut a striking figure in her dark-green, gold-embroidered velvet riding suit and plumed hat. The men called her "La Brigadiera" (the Brigadier). Upon her father's death, Doña María lived in the Spanish Governor's Palace, where she entertained international visitors at elaborate balls. Three years after her first husband's death (1823), she married José Cassiano, a wealthy Italian.[43]

Other elite women also enjoyed prominent public roles. In 1776 María Josefa Granados, member of a Canary Islander family, married Fernando Veramendi, a merchant and public figure. By 1787 she owned San Fernando de Béxar's largest general store, which carried an array of merchandise—from pins to saddles, from diapers to party dresses. She even sold chamber pots without handles. One observer noted, "Most people in town owed her money, and her list of debtors is a good census of her community for that year."[44] María Becerra de Seguín was the wife of Juan Erasmo Seguín, San Antonio political figure, postmaster, and businessman. In 1824 she wrangled with city authorities over water rights while her husband attended congressional sessions in Mexico City.[45]

In general, the Canary Islanders viewed themselves as the elite class of San Fernando de Béxar. Refusing to mingle with Native Americans at San Antonio de Valero Mission, they erected their own parish church. They were pleased, however, to welcome soldiers from the presidio as husbands for their daughters.[46]

THE END OF THE MISSION PERIOD

The missions generally provided only a precarious existence for their inhabitants. Thus, the effort to secularize them grew, beginning in the late eighteenth century. Following Mexico's independence, many missions were completely abandoned. Although the missions situated around present-day San Antonio were once the most successful of Spanish Texas, authorities nonetheless completely secularized San Antonio de Valero Mission in 1793, and its members were absorbed into the local parish. From 1801 to 1825, the former mission served as the encampment for soldiers and their families assigned to the Flying Company of San José y Santiago del Alamo de Parras and became known as the Alamo. In 1794 the four remaining missions along the river and south of present-day San Antonio were all partially secularized, with some of the properties allocated to the neophytes still living in them.[47]

As part of the secularizing process, each Indian woman was given "a blouse, white woolen skirts, flannel skirts, a blanket, a hair brush, necklaces, earrings, pendants, a plate, a cup, a basket, a long shawl, except two women who already possessed shawls of a better quality."[48]

Secularization turned the missions in San Fernando de Béxar into civilian communities. With the transformation of the mission system completed in 1824, San Fernando became the largest and most successful community in Texas. Females outnumbered males 1,021 to 973. An anticipated visit in 1822 of Ana María García de Trespalacios, the wife of Coahuila y Texas governor Félix Trespalacios, caused excitement and prompted letters from such prominent women as María Becerra de Seguín requesting invitations to the welcoming banquet.[49]

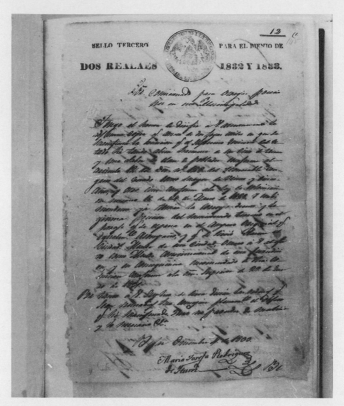

This land grant was issued to María Rodríguez in 1833. Many Spanish Mexican women were among Texas's earliest landowners. Courtesy Archives, General Land Office, State of Texas.

LAND GRANTS, LANDOWNERS, AND WOMEN'S PROPERTY RIGHTS

Soldiers, who were often awarded land grants near their posts in San Antonio, generally left land to their widows. In a 1752 will, Miguel de Castro left his widow six cows, nineteen head of cattle and sheep, ten horses, two mules, two *suertes* (about 53 acres), a stone house and lot, and tools. He also bequeathed to her a mattress, sheets, cooking utensils, a clothes chest, and other household furnishings. To his daughters upon their marriages he left dress aprons, lengths of gauze, shirts, pantaloons, quilts, silk stockings, mattresses, and pillows. By 1793 a census of San Fernando de Béxar listed forty-five native-born Tejana widows as heads of household. A number of the women belonged to prominent Bexareño families and were landowners.[50]

A number of Tejanas benefited from Spanish laws that allowed them

TABLE 1. *Examples of Spanish Land Grants Awarded to Women in 1767*

Name	Acreage	Present-day Counties
Margarita Gonzáles	6,218 acres	Starr County
María Josefa Guerra	6,525 acres	Zapata County
María Gertrudis Sánchez	5,570 acres	Webb County

SOURCE: *Guide to Spanish and Mexican Land Grants in South Texas,* nos. 155, 165, 287.

to retain title to the property they had held at the time of their marriages. In addition, wives could lay claim to an equal share of assets earned while married (community property), and their husbands could not dispose of the property without their consent. Women were permitted to negotiate contracts, and widows and unmarried daughters had the right to manage their own estates. Both Spanish and, later, Mexican laws protected women's property rights and awarded them inheritance rights equal to males'. Moreover, many women received land grants in their own names or inherited them from their husbands or families. They were entitled to land if they were the head of household or if their husbands had died while a grant was being finalized. This system ensured that wealthy women held significant economic power as large property owners, since it granted them ownership and control over vast amounts of land and wealth. During the colonial period, 60 Tejanas, from a total of 4,200 names listed by the Texas General Land Office, were original grantees (see Table 1). Many were widows with children. Others, with the permission of their husbands, applied for more land due to their large families or the large number of stock they were grazing.[51]

In about 1767 María Gregoria Martínez and her husband, Bartolomé de Lizarraras y Cuellar, founded the Treviño Circle T Ranch in Zapata County. In the 1780s María Gertrudis de la Garza Falcón inherited from her husband, José Salvador de la Garza, almost 300,000 acres—the Espíritu Santo grant—in present-day Cameron County. Her holdings included Rancho Viejo, cattle, horses, mules, sheep, and goats. In 1791 the Béxar *cabildo* (town council) compiled a list of fourteen area ranchers, including four women: Doña Manuela Móntes, Doña Antonia de Armas, Doña Josefa Quiñones, and Doña Leonor Delgado. In the 1830s a number of Tejanas received land grants in Robertson's Colony in Central Texas. For example, in 1833 María de la Concepción

Márquez applied for eleven leagues on the banks of the Guadalupe and San Marcos Rivers. Her grant amounted to 36,534 acres and 12,178 acres in present-day Robertson and Leon Counties, respectively.[52] Some of the land that these wealthy Tejanas originally held has remained in the same families for generations.

Women continued to receive land grants until Texas became a republic. In approximately 1790, Gertrudis de los Santos and her husband, Antonio Leal, owned a ten-league grant later known as the Edmund Quirt grant, on which the city of San Augustine, in San Augustine County, was built. The couple raised cattle and captured and sold mustangs. Doña Gertrudis also sold bolts of cloth and other duty-free merchandise from their ranch house.[53] María Josefa Rodríguez de Iturri, another landowner, applied for land in 1830, when she was twenty-eight and married. She explained that she did not have enough land to pasture her numerous livestock. In 1833 she received two leagues and one labor of land, which she located in present-day Bexar County. In 1835 Juana Camuñez de la Vina, a Nacogdoches widow and mother of three, acquired a land grant to raise crops and livestock. Her one league of land was located in present-day Rusk County, near Henderson.[54]

CATTLE QUEENS AND COMMUNITY BUILDERS

In 1770 the widow María Ann Cubelo owned three hundred head of cattle, the second-largest herd in Béxar. In 1809 two wealthy widows were listed in the Census of La Bahía and Refugio Missions. Doña Gertrudis Básquez owned seventeen mules with harness, one team of oxen, and thirty head of cattle. Doña Petra Contreras owned two teams of mules with harness, twenty-six head of cattle, and two horses.[55]

One of the largest landowners of the day was Rosa María Hinojosa de Ballí who in 1798 owned approximately 642,755 acres—one-third of the present-day Lower Rio Grande Valley. Today some have labeled her Texas's first cattle queen. Her contemporaries referred to her as "La Patrona" (the Landowner). Doña Rosa was the daughter of Spanish aristocrats, born in 1752 in what is now Tamaulipas, Mexico. The family moved to Reynosa, Mexico, in 1767, where her father was the *alcalde* (mayor). She was educated there, perhaps by the parish priest. On July 4, 1776, her husband, José María Ballí, and her father, Juan José de Hinojosa, jointly applied for a large land grant. By the time that the land grant was approved in 1790, both men had died. Nonetheless, because Spanish law protected widows' rights, Doña Rosa inherited her husband's full authority to act on her own.[56]

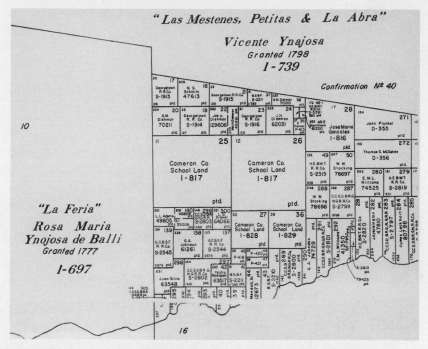

Doña Rosa María Hinojosa de Ballí (1752–1803) inherited land grants from her husband and father after their deaths. She continued acquiring land until she owned one-third of the present-day Lower Rio Grande Valley, around 1800. The original grantee map shown here is in Cameron County. Courtesy Archives, General Land Office, State of Texas.

Left with three young sons and an estate heavily encumbered by debt, Doña Rosa had the land grant completed in her name and later obtained several other large grants. She lived on what is now the Mexican side of the border, but her ranch headquarters were on the present-day Texas side, in La Feria, which was named after her land grant. She eventually doubled her property and made extensive improvements. The city of Harlingen is located on part of what was once her land. Her holdings included the 53,000-acre La Feria grant in present-day Cameron County and extensive acreage in present-day Hidalgo County. Her son and business associate, Padre Nicolás Ballí, eventually owned Padre Island, which was named for him.[57] She took possession of her land "in the colorful ceremony prescribed by Spanish law" by pulling up herbs and grasses and tossing soil and water to the four winds.[58]

Doña Rosa exercised unquestioned authority over the area. She was the godmother of many children baptized at Our Lady of Guadalupe Church in Reynosa Viejo. She also built a family chapel and donated funds for churches in three Mexican cities. Neighboring ranchers kept their papers and valuables in her strong box, sought her advice, and borrowed her farming tools. Apparently well educated, she kept meticulous records of her activities. By the time of her death in 1803, she controlled more than a million acres of land in the Lower Rio Grande Valley, including parts of present-day Hidalgo, Cameron, Willacy, Starr, and Kenedy Counties. Although her ranching empire declined after her death, her memory was cherished because of her warmth, generosity, and piety. Many citizens on both sides of the border trace their heritage back to her family.[59]

In her will Doña Rosa testified to her religious faith and listed her extensive property. She noted her ownership of La Feria, which, she said, "I inherited from my father [and] . . . a chapel that is on said land." She declared her ownership of large numbers of animals: forty herds of mares, two hundred mules, 2,001 sheep, forty steers, and three yoke of oxen. She stated that she owned a ten-room house in Reynosa and two carriages. Doña Rosa also listed altar ornaments, ribbons, tablecloths, chalices, and other religious items, as well as an assortment of silver plates and silverware, gold bracelets, rosaries, crosses, earrings with green stones, golden and silver reliquaries, trunks, and copper plates of Our Lady of Dolores and Saint Joseph. In addition, she declared that she owned bed linens and calico petticoats, a canoe, a sidesaddle, and a bridle with silver buckles. Doña Rosa's property included "a mulatto girl fifteen years old, named María Dolores, the document for whom from her mother will be found among my papers." Doña Rosa also noted that when she gave the wife of her son, Juan José, a dowry of $500, he had complained that the gift was too much. She answered, "I did not need him to tell me what I should give to my daughter-in-law."[60]

The heirs of Doña Rosa Hinojosa de Ballí retained ownership of Padre Island until 1938, when they sold their title to a section of the island to Gilbert Kerlin, a New York attorney. Although Kerlin promised to pay them a portion of future oil and gas royalties, they never received a cent. In 1993 the family filed a lawsuit against Kerlin, claiming he had cheated them out of royalties and land. When the case finally came to trial in 2000, a Brownsville jury made up of Tejanos found that Kerlin and his lawyer had conspired to defraud the Ballís and awarded them $1.1 million in lost royalties and $1.5 million in attorneys' fees. The Ballí heirs saw the verdict as a vindication for their family and for the many Mexican American families in the Southwest who have spent

Woman on horseback, copied from Julio Michaud y Thomas, *Álbum pintoresco de la República Mexicana*. Courtesy University of Texas Institute of Texan Cultures.

generations trying to reclaim what they call "*las tierras perdidas*" (the lost lands). Mexican Americans hailed the decision, recalling their own families' accounts of "being cheated, unfairly taxed, threatened, and even murdered for their land by Anglo settlers since the mid-1800s." Kerlin appealed the jury's decision, and the case remained in litigation as the twenty-first century began.[61]

DOÑA MARÍA DEL CARMEN CALVILLO: "THE BLACK-HAIRED BEAUTY WHO RODE THE WHITE STALLION"

In 1814 María del Carmen Calvillo, a Canary Island descendant, inherited El Rancho de las Cabras (Ranch of the Goats) in present-day Wilson County from her father. Doña María married Juan Gavino de la Trinidad Delgado, but the couple had separated by the time she came into her inheritance. She allegedly scandalized her neighbors because she let her long hair fly loose in the wind as she rode a large white stallion, supervising her workforce of twenty families. She increased the livestock of Rancho de las Cabras to fifteen hundred cattle and five hundred goats, sheep, and horses, and built an irrigation system, a sugar mill, and a granary. Although her neighbors had trouble with Native

Augustina de León and Ismael Alderete, her husband. She was a great-granddaughter of Patricia de la Garza de León and Martín de León. Courtesy Henry J. Hauschild, Victoria.

Americans, Doña María maintained peaceful relations by providing them with cattle and grain. They, in turn, never attacked her ranch. She continued acquiring land until 1833.[62]

DOÑA PATRICIA DE LA GARZA DE LEÓN: ARISTOCRAT, COLONIST, AND REFUGEE (1775–1849)

Doña Patricia de la Garza de León was one of the earliest pioneer women to colonize Texas. She and Don Martín de León, her husband, founded the town of Victoria in 1824, using her sizable dowry, which included 9,800 pesos and a considerable number of mares, cattle, cows, and oxen. After Don Martin's death in 1834, Doña Patricia managed their property and was soon one of the richest persons in Texas.

Though lacking a formal education, "she proved to be a smart and sensible business woman." Doña Patricia brought religion, schools, and an enriched social and cultural life to South Texas.[63]

Doña Patricia and Don Martín were both born in Mexico. His aristocratic Spanish parents offered him a European education, but he instead became a trader, serving the miners of western Mexico. Later he was an Indian fighter in the Spanish army. Don Martín reached the rank of captain, the highest rank available to one not born in Spain.[64]

Doña Patricia was born in about 1775 on the east coast of Mexico, not far from present-day Brownsville. Family wealth allowed her to grow up wearing expensive dresses and live amid luxurious surroundings. She was approximately twenty when she married thirty-year-old Martín de León in 1795. The couple started a ranch near Cruillas, Mexico, and in 1798 she gave birth to Fernando, their first of ten children. The other nine children were born in Texas.[65]

Her restless husband traveled north into the unexplored Tejas territory and returned with tales of abundant grasslands and large herds of unbranded cattle left behind when Spanish missions were abandoned. In 1799 the couple moved, with their baby and belongings, to a site on the east bank of the Aransas River, north of present-day Corpus Christi. They built a home and raised cattle, horses, mules, and goats. In 1807 they registered the first brand in Texas—a connected E and J—that had been a Jesuit brand for hundreds of years in Europe. The letters stand for "Espíritu de Jesús" (Spirit of Jesus).[66]

In 1809 the de León family, consisting of Martín and Patricia and their children—Fernando, Candelaria, Silvestre, Guadalupe, and Felix —were among the 4,000 Spanish-Mexicans who lived in what is now Texas. Soldiers comprised about one-fourth of the population, a number deemed insufficient to provide much protection on the frontier. Doña Patricia's family kept a cannon handy but relied on friendly methods to keep the peace, plying Indians who stopped at their home with blankets and beef.[67]

By 1810 the de León family had moved south to the Nueces River, enclosed a pasture, and begun domesticating wild mustangs. When the Spanish government pulled most of its troops back to Mexico to fend off revolution, Indian raids on settlers increased. With seven children, two under the age of two, Doña Patricia's family moved to a ranch outside of present-day San Antonio. Three more children were born there: Refugia, Augustina, and Francisca (born in 1818 when the oldest was

Doña Patricia de la Garza de León (1775–1849), a founder of Victoria with Don Martín de León, her husband, built this ranch house there in 1836. Courtesy Texas State Library and Archives.

twenty). Martín de León continued to travel to sell mustangs, cattle, mules, and horses in New Orleans, returning from his trips with wagon-loads of provisions.[68]

Their success encouraged the de León family to establish their own colony, but the Spanish government twice refused their land grant applications. However, in 1821 Mexico won independence from Spain, and Guadalupe Victoria was named president. Doña Patricia and Don Martín petitioned the new government and received permission to start a new colony with forty-one Mexican families "of good moral character" on the north bank of the lower Guadalupe River. Doña Patricia put up her dowry to fund the venture.[69]

Thus, in October 1824, when she was nearly fifty years old, Patricia de León moved with her family and eleven other families to the town of Nuestra Señora de Guadalupe Victoria (named for the first Mexican president). Twenty-nine more families arrived from Mexico the following spring. By then, the first group of settlers had cleared and planted the fields and replaced the adobe shelters with log homes. Victoria colony was a multiethnic town from its beginning because Don Martín had agreed to accept settlers of any race, creed, or color who swore allegiance to Mexico and upheld the Catholic religion. Thus, although the new settlement was the only predominantly Mexican colony in Texas, Anglo and Irish families joined it as well.[70]

As *empresario* (contractor), Don Martín acquired additional grazing land for each family he could settle. In turn, each family received a town lot consisting of more than 4,000 acres of grazing land and about 177 acres of farming land. Don Martín was awarded another 21,000 acres once the forty-one families were settled. Victoria colony was blessed with fertile land and many streams, allowing for the production of good crops of beans, corn, potatoes, and sugarcane. The land also supported livestock, and fish and game were abundant.[71]

When lots were laid out for the town center, Doña Patricia made sure that a plot for a church was set aside. She also donated $500 in gold for constructing and equipping the church. Moreover, she made certain that schools were immediately set up for the colony's children. She also attended to her own home, decorating it with fine furniture that her relatives in Mexico provided her.[72]

As her family's wealth grew, Doña Patricia oversaw personal and community activities. She sent her children to Mexico and Europe to be educated and set aside time and resources for religious and social activities that were essential to building a community. She also hosted one of the first celebrations in the new town: the wedding of her daughter Guadalupe. Doña Patricia witnessed the ascension of three of the de León sons-in-law as important members of the colony's governing structure and Victoria colony's attendance to basic needs: providing for a fort, a militia, a courier service, and visits from priests. Although the colony was under threat from some Native Americans and outlaws, Patricia de León refused to allow her children to use guns against anyone, declaring that she did not want them to be known as bandits.[73]

As both a prominent Mexican and a Catholic, Don Martín received preference in most legal matters, and he took advantage of his status. In 1829 he received permission from the Mexican government to add another 150 families to Victoria colony. This opportunity led him to displace the neighboring DeWitt colony to make room for the new settlers. He and his militia also worked with the Mexican government to control tobacco smuggling, and arrested Green DeWitt in one incident.[74]

Martín de León died suddenly in a cholera epidemic in 1834, the same year that Antonio López de Santa Anna was elected president of Mexico on a liberal platform. The following year Santa Anna declared that Mexico was not ready for democracy and set about ruling the country as an "autocratic centralist." It would be Santa Anna whom the Texian forces would confront at the famous battle of the Alamo in 1836.

The family of Doña Patricia was divided over the issue of Texas independence.[75] Plácido Benavides, husband of Doña Patricia's daughter Augustina, was a prominent officer on the Texian side, and Doña Patricia's sons Fernando and Silvestre fought for Texas independence. Some members of the family also risked their lives to smuggle arms and munitions from New Orleans. Although the war succeeded with their help, the de León family did not reap a harvest of gratitude for their allegiance. Patricia de la Garza de León did, nevertheless, earn respect for her many accomplishments as a pioneer, community leader, church benefactor, wife, and mother.[76]

Although Doña Patricia was one of the early prominent members of the Spanish-Mexican settler population in the state, she has only recently been seriously considered an important actor in Tejano history. Likewise, Angelina, the "learned" Caddo translator and a cofounder of San Antonio de Valero Mission, has not readily been acknowledged as a significant indigenous ancestor to Tejanas. Beginning in the 1700s, a great many more courageous, unknown, and unnamed native and Spanish-Mexican women began to shape the state's mestiza history, one that succeeding generations of Tejanas have inherited.

CHAPTER TWO

The Status of Women in the Colonial Period

Women worked hard preparing food for their families, as shown in *Les Tortilleras* (The Tortilla Makers). Copied from *Le Tour du Monde,* edited by Edouard Charton. Courtesy University of Texas Institute of Texan Cultures.

RICH AND POOR: THE ECONOMIC ROLE OF WOMEN

Tejanas . . . were the oldest (and often the wealthiest) on the Texas frontera.[1] ANDRÉS TIJERINA

Colonial Texas society was divided into landowners and laborers, with a marked caste system. Laredo, one of the earliest colonial settlements, provides an interesting example of social status. Before the 1824 census, the city classified residents as *españoles* (Spaniards), *castas* (racially mixed persons), Indians, mestizos, and mulattos. Upper-class *españoles* were honored with the titles "Don" and "Doña." These distinctions continued informally into the 1830s.[2] Tejanos have in later centuries employed the terms

"Don" and "Doña" to address elders or others respected by the community, regardless of social station.

Elite women derived power from landownership and marriage, and from kinship to military officers, government officials, and landowners. Doña Patricia de la Garza de León, cofounder of Victoria, and businesswoman María Josefa Granados of San Antonio were wealthy women of the period. Doña Patricia and Martín de León, her husband, made money selling horses, mules, and hides. Other rich women, such as some of the widows listed in the 1809 census of La Bahía and Refugio missions, owned medium-size *ranchos*. Among them were the widows Doña Petra Contreras, who owned two teams of mules with harness, twenty-six head of cattle, and two horses, and Doña Gertrudis Básquez, who owned seventeen mules with harness, one team of oxen, and thirty head of cattle.[3] Most Tejanas, however, worked on small, family-owned plots or were poor, landless female servants and ranch workers.[4] Women elites exploited poor women, and indentured service was also prevalent.[5]

Regardless of class, Tejanas held key economic roles. Female ranch owners bought and sold land and cattle, supervised foremen and ranch hands, handled finances, and managed estates. Wealthy women employed domestic servants to assist with child care and housework. Poor women worked as cooks, laundresses, gardeners, farmers, day laborers, cattle herders, seamstresses, midwives, and healers. Their lives also revolved around child care, cooking, sewing, and washing clothes. They often labored alongside men and children on *ranchos,* gardening and caring for domestic animals. To provide food for their families, they planted a few rows of corn, beans, or pumpkins behind their *jacales* (huts). A few women and girls in the *pueblos* (towns) took jobs as shepherds, tailors, peddlers, animal skinners, vendors, and prostitutes.[6]

Women were almost exclusively responsible for medical care. Midwives delivered most of the babies; *curanderas* (folk healers who used medicinal herbs and ritual cures) were also valued.[7] Even elite women could not count on good medical attention. Indeed, because the military barracks in San Antonio were so inadequate, in 1780 Governor Baron de Ripperda and his wife moved into the local jail, where she gave birth.[8]

THE BEXAR ARCHIVES AND WOMEN'S LEGAL ACTIONS

The Bexar Archives, a collection of legal and administrative documents at the University of Texas at Austin, cover the period from 1717 through

Entierro de un ángel (The Funeral of an Angel). A mid-1800s painting by
Theodore Gentilz. Courtesy Daughters of the Republic of Texas Library at
the Alamo, San Antonio.

1836. They are regional in scope and include materials on the borderlands of the eastern Spanish interior provinces—Texas, Coahuila,
Nuevo León, and Nuevo Santander (Tamaulipas). Numerous documents cover San Antonio, La Bahía (Goliad), Nacogdoches, and the
Texas-Louisiana border. Further, the Bexar materials reveal women's
legal right to own property in their own names, regardless of marital
status; their right to engage in legal actions; and their right to judicial
redress.[9]

The archives record a number of instances from the 1770s to the
1790s in which women sought justice regarding their property rights.
María Egeciaca Rodríguez brought a case against Domingo Delgado
for land possession, and Rosalia Rodríguez petitioned for a town lot in
San Antonio. Antonia Rosalia de Armas sued Pedro Granados for division of the family estate, and María Antonia Granados filed suit against
María Pérez de Granados, disputing their inheritance. (María) Josefa
Granados addressed the rights of way for roads and *acequias* (irrigation
ditches). Women also brought cases involving livestock. María St. De-
nis applied for a license to take stock to Natchitoches, and Ventura
Garza and María Ignacia de Urrutia requested licenses to round up un-

branded cattle. María Catalina de Urrutia called for an investigation to determine ownership of some mares. María Magdalena Vásquez asked the Texas governor for permission to send an agent to San Juan Bautista to collect debts. In addition, in 1824 businesswomen began to appear in the Bexar records: Teresa Arreola paid taxes for dances and grocery stores, and María Guerra paid custom duties.[10]

MARRIAGE, WIDOWHOOD, AND PROSTITUTION

Laws of honor and chastity ruled marriage.[11]

CYNTHIA E. OROZCO

Most women in colonial Texas were married, and the courtship ritual leading to the married state was strictly governed by social mores. Custom dictated that men and women meet at the plaza or in other public settings. In Laredo, for instance, socializing by the river, where women washed clothes and bathed, was frowned upon. After marriage the majority of women bore and reared children within a family structure. In Laredo, for instance, two parents headed most households. Adulterous women could be severely punished. Women could and did file charges for rape and abandonment. Husbands, however, were permitted to be unfaithful and still avoid punishment. On one occasion, an adulterer was banished from the town.[12]

Unfaithful women were deemed unacceptable, and they could be punished and their property confiscated. Although divorce was rare, divorcees tended to be ostracized. The law could also compel wives to stay in an unhappy marriage. In 1816 the Laredo *alcalde* (mayor) denounced common law unions as "a menace to the community's well-being." Despite the efforts of the clergy and colonial officials to maintain moral standards, illegitimacy rates were high. In 1799 Texas church records reveal an illegitimacy rate of 20 percent, and high rates continued throughout the period. The lack of priests to perform sacramental weddings may have contributed to the situation.[13]

Besides married women, many widows resided in colonial Texas, although some remarried. For instance, soon after the arrival of Spanish-Mexican soldiers and colonists in San Fernando de Béxar (San Antonio) in the 1720s, four widows married military men.[14] Nevertheless, a large number of women remained alone after the death of a spouse, making widows in the area 30 percent of all heads of household by 1824. In Laredo the number of widows was still high in the 1830s. Some of these women may have actually been abandoned wives, unwed mothers, or women in common-law marriages who called themselves widows to enjoy certain legal privileges and gain a measure of social respectability that such a designation permitted.[15]

Some women worked as prostitutes. In Nacogdoches, "the presence of large numbers of unmarried soldiers, slaves, and transients" may have been partly responsible for the prostitution among married women, "causing authorities to threaten severe punishment."[16] In 1783 the town passed an ordinance forcing husbands to bear some of the responsibility for their wives' behavior:

> Any man who shall assent to the prostitution of his wife, will for the first offense, be exposed in public, being feathered, rubbed with honey, wearing a fool's cap with a string of garlic and a pair of horns, receive 100 lashes and be sent to the galleys for 10 years; and for [the] second offense, he shall remain in the galleys for life.[17]

During the same year an ordinance to control morality was also passed in San Antonio. The new law required that "both honorable men and honorable women should remain at home at night." Individuals participating in fandangos and similar social activities were described as people "of ill repute," and their activities were branded as "notorious." The decree stipulated that after certain hours of the evening fandangos had to be limited to the interior of homes.[18]

MARRIAGE CASES IN THE BEXAR ARCHIVES

The Bexar Archives include cases related to marital and family issues. Ignacio Menchaca filed suit against Feliciano Villeda, alleging that Villeda had illicit relations with Menchaca's wife. María Josefa de la Santa, along with many other women, requested a license to get married. Rafaela de la Garza, a widow who had remarried, sued her son from her first marriage for property. María Gertrudis de Estrada asked for permission to join her husband, Pedro Lambremont, who was apparently stationed in another location. María Antonio de Abrego filed a petition to investigate her husband's gambling loss of 200 pesos, and Francisco López requested a divorce from Juana Antonia Ocona due to her infidelity. María del Refugio Sánchez and her family in Monterrey brought complaints of negligence regarding receipts of payment against Severo Ruiz, despite his paying a monthly allowance to María, his wife. Ruiz,

Religious processions and festivals were part of the spiritual and community life in nineteenth-century San Antonio. Illustration by Dean Louis Cárdenas. Courtesy Timothy Matovina.

in turn, requested permission to arrange a property settlement and a divorce. María Antonia Rodríguez petitioned to assume responsibility for the education of her nieces. María Petra Castañón requested help in obtaining the return of her runaway daughter.[19]

CHURCH, COMMUNITY, AND SOCIAL LIFE

> They knew that we were in charge
> of the rosaries and weekly prayer gatherings,
> the collection plate
> for hungry families, the garden rotations.
> They knew that our visitas were the corazon de todo.[20]
> > TERESA PALOMO ACOSTA, "In the territory of Bexar"

Women in colonial Texas were responsible for maintaining family life and building community institutions that created a civil society. Whether in the missions and presidios or on the *ranchos,* women kept cultural patterns alive, adapting those brought from Mexico and developing others to meet the new conditions of life. Women were especially influential in maintaining religious faith among Tejanos. Wealthy women contributed by erecting places of worship. For instance, in her 1798 will Doña Rosa María Hinojosa de Ballí wrote, "I declare as mine a chapel that is on said land [La Feria]." The chapel to which she referred was located on her property, most likely making it the only church in the area available to the populace. Doña Rosa also owned numerous chalices, rosaries, and other religious articles that could be used in services and for prayer, and she was a godmother many times over. In her will she confirmed her religious faith as a "Roman Catholic Christian" who truly believed "in the great mystery of the Holy Trinity, Father, Son and the Holy Ghost." She also acknowledged the "marvelous mystery of the Encarnation of the Holy word in the chaste bowels of the Virgin Mary, Holy Divine Mother, Our Lady and our Intercessor," and "in all of the other mysteries of our Holy Faith." After her son, Nicolás Ballí, was ordained, she always referred to him as "my

Patricia de la Garza de León brought religion, schools, and a cultured lifestyle to Victoria. Her homesite was donated to the parish there at her death and is the location of the present Saint Mary's Catholic Church, shown here. Courtesy Madeline Fleming O'Connor. Print from University of Texas Institute of Texan Cultures.

This purse belonged to Doña Patricia de la Garza de León. It held $500 in
gold, which she donated for the construction of Nuestra Señora de Guadalupe
Church in Victoria. Courtesy Victoria Public Library. Print from the Woman's
Collection, Texas Woman's University.

son, the priest." Doña Rosa celebrated the event with a three-day fiesta
at her ranch in La Feria.[21]

Both she and Doña Patricia de la Garza de León were among "the
most generous contributors to pious funds and social drives" for the
benefit of the Catholic Church. Doña Patricia donated $500 in gold
and furnishings to help found Nuestra Señora de Guadalupe (Our Lady
of Guadalupe) Church, the first Catholic parish in Victoria. After her
death, her home site was donated as the site of the present Saint Mary's
Catholic Church in that city. Elite women were not the sole contributors to the religious faith of the community. Indeed, women of all social classes served as spiritual guides. They instructed their children in
religious doctrine in the absence of a priest. In addition, they set up
small altars in their homes, with a statue or image of Nuestra Señora de
Guadalupe at the center. Mothers led family prayers before their altars
and planned religious commemorations to observe the feast days of the
Immaculate Conception of Mary and Our Lady of Guadalupe, both
celebrated in early December.[22]

Upper-class women supervised the education of their children, frequently sending them to Mexican schools in Monterrey and Saltillo.

The children of the wealthy were also often educated at home or in private schools along the border and in other states. Doña Patricia de la Garza de León ensured that a school was established in Victoria immediately after her arrival there in 1824. Petra Vela de Vidal Kenedy sent three sons, Thomas, John Gregorio, and William, to the Spring Hill Boarding School in Mobile, Alabama, and she registered her daughter Sarita at the Ursuline Academy in New Orleans.[23]

Following Mexican independence in 1821, the Constitution of the State of Coahuila y Texas of 1827 required that a uniform system of public instruction be established throughout the state. In San Fernando de Béxar, a school fund was established, but collecting money was difficult. San Fernando de Béxar had 334 school-age females and 297 school-age males within its walls; however, no one knows how many from each group attended the local school. Well-to-do parents were required to pay tuition for their children, but the educational costs for the handful of poor children who attended were covered through special provisions. In addition, citizen contributions helped maintain the school system. In 1832 Doña Gertrudis Pérez provided 100 pesos, apparently the largest single donation that the educational system received.[24]

Women took an active role in patriotic festivities. In 1825 Bexar citizens celebrated the Diez y Seis de Septiembre with three days of commemoration and revelry that included a *baile* (dance), a torchlight parade, and a Te Deum mass. In 1832 citizens of Goliad produced a dramatic play, with local women playing the opposing forces of the War for Independence. Twelve females (the antagonists), dressed in silks, laces, and jewels, held up white ribbons as they walked alongside a carriage carrying an Indian girl (the protagonist), dressed in traditional attire.[25]

Celebrations sometimes grew boisterous. In 1781 the Spanish governor banned horse racing on the streets of San Antonio on the Feast of Saint John, because the event often caused "breaches of good etiquette, and other disgraces." On one occasion in Goliad, a priest "arrested a girl, shut her up with other females, and made her pray a *salve* [Hail Mary] in the chapel of Espíritu Santo because she had participated in a horse race on Saint Anne's Day."[26]

Among the *patrón* (landowner) class, women and men held clearly defined roles when socializing. Moreover, both municipal and ranch events were separated by social class. Women sustained a female culture through *visitas* (home visits), which helped maintain community health and a spiritual life. Elite women extended charity to the poor. Poor women helped one another as their circumstances allowed.[27]

SEXUAL ABUSE AND VIOLENCE

Women of all ethnic groups were vulnerable to rape and violence. Spanish soldiers regularly molested Native American women, creating a major problem for the commanders to resolve. In fact, the "immorality of the soldiers with Indian women, single or married, knew no bounds." Military leaders and priests also abused their authority. In 1751 Captain Felipe de Rábago y Terán, presidio commander of San Xavier, "scandalized the religious" by his promiscuous contact with women. In San Antonio "he seduced the wife of Juan José Ceballos, a member of his command." When Ceballos threatened him, Rábago jailed him. The commander then ravished Ceballos's wife, forcing him to watch. Ceballos was later murdered. Rábago was relieved of his command, incarcerated, and investigated for eight years before finally being cleared. Other soldiers also committed questionable acts. In 1752 priests excommunicated the entire San Xavier military complement for immoral behavior. Members of the Roman Catholic clergy were themselves accused of failing to live celibate lives, as their vows dictated. In the 1800s, for instance, a San Antonio mission priest, Juan Zambrano, and María Guadalupe de la Garza, were the parents of two sons. Zambrano was ordered to leave San Fernando de Béxar in 1807 "for licentious behavior." In 1823 he left his house and land to María and her two sons, whom he identified as his own.[28]

Women also filed charges against men, alleging murder and rape. Juana García obtained a judgment against Tomás Travieso for the murder of her husband, Juan de Escamilla. In 1824 a woman's reputed lover murdered her husband. The case dragged on for four years until a local court finally dropped the charges. In 1832 Patricio Loy was tried in court at Goliad for murdering his wife.[29]

The Bexar Archives list a number of rape and sexual abuse cases. Miguel de los Santos was charged with raping María Cruz; María Josefa Ríos accused Francisco Gutiérrez de la Lama of statutory rape; María Luisa Hidalgo brought charges against Francisco de los Santos for forcing her to have illicit relations with him; María de la Concepción Losoya filed charges against José María Martínez for rape. José Vásquez was imprisoned for assaulting his wife, Concepción Villaseñor. When he escaped, she tried to secure her clothing, as well as the furniture in their home, from him. In the 1830s the legality of Manuel Monjaraz's marriage to María Josefa Salinas was questioned, and a *sumaria* (indictment) was issued against him for mistreating her.[30]

SLAVERY

Both Native Americans and the Spanish practiced slavery long before the arrival of Anglo American *empresario* (contractor) Stephen F. Austin and his colonists, the Old Three Hundred. Native people, for instance, enslaved the Spanish, mestizos, and mulattos. The Tejas, for example, held a Spanish girl in slavery in 1767. An inspection party tried to win her release, but "the captors preferred to keep her as their slave." In 1748 Governor Pedro del Barrio y Espriella ordered soldiers at the San Xavier mission to send their wives and children to safety for fear of attacks by the Apaches.[31]

On the other hand, Spanish soldiers also captured and enslaved Indians. After an inspection tour of presidios in 1729, Brigadier General Pedro de Rivera y Villalón stated that "no officer would be permitted in the future to capture Indians during a military campaign and keep them as his own, as slaves, or give the Indian captives to others." He further declared that captive males "were to be sent to Mexico City," whereas "captured women and children should be returned to their respective parents or spouses."[32]

Rivera y Villalón's stance was understandable, since Spain recognized free people of color. By 1792 the Spanish census of Texas recorded 186 *mulata* and Negro women as "free citizens." Thus, the region became a haven for runaway and freed slaves from the U.S. South. In one instance, Felipe Elua, a Louisiana creole and slave, purchased freedom for himself and his wife, Mary Ortero, a *mulata,* and their children. In 1807 they settled in San Antonio, where they acquired land and became farmers. The couple educated their children in Spanish and French.[33]

Even as the Spanish sought to protect free persons of color, women became part of the trade in slavery in New Spain's borderlands. For the period from 1778 to 1823, the Bexar Archives record a number of female slaves bought and sold, some by other females. For instance, the widow Antonia Morales sold María de la Candelaria Fierro, and María Catarina Gonzáles purchased a mulatto slave. María del Refugio de Jesús Santa María (an Indian) was transferred to Pedro Villareal at Boca de Leones. However, Rosa de la Rosa y Rúa granted freedom to her slave, María Rosa de la Rosa y Valle, and Ángel Navarro also freed María

Gertrudis de la Peña. Josefa Cerda escaped to Natchitoches to appeal for U.S. protection.[34]

THE ANGLO AMERICANS BRING THEIR SLAVES TO THE BORDERLANDS

Anglo Americans began moving into the Spanish borderlands in the 1800s, bringing their slaves with them. At the same time, the Mexican government, having won independence from the Spanish Crown, espoused antislavery sentiments and equality for all people. Indeed, in its 1821 treaty of independence, the government promised citizenship and equal rights and opportunities for all the people. The Mexicans also passed the first law against slavery in the Western Hemisphere. Nonetheless, Mexico clouded the situation regarding the freedom of human beings in the borderlands, including the state of Coahuila y Texas, by passing a number of ambiguous and contradictory measures relating to the legal status of slaves. In 1823, for instance, Mexico's Imperial Colonization Law provided that "there shall not be permitted . . . either purchase or sale of slaves that may be introduced into the empire. The children of such slaves, who are born within the empire, shall be free at fourteen years." Yet during the same year the Mexican government approved a request by Stephen F. Austin to bring settlers and their slaves from the United States into Mexican territory. The 1823 law was annulled the following year, when a new constitutional congress decreed that slave trade be prohibited forever. The law made clear that any slaves brought into Mexico in violation of this decree must be freed. However, in order to placate Anglo American cotton planters, the Legislature of Coahuila y Texas rephrased a clause in the colonization law, specifying that slavery would be allowed under the guise of "indentured servitude." Slave owners "obliged" by "freeing their slaves," then signing them on as lifetime indentured servants.[35]

WOMEN IN THE WAR OF INDEPENDENCE OF 1810–1821 THROUGH THE TEXAS REVOLUTION OF 1836

For more than twenty years, from the beginning of the 1810 Mexican War of Independence from Spain through the Texas War of Independence, which ended in 1836, women lived under conditions of intermittent warfare.

A number of them became involved in the struggle to gain independence from Spain. María Josefa Ortiz de Domínguez and Leona Vicario were two of the most important women involved in the long battle

María Josefa Ortiz de Domínguez (left) and Leona Vicario (right) were two of
the most important women involved in the struggle for Mexican independence
from Spain, from 1810 to 1821. Ortiz de Domínguez, known as La Corregidora
(the Magistrate), leaked information to the insurgents. Vicario published articles
and financed a cannon factory. They were precursors of later generations of
Tejana activists. Courtesy Benson Latin American Collection, University of
Texas at Austin.

for Mexican independence, which called for the establishment of a republic guaranteeing equality for all races, ending the special privileges
of the Roman Catholic Church and the army, and dividing large estates
into small farms. They joined women from all social levels—count-
esses, nuns, and housewives—who served as spies, *soldaderas* (female
soldiers), nurses, conspirators, strategists, and couriers. Ortiz de Domínguez, also known as La Corregidora (the Magistrate), participated
in a plot to overthrow the Spanish government and free Mexico from
Spanish rule. She leaked information to the insurgents, and her warn-
ing to Father Miguel Hidalgo about plans to arrest him triggered his
famous "El Grito de Dolores" (The Cry from Dolores), which marked
the beginning of the armed rebellion. For her action, Ortiz de Domínguez was denounced as "notoriously scandalous, seductive, and de-
structive," "impudent, bold, and incorrigible." She was imprisoned on

a number of occasions, including during a pregnancy and after the birth of her fourteenth child. Leona Vicario, another female freedom fighter, developed a communications network, published articles written by the insurgents, sold her jewels to buy weapons, and financed a cannon factory.[36]

The war to free Mexico from Spain evoked a mixture of support and opposition among Tejanos, who would later also be divided over the Texian revolt against Mexico.[37] After the 1813 Battle of Medina, the victorious Spaniards swept through San Antonio, turning it into a "scene of barbarity" by executing 300 suspected rebels and locking up women. Spanish soldiers with long whips reportedly forced the women to kneel for hours grinding corn at *metates* (long curved stones) and making tortillas until the flesh was worn from their palms and knees. After several weeks, the troops freed the women and left town.[38] However, the soldiers continued to suffer food shortages. In 1814 Doña María Josefa de la Garza pledged to alleviate the suffering of the Spanish troops under the leadership of Colonel Joaquín de Arredondo. She donated ten head of cattle to feed his soldiers and promised that, if necessary, she would donate the rest of her herd and all her property in defense of "her beloved king and master, Fernando VII."[39]

As a result of the war, Tejanas filed claims against the Mexican government, demanding pensions based on their husbands' services. Juana Francisca de la Garza, the widow of Leonardo de la Garza, petitioned for a widow's pension to support herself and her daughter. Adriana de Mier, the mother of Domingo de Ugartechea, received a military pension and payments from his salary. María Catalina de Urrutia, a widow, requested her husband's back pay and a pension. María Luisa de Urteaga asked that her petition for a widow's pension be forwarded to the president, since she had received nothing since her husband's death.[40]

Women also sought reimbursement for property rented or confiscated and for debt payments. For example, Luisa Gertrudis de la Rúa demanded payment of a debt the government owed to her deceased husband. María Antonia Ibarvo and Ponciano Ibarvo petitioned for rent due on buildings occupied by troops, while María Nieves Travieso petitioned for the return of her confiscated mule.[41]

UNDER THE MEXICAN FLAG (1821–1836): A TIME OF TRANSITION

After Mexico won its independence from Spain in 1821, Tejanos became citizens of the state of Coahuila y Texas. They struggled to protect their political and economic interests as citizens of a multiethnic Mexican nation in transition from a colonial state to an independent republic.[42]

The Mexican government continued to encourage settlement in Texas. The Colonization Law of 1823 promised single men one-third of a league of land, but they could qualify for an additional one-quarter league if they married a Tejana. As a result, a number of Anglos sought to marry the daughters of wealthy Tejano families.[43] Marriages between Anglo men and Tejanas had other attractive economic benefits for both. Take, for example, the case of James Bowie (who later fought at the Alamo). In 1831, Bowie married Ursula de Veramendi of San Antonio, the daughter of Juan Martín de Veramendi, the governor of Coahuila y Texas. The father and son-in-law soon formed a partnership to establish cotton mills in Saltillo.[44]

Concerned that Anglo Americans would overrun Coahuila y Texas, the Mexican government passed the law of April 6, 1830, to halt further North American immigration and to encourage Mexican citizens to move to the area. Under the provisions of the April law, the Mexican government offered to pay the expenses of any qualified citizen willing to relocate. Three women whose husbands were in prison were the first to apply.[45]

THE TEXAS REVOLUTION AND WAR FOR INDEPENDENCE (1835–1836)

During the 1820s and 1830s, thousands of Anglo American colonists flooded Texas. During this same period, about 2,000 slaves also resided in the area. Friction between the Anglos and the Tejano community began almost immediately. By the fall of 1835, when the 30,000 Anglo Americans outnumbered the 5,000 Tejanos by 6 to 1, conflicts boiled over into a revolution. The Texians organized an army and held a meeting at San Felipe in November 1835, calling for immediate independence. The motion was defeated, but the delegates adopted a "Declaration of the People of Texas," stating that they had taken up arms only to defend themselves, to oppose the rule of Santa Anna, and to struggle for a democratic government. Some Mexican origin women supported Santa Anna, while others backed the Texians. For instance, in December 1835 María Francisca de los Reyes rendered service as a geographic guide to Santa Anna's army as it advanced into Anglo areas. On the other hand, María Jesusa de García "was wounded and permanently disabled in rendering extraordinary services to the army of Texas at San

TEXAS
FOREVER!!

The usurper of the South has failed in his efforts to enslave the freemen of Texas.

The wives and daughters of Texas will be saved from the brutality of Mexican soldiers.

Now is the time to emigrate to the Garden of America.

A free passage, and all found, is offered at New Orleans to all applicants.   Every settler receives a location of

EIGHT HUNDRED ACRES OF LAND.

On the 23d of February, a force of 1000 Mexicans came in sight of San Antonio, and on the 25th Gen. St. Anna arrived at that place with 2500 more men, and demanded a surrender of the fort held by 150 Texians, and on the refusal, he attempted to storm the fort. twice. with his whole force, but was repelled with the loss of 500 men, and the Americans lost none   Many of his troops, the liberals of Zacatecas, are brought on to Texas in irons and are urged forward with the promise of the women and plunder of Texas.

The Texian forces were marching to relieve St. Antonio, March the 2d. The Government of Texas is supplied with plenty of arms, ammunition, provisions, &c. &c.

An 1836 advertisement for land in Texas. Courtesy Center for American History. Print from University of Texas Institute of Texan Cultures.

Antonio" when she attempted to carry water to the Texians on December 5, 1835, in spite of a heavy Mexican barrage. She was later commended in an act passed by the Texas Congress.[46] Mexican women took on other burdens as the armed struggle for independence grew. For instance, some Texians forced Mexican women to cook and work for them.[47]

On March 2, 1836, a convention of fifty-nine delegates, including two Tejanos, signed the Texas Declaration of Independence, which stated that the Mexican government had violated liberties guaranteed under the Mexican constitution. The declaration also asserted that Mexico had deprived citizens of freedom of religion, the right to trial by jury, the right to bear arms, and the right to petition. The document stated further that Mexico had failed to provide a system of public education.[48] Following the declaration of independence, Mexican general Antonio López de Santa Anna led his army into the region to defend Mexican territory against insurrection. Sam Houston led the Texian soldiers.

THE TEJANO COMMUNITY'S SUPPORT FOR TEXAS INDEPENDENCE

Some Tejanos joined the Anglo American rebels, others remained loyal to Mexico, and still others were ambivalent. Mexican general Vicente Filisola complained, "All the individuals of the [Victoria] families were the most assiduous collaborators in the Texas revolution."[49] The family of Doña Patricia de la Garza de León was among the prominent families divided over the conflict, with some members siding with the Texians and others remaining neutral. The de León family's support for an independent Texas included an effort to smuggle arms and ammunition from New Orleans to the Texians.[50]

Despite their support of the Texians' cause, the de León family fell victims to the anti-Mexican sentiment that swept Texas after the revolution. Soon after the Battle of San Jacinto, Victoria was plagued by lawless volunteer U.S. troops. Doña Patricia and other settlers sought the assistance of Texas general Thomas Rusk, demanding that he protect them. The general's response was to order them to sail for New Orleans. The de León family believed that their banishment would be short-lived; instead, it turned into a long exile that lasted until 1845. While living in New Orleans, Doña Patricia sold her Victoria ranch to Pleasant B. Cocke for $10,000 and invested in Louisiana mortgages. Her action enabled the family to survive in comfort while in exile. When Doña Patricia returned home in 1845, she found her possessions scattered and her influential position gone. However, the family still had considerable wealth, part of which they used to press their claims in court. Doña Patricia also sold her home in Victoria to an Anglo couple but retained the mortgage. When the two stopped making the $700 payment, she sued them. Doña Patricia died during the court proceedings, but her son Fernando pursued the case, and the suit was eventually settled in the de León family's favor.[51]

The Alamo in San Antonio was originally a religious site called San Antonio de Valero Mission. Courtesy San Antonio Convention and Visitors Bureau.

Another well-regarded family, the Seguíns of San Antonio, donated grain and livestock worth more than $4,000 to the independence effort. At least one Tejana who aided the Texian cause, the aforementioned María Jesusa de García, received a pension from the Republic of Texas for serious wounds received from Mexican gunfire.[52] María Antonio de la Garza of Victoria surrendered about sixty head of cattle, worth about $10 each, to the Texian Army, an act for which she was praised by General Thomas J. Rusk. She later filed a claim for compensation from the Republic of Texas.[53]

TEJANAS AT THE ALAMO AND GOLIAD

At least three Tejanas were present during the famous Battle of the Alamo, from February 23 through March 6, 1836. They all survived. Juana Gertrudis Navarro Alsbury and Andrea Castañón Villanueva nursed Jim Bowie. Alsbury and Castañón were later rewarded with state pensions. However, it took the state more than fifty years to award Castañón's compensation of $12 a month. She finally received it in 1891.[54] Another Tejana, Ana Salazar de Esparza, and her children re-portedly entered the Alamo to seek refuge or to join her husband, Enrique Esparza. She refused to leave when ordered to do so. Her husband was killed during the battle. Her heirs received land for both her husband's military service and his death at the Alamo.

Francisca Álvarez took pity on captured prisoners of war. Following the execution of Colonel James W. Fannin and most of his Texian soldiers by Mexican troops at Goliad in March 1836, she cared for the remaining prisoners and helped several avoid death. The survivors referred to her as the "Angel of Goliad." A bust honoring Álvarez was placed at Presidio La Bahía to honor her role at Goliad.[55]

AFTER SAN JACINTO

The Mexican victory over the Texians defending the Alamo was fleeting. On April 21, 1836, with shouts of "Remember the Alamo" and "Remember Goliad" filling the air, Sam Houston's army attacked and

Fifty years after the fact, Andrea Castañón Villanueva (Madam Candelaria) received a state pension of $12 a month for her nursing services to Jim Bowie at the Alamo in 1836. Courtesy San Antonio Conservation Society. Print from University of Texas Institute of Texan Cultures.

captured Santa Anna at the Battle of San Jacinto. The Texian army, moved by a spirit of revenge, carried out a mass slaughter of Mexican soldiers, and Houston was declared the president of the Republic of Texas.[56]

In the newly independent nation, Tejanas would soon enough find themselves outsiders.

CHAPTER THREE

From the Republic of Texas to 1900

Petra Vela de Vidal Kenedy (1823–1885) was a South Texas rancher and philanthropist. She and Mifflin Kenedy, her husband, prospered with a number of business enterprises and ranches. From the Collection of the Corpus Christi Museum of Science and History, Corpus Christi.

Only now someone asks
About you
Wants to know the truth
And insists on loving you—
Myth, legend, lie. All.

But all the truth
Is buried deeper still
—within your dust.[1]

TERESA PALOMO ACOSTA,
"Chipita"

In 1863 Chipita Rodríguez, an elderly innkeeper in San Patricio, was legally hanged for a murder she probably did not commit. She had pleaded "not guilty" during her trial but was convicted on circumstantial evidence. Although the all-white, all-male jury recommended leniency, she was put to death. Her fate symbolizes the suspicion and violence that plagued the lives of

Tejanas and Tejanos in the nineteenth century.[2] In general, neither Tejanos nor slaves enjoyed freedom and safety in the new Republic of Texas following independence from Mexico in 1836. Anglo Texans in control of the government sought to maintain slavery, restrain or rid the republic of Native Americans, and dispossess the Mexicanos of their land.

AFTER THE TEXAS REVOLUTION

Always remember these words: Texas is ours. Texas is our home.[3]
RAMONCITA, great-grandmother of Jovita González de Mireles

Mexicans are no better than Indians . . . I see no reason why we should not . . . take their land.[4]
SAM HOUSTON, *New York Herald,* January 30, 1848

When Texas became a republic in 1836, its Anglo leaders claimed the land between the Nueces River and the Rio Grande. The political alliance between Anglo Texans and Texas Mexicans began unraveling soon after, and by 1842 their bond was tenuous.

Anglo violence against Tejanos, which had increased during the Texas War for Independence, continued, with Tejanos finding themselves unwelcome in their homeland. Most Tejano exiles returning in the late 1830s found that they had lost their holdings, including land and cattle, to Anglos.[5] Historian Armando Alonzo notes that only where Tejanos retained their land along the lower border, or where they and Anglos worked together in stock raising or trade, were relations between them "amiable." Alonzo also notes that periods of intense conflict and violence existed between the groups.[6]

In the hostile environment that prevailed after the Texas Revolution, Mexicans also began to lose political power. For instance, in June 1841 María Gertrudis Flores de Abrego, the wife of San Antonio mayor Juan Seguín, was a member of the power structure—she had the first dance with the president of the Republic of Texas, Mirabeau B. Lamar, at a grand ball. By April 1842 anti-Mexican sentiment and murder threats forced her husband, Juan N. Seguín, to resign and flee for his life to Mexico. Believing that it was possible to be "both a proud Mexicano and a loyal Tejano," he and his family had donated grain and livestock worth $4,000 to the cause of Texas independence. Seguín had also fought with the Texians at the Battle of San Jacinto. Neither of these examples of patriotism, however, saved him from anti-Mexican

Women worked alongside their families on goat ranches like La Mota Ranch in La Salle County. Photograph attributed to I. N. Hall. Courtesy University of Texas Institute of Texan Cultures.

sentiment in the period following Texas independence. All told, some 200 Tejano families were driven out of San Antonio. By 1856 the Tejano population, once the overwhelming majority in the city, was cut in half.[7]

Moreover, from approximately 1848 to 1885 over 80 percent of the land in South Texas changed hands, with many Texas Mexican families losing their property through lawsuits, sheriff's sales, and questionable transfers of titles. There were notable exceptions—Tejano couples and widows who sold their land voluntarily or were able to hold on to land that had been in their family for generations. Others kept their property by winning lawsuits in court.[8]

For instance, in 1849 the heirs of Doña María Gertrudis de la Garza Falcón filed suit to recover the Espíritu Santo grant, on which Brownsville was located. They claimed that holders of faulty titles had improperly conveyed their land to Charles Stillman and the Brownsville Town Company. Although the Falcón heirs won the suit, they soon sold the Brownsville tract for one-sixth of its appraised value to Stillman's lawyers. The lawyers then sold it back to Stillman. This litigation fueled the bitterness of Juan N. Cortina, a great-grandson of María Gertrudis, who later tried to avenge this and other inequities in what became known as the Cortina Wars.[9]

One of the most famous cases of land transfer for a paltry sum of money involved the widow of Juan Mendiola. On July 25, 1853, she, her three sons, and their wives appeared in Rio Grande City to "set their hands and seals to a warranty deed" conveying their 15,500-acre Rincón de Santa Gertrudis land grant in Nueces County to Captain Richard King for $300. Richard King received more than a bargain when he attained the land that the widow had inherited from her husband. The 15,500 acres cost him less than 2 cents an acre. They formed the basis for the famous King Ranch in present-day Kingsville. The captain imported the entire population of a drought-stricken Mexican village, together with its cattle, to supply his ranch with workers and cattle herds. He promised homes, jobs, and regular cash wages to the 100 men, women, and children. The group became known as *los kineños,* the people of the King Ranch. These new landless Tejanos were essentially wage laborers, whose work was critical to the success of the ranch. Richard King continued to buy land to expand his ranching operation. In 1878 he bought 2,000 acres from Miguel Gutiérrez for unspecified "valuable considerations," and he paid $240 in back taxes to get the title to an additional 27,872 acres of Gutiérrez's Santa Gertrudis grant. He acquired the remaining 24,534 acres for $4,000 in 1881 from Gutiérrez's widow, María Gutiérrez. By then 500 workers and their families lived on the King Ranch. After King's death in 1885, his widow, Henrietta King, ran the ranch with her son-in-law, Robert J. Kleberg, until 1925. They eliminated a $500,000 debt and doubled the size of her holdings to over one million acres.[10]

The King Ranch, created out of previously Mexican-held land, dominated the ranching industry. Nevertheless, Mexican citizens who moved to Texas during this time also became landowners and ranchers. In 1857 Francisca Ramírez and her husband, Milton Faver, moved their family, vaqueros, and cattle over the border to establish a ranch in Presidio County. There they built an adobe castle with huge towers on the banks of a spring to serve as their home and headquarters. Their ranch supplied U.S. soldiers at Fort Davis with mutton, beef, vegetables, grain, and peach brandy.[11]

Tomasa de la Peña and her husband, Valentín de las Fuentes, who had founded the Alberca de Arriba Ranch in Webb County while Texas was still part of Mexico, also owned a large amount of land. After de las Fuentes's death, the Mexican government granted Tomasa de la Peña title to their 22,142-acre grant in 1834. In 1836 Native Americans, probably fighting for their seasonal camping site by the Alberca spring, forced de la Peña, her workers, and her tenants to flee. However, she soon returned and reestablished her ranching spread, which included forty stone buildings. In nearby Duval County, Vicente Barrera inherited land grants where present-day San Diego was built. Following her marriage to Pablo Pérez in 1850, the couple continued to acquire land. By the time she died in 1876, they had accumulated considerable property.[12]

From 1848 to 1860, Tejana ranch owners continued to prosper, and women registered seven of the 109 cattle marks and brands recorded in Webb County. In 1850 Doña Rita Domínguez, a widow, ran the Rosario Ranch in the Lower Rio Grande Valley with the help of a household of thirty-seven male laborers. Other women acquired land through dowries and marriages. For instance, in 1852 Sixto Domínguez of Hidalgo County promised his prospective bride, Salomé Vela, four yoke of oxen, a cart, 130 head of sheep and goats, twenty-two hogs, three cows, the rights to fourteen *sitios* (sites) in the Santa Anita grant, and rights and interests in three additional *porciones* (portions) of land in Hidalgo County.[13]

INTERMARRIAGES AMONG TEJANA LANDOWNING ELITES

After Texas joined the Union in 1845, U.S. law upheld Tejanas' right to inherit land in their own names. This entitlement was not lost on Anglo men, who could acquire economic power and political authority by marrying wealthy, land-owning women like Salome Ballí and Petra Vela de Vidal.[14]

Salomé Ballí was a descendant of one of the early owners of the Santa Anita land grant in Cameron County. After John Young married her in 1848, the couple expanded her family ranch, making it one of the most prosperous in the state. In 1860, a year after her husband's death, the young widow was one of Texas's wealthiest citizens. She owned $100,000 in real property and $25,000 in personal property.[15]

Petra Vela de Vidal, rancher and philanthropist, was born in 1823 along the Rio Grande at Mier, Mexico, where her father was the Spanish provincial governor. When Doña Petra was seven, Comanches captured her and her two sisters. She was ransomed, one sister escaped to freedom, and the third was never heard from again. Doña Petra's first husband, Luis Vidal, was a colonel in the Mexican Army. They had six children before he died, sometime between 1849 and 1852. According to family stories, she inherited a fortune in silver from the Vidal family mines in Durango, Mexico.[16]

The beautiful and wealthy young widow attracted the attention of

Petra Vela de Vidal Kenedy owned this carriage, which was known as a mud wagon. She used it for her numerous trips to Brownsville, Corpus Christi, and Mexico. From the Collection of the Corpus Christi Museum of Science and History, Corpus Christi.

Petra Vela de Vidal Kenedy's crest adorned her china and her coach. From the Collection of the Corpus Christi Museum of Science and History, Corpus Christi.

Mifflin Kenedy, a Quaker steamboat captain from Pennsylvania who ran his boats on the Rio Grande. The couple married in Brownsville around 1854, and he converted to Catholicism. Within a few years, the Kenedys owned a ranch in Hidalgo County with ten thousand sheep. The couple had five children of their own and adopted another. One daughter, Sara or Sarita, later became known as the "Belle of Corpus Christi." [17]

Doña Petra used her horse-drawn coach emblazoned with her family crest to make frequent trips to Matamoros, Mexico, and to Brownsville to visit her daughters and grandchildren. She also used it to travel to Corpus Christi. The coach, while magnificent in appearance, was known as a mud wagon because of its durability. [18]

Mifflin Kenedy, Doña Petra's second husband, became a partner with Richard King in land and livestock. During the Civil War, the Kenedys and the Kings prospered through the cotton trade and steam boating. In 1869 the Kenedys established Los Laureles, a 172,000-acre ranch in Nueces County. One hundred sixty-one workers, including vaqueros, shepherds, and laborers, maintained the ranch. More than twenty Tejano families lived there, with wives keeping house for their husbands and tending to more than forty children. Doña Petra had six household servants to assist her. The 1870 federal census listed the Kenedys as residents of Duval County. Their real estate was valued at $21,000 and their personal assets at $139,600. [19]

When Doña Petra visited her ill mother-in-law in Pennsylvania, local newspapers described Petra as "a quiet, elegant, affluent woman" who spoke only with her maid. Doña Petra was nonetheless sufficiently comfortable among her Anglo relations to prefer that her daughters marry Anglo settlers. Three of them followed her advice. A fourth daughter married a Tejano, Manuel Rodríguez, the mayor of Laredo. [20]

For almost twenty years, Doña Petra suffered from uterine cancer, for which she received increasing doses of morphine. Her husband built her a luxurious home in Corpus Christi, which was finished in 1885, but she died within a month of moving into it. [21]

Juana Cavasos, whom the Comanches also captured, held no animosity toward Native Americans. After she was ransomed, she married Charles Barnard, the brother of her rescuer. Doña Juana and her husband opened a trading post in 1849 in Somervell County and began to trade with the Indians. They accumulated wealth through landholdings, trade, and a gristmill, which they built with slave labor. By 1860 they held real estate worth $50,000, and their personal estate was valued at $60,400. Doña Juana was reportedly an excellent horsewoman.

She was also a midwife skilled in the use of medicinal herbs, the latter a skill she may have learned from a Comanche medicine woman during her captivity. Doña Juana, who gave birth to fourteen children, also relied on midwives, some of whom were slaves and Native American women.[22]

INTERMARRIAGES AMONG SAN ANTONIO'S UPPER CLASS

The San Antonio area—populated with landed families, small ranchers, and laborers—reflected the class divisions of society during this period. Scores of mutually beneficial intermarriages between wealthy Tejanas and Anglos who aspired to the women's wealth occurred. Merchants, lawyers, and politicians positioned themselves atop the Mexican elite by marrying into landed families.[23]

From 1837 to 1860, 906 Tejanas wed Tejanos, while 88 married Anglos. Almost half of the Tejanas who married Anglos were from elite families. Although no one has ever determined how the brides felt about their planned marriages, the unions likely pleased their Anglo partners, who gained land, inherited wealth, and attained high social status. For their part, the Tejano families acquired allies to protect their landholdings. A soldier stationed in San Antonio reported that land-rich parents of Tejanas were determined to have their daughters marry "genuine Americans."[24]

Since Mexican daughters customarily inherited property, often on an equal basis with sons, these arranged marriages could unite Mexican landed wealth with Anglo political influence. Indeed, John W. Smith, who served three times as mayor of San Antonio between 1837 and 1844, and Edward Dwyer, who was mayor in 1844 and 1845, married Tejanas, and one of the de la Garza women married the sheriff. A daughter of José Antonio Navarro also married a member of the ruling elite, the new republic's adjutant general. Since the Navarros owned fifteen town lots and 20,000 acres of land, the marriage created an important base of power among rich Texas Mexicans and the Anglo newcomers who aspired to great wealth and political clout. Some Anglo Texans may have also looked upon marrying Tejanas as a means to pocket the Mexican vote. Although by 1850 Tejanos were less than half the city's population, they nonetheless had political influence. In some cases Mexican women attained a measure of individual economic power by marrying Anglos. For example, in the 1840s Guadalupe Ruiz Durán, the widow of Erastus "Deaf" Smith, ran a successful boardinghouse where most local and transient bachelors lived.[25] Mutually beneficial intermarriages between Tejanas and Anglos continued through the 1870s.[26]

Marriage to an Anglo for an upper-class Tejana initiated a process of acculturation, which often led to the virtual assimilation of their children in a society increasingly dominated by Anglos. However, the woman's Catholic Church affiliation usually resulted in the children being reared as Catholics. The children's godparents—*madrinas* and *padrinos*—were often chosen from among the mother's relatives. Nevertheless, most upper-class children of mixed marriages identified with their father's ethnic group, and their assimilation was aided greatly through their attendance at school. (According to the 1850 census, all children of mixed marriages were attending school.) A few were sent to boarding schools and colleges in other states. Josephine Tobin, whose maiden name was Josefa Agusta Smith y Curbelo, attended a boarding school in Newark, New Jersey. Anita Dwyer, whose parents were Mariana Leal and Edward Dwyer, attended college in Bardstown, Kentucky. With rare exceptions, the offspring of Tejana–Anglo marriages also married Anglos and became ever more assimilated into Anglo American society.[27]

A few Tejanas in San Antonio became Protestants, some as a result of intermarriage. For example, several members of the Navarro family joined the Methodist Church around 1860, and two of the young Navarro women taught classes for Mexican children in Methodist Sunday School in 1861 and 1862. Several other Tejanas who married Anglo men joined Saint Mark's Baptist Church, and Ángela María de Jesús Cooke (nee Navarro), a niece of José Antonio Navarro, was among the thirteen charter members of the First Baptist Church in 1861.[28]

STEREOTYPING OF TEJANAS PAVED THE WAY FOR DISCRIMINATION

Very few of the Mexican ladies could write but they dressed nicely and were graceful and gracious of manner.[29]

MARY A. MAVERICK, *Diary,* 1841

The upper class of women . . . have a certain indescribable charm; a dreamy, soft, subdued, almost languid manner, covering an enthusiasm almost startling when roused.[30]

TERESA VIELÉ, Fort Brown, Brownsville, 1850s

The larger part of each [Mexican] family appeared to be made up of black-eyed, olive girls, full of animation of tongue and glance but sunk in a soft embonpoint which added a somewhat extreme good-nature to their charms. Their dresses seemed lazily reluctant to cover their plump persons.[31]   FREDERICK LAW OLMSTED, 1857

The racial labeling of Tejanas served to bolster Anglo domination. Stereotypes were an "integral part of an ideology that helped justify the Mexican-American War [of 1846–1848] as well as subsequent repression in the conquered territory."[32]

White men and women alike gave voice to racist opinions of Texas Mexicans, whom they described as a "race of mongrels" who were "ignorant, cunning, treacherous," childlike, unambitious, and immoral. Tejanas were described as flashy and morally deficient.[33] Anglo men of the 1840s and 1850s "delighted in recounting tales of the passionate and pleasure-loving señoritas of San Antonio." The Anglo males' wishful thinking likely prompted considerable exaggeration. Some Anglos found Tejanas' practice of nude public bathing offensive, although they also took pleasure in watching the women bathe. Ferdinand Roemer recalled that in San Antonio all inhabitants bathed in the river. "It was quite a startling spectacle to see . . . in the heart of the city, a number of Mexican women and girls bathing entirely naked. Unconcerned about our presence, they continued their exercises while laughing and chattering."[34]

Anglo men also attended the popular, almost nightly, fandangos, where they could observe the "sensuous movements of the Mexican women," whose low-cut and uncorseted dresses were deemed immodest in the eyes of Anglo observers. Their critics rarely took note that families closely supervised unmarried daughters at social gatherings. A Frenchman visiting Castroville in the 1840s did, however, note that after a dance, the "cavalier" accompanied the young lady first to the buffet, then "to her mother or to her chaperon." One Anglo traveler in 1835 was shocked to see "females betting at a public game rabble. I do not suppose they were of respectable standing in society, . . . but I am told that it is not at all uncommon for Mexican ladies to be gaming in public."[35]

The subject of interracial sex preoccupied white males, who claimed that Mexican women had a preference for "foreigners" (whites) and willingly agreed to marry them. Their view of Tejanas as erotic, sensuous, and voluptuous provided them with a pretext for associating with the women of an ethnic group that white society generally considered racially unacceptable. Although Mexican descent women were usually

Fandangos were popular recreational activities in San Antonio's Tejano community. Painting by Theodore Gentilz. Courtesy Daughters of the Republic of Texas Library at the Alamo, San Antonio.

brown-skinned mestizas, some were transformed into light-skinned "ladies" of "Spanish ancestry" in an effort to make them acceptable; their men, however, remained dark-skinned "Mexican[s]." "This new image of Tejanas justified . . . the union of a racially, morally superior Anglo man to a woman of an inferior race." Further, such a woman possessed "racial purity, morality, and economic worth [that] elevated her status, making her worthy of marrying an Anglo while dispossessing her of her racial, historical, cultural and class roots."[36]

TEJANOS IN THE AFTERMATH OF THE U.S.-MEXICAN WAR OF 1846–1848

Mexicans were killed for a cow or horse, for no reason at all. . . .
The Rangers hated the Mexicans, who hated and feared them
in return. . . . There was turmoil and strife unending. There
was blood: Texas dipped a pen deeply in it, and wrote its history
with it.[37]

JOVITA GONZÁLEZ AND EVE RALEIGH, *Caballero: A Historical Novel*

Women earned money by selling birds in the market in San Antonio. Courtesy Daughters of the Republic of Texas Library at the Alamo, San Antonio. Print from University of Texas Institute of Texan Cultures.

In 1845 the United States annexed Texas, precipitating a war with Mexico that ended with the Treaty of Guadalupe Hidalgo in 1848. The treaty had a devastating impact on Mexico, which lost a large part of its territory—most of the present-day U.S. Southwest. The ending of the war also meant that Anglos, taking advantage of their growing economic power, sought to acquire land that Tejanos had held for generations. Nevertheless, numerous Tejanos were able to keep their land, aided by the adjudication process that the state carried out.[38]

Women in the state—whether Mexican or Anglo—suffered significant losses as a result of the Texas Constitution of 1848, which effectively ended some of their legal rights. New laws enacted provided that husbands could manage their wives' separate property and act as the sole administrators of their community property. The constitution did recognize, however, that assets acquired by gift, devise, or descent constituted women's separate property, before or after marriage. It also declared that women could retain land and slaves after marriage and inheritance.[39]

Tejanos were now divided into at least two distinct classes. One group was comprised of landowners who had held on to their land legally and those who had the funds to purchase land for farms or cattle and sheep *ranchos*. Another group was composed of individuals who lost their land as "war veterans and unscrupulous swindlers" found ways of acquiring land from them. This landless class of Tejanos now had to earn a living working as ranch and farm hands for new white owners.[40]

Mexican women also took up wage labor. In Laredo they worked as cooks, housekeepers, and servants in 1850. In 1860, perhaps because of the large number of military troops in Laredo, thirty-six Tejanas earned money as laundresses and fifty-three worked as seamstresses. These occupations had not existed ten years before. Other women worked as cooks and housekeepers. The number of women over fifty-one had also doubled during the decade.[41]

THE CIVIL WAR (1861–1865)

> A party of Mexican American abolitionists renounced allegiance to the Confederacy and pronounced for the U.S. government.[42]
>
> *Corpus Christi Ranchero,* April 20, 1861

Although Tejanos were largely indifferent to the Civil War, most were opposed to slavery, and they escorted many slaves to freedom in Mexico. Some Texas Mexicans intermarried with slaves, and Mexican and black men and women often ran away together. An estimated 900 Tejanos served in the Union Army, while an estimated 3,000 fought for the Confederate Army. Union sympathizers led by Cecilio Valerio and "irregulars" such as Juan Cortina harassed Confederate troops, seizing cotton and livestock for the Union Army. On the other hand, Santos Benavides was appointed a colonel in the Confederate Army, becoming its highest-ranking Tejano.[43]

Some Texas Mexicans prospered during the Civil War because jobs were readily available and wages were higher. Whereas Tejano *carteros* (wagoners) had been threatened and ill-treated in 1857, they were now in great demand to transport goods for the Confederacy. San Antonio, the largest city in Texas at the time, enjoyed an economic boom. It became a key army supply center and cotton-trading hub. Employment opportunities improved throughout South Texas, bringing prosperity to Brownsville and Laredo. Some of the landed Mexican elite provided political and military support for the Confederacy. Petra Vela de Vidal Kenedy and Mifflin Kenedy of Hidalgo County continued to add to their wealth through cotton trading, steam boating, and entering into a partnership with Richard King in land and livestock.[44]

RACISM AND VIOLENCE AGAINST TEXAS MEXICANS: THE CASE OF CHIPITA RODRÍGUEZ, HANGED IN 1863

We the jury find the defendant Chepita [sic] Rodríguez guilty of murder in the first degree but on account of her old age and the circumstantial evidence against her do recommend her to the mercy of the court.[45]   JURY VERDICT, SAN PATRICIO COUNTY, 1863

During the Civil War, Chipita Rodríguez, a woman in her sixties who ran a San Patricio inn on the Aransas River, was convicted of the murder of a traveler, John Savage. The only evidence found against her was circumstantial. Savage's body was found near her house in San Patricio. Possibly a Confederate gunrunner or horse trader, Savage had spent the night at Rodríguez's inn. A few days later his body, wrapped in burlap bags, was discovered floating down the river, and the $600 in gold he had been known to be carrying lay nearby. He had been murdered with an ax.[46]

Rodríguez and Juan Silvera, possibly her son, were arrested and charged with Savage's murder. From the start, judicial proceedings against the two were tainted. The arresting sheriff was also the foreman of the grand jury that returned indictments against Rodríguez and Silvera. Moreover, three members of the grand jury also served on the trial jury, and members of both juries (all white males) faced indictments for crimes ranging from cattle rustling to murder.[47]

During a two-day trial, Rodríguez spoke only the words "not guilty." Silvera was convicted of second-degree murder and sentenced to five years in prison. Rodríguez was found guilty of first-degree murder. The jury recommended mercy for her both because of her advanced age and because the only evidence against her was questionable. Her defense counsel made a motion for a new trial but withdrew it when the "said defendant Chipita Rodríguez . . . having been asked if she had anything to say why judgment should not be rendered and sen-

tence pronounced against her said nothing but that what she had here-
tofore said." The presiding judge, Benjamin Neal, ordered her executed
on Friday, November 13, 1863.[48]

While awaiting execution, Rodríguez was chained to the wall of the
courthouse. Children brought her corn shucks for cigarettes and candy
to eat. Reportedly, most of the townspeople, especially the women—
Tejanas and Anglos alike—believed her to be innocent. Betty Mc-
Cumber drove off the hangman, John Gilpin, when he arrived at her
house to borrow her wagon to transport the condemned woman to the
execution site. Gilpin located another cart and drove Rodríguez to her
execution. She reportedly rode seated atop her coffin, smoking a corn-
husk cigarette. Local citizens silently gathered to watch her being
hanged. Afterward, Rodríguez's body was dropped into a wooden box
and buried in an unmarked grave beneath the tree from which she had
been hanged.[49]

Numerous legends sprang up almost immediately following Rodríguez's execution, and she has since been the subject of two operas,
books, and numerous articles. Twenty-five years later, an old man apparently confessed to the murder on his deathbed. In 1985 State Senator Carlos Truan of Corpus Christi asked the Texas legislature to ab-
solve Chipita Rodríguez of murder. The 69th legislature passed his
resolution, and Governor Mark White signed it on June 13, 1985.[50]

Historian Yolanda Chávez Leyva considers Chipita Rodríguez's
questionable conviction and hanging a tragic example of how bad race
relations in Texas were then. "She represents the thousands of now-
nameless Tejanas and Tejanos who confronted the intolerance, violence, or benign neglect of Texas society in the nineteenth century."[51]
Historian Arnoldo De León has characterized the case as the "product
of vindictive emotions desiring recompense for the murder of a white
man." To protect its stability, white society was willing to execute an
innocent woman.[52]

GENERALIZED RACISM AND VIOLENCE AGAINST TEJANOS

Following the Civil War, lynchings and other atrocities perpetrated
against the Tejano community grew. In South Texas in the 1860s and
1870s, violence took the lives of many innocent Mexicans who were
implicated in cattle raiding.[53] In the 1870s and 1880s, vigilante groups,
local law enforcement officials, and Texas Rangers commonly carried
out acts of brutality, including lynchings. A large number of Tejanos

who fell victim to Anglo ire were coldly murdered. In 1874 Juan Moya and his sons were lynched without a trial after being jailed in Goliad County, accused of murdering an Anglo family.[54] In another case, Anglos killed Benito Bontán, a former guard at the Alamo, and his son, José, after losing a horse race to the two men.[55] On June 21, 1875, the *San Antonio Express* stated that Mexicans were being killed "promiscuously" on public highways because Governor Richard Coke had proposed resolving border troubles by killing Mexicans. At the root of Anglos' discrimination and violence was their sense of racial and cultural superiority. Indeed, white Texans considered Mexicans and African Americans, who were lynched in greater numbers than whites, as innately inferior and thus obstacles to economic and political progress.

Tejanas also faced violence. In 1877 Trinidad de la Garza's husband, Juan Elías Lozano, was murdered on their 300-acre ranch in Refugio County. After his death, de la Garza slept with a loaded rifle pointed at the door to protect herself and her child. She dreaded dawn because "she knew that death had struck her livestock during the night." Her niece recalled frequent visits from "an American man [who] used to come from a nearby town to tell my aunt to vacate the ranch and land because it was not theirs." Having no male relatives to offer protection, the widow moved in 1878 to a 187-acre ranch in La Bahía (Goliad).[56]

Besides using physical intimidation and violence against people of color, Anglos undertook organized means to disenfranchise them. On February 8, 1892, the *Corpus Christi Caller Times* reported, "The citizens of Duval County have organized a 'White Man's' Party." Along with Jim Crow laws in the late nineteenth and early twentieth centuries, which were intended to separate blacks from whites in such public accommodations as trains and restaurants, white male–only vigilante groups grew up around the state, reinforcing Anglo domination through violence. In 1896 the U.S. Supreme Court supported the notion of racial superiority when it gave judicial approval to segregated public accommodations in *Plessy* v. *Ferguson.* The decision subjected African Americans to the "separate but equal" law of the land. Although Tejanos were not legally excluded under the "separate but equal" provisions of *Plessy,* they were excluded from public accommodations by custom. Other laws were also oppressive. In 1899 a seventy-year-old Mexican in San Antonio "was saddened" when he was denied an application for a marriage license to a fifty-two-year-old Negro woman because of the state's miscegenation laws.[57]

Francisca de la Garza, the widow of Goliad deputy sheriff Juan Rubio, was left
with nine children to support in 1903. She kept her family alive with a small
pension and by planting corn, beans, and chili peppers on land her father gave
to her. Courtesy Abel Rubio, Houston.

One of the first cases involving the civil rights of Tejanos occurred
in 1896, when Ricardo Rodríguez, a Mexican who had lived in San Antonio for ten years, went before a federal judge for final approval of his
application for United States citizenship and thereby the right to vote.
In 1897 the judge ruled in Rodríguez's favor, legally affirming the right
of Texas Mexican males to vote.[58]

TEJANAS AND LANDOWNERSHIP

Many Mexican Americans arrived in Concho County as day laborers
between 1868 and 1872, later acquiring land and wealth. Doña Ramona
and her husband, Don Pablo Alderette, were among the most prominent. The couple held dances at their ranch, with both Anglos and

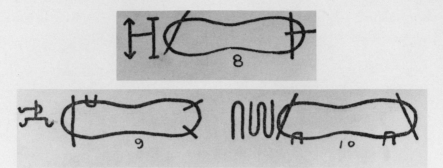

Tejana ranchers registered their cattle brands (ear marks) in Nueces County in 1867, 1868, and 1869. No. 8, Margarita Villareal; no. 9, Florencia Benavides; no. 10, Paula Rodríguez. Copied from Hortense Warner Ward, "Indian Sign on the Spaniard's Cattle," *From Hell to Breakfast,* edited by Mody Boatright. Courtesy Publications of the Texas Folklore Society, XIX, 1944.

Mexicans attending. Don Pablo also served as a member of the first county commission and as justice of the peace for his precinct. After his death in 1882, Doña Ramona moved with her children into San Angelo, where the family also owned land. She remarried and became an active participant in the community.[59]

A number of other Tejanas—Margarita Villareal, Florencia Benavides, and Paula Rodríguez—registered cattle brands at the Nueces County courthouse in the late 1860s.[60] From 1870 to 1898 about forty Spanish-surnamed women filed homestead claims, usually for 160 acres, in such counties as Atascosa, Bexar, Duval, and Webb. One woman, Petra López, even pioneered an urban homestead in downtown El Paso, claiming three town lots in 1873. She was reportedly the only person, woman or man, who claimed city lots as a homestead in Texas.[61]

In 1878 Rafaela Hinojosa and her husband, José Anastacio Barrera, moved from Mier, Mexico, to work the 19,000-acre Los Braziles Ranch near Falfurrias in Brooks County. They raised cattle, horses, sheep and goats, and harvested corn, beans, and cotton.[62] Besides operating ranches alone or with their husbands, Tejanas also participated in the sheep industry. In Duval County, prosperous sheep owners in the 1880s included Refrigia Vela de Guerra, María Antonio Jiménez, Victoria Guachola, and Macaria Muñós.[63]

During the 1870s and early 1880s, New Mexican *pastores* (sheep herders) moved to the Texas Panhandle with their families and flocks. The largest group arrived in 1876 with Salomé and Casimero Romero, a prominent and wealthy New Mexican couple. The Romero family moved themselves and five thousand sheep, horses, and other livestock to what is now Tascosa. The Romeros traveled to their new home in a large caravan that included a coach and fourteen wagons purchased from the army and painted regulation army blue. Four yoke of oxen pulled each vehicle. In 1882 the Romeros lost half their sheep in a blizzard. By 1896 both encroachment by Anglo ranchers and the arrival of railroads drove the Romeros to sell their holdings and return to New Mexico.[64]

The Romeros' experience became a familiar one among Tejanos who lost land to railroad companies. Indeed, the State of Texas encouraged these corporations to construct railroads by granting them millions of acres of public, supposedly vacant, land as bonuses. Some of this land, however, belonged to Tejanos. Antonia Cruz, the widow of Carlos de la Garza and owner of the 2,000-acre Becerra grant in Refugio County, was the victim of fraud involving land scripts that the General Land Office granted to the International and Great Northern Railroad Company in 1875. Unfortunately for her, some of these scripts fell within the boundaries of her grant. By 1884 Antonia Cruz no longer appeared in the county tax records.[65]

After Texas became a state, the legal status of Spanish and Mexican land grants became a major issue for Tejanos. In most cases, "the state acted swiftly to validate land-grant claims presented to the board of commissioners in 1851 and 1852." Tejano families fought until the 1920s to receive formal validation of their land titles. Later, state courts considered almost three hundred more land title cases; they validated most of these as well, rejecting only a handful.[66]

RURAL LIFE: CHANGES IN TEJANO LIFE ON THE LAND

The Mexicans have sold the great share of their landholdings and some work as day laborers on what once belonged to them. How sad this truth![67]   NICASIO IDAR, ca. 1911

Tejanos were a majority of the population in the Lower Rio Grande Valley from 1850 to 1900 (increasing in numbers from 10,000 to almost 90,000).[68] As Tejanos were dispossessed of their land, they began to work for wages on land they once owned. Women were also forced into wage work as field hands, shepherdesses, cooks, domestics, and gardeners. Tejano elites, once major landowners and ranchers, could not escape these changes for long either. By the 1870s and 1880s, many faced declining fortunes. Nevertheless, some women property owners continued to fare well. In 1894 four Tejanas in Brownsville owned property valued at more than $5,000. The estate of María Josefa Cavazos was worth $48,625 and Antonio Ysnaga and his wife had assets amounting to $10,079. Julia P. de Beastero's property was valued at $11,020, and Caledonia Garza's holdings were set at $5,868.[69]

The introduction of barbed wire had a devastating impact on Mexican and Anglo owners of small ranches, who had little money with which to fence their land. Changes in landownership placed Tejanos into two servant classes: vaqueros, whose work was restricted to cattle, and *peones* (laborers), who tended goats and sheep, worked the fields, and performed menial labor, including housework. The *patrón* system —a form of labor relations involving paternalism, reciprocal obligations, and permanency—ruled the lives of the *peones*.[70]

In 1850 Tejana wage laborers partly supported about 5.2 percent of Tejano households across the state; fifty years later, by 1900, the percentage of Tejanas who worked for wages stood at 15 percent in South Texas. In the 1880s Amanda Burke employed Tejanas as goat herders on La Mota Ranch, her ranch in La Salle County.[71] In the latter part of the nineteenth century, Tejanos and their families, including the women, became the mainstay of the cotton-picking force in South Texas, working as wage laborers and tenant farmers. Others joined the migrant stream to find work in other Texas counties.[72]

CHANGES IN THE ECONOMY: THE RAILROADS AND URBANIZATION

> Complaints are frequent among the [white] ladies of El Paso, on account of not being able to secure female help.
>
> *El Paso Times,* February 28, 1891

Between 1880 and 1900, the rise of commercial farming and the railroads curtailed ranching, significantly altering the Texas economy and the lives of Tejanos.[73] The railroads promoted urban growth and provided jobs for displaced ranch workers. Railroads also reinvented the border by creating new urban centers and transporting people to them, and by linking the U.S. Southwest to northern Mexico.[74] Tejanos also moved to Houston in the 1880s, seeking a better life. By the 1890s the city directories listed Mexican peddlers, mainly as tamale vendors. At the century's turn, although the city's Mexican population had grown, it remained at under 500.[75]

El Paso boomed with the arrival of the railroads. In 1881 the city's population was 1,500; by 1890 it had reached 10,000. As early as 1883, the *San Antonio Express* noted that Mexicans in El Paso would work as servants only if the employer spoke Spanish.[76] Immigration from Mexico began to increase in 1880 as entire families, along with single men and female heads of household, arrived in the border city. Women, single and married, worked to supplement the family income. According to the *El Paso City Directory* of 1889, almost one-half of working Tejanas were domestics (61), and about one-third were laundresses (40). Although laundry work was backbreaking and underpaid, home-based washerwomen led more independent lives than domestics. The business required little investment for equipment, and since many women washed the clothes at home, they controlled their own time and combined the job with household duties and child care. By 1900 census takers found that 17.11 percent, almost one-fifth, of El Paso Tejano households included a female wage earner. Since both the census and city directories failed to count many Tejanos and Tejanas, these figures are probably low.[77]

Some Tejanos in small towns and cities began entering the middle class as entrepreneurs and small business owners. By 1900, 7.5 percent of Tejanos were urban entrepreneurs. In the Del Rio area, the "Tejana-managed San Felipe farms prospered as a corn producing enterprise." In 1883 a woman described in one account as the Mexican (and bilingual) wife of a man named Taylor ran several corn mills. The woman was likely Paula Losoya Taylor, who cofounded Del Rio.[78] In Brownsville the 1880 census recorded thirty-eight "Mexican" dressmakers, forty-five "washers," seventy-two "laundresses," twenty-one "hucksters" (peddlers), and five sewing-machine operators. The numbers are probably low, as many women kept boarders, performed odd jobs for pay, and may not have been included in the census.[79]

A small number of Tejana workers found new opportunities. The May 7, 1887, *San Antonio Express* reported from Laredo, "Mrs. Fernández is acting as inspectress at the ferry on the river." Most other women continued working in such traditional jobs as midwives and healers. Caterina Flores de Guerrero, mother of twelve, was a midwife for the area around San José Mission in San Antonio. She delivered more than three hundred babies from 1874 to 1940. A few Tejanas joined nursing

Elena Villarreal de Ferrer around 1872 in Victoria. Courtesy Local History
Collection, Victoria College.

and religious teaching orders. In 1871 María Josefa Esparza became one
of the first San Antonio (and Mexican origin) women to be invested in
the Sisters of Charity of the Incarnate Word when she became Sister
Claude. The Sisters of Charity founded the first hospital in San Antonio in 1869—the Santa Rosa Infirmary—and recruited members from
Mexico, as well as from Europe and the United States.[80]

COMMUNITY BUILDERS AND LEADERS

The poor never appealed to her in vain and their wants were often anticipated.[81]   OBITUARY OF PETRA VELA DE VIDAL KENEDY, 1885

Women were at the center of community life in Texas as early as the 1730s, when Canary Islanders settled in San Antonio. In the early 1800s, Doña Rosa María Hinojosa de Ballí and Doña Patricia de la Garza de León were prominent church supporters in La Feria and Victoria, respectively. In 1833 Josefa Flores de Barker donated 200 acres of her land to establish the town of Floresville, and in the 1840s the home of María Josefa Menchaca and her husband, José Garza, served as church, school, and community center in southeastern Bexar County.[82]

Petra Vela de Vidal Kenedy, a devout Catholic, was a philanthropist who was well known for her generous gifts to the poor. She also gave money to Saint Mary's Church in Brownsville, and after the Kenedys moved to Corpus Christi, Doña Petra again helped the church and the poor. She donated three bells for the tower and other gifts to a new Catholic church.[83]

Doña Paula Losoya Taylor also served as a community builder and benefactor. She was a key figure in the founding of Del Rio in 1860, and also contributed land for a school and a cemetery. Doña Paula divided up other land among a group of settlers, supervised the planting of sugarcane, corn, and other vegetables, and built a sugar mill. She introduced irrigation and the growing of grapes into the area. After the death of her second husband, James Taylor, she opened her home as a boardinghouse.[84]

Adina De Zavala of San Antonio, who was a charter member of the Texas State Historical Association in 1897, contributed to the preservation of the Alamo (originally San Antonio de Valero Mission). She led a long, sometimes bitter, and ultimately successful campaign through her chapter of the Daughters of the Republic of Texas to save the Alamo's historic long barracks from destruction. To emphasize the importance of her crusade, she locked herself in the barracks during a three-day hunger strike and protest in 1908.[85]

Numerous other women participated in the Tejano community's *sociedades mutualistas* (mutual aid societies). The groups had originated in Mexico in the 1870s to provide self-help and community service, including low-cost funerals and low-interest loans, as well as assistance to the poor. *Mutualistas* sprang up in San Antonio, Laredo, Brownsville,

Adina Emilia De Zavala, granddaughter of Lorenzo de Zavala, a vice president
of the Republic of Texas, was a teacher and one of the founders of the Texas
State Historical Association (1897). She was instrumental in preserving the
Alamo from commercial exploitation. Courtesy Center for American History,
University of Texas at Austin.

These young girls, some holding books and one a slate, attended the Incarnate
Word Convent School in Brownsville around 1890. Courtesy Nazareth Convent.
Print from University of Texas Institute of Texan Cultures.

Eagle Pass, and Corpus Christi. Women may have organized the first female-led *mutualista,* the Sociedad Mutualista de Beneficencia de Señoras y Señoritas, in Corpus Christi in 1890. On April 1, 1892, the *Corpus Christi Weekly Caller* reported, "The better class of Mexican citizens attended a ball given by the Ladies Mutual Aid Society."[86] In the 1890s women organized the Sociedad Josefa Ortiz de Domínguez in Laredo.[87] In the coming twentieth century, women would continue to participate in *mutualistas* both to support the needs of women and to bolster the Tejano community. Moreover, women would shape an array of efforts to support the Mexican Revolution of 1910 and provide the leadership to carry them out. They would also resist continuing Anglo racism in the coming century.

CHAPTER FOUR

Revolution, Racism, and Resistance: 1900–1940

Jovita Idar was a journalist for *La Crónica,* her family's Laredo newspaper. She helped establish and lead the Liga Femenil Mexicanista, one of the earliest known twentieth-century organizations of Mexican American women. Courtesy A. I. Idar. Print from University of Texas Institute of Texan Cultures.

As the twentieth century began, the Texas-Mexico border was sparsely populated with small settlements and cities. The Mexican American population was dominant in the region, much as it is today. At the turn of the century, Mexican Americans were the overwhelming majority of present-day Webb, Cameron, and Starr Counties. Along the El Paso–Juárez border, they comprised more than 50 percent of the population. In a region where agriculture and trade formed the economic backbone, women entered the paid labor force as servants, laundresses, and seamstresses. Men worked as day laborers, vaqueros, shepherds, farmers, artisans, merchants, and professionals.[1]

The anti–Porfirio Díaz senti-

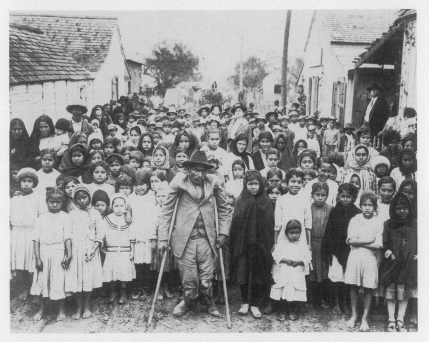

Refugees like these fled across the Rio Grande into such border towns as Brownsville in 1913. Photograph by Robert Runyon. Courtesy Runyon Collection, Center for American History, University of Texas at Austin.

ment leading to the Mexican Revolution of 1910 began even before the turn of the century. Indeed, the short-lived Garza War was an effort to launch a Texas-based attack on Porfirio Díaz in 1891–1892.[2]

Mexican origin women along the border took part in the Mexican Revolution, fighting on all fronts of the struggle. In addition, from 1900 to 1940, women influenced all the major efforts within the Tejano community to address economic, political, and social injustice and to retain its cultural heritage. Santa Teresa Urrea, Sara Estela Ramírez, Andrea and Teresa Villarreal, Jovita Idar, and Leonor Villegas de Magnón were among those who created a resistance movement on behalf of Texas Mexicans and worked to advance the cause of the Mexican Revolution.

SANTA TERESA URREA

Santa Teresa Urrea, a healer associated with the revolutionary Lauro Aguirre, lent her support to the turn-of-the-century movement against Porfirio Díaz. Several years prior to the start of the Mexican Revolu-

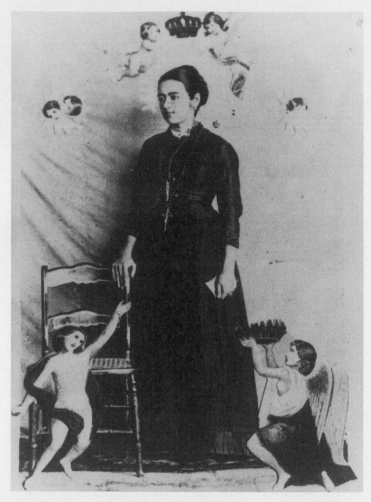

Teresa Urrea, also known as Santa Teresa and the Niña de Cabora, was a healer, political figure, and a symbol of hope for the Yaqui and Tomochi Indians. She lived in Texas in approximately 1896. Courtesy Arizona Historical Society, Tucson, Arizona.

tion, she became a political force among the Yaqui Indians, who represented indigenous resistance to Díaz. Urrea was the child of Tomás Urrea, a wealthy rancher and supporter of the liberals in Mexico, and Cayetana Chávez, a Tehueco Indian who worked in his household. Because the Díaz government harassed Tomás Urrea, a political moderate, the Urrea family left Sinaloa for Cabora, Sonora, Mexico. There Teresa

Urrea attended school and learned to read. She was also instructed in healing by María Sonora, an Indian who was reportedly a *curandera*.[3]

Urrea fell into a cataleptic state lasting three months and eighteen days after the family arrived in Cabora. When she recovered, she began to perform healings by the laying on of hands. As word of her miraculous abilities spread, many poor Indian pilgrims sought out Urrea, who did not charge for her services. She espoused justice for the downtrodden, and her attitude apparently inspired a series of rebellions among the indigenous people. In 1891 the Tarahumara Indians from the village of Tomochi rose up against the Mexican government to protest the injustices perpetrated against them. Díaz ordered Santa Teresa and her father deported in 1892 on the pretext that they were responsible for the insurrection. The family settled first in Arizona but moved to El Paso in 1896, fleeing unremitting government harassment.[4]

Shortly after her arrival in El Paso, Yaqui and Tomochi Indians calling themselves Teresitas attacked the Mexican customs house in Nogales, and Urrea was accused of helping them. The United States government sought to extradite her, although she denied any involvement in the attack. After three assassination attempts on her life, Urrea left Texas for Clifton, Arizona. From there she traveled to major U.S. cities, working as a healer. She eventually returned to Clifton, where she died in 1906.[5] Urrea's support of the poor made her part of the groundswell of women whose concern with the downtrodden on both sides of the border propelled them into political activism as community leaders, nurses, and *soldaderas* (female soldiers) during the Mexican Revolution.

WOMEN INTELLECTUALS JOIN THE REVOLUTIONARY MOVEMENT

¡Surge! Surge a la vida, a la actividad, a la belleza de vivir realmente. [Surge! Surge to life, to liveliness, to the beauty of truly living.][6]   SARA ESTELA RAMÍREZ

By the time the Mexican revolution to end the thirty-four-year rule of Porfirio Díaz broke out in November 1910, the passion among women intellectuals to see him overthrown had grown steadily, and a sizable number of them joined the struggle. Historian Emma Pérez has written that women developed their own "particular agenda" and brought a feminist perspective to the revolution. Thus, between 1900 and 1910 they both promoted and shaped the larger revolutionary cause in numerous ways and fought to ensure that women's abilities and concerns were not ignored. Their support of the Partido Liberal Mexicano (PLM), the major opposition political party, was especially important. The PLM, which began to operate in Texas in 1904, was first organized at the Congreso Liberal in San Luis Potosí in February 1901.[7]

Afterward, Ricardo Flores Magón and his brother Enrique, PLM leaders, were arrested and imprisoned several times for their revolutionary activities. The two eventually fled to Laredo, Texas, arriving on January 3, 1904.[8] Tejanas in the border city, in surrounding communities, and in San Antonio welcomed the PLM.

In 1904 Sara Estela Ramírez, a poet, political activist, and trusted confidant of Flores Magón since 1901, took up the cause of the PLM, becoming one of its principal contacts in Laredo. Ramírez, who had been educated at Ateneo Fuentes, a teacher's college in Saltillo, Coahuila, Mexico, had arrived in Laredo at the age of seventeen. There she assumed a position as a teacher of Spanish at the Seminario Laredo. When Flores and Enrique Magón escaped to Laredo, Ramírez offered her home as their headquarters. Because the PLM was under the watchful eye of local authorities, as well as of Pinkerton and Furlong detectives, the Magón brothers had to exercise great caution, so Ramírez took on the role of spokesperson for the party.[9]

Ramírez worked in the Tejano community as a political activist, writing essays that supported the working class. She published some of these works and her poetry in at least two Spanish language newspapers in South Texas, *El Demócrata Fronterizo* and *La Crónica,* between January 8, 1908, and April 9, 1910. Her works provide important insights into women's roles in society and revolutionary politics. Because she was a highly sought-after speaker, some of her essays were based on her public speeches before Tejano organizations. Ramírez first presented "Alocución" (Address) and "Igualdad y progreso" (Equality and Progress) as lectures to the Sociedad de Obreros, Igualdad y Progreso, a *sociedad mutualista* (mutual aid society). In both works, she urged workers to remain united for the good of all and insisted that they practice altruism in their struggles against exploitation.[10]

Sara Estela Ramírez was also a publisher, overseeing two newspapers. One of these, *La Corregidora,* which featured literary works, was printed in Mexico City and distributed in Laredo and San Antonio. She published another newspaper, *Aurora,* which was printed in Laredo.[11] As a journalist and PLM advocate, Ramírez allied herself with other women in the resistance movement, including Dolores Jiménez y Muro, Juana Belén Gutiérrez de Mendoza, and Elisa Acuña y Rossetti.[12]

Dolores Jiménez y Muro served as president of Hijas de Cuauhté-

moc, a women's political resistance organization, and edited several revolutionary journals. Gutiérrez de Mendoza established the newspaper
Vésper: Justicia y Libertad in 1901, using money from the sale of goats that
she owned. Elisa Acuña y Rossetti served as coeditor of the newspaper.
The appearance of *Vésper* netted a compliment from the Magón brothers. They praised Gutiérrez de Mendoza as "la mujer animosa y va-
liente" (a brave and valiant woman). Like Sara Estela Ramírez, Gutiérrez de Mendoza was also a teacher who dedicated herself at an early age
to educating poor Indian children and to improving the lives of agricultural and industrial workers.[13]

Juana Gutiérrez de Mendoza began her career in journalism in Chihuahua for the liberal newspaper *La Voz de Ocampo*. She was imprisoned in Mexico in both 1902 and 1903 for her outspoken criticism of
the Díaz regime, and her newspaper *Vesper* was impounded. From her
jail cell, where she met Jiménez y Muro and Acuña y Rossetti, Gutiérrez de Mendoza continued her revolutionary activities, editing *Fiat
Lux,* yet another opposition newspaper.[14] The resistance publications
that the four women oversaw lobbied strongly against the Díaz dicta-
torship. Their newspapers also reinforced community solidarity and
called for societal changes.[15]

Juana Gutiérrez de Mendoza lived to an old age, continuing her political work and later publishing *Alma Mexicana*. Sara Estela Ramírez,
however, died at the age of twenty-nine on August 21, 1910, of un-
specified causes. Her passing was deeply felt and mourned in the Tejano
community. Fellow journalist and activist Jovita Idar lauded her as a
woman of "intelligence, tenderness, and talent."[16]

THE REBEL

> The Rebel established a bureau of secret service. News of impor-
> tance was given directly to her regarding movements of troops
> so that she could supply loyal nurses and doctors as territory was
> gained.[17]   LEONOR VILLEGAS DE MAGNÓN

With the death of Sara Estela Ramírez, the service of other women
working for the Mexican Revolution took on an even greater significance. One of them, Leonor Villegas de Magnón, wrote a memoir
of the revolutionary era, *The Rebel*. Years later, her great-great-niece
Claire Keefe noted that Villegas de Magnón was considered the "black
sheep of the family."[18]

Villegas de Magnón's father had "affectionately" first called her "La

Leonor Villegas de Magnón (top row, beneath flag) and members of La Cruz Blanca, a medical relief organization she founded to provide aid to Carrancista soldiers and civilians injured during the Mexican Revolution. Also pictured are U.S. doctors who helped the organization. Laredo, around 1913. Courtesy A. I. Idar. Print from University of Texas Institute of Texan Cultures.

Rebelde" (the Rebel) after soldiers searching the family's neighborhood mistook her cries as a newborn for the voices of insurgents. In time, Villegas de Magnón gave up her privileged background to join other women involved in the rebellion against Díaz. She ultimately became a writer, nurse, teacher, political activist, and founder of La Cruz Blanca (The White Cross), the medical field nurses organization that assisted the troops of Venustiano Carranza during the Mexican Revolution.[19]

Villegas de Magnón's well-to-do family educated her to be a teacher, sending her to the Ursuline Convent in San Antonio and later to the Academy of the Holy Cross in Austin. Afterward, she graduated from Saint Ursula's Convent in New York with honors and returned to Laredo, planning a career as a teacher. However, following her marriage to Adolfo Magnón on January 10, 1901, she moved to Mexico City, where she enjoyed the privileges of the wealthy class. Apparently, as she relates in her memoir, she grew both disenchanted with her position and intolerant of Porfirio Díaz's repression of the poor.[20]

Villegas de Magnón eventually began associating with the antigovernment forces in Mexico City, keeping from her husband her meetings with Francisco Madero, a leader of the liberal faction. Her career as a journalist began in this period, as she dashed off "fiery articles" in opposition to Díaz. In 1910, prior to the outbreak of the revolution, Villegas de Magnón returned to Laredo with her children to tend her ill father. After his death, she remained in Laredo and became involved in the revolutionary struggle with the opposition group, Junta Revolucionaria. Villegas de Magnón also began to work with journalist and community leader Jovita Idar and to write articles for *La Crónica,* the newspaper owned by Idar's family. She also wrote for *El Progreso* and *El Radical,* both revolutionary journals, and she turned her Laredo home into a shelter for Mexicans fleeing from persecution by the Díaz regime. Equally concerned with the welfare of the future Texas Mexican generation, she established one of the first bilingual kindergartens in the region during this period.[21]

On March 13, 1913, Villegas de Magnón recruited Jovita Idar, then a writer for *El Progreso,* to join her in crossing the border to nurse opposition soldiers wounded in the war. The two persuaded four other women to go with them. The women's spontaneous effort led to the founding of La Cruz Blanca. After Nuevo Laredo was attacked on January 1, 1914, Villegas de Magnón threw all of her financial resources behind the medical corps, officially launching it.[22]

The kindergarten students of Leonor Villegas de Magnón around 1910. Villegas de Magnón was a kindergarten teacher who organized La Cruz Blanca with the assistance of Jovita Idar during the Mexican Revolution. Copied from *We Can Fly,* edited by Mary Beth Rogers et al. Courtesy Ellen C. Temple.

With the attack on Nuevo Laredo, she transformed her home into a hospital where she, Jovita Idar, and fellow members of La Cruz Blanca tended to more than a hundred soldiers of Venustiano Carranza's forces. She also fought efforts by U.S. authorities to arrest and detain the soldiers in her care and sought legal counsel to obtain the release of soldiers who had been arrested and taken to Fort McIntosh. U.S. Secretary of State William Jennings Bryan had the men freed after Texas governor Oscar B. Colquitt refused to intervene on the soldiers' behalf. Later that year, leaving her children in the care of her family, she led La Cruz Blanca across the border at El Paso to head the medical team for the Carrancista forces.[23]

THE VILLARREAL SISTERS: ANDREA AND TERESA

It is now time for woman to become independent and for men to stop considering themselves the center of the universe and to stop oppressing her and to give her in daily life the position of comrade and companion that corresponds to her.[24]

WOMEN'S STATEMENT, *Regeneración,* February 25, 1911

Andrea and Teresa Villarreal were contemporaries of Sara Estela Ramírez and Leonor Villegas de Magnón. Andrea Villarreal received the honorific title Joan of Arc from the *San Antonio Light and Gazette*. The pronouncement appeared in the newspaper on August 18, 1909, the day on which Andrea joined Mother Jones, the labor activist, in making public speeches calling for the release of Mexican revolutionaries imprisoned in San Antonio.[25] Andrea Villarreal disagreed with the statement, saying: "It is not good to call me the Mexican Joan of Arc because I cannot go to Mexico on a horse at the head of my soldiers and I cannot fire a gun, my hands are too small."[26]

Teresa Villarreal, Andrea's sister, established the socialist paper *El Obrero* (The Worker). By 1910, working as a team, the Villarreal sisters had founded *La Mujer Moderna* (The Modern Woman), a San Antonio-based newspaper that championed the emancipation of women. The two raised funds and organized activities with Leona Vicario, a feminist organization, and worked with the Liberal Union of Mexican Women.[27] They were also actively involved in the San Antonio group Regeneración. Teresa Villarreal served as president of the group, which called for the liberation of women as a crucial outcome of the Mexican

ANDREA VILLARREAL
Mexican ''Joan of Arc,'' who will speak in Spanish at meetings in old tent
Theater on Houston Street.

Andrea Villarreal addressed a San Antonio rally on August 18, 1909, demanding freedom for jailed Mexican revolutionaries. She and her sister Teresa published *La Mujer Moderna* (The Modern Woman). Print from Center for American History, University of Texas at Austin.

Revolution. Other officers included Isidra M. de Ibarra, secretary, and Concepción Ibarra, director.[28]

Since the male leadership of the PLM was often under duress politically, the work of Andrea and Teresa Villarreal in San Antonio, like that of Idar and Villegas de Magnón in Laredo, was essential to the insurgent cause. One observer noted, "Women in Texas were particularly active since [they] had to continue the work [that] men were now too intimidated to do."[29] Other women who publicly affirmed their commitment to the PLM included Margarita Andejos, Domitila Acuña, Severina Garza, María Cisneros, Concepción Martínez, and Carmen Luján, all of Dallas. The women wrote a letter to Flores Magón on March 4, 1911, offering their support to the PLM and demanding that he "go hard on the bourgeoisie," who, the women noted, preferred to keep the working class under its yoke.[30]

FEMALE POLITICAL REFUGEES: THE CASE OF FLORES DE ANDRADE

> Later when everything was ready for the revolutionary movement against the dictatorship, Don Francisco [Madero] and all those who accompanied him decided to pass over to Mexican territory. I prepared an afternoon party so as to disguise the movement.[31]
>
> FLORES DE ANDRADE

Many other women—often unnamed and unknown—were part of the contingent involved in the Mexican Revolution. Oral history has provided a window into the lives of these less known women, who entered Texas as political refugees and continued their political participation on the U.S. side of the border. Indeed, the story of Flores de Andrade's involvement in the Mexican Revolution might have gone unnoticed had she not recounted her memories to anthropologist Manuel Gamio.[32]

Born into a wealthy family in Chihuahua, Mexico, Flores de Andrade spent her childhood on her grandparents' estate. When she was thirteen, her grandparents died, leaving her a large inheritance. She soon set all the workers on the family estate free of their debts, and provided them with animals and tools to continue to work the land for as long as they desired.[33]

Flores de Andrade married and had six children. Following her husband's death, she took her children to live in Chihuahua City. Once there, she turned her empathy for the poor workers on her family's estate into political action, joining with Elisa Acuña y Rossetti to work with the Hijas de Cuauhtémoc. Flores de Andrade's activism subjected her to criticism and poverty. In 1906, with her companion, PLM member Pedro Mendoza, she moved her family to El Paso, where she worked for both Flores Magón and Francisco Madero, raising funds and gathering medicine, clothing, arms, and ammunition. U.S. officials apparently ordered her to marry Mendoza. She later divorced him, charging him with infidelity and abuse.[34]

Flores de Andrade's life is similar to the lives of other women who, leaving behind either great fortunes or the confines of married life, took on the revolutionary cause on either the federal or the insurgent side. In doing so, many of them forged new identities and new roles.

María Catherine Villagómez (left) and Delfina Martínez Villagómez, her mother (right), were among the thousands of Mexican citizens who arrived in Texas during the Mexican Revolution. They carried $800 in gold and silver, proceeds from the sale of their house in Morelia. While crossing a creek, Delfina accidentally dropped the gold but luckily saw it shining in the moonlight and retrieved it. Photographed around 1915. Courtesy Lyndon Baines Johnson Library and Museum and Mary Catherine Villagómez, Houston.

THE REVOLUTION'S IMPACT ON WOMEN

Women who crossed the Mexico-U.S. border during the revolution were especially vulnerable to exploitation by U.S. authorities. *Solas* (single women) traveling on their own or as single mothers with children could count on immigration authorities questioning or threaten-

Some refugees from the Mexican Revolution crossed into Texas around El Paso.
Courtesy Aultman Collection, El Paso Public Library.

ing them as they entered Ciudad Juárez or El Paso. Women were also
economically at risk, often lacking the funds needed to cross the border. Pasquala Esparza suffered such a fate and was forced to remain in
Juárez as a housekeeper. Jesusita, her nine-year-old daughter, had to
care for her younger siblings while their mother worked to support the
family. In other instances, women who needed to cross the border challenged border officials. This strategy sometimes worked to their advantage, as happened in the case of Trinidad Orellana, who was defiant in
answering border guards' queries. She was ultimately admitted to the
United States and joined her mother and sisters, all actors at El Paso's
Star Theatre.[35]

Many women witnessed the horrors of war, including starvation,
rapes, and kidnappings.[36] One female refugee recalled:

> There were hardly any provisions left . . . because the soldiers
> didn't leave a thing. They dumped over the small pails and fed
> their horses everything that had been harvested. Many people died
> of hunger. One of our aunts died of hunger and she had four chil-
> dren and one of them also died.[37]

Women served as *soldaderas* during the Mexican Revolution. Although leaders such as Pancho Villa on the rebel side and Salvador Mercado on the federal side opposed female soldiers, they were powerless to keep women from joining their armies. As a result, *soldaderas* took part in gun running, spying, fighting, nursing, burying soldiers, and cooking.[38]

Soldaderas were part of the dispersed sections of Salvador Mercado's *federales* (federal troops), who crossed the border in retreat from Pancho

These *soldaderas*, who fought in the Mexican Revolution, were photographed in Matamoros, Mexico. Courtesy Hidalgo County Historical Museum, Edinburg.

Villa's constitutional forces in January 1914. The Mercado army consisted of 3,557 men, 1,256 *soldaderas,* and 554 children. The United States military incarcerated Mercado's troops from January to May 1914, initially at Presidio, then at Fort Bliss, Texas, and later at Fort Wingate, New Mexico. While living in the prison camps, women continued to carry out some of their regular roles—aiding wounded soldiers and cooking. One *soldadera,* Captain Clara Ramos, who led a faction of women irregulars under Orozco, a foe of Mercado, successfully infiltrated the Presidio camp and convinced at least seventy *federales* to escape with her. The group avoided capture by both U.S. soldiers and Villa's army and made it back to Mexico City.[39]

The presence of women in the Mexican Army complicated matters for U.S. Army officials, who were not accustomed to female soldiers. Conditions for Mercado's troops in the camp at Presidio were atrocious, and the U.S. Army could not adequately provide them with basic necessities. Rather than allowing the Mexican soldiers to cross back into Mexico at a safe point, the Americans marched them to Marfa, Texas, a distance of about sixty-seven miles. Initially they feared that the lengthy march would exact a great toll on the women. Mercado allayed their fears, assuring the U.S. Army that the *soldaderas* were familiar with the rigors of "outdoor life and capable of enduring fatigue." The women proved him right and marched to Marfa, bearing the weight of their usual cargo: "small children, pots, pans, kettles, and bedding."[40]

JOVITA IDAR, THE LIGA FEMENIL MEXICANISTA, AND TEJANO RIGHTS

As the Mexican Revolution was being waged, the Mexican descent population in Texas continued to suffer from limited political and economic power, segregated schooling, and racial violence, including lynchings.

Journalist Jovita Idar, whose family published *La Crónica* in Laredo, was one of a number of women who banded together to address these issues. Idar led the Liga Femenil Mexicanista (Female Mexicanist League), a women's group established during El Primer Congreso Mexicanista (The First Mexicanist Congress), held in Laredo from September 14 through 22, 1911. The Liga is likely the first well-known twentieth-century effort that Tejanas created to work on behalf of the Mexican origin population in the state. Established principally to promote free education for Texas Mexican children, the Liga also organized social, cultural, and charitable activities. It took as its motto "Por la Raza y para la Raza" (For the People and by the People).[41]

Both professional and working-class women were members of the Liga, which met at Idar's family home. The group sponsored theatrical and other literary performances to raise funds for its work, and news of its activities appeared in *La Crónica*. Besides Jovita Idar, members included Luisa Cabrera, María de Jesús de León, Aurelia Peña, Soledad Flores de Peña, María Rentería, Señora de Silva, Rita Tarvín, and María Villarreal. One of the members, Soledad Flores de Peña, spoke on behalf of women's education at the Congreso Mexicanista.[42]

The Liga's president, Jovita Idar, like many of the educated Tejanas of her era, had initially entered teaching, the profession most commonly open to women. Educated at the Holding Institute, a Methodist school, she earned a teaching certificate in 1903 at the age of eighteen and then taught school at Ojuelos, Texas. Very poor conditions at the school ultimately forced her to resign. She then began to write for her family's newspaper, *La Crónica,* which covered all manner of events taking place in Laredo. As a result, Idar reported on the economic, political, and social struggles that the Texas Mexican community faced.[43]

Like Leonor Villegas de Magnón, Jovita Idar publicly condemned the maltreatment of Mexicans by U.S. authorities. In an editorial for *El Progreso,* another paper for which she worked, she protested President Woodrow Wilson's sending of U.S. troops to the border. Her words elicited great opposition from both the Texas Rangers (disparagingly called *los rinches* by Tejanos) and the United States Army. When the Texas Rangers attempted to shut down *El Progreso,* Idar blocked their entrance by standing in front of the office doors. The Rangers ultimately succeeded in closing down the newspaper, and Idar returned to work for *La Crónica.* Following the death of her father, Nicasio Idar, in 1914, she and her brothers Clemente and Eduardo Idar oversaw the family newspaper.[44]

Jovita Idar married Bartolo Juárez on May 20, 1917, and they settled in San Antonio. There she continued to work in the Tejano community and joined the Democratic Party. She also set up El Club Democrat, an organization that helped facilitate Tejano political activity in the city. Continuing the tradition that the women of the Liga supported, she opened a free kindergarten for Tejano children and taught them Spanish and English. She also served as an interpreter at the Robert B. Green Hospital Clinic and worked as a writer and coeditor for *El He-*

raldo Cristiano, the official news organ for Spanish-speaking Methodists. In addition, Idar wrote for two Italian newspapers in San Antonio, *La Voce de la Pattria* and *La Voce Italiana.*[45]

VIOLENCE AGAINST TEJANOS IN THE NEW CENTURY

Anglo Texan violence against Tejanos continued in spite of El Congreso Mexicanista of 1911, in part motivated by the tensions brought about by the Mexican Revolution. As a result, some in the Texas Mexican community banded together under the Plan de San Diego of 1915, a revolutionary manifesto declaring armed struggle against Anglo Texan violence. The plan called for a force of Mexican Americans, African Americans, and Japanese to liberate the states of Texas, New Mexico, Arizona, California, and Colorado from the United States and create a free society comprised of people of color. Many Texas Mexicans—seditionists and innocent citizens alike—were killed in the bloodshed that resulted from the guerrilla warfare. Américo Paredes and Walter Prescott Webb estimated that the total number killed was 5,000.[46]

Indeed, between 1885 and 1942 white Texas citizens killed many people of color. Texas was third, after Mississippi and Georgia, in the number of lynchings carried out during that era. One account of this fifty-seven-year period reported that 339 blacks, 77 whites, and 53 Mexican Americans were lynched in Texas. More than one-half of the Tejanos who were lynched were put to death around 1915, the same year that the Plan de San Diego was launched.[47]

THE CASE OF GREGORIO CORTEZ

For Tejanos, the case of Gregorio Cortez may perhaps be the best-remembered early twentieth century act of police action and incompetence, as well as the best-known act of early twentieth century resistance by the Tejano community.[48]

On June 12, 1901, poor interpretation during Sheriff W. T. "Brack" Morris's questioning of Cortez concerning a case of horse thievery left Morris dead just outside of Kenedy and Gregorio's brother Rómulo wounded. Rómulo Cortez later died in the Karnes County jail from his wounds.[49]

Following the event, many other Tejanos became the victims of retaliatory violence in at least eight cities and four counties. Public reaction to the shooting of Morris was divided along ethnic lines. While the Tejano community banded together and raised funds to defend Cortez, many non-Tejano newspapers such as the *San Antonio Express* worried that he had not been lynched. The *Seguin Enterprise* stated flatly that Cortez was an "arch fiend." After several trials, Cortez was given a life sentence, but he served only approximately nine years. In July 1913 Francisco A. Chapa, the editor of San Antonio's *El Imparcial,* helped Cortez win a conditional pardon from Governor Colquitt.[50]

1920 AND BEYOND: NEW ORGANIZED RESPONSES TO COMMUNITY NEEDS

The Mexican Revolution was responsible for the first and largest single wave of Mexican immigrants to the United States in the twentieth century. Many who came joined family members already living on the northern side of the Rio Grande. As the numbers of Mexican origin people in the country increased, they faced anti-immigration laws that would continue to plague them through the rest of the twentieth century as American authorities, often at the behest of conservative politicians, sought legal means to limit their entry.

The Immigration Act of 1917 contained provisions designed to bar immigrants deemed undesirable, a category in which Mexicans found themselves. For instance, the 1917 legislation included a literacy test and a head tax. Immigrants crossing the Rio Grande were also at the mercy of the immigration authorities. Tejanos referred to these officers as "la Migra" and considered their treatment of Tejanas particularly odious. In general, many immigrants faced detention in holding tanks and poor living conditions, without even the basic necessities of toilets or water provided to them.[51]

In the face of anti-immigration legislation and ill treatment, Mexican Americans continued to organize for self-improvement through the *sociedades mutualistas* and other civic organizations that promoted educational and economic opportunities. The *mutualistas* served both immediate and long-term goals, helping with medical assistance and burial insurance and promoting economic progress.[52]

The *sociedades mutualistas* had originated in Mexico in the last quarter of the nineteenth century, and their numbers grew as more immigrants arrived in Texas during the Mexican Revolution. By the 1920s mutual aid societies could be found in every barrio in the United States. In Texas, Corpus Christi was home to about a dozen. There were ten in El Paso and more than twenty in San Antonio. Although most mutual aid societies were exclusively male, women participated in them in a variety of ways. In San Antonio, of the nineteen *mutualistas* established between 1915 and 1930, only seven allowed women to join and hold office; two others allowed women's auxiliaries, and two consisted exclusively of women.[53]

The *mutualistas*' promise to provide insurance to cover sickness and burial costs initially attracted most members. Nevertheless, the groups' leaders had a more far-sighted vision of their role in the Tejano community and sponsored programs to meet a wide variety of needs and interests: legal aid, libraries, adult education, and cultural programs. Despite male dominance of many *mutualistas,* women formed auxiliaries in some of the larger groups, and Luisa M. González of San Antonio headed a *mutualista* with both female and male members, the Alianza Hispano-Americana, which had originated in Tucson, Arizona. Thanks to the female *mutualistas,* as well as the women's auxiliaries within the male-dominated *mutualistas,* families were provided for during illnesses. The female *mutualistas* also tended to women's needs during childbirth and afterward assisted with child care. Indeed, women's efforts to create informal alliances within the *mutualista* movement formed the backbone of the group's pledge to assist the Tejano community.[54]

MARÍA L. DE HERNÁNDEZ

Acting individually, women leaders also assisted the Tejano community in the 1920s to develop new organizations that would help in the struggle for equality. María L. de Hernández was one of the most important of these leaders. On January 10, 1929, Hernández cofounded the Orden Caballeros de América (Order of Knights of America) in San Antonio with Pedro Hernández Barrera, her husband. They created the organization to involve Mexican Americans in defending their rights and to increase their participation in civic and political activities. Given the continuing segregation of Mexican American children in public schools, the group was especially concerned with educational matters. In 1933 Hernández also established the Asociación Protectora de Madres, under the sponsorship of the Orden Caballeros, to provide financial assistance to expectant mothers. The mothers' group lasted until 1939.[55]

Shortly after setting up the mothers' association, Hernández and her husband collaborated in establishing La Liga de Defensa Pro-Escolar. La Liga was another effort to focus attention on the poor educational op-

María L. de Hernández, a Tejana leader and orator, spoke out eloquently and fought for the rights of her people for more than forty years. Copied from the dedication page of her publication *México y los cuatro poderes de dirigen al pueblo.* Print from Benson Latin American Collection, University of Texas at Austin.

portunities offered to children of Mexican descent on the west side of San Antonio, where most Mexicans lived. There the schools were among the worst in the city, staffed with less experienced teachers and supplied with antiquated textbooks. Hernández, an excellent orator, organized the community to protest these conditions and appeared before the state superintendent of schools to appeal for changes.[56]

The daughter of a professor, Hernández had studied to be a teacher. After completing her training, she taught in primary schools in Monterrey, Mexico. She later moved with her family to San Antonio and took up important community work, often in conjunction with her husband. Hernández's activism on behalf of the Tejano community was not a youthful fancy; she continued her involvement well into the 1960s and 1970s, making several hundred speeches throughout her life on behalf of the Tejano community. As an elder, Hernández became a well-respected member of the Raza Unida Party, the political party organized during the Chicano movement.[57]

LADIES AND LULAC

As the 1920s drew to a close, the growing Mexican American middle class in the state sought another means to help them become full-fledged Americans. Longing to attain the American dream and to protect their rights, they established the League of United Latin American Citizens (LULAC) on February 17, 1929, in Corpus Christi. Originally called the United Latin American Citizens, LULAC holds the record as the longest continually active civil rights organization for Mexican descent citizens in the United States. From its inception, LULAC took on such issues as jury exclusion of Mexican Americans, white-only primaries, and segregation in all sectors. Despite surveillance by the Federal Bureau of Investigation in earlier decades, the organization has thrived.[58]

Women have played an important role in LULAC from its beginning. By 1932, three years after the group's founding, Tejanas had organized women's auxiliaries within the organization. A year later, in 1933, Ladies LULAC was founded at the LULAC state convention in Del Rio, Texas. Granted permission to "organize on the same basis as men," the Ladies LULAC chapters replaced the women's auxiliaries. In that same year, LULAC set up the post of "ladies organizer general" to establish women's chapters throughout the United States. The position existed at least through 1942. Tejanas who have held the position include Estefana Valdez of Mission, in 1934–1935; Gladstone Swain of San Antonio, in 1936–1938; and Esther Machuca of El Paso, in 1938–1939.[59]

Most of the members of Ladies LULAC were drawn from the Mexican American middle class. They were often high school graduates, and some had completed college. A small number of professional women eventually joined the group. In the 1930s mother-daughter teams joined

Alice Dickerson Montemayor, top row, fourth from right, organized a coed
Junior LULAC Council in Laredo in 1937. Copied from *LULAC News,* May
1939. Print from Benson Latin American Collection, University of Texas at
Austin.

in Houston. Members ranged in age from twenty-one to over sixty-
five. The Ladies Councils were fairly independent of one another and
the men's councils. The councils nonetheless shared similar interests:
children, the poor, women, and elders. They also organized youth
groups known as Junior LULAC Councils.[60]

SHAPING LADIES LULAC IN THE 1930S: ALICE DICKERSON MONTEMAYOR AND ESTHER NIETO MACHUCA

> If a woman is qualified to fill a general office and some of our
> membership draw the line on her just because of her sex, then they
> are not true Lulackers and are not complying with that which is
> provided for in our Constitution.[61]
>
> ALICE DICKERSON MONTEMAYOR

Alice Dickerson Montemayor of Laredo and Esther Nieto Machuca of
El Paso took on significant roles in shaping both Ladies LULAC and its
umbrella organization, LULAC.

A social worker in Webb County during the Great Depression,
Montemayor became a charter member of Ladies LULAC no. 15 in
1936 at the invitation of Esther Nieto Machuca. Montemayor rose

OUR LADIES ORGANIZER GENERAL

Mrs. J. C. Machuca

THE FIRST GENERAL OFFICER TO BE APPOINTED
BY PRESIDENT GENERAL FILEMON T.
MARTINEZ IMMEDIATELY AFTER
HE TOOK OFFICE

SUCCESSFULLY PUTS THROUGH HER ORIGINAL
PLAN OF HAVING THE LADIES COUNCILS
OF OUR LEAGUE TO SPONSOR AN
EDITION OF LULAC NEWS

SHE HAS AN ENVIABLE RECORD TO HER CREDIT

By Mrs. F. I. Montemayor

Associate Editor

In the historic and romantic town of Ojinaga — formerly El Presidio del Norte—Distrito de Iturbide, State of Chihuahua, Republic of Mexico, our Ladies Organizer General, Mrs. J. C. Machuca (nee Esther Nieto), was born on the 10th day of October, 1895. Her parents, Juan Nieto and Carolina Rodriguez. On her paternal side she is the grand daughter of Dicnicio Nieto and Jesus Franco, and on her maternal side Dario Rodriguez and Lucia Baeza were her grandparents. All families mentioned being among the pioneer and leading families in the Presidio del Norte region.

Her father, Juan Nieto was a lawyer and civil engineer, who during his lifetime enjoyed a very lucrative practice in both professional fields. Mrs. Machuca is the fifth child of a family of twelve. Almost all her relatives have been blessed with large families. On November 22, 1936, her parents celebrated their golden wedding anniversary at which time a family reunion was had and over 100 persons direct descendants of the Nieto and Rodriguez families attended. Half of these were children, grand-children and great-grandchildren of Don Juan and Doña Carolina. Today Mrs. Machuca has many kinsmen on both sides of the Rio Grande. Among those who are very closely related to her and who live on the north side of the Rio Grande are the Burgess, Kleinman, Russell, and Spencer families.

On June 26, 1915, she married Juan C. Machuca, at Presidio, Texas, who is known to Lulackdom as the most outspoken and dynamic Director of Publicity that Lulac has yet produced. In April 8, 1932, the Machucas became the proud parents of a son, whose name is Louis. They have no other ambition in life than to train and educate Louis to become a model Christian, a loyal American citizen, and incidentally an active and true Lulacker.

Our Ladies Organizer General does not belong to any particular social group. Her hobby is housekeeping and making that "terrible" husband of hers as well as her sonny boy as comfortable and happy as possible. Though a recipient of many invitations to join various social clubs and recreation groups, Mrs. Machuca has very graciously declined them. She admits that Lulac has really been the only organization that has attracted her attention. She is very much interested in good literature and devotes a great deal of her leisure time in reading educational and literary works of Spanish authors.

In 1934, when the El Paso Ladies Council No. 9 was first organized, Mrs. Machuca took an active part in the organization work. She was among the charter members and had the honor of being its first Treasurer. In 1936, because of the failure of the General Office —at that time—to cooperate with Council No. 9, Mrs. Machuca was among the first to accept the decision of the majority of the membership to withdraw from the League. This was not done because of lack of Lulac spirit, but because it was found impossible for the council to function properly without the cooperation of the General Office. She is a firm believer in constructive work and in 1937, when El Paso Ladies Council No. 9, was reorganized, Mrs. Machuca took a very prominent part in the reorganization of her local council.

In recognition for her constant activity and her executive ability, she was elected Official Hostess for the 1938 National Convention of Lulac, held in El Paso, last June. She was in charge of the entertainment of the women delegates and visitors at the social party given at the Pent House of the Hilton Hotel. The writer having been present at this charming affair will vouch for Mrs. Machuca's ability and personality as a gracious hostess.

Mrs. Machuca was the first General Officer to be appointed by President General Filemon T. Martinez,

Esther Machuca of El Paso was the ladies organizer general of the League of United Latin American Citizens (LULAC) in 1938–1939. Copied from *LULAC News,* May 1939. Print from Benson Latin American Collection, University of Texas at Austin.

quickly in stature in the organization. In 1937 she was the first woman elected second national vice president general of LULAC. In 1938–1939, she was president of Ladies LULAC no. 15. She also soon established a reputation as an outspoken defender of women's rights. In 1937, at the funeral of Ben Garza, the first president of LULAC, Montemayor discussed women's roles in politics. As an associate editor of the *LULAC News,* she wrote essays in support of women. In October 1937 Montemayor wrote "Woman's Opportunity in LULAC," declaring that women must assume roles within the organization that improved their lot. She followed this essay with an editorial in March 1938 in which she discredited male domination and called for full and equal participation of women in LULAC. She entitled the piece "Son muy hombres(?)." [62]

Montemayor also put her skills to use in promoting LULAC among Mexican American youth. As the major convener of the Junior LULAC, she wrote its first charter and served as its president general in 1939–1940. She also established a coed youth group as an example for adult LULAC members. In 1940 she gave up her work with the organization. In later years, Montemayor became a famous folk artist. [63]

Esther Nieto Machuca, Montemayor's colleague, established Ladies LULAC no. 9 in El Paso in 1936. Two years later, angered over the refusal of LULAC's state-level male leaders to answer the group's correspondence, she led the women in disbanding the council. She also helped reorganize it a year later after the issue had been resolved. [64]

When the national convention of LULAC was held in El Paso in June 1938, Machuca was the official hostess for the delegates. With the election of Filemón T. Martínez as the LULAC president in 1938, she was appointed ladies organizer general. During her one-year tenure (1938–1939), Machuca increased the number of chapters outside of Texas, thereby giving Ladies LULAC a national presence. At the end of her term, Ladies LULAC Councils were operating in California and Arizona as well as in Texas. [65]

JOVITA GONZÁLEZ DE MIRELES: DOCUMENTING THE EXPERIENCE OF TEJANOS IN THE ERA OF VIOLENCE AND TEJANO RESISTANCE

There is a group of advanced progressive Texas Mexicans who, realizing that the future of their children depends upon their getting an American education, are sending their sons and daughters to American colleges and universities. [66]   JOVITA GONZÁLEZ

In South Texas, folklorist, educator, historian, and writer Jovita González (later Jovita González de Mireles) responded to the Tejano experience in the era of violence and cultural loss from another perspective. In an article entitled "America Invades the Border Towns," published in the *Southwest Review* in the summer of 1930, she addressed the struggles of Tejanos to gain equality in the United States.[67] The daughter of land-rich Mexicans who lived in Roma, Texas, González was educated at Our Lady of the Lake University in San Antonio, where she completed a bachelor's degree in Spanish in 1927. As a young woman, she became the first Texas Mexican to record her people's folklore in English and one of the first Tejanas to attain a Master of Arts degree at the University of Texas at Austin, on August 29, 1930. She completed a master's thesis based on her knowledge of Mexican life in South Texas, calling it "Social Life in Webb, Starr, and Zapata Counties." She later noted that her thesis arose from "a lifetime of love and understanding of my people." Eugene C. Barker, her graduate advisor, had initially rejected her topic. However, Carlos E. Castañeda, a Tejano historian and González's mentor, convinced Barker that her work would be "used in the years to come as source material."[68] As one of the first university-educated Tejana intellectuals in the twentieth century, González ultimately turned writing about Texas Mexicans into a powerful tool of resistance against efforts to erase them from the historical record of Texas.

González, like the Tejanas who shaped organizations such as the Orden Caballeros de América, the *sociedades mutualistas,* and Ladies LULAC, became involved in the struggle for educational justice. She and Edmundo Mireles, her husband, were associated with the Texas Mexicans involved in the *Salvatierra* v. *Del Rio ISD* desegregation lawsuit in 1929, the first official court challenge to the segregation of Mexican descent students in public schools in the state. The couple's involvement in the effort led them to work with the San Felipe School that Tejanos set up to protest their treatment in Del Rio schools. González became an English teacher at San Felipe, and Edmundo Mireles worked as its principal. The two spent the next four years helping shape the education of Tejanos at San Felipe.[69]

CHAPTER FIVE

Life in Rural Texas: 1900–1940

Sabina Palomo (left) and María Acosta (right) in front of the Fall family ranch in McGregor around 1934. Both women worked in harvesting Central Texas's cotton crop during the Great Depression. The two became permanent residents of the area. Teresa Palomo Acosta Collection, Benson Latin American Collection, University of Texas at Austin.

RULERS IN THE HOUSE

"La mamá era todo." (The mother was everything.) Without the mother there would be no family.[1]

AN ELDERLY MEXICANA
RECALLING HER FAMILY LIFE

After many Tejano families living in South Texas lost their land in the early twentieth century, they took up life on Anglo-owned ranches. The women contributed to the family economy through their daily homemaking chores, which could begin as early as four o'clock in the morning. One Tejana who lived on a ranch from 1915 to 1932 recalled a typical morning:

I woke up first in the house and put some water to boil in a pan
for the children's baths. . . . I'd bathe all the children, one by one,
and dress the smaller ones. . . . I prepared the *masa* (dough) for
the tortillas. . . . Then I'd have to start preparing lunch for my
husband.[2]

A woman who lived in the countryside had scant time to relax because she was bound to a variety of around-the-clock responsibilities: organizing the family's daily life, caring for her children and in-
structing them in household tasks, and nursing those who fell ill. She
also endeavored to keep her house clean and her children dressed in
neat, though worn, garments. As a self-respecting housekeeper, she had
no desire to be known as a *dejada* (lazy woman) who did not tend to
her home.[3]

Although in many families a husband had the last say on most issues,
women exercised much authority in household matters and in the children's upbringing. A Tejana who lived on a ranch in 1910 recalled her
parents' relationship:

My mother *mandaba en la casa* (was the boss in the house), but
decisions were made by both her and my father. If my father
wanted to sell all the *maíz* or a cow, he first consulted with my
mother. . . . They were good to each other.[4]

Tejanas recalled family life on the ranches as physically hard but
close-knit. Women rarely had time to socialize, but they did pay *visitas*
(visits) to female friends' houses. Sometimes they stayed overnight, taking advantage of the opportunity to maintain a sense of solidarity with
other women. Besides going on *visitas,* they made occasional forays to
the nearby towns to watch silent movies.[5]

FOLLOWING THE CROPS

As the twentieth century progressed, an increasing number of Tejanas
and their families were reduced to a state of extreme poverty. In 1911
Laredo's *La Crónica* editorialized about Tejano land loss and the resulting poverty caused by the sale of land to Anglos in South Texas. "The
Mexicans have sold the great share of their landholdings and some work
as day laborers on what once belonged to them. How sad this truth!"
By 1920, as the Mexican Revolution drew to an end, Texas Mexicans

María (Chata) Sada and her husband, Juan Sada, ran Chata's Place in the Big Bend area, offering miners and other visitors hot meals, lodging, and loans in the 1920s and 1930s. Beginning in the late 1920s, María Sada also acted as a midwife and teacher for people living on both sides of the border. Photography Collection, Harry Ransom Humanities Research Center, University of Texas at Austin.

"had generally been reduced, except in a few border counties, to the status of landless and dependent wage laborers." Thus, in the new century, a large number of Tejanas and their families became the seasonal and migratory workforce for the commercial agriculture that developed in the state in the late nineteenth and early twentieth centuries.[6]

Both immigrant and native-born Tejano families labored in the fields, whether harvesting spinach in Crystal City or picking cotton in

Tejano laborers in a cotton field on the Fall family ranch in McGregor around 1937. Women and men worked together in the fields to support their families. Photograph by Lucía Alderete. Teresa Palomo Acosta Collection, Benson Latin American Collection, University of Texas at Austin.

Central Texas. Two sisters who ultimately settled in Central Texas, Sabina Palomo Acosta and Juanita Palomo Campos, were among the many Tejanas who, as daughters of landless Mexican immigrants, worked the spinach and onion fields owned by white South Texas farmers. The sisters' family arrived in Texas in approximately 1918, pushed out by the Mexican Revolution. Sabina was approximately four years old. Juanita, her sister, was born in Crystal City in 1922. Maximino Palomo, their father, had worked on a ranch in San Luis Potosí, Mexico. The Palomos arrived in Texas as part of the estimated 1.5 million immigrants who left Mexico for the United States between 1890 and 1930.[7] As migratory agricultural workers, the Palomos traversed the state from their base in Crystal City for a number of years before they settled in McGregor, joining the many Mexicans who eventually made their permanent homes in Central Texas.[8]

As more Mexicans arrived in the state to fill jobs in the fields, South Texas towns such as Asherton, Donna, and McAllen became a "reconstructed rural society" where white farmers owned much of the land and Mexican families worked it.[9] In Cotulla, the farmers hired so many Mexican field hands that the town's population swelled with Tejanos. Indeed, by 1928 Mexican Americans made up 80 percent of Cotulla's total population of 3,000. Labor contractors, including some Tejanos, often recruited workers directly in Mexico to work in the fields. As a result, Mexicans poured into the state by the thousands, seeking a promise of jobs and better wages in the commercial agricultural economy.[10]

They found plenty of work in harvesting tomatoes, cabbages, carrots, potatoes, beets, corn, green beans, and onions—the staples of the

Martha Vela and Lucía Zambrano lived in Bee County in the late 1910s. Courtesy Tensy Quinbar. Print from University of Texas Institute of Texan Cultures.

Lower Rio Grande Valley cornucopia. Farmers had introduced citrus, the most important produce of the region, as a commercial crop in 1904.[11] Better wages were offered the immigrants than they received in Mexico. For instance, in 1910 a Mexican family could earn $5 a day picking cotton in Collin County, in comparison to the 12½ cents each member would earn in Jalisco, Mexico. In 1923 workers could each earn $3 a day in Texas, but only 50 cents in Mexico.[12]

By the 1920s the new cotton-based agriculture of the state relied on vast numbers of Tejano farmworkers. They worked the land from the southern tip of the state to Central Texas and then to West Texas. Many traveled as multiple family units for companionship and assistance as they moved from region to region.[13] Still other families extended their stays after the cotton harvest and became residents of West Texas towns, including Lamesa, Rotan, Sweetwater, Muleshoe, Lubbock, and Plainview.[14]

Indeed, between 1912 and 1920, migrant workers began to remain in Lubbock County after the end of the cotton harvest. In 1912 Ventura Flores was the first Mexican American to settle permanently in Lubbock, when he pitched a tent by the railroad depot. Four years later he was the first Mexican American to acquire a home in that city. A barrio of Mexican American families sprang up around him. The presence of Tejanos in Lubbock increased in later years, with many of the field workers moving to that city from other parts of Texas. In 1939 the U.S. Employment Service reported that 85 percent of the labor force in the fields was Mexican, while 10 percent was black. Women comprised approximately 15 percent of all laborers in the Panhandle.[15]

Traveling from one place to the next on their journeys from Crystal City to Robstown to Plainview, families might stop to eat a meal and spend the night along the road. Following an overnight roadside stay, mothers and daughters rose early. After "quickly dashing water" on their faces, they prepared the family's breakfast. Because they often did not carry corn with them or lacked the time to grind it into *masa,* the women reverted to making white flour tortillas, which took less time to prepare. They also cooked the traditional staples of *arroz* (rice) and *fideo* (vermicelli), but they rarely prepared pinto beans, which took a much longer time to cook. The women made everything on their portable *comal* (cast iron griddle), which was placed atop stacked firewood that they gathered from the side of the road.[16]

Once they reached their destination, Tejana farm laborers worked hard in the fields, with employers usually dictating the conditions. One descendant of a family that worked for the giant Callaghan Ranch near Cotulla recalled that the working circumstances were "feudal." Tejanas were also part of "large labor gangs" for the agribusiness companies that developed in the new era. The 200,000-acre Taft Ranch near Corpus Christi was perhaps the best-known corporate farming effort of the period, employing new technologies and worker management strategies to produce cotton.[17]

Some labor union sympathizers stepped in and organized farmworkers in South Texas. One of these union leaders, Manuela Solis Sager, would later organize factory workers. In 1932, in the midst of the Great Depression, she turned her attention to Tejano field hands in Laredo, where she helped establish unions for onion field workers. By 1935, working with James Sager, she succeeded in getting the workers to go out on strike. She and Sager also organized about 1,000 farm and packing shed workers in the Rio Grande Valley into the United Cannery, Agricultural, Packing, and Allied Workers of America (UCAPAWA). The company bosses, however, took pains to keep their labor movement in check, preventing the workers from making significant improvements in their conditions.[18]

In Cotulla, where Lyndon Baines Johnson taught in one of the segregated Mexican schools, Tejana agricultural workers lived in shacks in farm labor camps.[19] These inadequate shelters provided scant haven from the heat and cold. In addition, the workers' wages reflected their employers' neglect of them. When Johnson arrived in Cotulla in the late 1920s, a family of four working in the Winter Garden area earned $600 in annual wages. Many Tejano families, seeking to improve their lot, attempted to find a better situation, only to be restrained by state laws. The Texas legislature, for instance, passed the Emigrant Labor Agent Act of 1929 to prevent labor contractors from other states from setting foot in Texas to recruit workers for their regions.[20]

The state coveted Mexican field hands because its agriculture-based economy flourished with cheaply paid labor. Unquestionably, the work that Tejanas and their families accomplished in harvesting cotton, the state's principal cash crop, was extremely important. When small local farmers called for an end to the immigration of Mexican workers, the agribusiness corporations, whose profits depended on Mexican labor, did not heed them.[21]

Mexican American girls who sought to improve their lot through a public school education often failed to make any headway. Julia González de Toro, a young Tejana in La Salle County, was typical of the

The daughter of a farm family is surrounded by family photographs in her home near Santa María, twelve miles southeast of Harlingen. Photograph by Russell Lee. FSA 606-32126-D. Courtesy Library of Congress.

young females whose families could not afford to educate them. Instead she picked cotton all day, contributing her wages to the family's support. Only the more fortunate children of the "shopkeepers" attended school. Thus, a majority of young Tejanas and their families worked in the local fields and then boarded "rickety" trucks to cross the state on the migrant trail, following a variety of crops—cotton, tomatoes, onions.[22]

Cotton growers prized the Mexican field hands because they often worked as a family unit. Moreover, the farmers could count on the Mexicans' large families, including daughters, to pick a great deal of cotton. In fact, by 1920 women were quickly becoming a sizable portion of Texas field workers, partly because an estimated 50 percent of all immigrants who came to the state from Mexico were females and children. Some of the women traveled alone—*solas*—finding work on their own through labor contractors. They sent a portion of their earnings to the families they left behind in Mexico.[23]

The Great Depression, which followed the stock market crash of October 29, 1929, created a severe economic crisis in the state. Conditions worsened after 1931. In the rural areas, the situation degenerated even beyond the poverty to which sharecroppers and tenants were accustomed.[24] Tejanas, already near the bottom of the economic scale, would experience even more severe conditions as farm laborers during the depression.

Focused on earning a living, few Mexican American women in the rural areas took full advantage of the opportunities that the National Youth Administration (NYA), established by the Roosevelt administration during the depression, offered. Lyndon Baines Johnson, the former Cotulla teacher, headed the Texas NYA, which provided scholarships and work opportunities to unemployed youth in federally funded works projects.[25] While a number of Tejanas enrolled in NYA projects, they were subjected to discrimination. Although Manuela González, who became a lifelong friend of Johnson, found work as a library aide in the Cotulla school, most Tejana NYA participants were sent to poorly equipped and segregated training sites. Worse, by agreement between government officials and county farm agents, NYA relief was not available during the harvest season, when all hands were needed.[26] This action effectively ensured that Tejana field workers could not pursue training opportunities year-round.

THE LABOR OF TEJANAS IN RURAL CENTRAL TEXAS

Later I realized that they didn't like us for anything except for work—poorly paid work.[27]   SABINA PALOMO ACOSTA

From November 1928 through January 1930, sociologist Ruth Allen conducted a study of Mexican American, black, and white women who worked on Central Texas farms in Bastrop, Burnet, Caldwell, Travis, and Williamson Counties.[28] Allen included approximately 269 Tejanas in her research. Of this total, 79.2 percent were members of tenant farm families and 20.8 percent belonged to farm laborer families. Approximately 56 percent of the women Allen interviewed were married,

32 percent were single, and 12 percent were widows. More than 50 percent of the women worked in the fields for their families, with a much smaller percentage engaged in field work for hire. About 45 percent of the women's families owned an automobile, which provided them important mobility for seeking better-paid work.[29]

In her study, Allen noted that a small number of the Mexican women also did other farm labor, such as baling hay, plowing with a walking plow or a riding plow, and cutting feed. She reported that none of the women collected a salary for their work. Instead, the man in the family received their wages.[30]

More than 50 percent of the women owned a sewing machine and 71 percent raised chickens, but only 22.3 percent had a cow, and a mere 3.7 percent preserved food for their families. Mexican women's sole recreation away from the drudgery of hard work, Allen suggested, centered on church attendance. Adelaida Torres Almanza and her family, who lived in the Central Texas blacklands, made every effort to attend mass as often as possible, using a borrowed wagon to travel twenty miles to a church in Waco. However, other Tejanas who lived and worked in Central Texas cotton country attended mass only about once a year, because they had no means to travel such a distance on a regular basis.[31]

Allen's work provides important facts about the lives of Tejana cotton workers in Central Texas. The personal stories of women cotton field workers, however, can supply uniquely important information and insights about their lives. The stories of four Tejanas who worked in Central Texas cotton fields are the focus of the rest of this chapter. All of them lived in the Central Texas blacklands, in McLennan County, a region that lies north of the area that Allen studied.

FOUR TEJANAS IN THE CENTRAL TEXAS COTTON BELT: NATIVES AND FUEREÑAS

Lucía Alderete Anaya, María Quiroz de León, Sabina Palomo Acosta, and Juanita Palomo Campos all lived and worked in the very productive cotton country of Central Texas during the Great Depression.

Two of the four were born in the area, and two were *fuereñas* (outsiders). Lucía was born in 1922 on the Holloway farm between McGregor and Waco. María was born in 1920 in Coryell City, in Coryell County to the west of McGregor. She later moved to Crawford and ultimately to McGregor. There she and her husband Refugio worked their own 150-acre farm. Sabina and Juanita, sisters and *fuereñas,* were born in 1914 on a ranch in the state of San Luis Potosí, Mexico, and in

1922 in Crystal City, Texas, respectively. Sabina was nineteen and Juanita eleven when they moved to the Fall farm in McGregor.

Lucía celebrated her first birthday in 1923 on the Fall farm in McGregor, where her father, Narciso Alderete, had taken up residence with the Fall family as a sharecropper. In 1927 at around age seven, María moved from her birth home in Coryell City to a farm near Crawford, north of McGregor. She briefly attended school and then went to work in the fields. After both of her parents died, her older sister, Beta Quiroz Leos, reared her.

The migrant trail life that Sabina and Juanita had followed for a number of years ended in 1933, when they arrived in McGregor with their father, Maximino, a widower, and their siblings, Antonio and María (Mari). The Palomos were traveling with the family of Felipa Alderete Acosta. In McGregor, Sabina and Juanita would become lifelong friends with Lucía and María. All four women became permanent residents of the area. They eventually married and reared their own families in McGregor and in nearby Moody.

Prior to their journey to the Central Texas cotton belt, the Palomos had met the Acostas in Crystal City, where both families worked in the spinach and onion fields. To facilitate their work and to help each other, the two families had formed an alliance. Traveling together on the migrant circuit, they journeyed in trucks from their home base in Crystal City to the fields near Robstown and then in the Panhandle before returning home.[32]

In 1933 Felipa Alderete Acosta, the matriarch of the Acosta family and a widow, learned that Narciso Alderete, her long-lost brother and the father of Lucía, was living on the Fall farm in McGregor. The Acostas, accompanied by the Palomos, headed to Central Texas to find Narciso. Once reunited with him, the Acostas decided to stay in the area because the Fall family and other farmers offered them work. The Palomos stayed as well. Years later, Sabina pointed out that the Palomos would not have been able to return to Crystal City even if they had wanted to, because they did not own a vehicle. Several years would go by before they could afford to buy one.[33]

WORKING ON THE LAND AND IN THE HOME

After holding a dance to celebrate the reunion of Narciso Alderete and Felipa Alderete Acosta and their families, everybody returned to the daily routine of field work. During the harvest season, the women rose before dawn to prepare a simple lunch of tortillas and beans that they had cooked the previous night. When their chores at home were light, Tiburcia, Lucía's mother, and Mari, Sabina's sickly younger sister, prepared and delivered a hot meal to the workers in the fields. Thus, these two females, one older and the other infirm, provided a support system for daughters and sisters who worked in the fields, relieving them of some of their cooking tasks.[34]

Sabina and Juanita lived with their family in a one-room *casita* (lean-to) close to Lucía on the Falls' place, and the three usually walked together to the fields. Narciso Alderete, Lucía's father, went ahead of the workers in a wagon. During hoeing and cotton-picking season, the women's routine was predictable. Sabina recalled, "We worked from sunup to sundown."[35] They had little time to rest during the day. During hoeing season, except for a brief lunch, they took no breaks. Married women usually brought their children with them to the fields. The older ones worked alongside them or tended to younger siblings.[36]

Everyone was responsible for her own work. Juanita, who weighed between eighty-five and ninety pounds, regularly picked at least one hundred pounds of cotton each day. Throughout the day, she filled her sack, carefully hoisted across a shoulder, then dragged it in for weighing.[37]

When the workday in the fields ended, the women usually returned to their *casitas* to prepare tortillas for the following day, make supper, and clean up afterward. They cooked on wood stoves, using simple pots and pans. On some evenings, they repaired their cotton sacks, using a paste fashioned from milk and flour. When night fell, everybody— parents and siblings alike—slept on the floor, sometimes on mattresses made from sacks filled with cotton. Sabina recalled that, except for a table or a chair, her family had no furniture for several years. They often kept the door of their lean-to open to let in air and light, because the structure had no windows. Bad weather presented them with additional burdens to bear. Lucía recalled that the leaky roof of her family's *casita* offered little protection during downpours. Nevertheless, the women adorned their homes with embroidered handiwork that they made out of recycled flour sacks. At times they used colorful photographs from fruit crates to decorate the interior of their *casitas*. They also papered the walls with newspapers to keep out some of the elements, using glue they made from cooked flour.[38]

Men rarely lent any assistance with housekeeping or cooking. Maximino Palomo, Sabina and Juanita's father, occasionally prepared coffee. "That was all he knew how to make," recalled Sabina. In addition to cooking and cleaning, the women chopped wood and hauled water for the household. All the families on the Falls' place drew their drinking water from a pump. The Falls required them to haul water for all other needs from a nearby creek that they shared with grazing animals.[39]

WORKING FOR WHITE FARMERS' WIVES

I learned to make American food—roast, custard pie, and fried chicken. I learned how to serve a dish properly at the dining table.[40]
                                                    LUCÍA ALDERETE ANAYA

In addition to working in the fields and in their own houses, Lucía, María, Sabina, and Juanita cleaned house, looked after children, and did odd jobs for the wives of farm owners. They often cleaned kitchens and washed and ironed clothes. Sabina remembered that the pay for this work was miserable—perhaps 25 cents at most, even though it could take at least half a day to wash and hang the laundry out to dry. On one occasion, a farmer's wife paid her sister Juanita in cloth rather than money. Juanita turned her paycheck into a dress. While the women were dismayed with the low pay level for hard domestic work, they swallowed their anger and tried to consider themselves lucky to add a few more cents to their wallets occasionally.[41]

Lucía worked longer in domestic service—approximately twelve years—than the other women. She started around 1940, when she turned eighteen. She quit when she turned thirty, married José Anaya, and left the Fall farm. Because she was required to work in the fields as well, Lucía's housekeeping and cooking roles for the Fall household did not begin until the end of the annual cotton harvest. When she first went to work for the family, she did not know how to cook Anglo American food. However, under the tutelage of the Fall family women, she learned to prepare family favorites, such as roast beef, custard pies, and other delicacies.[42]

On several occasions Lucía prepared fried chicken for Governor Pat Neff, a Fall family friend. In her own *casita,* her family fare, like that of other Tejano sharecroppers, consisted of *frijoles, arroz, fideo,* an occasional side of meat from the Falls' slaughterhouse, and the ever-present tortillas. With the advent of World War II, Gladys Fall, one of the Fall women, took a job in a bomb assembly plant in McGregor, and Lucía added the care of Gladys's children—Harry, Mary Lee, and John—to her domestic work.[43]

María began to work in the fields to help her family when she was about ten and entered domestic service when she was twenty, caring for a white teacher's children in nearby Crawford. A few years later, after María married Refugio de León, a farmer who owned a 150-acre farm, she turned her attention to her own family.[44] Besides doing laundry for farmers' wives, Sabina did odd jobs for the Fall family to bring in a trickle of money. She recalled that once she and three other friends picked poke salad, a favorite of the Fall family. For their efforts, the four friends earned a total of 40 cents, which they split four ways.[45]

VISITING, DANCING, AND COURTING

The women would fold their letter to a man into a tiny square and then place it in his palm as they danced.[46]

LUCÍA ALDERETE ANAYA

Although Lucía, María, Sabina, and Juanita spent many long hours in the fields, they also enjoyed recreation in their *casitas,* amid friends, in the surrounding rural towns of Crawford and Oglesby, and on infrequent trips to Waco, the largest city in McLennan County.

Sundays may have been created for offering praise to God, especially for many Tejanas raised in a Christian family. But for Lucía, María, Sabina, and Juanita, who lived too far away from Waco to attend mass regularly at Saint Francis Catholic Church, Sundays—albeit not on a weekly basis—were made for *visitas,* a tradition that has been part of Tejanas' lives since their earliest *rancho* settlements in the state.[47]

Thus, when the weather, time, and general circumstances permitted, the four women had Sundays for *visitas.* These occasions provided them the opportunity to spend time with friends who were also field workers. Sunday visiting likewise enabled them to meet men in a protected setting, chaperoned by older siblings or parents. In order to visit friends who lived at a distance, they went by horse drawn wagons and later in vehicles.[48]

Spending Sundays visiting new friends—Beta Quiroz or Fanny Blanco, for instance—meant that Lucía, María, Sabina, and Juanita could forget the work week that lay just behind or ahead of them. On Sundays they laughed and restored themselves from their labors. As the women visited, they often cooked a meal for the families gathered at a friend's *casita.* They exchanged ideas for embroidery or hand sewing projects. But they also played softball and listened to music on hand-cranked victrolas.[49]

Left to right: Sabina Palomo, María Acosta, Lucía Alderete, and Consuelo Acosta
holding instruments that Tejanos used to provide dance music at the *bodas de
ranchos* (country weddings) in Central Texas around 1933. Courtesy Teresa
Palomo Acosta.

Besides making and maintaining friendships through *visitas,* Tejanas
also took advantage of another cultural tradition: *bailes caseros* (dances in
homes). The women spread word-of-mouth invitations to these dances
as they worked or visited. On the appointed evening, families poured
into a *casita* for the infrequent and thus much appreciated event. "We
were packed in like sardines," recalled Lucía. Accordionists and guitarists known collectively as *músicos caseros* (house musicians) provided
the musical accompaniment for these gatherings. Occasionally, violin-
ists were engaged to play for the dances although the instrument was
not generally as popular for such events.[50]

Tiburcia Alderete, Lucía's mother, was one of the *músicos caseros* who
played for the dances. (Julia Martínez, another Tejana living in the area,
also played accordion although not necessarily for dances.) Tiburcia had
taught her son Manuel Pérez (Lucía's half brother) to play the accordion, and he usually played for all the dances. Tiburcia also knew how
to play the harmonica and taught the instrument to Lucía. However,
Lucía never had the opportunity to demonstrate her finesse with it at
the dances. Years later, in her late 70s, she could still play a tune on the
harmonica.[51]

While Tejanas met men at the dances, courting with men at these closely chaperoned events proved a tricky proposition. It was "poco strict," Lucía remembered.[52] *Solas* arrived at the dances in the company of family members, never with a beau because they were not allowed to date. Moreover, tradition held that the women sat together inside the *casita,* and all males remained outside between turns on the dance floor.[53]

As soon as the music struck up, the men entered and selected a dancing partner. Once the music ended, the men promptly stepped outdoors. If a woman attempted to linger for a chat with her male partner after a dance, a parent or other relative put a stop to this breach in social decorum by a firm look of disapproval or by physically separating the couple. "They would put their arms between the two and push them apart," remembered Sabina.[54]

Despite the restrictions on male-female interactions, the *bailes caseros* furnished one of the few publicly sanctioned social spaces where a woman and man might court. Dancing allowed men and women who had already evinced some interest in each other to communicate their attraction. As they danced, the couple conversed, but they also relayed their mutual interest in a unique way: the secret letter.

Lucía and Sabina recalled that women prepared their communiqués in advance. Literate women wrote their own notes or functioned as scribes for illiterate women. The "author" of the note then carefully folded it into a tiny square and hid it as best she could manage in her palm. As she danced with a prospective beau, she discreetly slipped the note into the man's palm for reading later.[55]

Besides courting at dances, women and men also courted through mailed or hand-delivered letters. Sabina recalled being the "go between" for her future sister-in-law, María Alderete Acosta, and Julio Quiroz, her friend María Quiroz de León's brother. By prior arrangement, Julio mailed to Sabina the letters he wrote to María Alderete Acosta. This tactic diverted attention from the budding relationship between the two, who later married.[56]

Sabina acknowledged that María Alderete Acosta's family was likely aware of the secret correspondence but chose to look the other way, thus upholding family honor. Tejanas also courted by leaving letters to sweethearts in certain agreed upon locations—near a particular flower pot or at a landmark familiar to the couple, who also arranged this method of communication in advance.[57] Thus through employing various covert methods for communicating with men, Tejanas found a way around the family's vow to protect women's morality.

The wedding of Eufemia Rodríguez and Eufracio Zambrano, outside the
Theodore Zambrano residence on a ranch near Kenedy in 1909. Courtesy
Ida Treviño. Print from University of Texas Institute of Texan Cultures.

The desired culmination of these secretive courting activities was the
boda de rancho (country wedding). A *boda* was apparently a major highlight of the cotton harvest, when the family of the couple could collect
sufficient funds to hold the event. Thus, no time was wasted when a man
asked for a woman's hand in marriage while the cotton season was in
full swing. The couple's relatives delivered wedding invitations through
word-of-mouth, quickly spreading news of the event from *casita* to *casita,* from cotton field to cotton field.[58]

Traditionally, the bridegroom paid for his bride's wedding gown,
and the pair, aided by family and friends, also prepared separate *castañas*
(hope chests) of items for their new lives—bed linens and kitchen towels, for instance. Friends and relatives of the wedding couple used their
artistic abilities to help provide the bride and bridegroom with these
basic necessities. To prepare the *castaña* for Manuel Pérez, Lucía's half
brother, Maximino Palomo, Sabina's father, drew the designs for the
linens, and the women embroidered them.[59]

Occasionally Tejano couples in McLennan County were married at
Saint Francis Catholic Church in Waco. Most, however, took their
marriage vows in a civil ceremony because they could not afford a tra-

ditional Mexican church wedding. Afterward, their friends joined them at the *boda de rancho* at a relative's *casita*. There the guests enjoyed a home-cooked meal of *mole* (Mexican chicken dish made with a chocolate sauce) and *arroz,* followed by a dance with entertainment by the *músicos caseros.*[60]

TAKING CARE: TEJANAS AND HEALTH IN CENTRAL TEXAS

Health care for Tejanas in the first four decades of the twentieth century was for the most part a family and cultural affair. Like most other people living on farms, they raised such herbs as *hierba anís* (anise) and relied on *remedios caseros* (home remedies) for stomach aches and other everyday ailments.[61]

Unable to afford doctors, many Tejanas confronted everything from the common cold to the more serious *tos ferina* (whooping cough) to the usually fatal *caída de la mollera* (sinking of a baby's fontanel or soft spot) on their own.[62] In addition, women usually endured childbirth without medical care or any pain relief. Some women relied on *parteras* (midwives) to deliver their babies, but many others faced childbirth with little help.[63]

Curanderas existed in most Mexican American enclaves. Tejanas relied on them for their skills with curative herbs or other healing techniques to relieve such ailments as *empacho* (digestive tract blockages), *mal de ojo* (evil eye), or *susto* (fear). Lucía recalled that families often called upon Doña Cristina, a local *curandera,* to heal a loved one of *empacho* or *mal de ojo.* The women also relied upon a local medical supplies salesman, who made the rounds of their *casitas* in his vehicle every several weeks, selling them simple health care concoctions.[64]

Tejana field workers sustained themselves on a diet of beans and rice. (The Palomos, for instance, often purchased pinto beans in bulk, around twenty-five pounds.) They rarely ate vegetables and fruits. While Lucía and María had family gardens, where they raised onions, tomatoes, garlic, and cabbages, most Mexican women could not rely on providing these nutrients to their families. Historian Rebecca Sharpless has reported that less than a quarter of Central Texas blacklands Tejana farm women kept gardens.[65]

The women's poor diets, coupled with harsh living and working conditions, caused poor health. Some women eventually suffered from serious, often contagious illnesses. For instance, as a young mother

Juanita lost a lung to tuberculosis. When her youngest child turned four years old, Sabina was confined to a tuberculosis sanitarium in Tyler for fourteen months. Their younger sister Mari likely died from malnutrition, which had stunted her growth, making her sickly throughout her seventeen years of life.[66] Other Tejanas in the cotton country of Central Texas also suffered similar and worse personal health conditions.

WOMEN'S EDUCATIONAL STRATEGIES IN THE CENTRAL TEXAS COTTON BELT

After I was married, I would drive alone in Moody, where we lived. . . [because] I had taught myself to drive a car.[67]

JUANITA PALOMO CAMPOS

At Winn's I ordered and sold goods. I wrote up orders. I was paid three dollars and fifty cents an hour. Later I took another job because it paid better—four or five dollars [an hour], as I recall.[68]

MARÍA QUIROZ DE LEÓN

Most Tejanas living and working in the Central Texas blacklands did not attend school. In the South Texas farm town of Crystal City, Sabina studied briefly at an *escuelita* (private Tejano school), gaining rudimentary reading and writing skills in Spanish. However, Tejanas could not depend on *escuelitas* in Central Texas, and the local authorities denied Mexican children an education in the McGregor public school until about 1935. With little access to school, illiteracy rates for Tejana farm laborers were high in the Central Texas blackland prairies.[69]

Lucía learned English from Christine Fall, daughter of the Fall farm owners and later a professor at Baylor University in Waco. Fall was interested in the education of other Mexican children as well. She apparently joined hands with H. G. Isbill, a few other Anglos, and some local Tejanos to demand that Mexican children be allowed into McGregor's schools.[70]

In the mid-1930s, when McGregor opened its doors to Mexican children, Lucía, who was thirteen years old, enrolled and was placed in first grade. On her first day as a student, Lucía wore an inappropriately fancy party dress that her mother, who was not familiar with school attire, had selected. Lucía, the oldest and tallest among the first graders, was extremely embarrassed by the experience. After two days of attending school, she never again returned to a classroom. Years later,

Sabina recalled that Antonio, her younger brother, attended public school in McGregor and later in Crawford. She had no memory of Mexican girls attending public school in McGregor in the 1930s.[71]

Given this environment, Tejanas in Central Texas taught themselves basic cognitive skills in informal ways. María and Juanita both employed the response "Yo solita me enseñé" (I taught myself) to describe their efforts to become educated. Almost all their everyday experiences whetted their desire to learn. For instance, the women's courtship ritual of communicating with a sweetheart through letters prompted their desire to become literate. Thus, Sabina read to her friend Rebecca Blanco and taught her to write so Rebecca could put her newfound skills to practical use—communicating with her future husband.[72]

Tejanas also employed other informal means to become literate. Lucía's mother, Tiburcia, who could read in Spanish, received a subscription to San Antonio's Spanish language newspaper, *La Prensa,* as a gift from Manuel Pérez, her son. Lucía, who had a strong yearning to read in Spanish, struggled to teach herself. Eventually, as a result of regularly pouring over the newspaper's coverage of events in San Antonio and Mexico, printed words began to make sense to her.[73]

Tiburcia also ordered stories that *La Prensa* offered to its subscribers. Lucía, Sabina, and Juanita greeted the arrival of the stories, some of them Spanish translations of such children's classics as *Snow White,* with elation. In the evenings, Tiburcia read and reread the stories to the three until the pages of the stories grew frayed from frequent turning. They also delighted in listening to Tiburcia read a Spanish language serial in *La Prensa* with characters named Julia and Gilberto. Tiburcia also helped them develop reasoning skills by purchasing picture puzzles. Sabina and Juanita regularly joined Lucía at her *casita* to solve them.[74]

In addition, the women developed their imagination by drawing, crocheting, doing *deshilado* (drawn work), and designing and hand-stitching clothes and linens. Juanita, at seventy-eight years of age, was proud to still own some of the *deshilado* and hand embroidery she had produced as a young woman. She had first learned to do needlework at age eleven when a Tejana elder, Señora Blanco, had instructed her in the art of crocheting. Juanita also recalled her love of drawing and sketching still lifes, which she taught herself. She often transferred her designs onto cloth for decorating linens. She, like many other Tejanas in rural Central Texas, used her creations to adorn her house. As Ruth Allen notes in her study of Mexican farm women, they beautified their houses with "some colored handwork on the table or the chair."

In other cases, they placed pictures on their walls or created "a tiny flower garden protected by wires and sticks" to add beauty to their surroundings.[75]

The opportunity for female field workers to learn from one another depended upon having time for informal visiting. Lucía and sisters Sabina and Juanita were fortunate to live close to each other, as it enabled them to hear Tiburcia read stories from *La Prensa* or work on puzzles together. Studying with friends on other farms meant relying upon the menfolk to ferry them around, because none of the women drove a vehicle during their adolescence. Several years later, however, all four of these Tejanas learned to drive a vehicle, and Lucía and María obtained a driver's license after they got married.

María, outgoing, alert, and still driving at nearly eighty, had a learning-to-drive story. After her marriage to Central Texas farmer Refugio de León in the early 1940s, she regularly drove the family tractor to prepare the ground for planting crops. Her husband offered to teach her to drive a car. Since he was an impatient teacher, María abandoned the idea after her first disastrous lesson. However, necessity forced her behind the wheel of a vehicle again—this time on her own. Because María was busy as a homemaker and farmer, delivering a midmorning snack to Refugio became an exercise in time management. One day, trusting that she remembered enough from her one driving lesson and determined to save herself precious hours for her many tasks, she boarded the family truck, turned the ignition key, and set off to deliver Refugio's snack. After that, she kept driving. Years later she proudly recalled, "Yo solita me enseñé" (I taught myself).[76]

After driving without a license for some twenty years, she took and passed the driving test in English on her first try, winning a $10 bet with her husband, who did not think she could master the test materials.[77]

Juanita also taught herself how to drive for practical reasons. She frequently needed to run errands for her family in Moody, where she settled after her marriage to Francisco Campos.[78] Sabina and Lucía also eventually learned to drive vehicles, and Lucía obtained her driver's license.

The informal education that Tejanas undertook in the cotton belt of Central Texas provided important avenues for attainment and self-worth. They gained and imparted basic skills and won for themselves some release from the cares and responsibilities of maintaining their households. Although they did not acquire a formal education, the four women found ways to use their minds. In old age, they all remembered

Signs refusing Mexicans admittance to public establishments were common throughout the state. This one was painted on the wall of a restaurant in San Antonio around 1935 to 1937. Russell Lee Photograph Collection, Center for American History, University of Texas at Austin.

having the dream that their children—male and female—would receive the benefits of a formal education. Wanting their children to advance beyond their own status, the women sent them off to McGregor and Moody public schools. They also succeeded in getting them into college or other employment training. Most of their children completed high school or obtained an equivalent education. A number of their children and grandchildren obtained undergraduate and graduate degrees. The four women remained in old age deeply impressed with Mexican Americans in the Central Texas community who were "muy educados" (very educated).[79]

CONFRONTING RACISM IN THE COTTON BELT

Racial dictates of the era limited the activities of Tejanas who lived in McGregor. When Lucía, María, Sabina, and Juanita ventured into McGregor to see a movie at one of the town's three theaters, enjoy an ice-cream cone, or purchase a record for their hand-cranked victrolas, they encountered either looks of welcome or repugnance in the eyes of the Anglo proprietors.

At the Texas Theater they could sit with the whites. However, at Ever's Drugstore, just down the corner from the theater, they could buy an ice-cream cone only if they ate it outside. The Krause Drugstore across the street from Ever's integrated first, with Ever's reluctantly following suit later. At Our Town Studio, where they purchased the small box cameras for the photographs they took at the *bodas de ranchos,* they could count on having their portrait made and purchasing records for their victrolas without being harassed.[80]

All four women knew about the deep dislike—at times outright hatred—that some Anglos in Central Texas had for Tejanos. None of them recalled protesting acts of racism. As far as they knew, law enforcement officials were generally set against Mexicans. In such an environment they minded their own business, hoping that their exclusion from society would eventually end.[81]

With the arrival of a new decade in 1940 and World War II, the lives of all four women gradually began to change. Sabina and Juanita married and moved from farms into town in McGregor and Moody, respectively, when both of their husbands took jobs with the Atchison, Topeka, and Santa Fe Railroad Company. At age thirty, María stopped working on her family's farm and took up jobs in local business and industry for approximately the next thirty years. In her first job, she worked as a saleswoman at Winn's, a local department store in McGregor. Lucia remained on the Falls' place until the early 1950s, when she married José Anaya, whose family had acquired a farm in nearby Crawford. She was thirty years old when she and José celebrated their marriage in the *casita* where she had lived virtually all of her life with her parents. The Fall family provided the cake for their wedding.[82]

Thus, Lucía, María, Sabina, and Juanita eventually left the hard life of harvesting the region's cotton crop to take up life as members of the Mexican American working class of Central Texas. However, their stories of surviving difficult times through a multitude of strategies, including their own informal schooling in reading and writing, in the arts, and in practical matters of self-reliance, remain important lessons in the region's history.

CHAPTER SIX

Life in Urban Texas: 1900–1940

In 1938 Emma Tenayuca led a Workers Alliance demonstration on the steps of San Antonio's city hall, protesting against discrimination toward Mexicans by the Works Progress Administration, against deportation, and for justice. *San Antonio Light* Collection, University of Texas Institute of Texan Cultures.

Jovita Idar worked as a hospital translator and writer and as an editor for *El Heraldo Cristiano,* a Methodist newspaper, after moving to San Antonio in 1917. Faustina Porras Martínez founded a restaurant in Dallas in 1918. Beatriz Escalona Pérez made her stage debut at El Paso's Teatro Colón in 1921. These women were three of a number of Tejanas who put their talent and business acumen to use in earning a decent living for themselves and contributing to the Tejano community's prosperity between 1900 and 1940. However, during this same period, the vast majority of Tejanas living and working in the cities earned a paltry sum of money as employees of commercial laundries, garment manufacturers, cigar makers, and pecan-shelling companies.[1]

FOOD EQUALS MONEY: TEJANAS AND MEXICAN RESTAURANTS

Tejana entrepreneurs have historically made a living by selling food. In the nineteenth century, Tejanas earned money as street vendors, offering Mexican dishes such as tamales and other delicacies to the public. Some women specialized in making chili and became known as "chili queens." Other women transformed their homes into informal restaurants.[2] These types of enterprises were likely the foundation of restaurants that many Tejanas subsequently established, investing their time and money in a promising trade.

Drawing on the human attraction to enticing food, many Tejanas turned their knowledge of Mexican cuisine into a successful business. Moreover, by becoming owners of restaurants, they ultimately stationed themselves in the manager's office rather than in front of the hot stoves in the restaurant's kitchen. Like other entrepreneurs, they hired others to work for them and spent their time overseeing their companies.

Tejanas opened restaurants in all the growing urban areas of the state. In Houston, Eciquia Castro operated a cafe in the early 1900s. As part of the founding generation of Mexican Americans in Houston, she contributed to the development of a Tejana entrepreneurial class. Later, in the 1920s, another Houstonian, María Sarabia, became a notable restaurateur with Raúl Molina, her husband. In Corpus Christi, Señora Reyes Ibarra, a graduate of Granger College, attracted wealthy tourists to her business, the Little Mexican Inn. She diversified her business interests, also purchasing real estate in San Antonio. In Dallas Faustina Porras Martínez became a highly regarded businesswoman. The daughter of a physician, she saved money for three years to open the Martínez Restaurant with her husband Miguel on McKinney Street in 1918, thus founding one of the first Mexican restaurants in the city. The restaurant chain El Fenix that grew out of her restaurant later extended its operations to the rest of the state.[3]

While running her business, Martínez reared a family of twelve children. They all worked in the family trade, the boys as cooks and the girls as hostesses, bookkeepers, and cashiers. In 1955, by then a prosperous woman, Martínez turned the operation of El Fenix over to her children. For a time, her daughter Irene put her skills to use with a law firm. She typed and took dictation at the rate of 77 and 125 words per minute, respectively. She later returned to work with the family business and ended her own career as chairperson emeritus of El Fenix's board of directors.[4]

Adelaida Cuellar started out as a tamale vendor in 1926 to supple-

Eciquia Castro owned a cafe in Houston around 1915. Castro Family
Collection, Houston Metropolitan Research Center, Houston Public Library.

ment the family's meager income as sharecroppers in Kaufman. From
this modest beginning, she and her sons opened their first restaurant.
Despite setbacks during the Great Depression, Cuellar's sons used her
recipes to operate restaurants in Terrell, Wills Point, Malakoff, and
Tyler throughout the 1930s. Afterward, the Cuellar sons took their
mother's recipes into Dallas, Fort Worth, Waco, and Houston, calling
the new establishments "El Chico's." As the restaurant's fame spread,
the Cuellar sons became known collectively as "Mama's boys." At
Cuellar's death in 1969, El Chico Corporation operated at least twenty
enterprises, ranging from restaurant franchises to canning companies.[5]

A COMPANY OF ONE'S OWN

María Luna started the Luna Tortilla Factory in 1924 in the Little Mexico barrio in Dallas. At the time, she was a mother with two children to support. During the first year of her business, Luna carried dishpans full of *masa* (corn dough) to the women who worked for her out of their homes. She picked up the tortillas later in the day and sold them. After a year, she had convinced the women's husbands, who were initially opposed to their wives working outside the home, that she was a serious businesswoman. As a result, by the second year of Luna's Tortilla Factory, twenty-five females took jobs in her factory, producing a daily quota of five hundred tortillas. Four years later, on the eve of the Great Depression, Luna began a home delivery service to other Mexican barrios—Cement City, West Dallas, and El Rancho Grande. A founder of the second Mexican Chamber of Commerce, María Luna's legacy had been passed down by 1996 to a fourth generation and production output reached fifteen hundred dozen tortillas a day.[6]

María Luna was one of the first Mexican origin businesswomen in Dallas. She opened the Luna Tortilla Factory in 1924. Courtesy Vivian Castleberry.

Anita Mongaras Nañez opened a beauty shop in her home in 1924, making her
one of the first women business owners in the Little Mexico barrio in Dallas.
When her house caught on fire, the first thing she rescued was her permanent
wave machine. Courtesy Vivian Castleberry.

Even as the deportation drives of the Great Depression began, forcing many Tejanas to return to Mexico, Herlinda Morales Rodríguez of
San Antonio found success as an entrepreneur. In 1929, following the
death of Guadalupe Rodríguez Jr., her husband, she became president
of Rodríguez and Son Bottling Company. The soft drink business that
she led was first established as a carbonated water company in 1918. She
became sole owner of the enterprise in 1933. A year later, in 1934, she
registered the business under the name Dragon Bottling Company and
expanded its offerings to include twelve different flavors. She also increased daily production to 120 boxes of sodas per hour. Under her
leadership, Dragon operated twelve distribution vehicles that covered a
160-mile radius. Her company was in business until about 1962.[7]

Other women operated other concerns out of their homes. In 1924
Dallas resident Anita Mongaras Nañez set up a beauty parlor in the fam-

ily's living room in Little Mexico. To help business along, she sent
Ninfa and Olivia, her two eldest daughters, off to study at the Marinello
Beauty School. Her daughter Anita Martínez, later a businesswoman
and the first Mexican American member of the Dallas City Council, recalled her mother as "a woman ahead of her time" and an inspiration to young women in the neighborhood. Nañez astutely opened
her shop when the nation's beauty salon business was in its infancy. By
1926, when her shop had been in operation for two years, beauty sa-
lons throughout the United States had increased from 5,000 to 21,000
shops.[8]

In the 1930s Tejanas also took other jobs in family-run businesses.
María Cristina Jiménez worked for her family's film distribution company, the Latin-American Film Exchange, which was originally located
on Soledad Street in San Antonio. In addition to Jiménez, three other
women worked for the company. In Dallas, photographer Guadalupe
Zambrano was an equal partner in Zambrano Photographers, a company that she and her two brothers ran. She specialized in retouching,
colorization, and makeup.[9]

BARRIO LIFE

> The Mexican people find it impossible to rent or buy in any
> decent section of town and are forced to live in dirty crowded
> conditions in houses out of which Americans have moved.[10]
>
> STELLA QUINTENELLA AND CARMEN CORTEZ,
> "Letter from Chapultepec" (Houston), June 11, 1937

Many successful women began their businesses in Mexican barrios
and often lived there as well. However, most Tejanas were not self-
employed and running successful commercial ventures. They worked
in poorly paid jobs and lived in impoverished conditions. Whether in
Dallas's Little Mexico, San Antonio's west side, El Paso's south side, or
Houston's east side, the majority of Mexican Americans lived in dilap-
idated housing. In Dallas's Little Mexico, no streets were paved, residents had no hot water, and three-quarters of the inhabitants had no
indoor plumbing. Disease and malnutrition haunted these neighborhoods, with many families losing children to a host of illnesses. Moreover, most Mexicans lived in segregated circumstances that did not allow them entry to movie theaters, banks, and other public places.[11]

In El Paso women who existed on extremely low wages called a single rented room their home, which they usually shared with at least one dependent. Female refugees fleeing from the Mexican Revolution to the border city found themselves at the mercy of white citizens. One Anglo reporter, Julia Sharp, declared that Mexicanas were hardy and therefore warranted no assistance. Their children, Sharp wrote, crossed the border without proper clothing and were accustomed to living in near nakedness. Hence, she reasoned, Mexicanas could subsist on the worst jobs and do with little education. This prevailing attitude consigned Tejanas to a cycle of poverty. In the city's segregated schools, school authorities dutifully instructed Tejano children in the "domestic sciences." Boys studied carpentry and girls learned how to sew and do laundry. By sixth grade many Tejano children left school to help support their families.[12]

In Houston the expansion of railroads and the growth of the city as a major commercial and industrial center brought many Mexicans to the area. They settled in neighborhoods that would become the north side barrio and El Segundo Barrio. In these neighborhoods, Tejanas tended to their families in "shoddy, unpainted two- and three-room frame houses." More than a dozen individuals often lived together to make economic ends meet. By 1920, a section of the city's Magnolia Park area had also become a Mexican barrio.[13]

Throughout the state, however, a small middle class emerged in the midst of economically and socially repressed conditions. In El Paso, Brownsville, and Laredo, some Tejanos worked in city and county government, and a few were physicians and attorneys. In Houston a small merchant class that included women arose. By 1920 Tejano-operated bookstores, pharmacies, and doctors' offices had sprung up. A Mexican-owned theater had also opened. María Sarabia and her brothers José, Socorro, Felipe, and Jesús had opened a variety of businesses.[14]

During the Great Depression, the poorest Mexicans and the fledgling entrepreneurial class inhabited the same barrios on San Antonio's west side. An unusually large number of Tejanas in the barrio operated cafes or sold food as vendors.[15] These women, independent members of the business community, contributed both to their families and to their community's productivity in the midst of great need.

A vital newspaper industry that reported on Mexican American issues and interests existed in the cities of the state. Some newspapers established during the Mexican Revolution continued to maintain a presence. In Houston, Spanish language newspapers published in the 1920s included *El Anunciador, La Gaceta Mexicana,* and *El Tecolote.* In

San Antonio, the feminist *La Mujer Moderna,* founded by sisters Andrea and Teresa Villarreal during the Mexican Revolution, directed its news coverage at the concerns of both women and the working class. Francisco A. Chapa, a conservative and a member of the small group of Texas Mexican Republicans, founded and operated *El Imparcial de Texas.* Ignacio E. Lozano established *La Prensa* in 1913, initially to keep Mexicans in exile (el México de Afuera) informed of the events of the Mexican Revolution. After Lozano's death in 1953, Alicia E. Lozano, his associate and widow, and Leonides González, his longtime business partner, took over management of the newspaper.[16]

In Houston the Club Moderno y Recreativo, a women's group, provided opportunities for girls to socialize. Women also founded the Club Femenino Chapultepec in 1931 under the sponsorship of the Young Women's Christian Association (YWCA). The club, which had met informally since 1928, was initially established to provide social, athletic, and recreational activities. It ultimately served the Tejano community in several ways, including organizing the celebration of Mexican holidays (*fiestas patrias*) such as Cinco de Mayo and Diez y Seis de Septiembre. Some members of Chapultepec had graduated from high school and worked in Anglo-owned businesses. One of its original members was Carmen Cortez, who would later serve as president of the League of United Latin American Citizens (LULAC) Council no. 22. Through its affiliation with the city's YWCA Business and Professional Department, Chapultepec instructed young girls in citizenship. Later, during World War II, the organization sold government bonds.[17]

Club Chapultepec members eventually expanded their outreach to include the welfare of all Tejanos in the city. Thus, on June 11, 1937, Stella Quintenella and Carmen Cortez, representing the organization, wrote a letter to Miss Leona B. Hendrix of Kansas City, Missouri, who was likely associated with the National Business and Professional Girls Council there. In a document entitled "Letter from Chapultepec," the women enumerated ten concerns facing the Tejano community. The authors of the letter and Olive Lewis, an Anglo woman who sponsored the club at the YWCA, signed the letter. In general, the letter described the negative impact of racial discrimination on Tejanos. For instance, the women wrote that young people's reactions to their segregation were alarming. Some denied their heritage and called themselves French, Italian, or Spanish "to get ahead." Others refused to become citizens, since changing their legal status apparently did not improve their standing. The letter was sent one week after the acquittal of two Anglo police officers for the murder of Elpidio Cortez, a Mexican man. As a result of signing the "Letter from Chapultepec," Olive Lewis was fired from her position and Stella Quintenella was subjected to many harassing visits from the FBI, which continued until 1942. She stopped attending the Club Femenino Chapultepec meetings in around 1942. The club apparently dissolved in 1945.[18]

Like Tejanas in Houston, others around the state involved themselves in their community as their interests and circumstances allowed. María L. de Hernández championed the cause of Tejano educational needs through La Liga de Defensa Pro-Escolar. She was also a founding leader of the Orden Caballeros de América, a civic organization for Tejanos. Carolina Malpica Munguía, a member of the Tejano middle class (and grandmother of Henry Cisneros), helped establish Munguía Printers and served as vice president of the family company. On June 12, 1938, she helped establish the Círculo Cultural Isabel la Católica, which dedicated itself to the needs of Tejanas and community uplift from a philosophy of female benevolence.[19]

TEJANAS AND THE SETTLEMENT HOUSE MOVEMENT

They were taught how to set the table, and how to serve the men. They learned also that they had to share, to cooperate, and to wait their turn.[20]   HOUCHEN HOUSE SETTLEMENT WORKER

As Tejanas and newly arrived Mexican immigrant women settled in cities, they became the focus of the settlement house movement, a late-nineteenth-century effort that drew scores of white middle-class women eager to provide educational and social programs to new Americans. The workers, however, also sought to Americanize the immigrants' habits. In Texas, at least eighteen settlement houses ultimately came into existence in the major urban areas.[21]

Settlement house workers set out to accomplish a number of things they believed would improve the lives of immigrant Mexican women, one of which involved training them to work as servants or seamstresses.[22] In addition, settlement workers, who considered the rice, beans, and tortillas that Mexican American women fed their families to be unhealthy, sought to convince them to bring new dietary habits into their households. Accordingly, the settlement workers urged the women to replace traditional foods with such Anglo American staples as white bread and lettuce. Indeed, the settlement workers deplored the deficit of "the right varieties of foods" in Mexican households. They considered this factor responsible for producing children who, lacking milk and fruit to consume, would "take food from the lunch boxes of more fortunate children." In the eyes of the settlement workers, children who consumed Mexican food took "the initial step in a life of thieving."[23]

In Houston, Sybil Campbell, a public school teacher in the Second Ward, founded the Rusk Settlement House in 1907. Three years later, in 1910, when the Mexican population in Houston reached 2,000, Rusk employed three full-time staff members and hired visiting nurses. The workers addressed a variety of perceived needs in the neighborhood. They organized children's activities, distributed clothing and food, organized English classes for adults, and provided limited health care. By 1929 Rusk was serving nearly 29,000 people. Settlement workers also supported legislation to end child labor, to institute an eight-hour workday, and to promote workers' right to unionize.[24]

While Rusk's settlement workers brought to the attention of city authorities the deplorable conditions under which Mexicans lived, they did not necessarily speak out against the causes of racial repression. Moreover, while they were quick to defend Mexicans' cultural heritage, they were also inclined to consider them quaint and victimized by a culturally inferior background. The Rusk settlement workers were also bent on socializing the Tejanas enrolled in their English classes "into roles as wives and mothers." Accordingly, the workers instructed them in a vocabulary related to homemaking responsibilities, teaching the women the names of foods, clothing, and furniture.[25]

In El Paso, the Rose Houchen Settlement House, a Methodist center founded in 1912 in the city's Segundo Barrio, also targeted Tejanas for "Americanization." Houchen's workers, like those at Rusk in Houston, sought to instill in the women who attended the center the values of Methodism and good Protestant American housewifery through classes on health, cooking, and sewing. To reach a wider audience of women, the staff carried out its Americanization efforts in a bilingual context. Tejanas, however, chose to participate only in activities they found helpful. They took advantage of Houchen's social, educational, and medical services. Moreover, although they rejected the staff's efforts to convert them, they enrolled their children in Houchen's kindergarten. They also allowed their daughters to take part in social activities. One Houchen participant noted, "My Mom had an open mind, so I participated in a lot of clubs. But I didn't become Protestant." Thus, like many other Americanization projects around the nation, Houchen's efforts were not a resounding success in the Tejano community.[26]

WORKING FOR A LIVING

> I find it difficult to live on my wages.[27]
>
> MANUELA HERNÁNDEZ, employee of Acme Laundry, El Paso

For a growing number of Tejanas in the state's urban areas, working for a living became, little by little, a reality. Americanization efforts to train them to work as servants or to feed their children cuisine considered acceptable in the United States were hardly the reasons for which they entered wage labor. In essence, they needed to earn money to support themselves.[28]

As a result, more Tejanas began to join the wage labor pool in the early twentieth century. They, like other poor and working-class women, dreamed of success and a good salary. "We felt that if we worked hard, proved ourselves, we could become professional people," recalled a Mexican American woman. Nevertheless, for the vast majority of Tejanas who worked in low-status jobs becoming professional people was a distant fantasy. Indeed, most Tejanas found employment in laundries, factories, and food-processing plants, carrying out jobs that resembled homemaking tasks.[29]

At the turn of the twentieth century, 15 percent of Mexican immigrant women were employed outside the home in South Texas. By 1920 at least 17 percent of them worked outside the home in El Paso. In Houston they went to work in the textile industry. So few were in professional positions that those who held them stood out. For instance, Praxedis Torres Mata became Uvalde's first Mexican American public school teacher in 1905. In San Antonio, the U.S. Census Bureau reported that by 1930 Mexican descent women comprised 40.2 percent of domestic and personal service workers but only 2.3 percent of professional employees. White women were 21.3 percent of domestic workers and 20.4 percent of professional workers. In addition, Tejanas in San Antonio were more likely than other women to be working heads of families that included adult males.[30]

Many Tejanas who remained in their homes earned money by taking in ironing and doing *deshilado* (drawn work). They also sewed and washed clothes. Young single Tejanas were among the first to undertake

During the Great Depression, Mexican American seamstresses earned a pittance
doing piecework in their homes. National Archives, photo no. 86-G-6E-8.

work outside the home, comprising about 30 percent in South Texas,
22 percent in West Texas, and 10 percent in Central Texas.[31]

In San Antonio married Tejanas pursued home-based work. In the
Depression era, they set the pace in the industry for the quality and
speed of their sewing, a skill that they owed to the instruction of mothers and grandmothers. Yet the pay scale for these skilled workers was
deplorable, with wages during the 1930s remaining at $1.10 to $3.30
per week, according to a study by the Women's Bureau.[32]

By 1910 Tejanas in Corpus Christi, San Antonio, Houston, and Dallas also began to take industrial jobs. Like their sisters elsewhere in the
state's growing urban areas, they worked as laundresses, seamstresses,
domestics, and pecan shellers. These women's efforts were likewise
poorly rewarded. In San Antonio, the Women's Bureau reported in
1932 that when Tejanas and Anglo women held similar jobs, the Tejanas
earned far less. For instance, Anglo women earned a weekly wage of
$4.15 for pecan shelling, while Tejanas earned $2.65 for the same work.
Likewise, Anglo department store clerks earned a weekly paycheck of
$12.45, while Tejanas could count on no more than $9.00 per week.[33]

TEJANA WAGE EARNERS IN EL PASO

In El Paso, according to a 1919–1920 study by the Texas Bureau of Labor Statistics, Mexican origin women and Anglo women worked principally in sales. The Tejanas tended to work in Mexican-owned stores, filling lower-status jobs. After sales, Tejanas filled the ranks of laundry establishments, while Anglo females were employed as telegraph and telephone operators. Tejanas took home weekly earnings of $8.69, while Anglo women earned $18.56 a week, a difference of $9.87. Race, more than education, accounted for the disparity in earnings, for even when Mexican American women had educational levels comparable to Anglo women's, they earned less. The Mexicanas were also younger than female Anglo workers, often lived at home, and contributed to their family's income.[34]

A 1900 study noted that 17.11 percent of El Paso households had at least one female working outside the home. Moreover, widows with children to support most certainly worked for a living. In 1920, two decades later, the census noted that 3,474 foreign-born females (principally Mexican) who were at least ten years old worked. A large number of these women washed clothes or worked as servants. A few Tejanas taught school or held jobs as typists or nurses. Some self-employed women were food vendors in Chihuahuita. Others went to work as dancehall girls in the red light district. None were known to hold white collar jobs with banks or the city's utility companies.[35]

Finding work as a maid was easy because "almost every Anglo-American family had at least one, sometimes two or three, servants: a maid and laundress, and perhaps a nursemaid or yardman." The Tejana servants usually journeyed each morning from their homes in the barrios to work from seven in the morning until five in the evening. In some cases, however, Anglos provided their maids with rooms. In 1907 these "house girls," as the servants were known, earned from $3 to $6 a week.[36]

In 1917 Spanish-surnamed employees of El Paso Laundry, the city's largest commercial laundry, constituted 134 of the company's 166 workers, with females comprising more than half of the Spanish-surnamed employees. At Elite Laundry, 76 of the 128 employees were Spanish-surnamed in 1917. At Acme Laundry, also one of the largest in the city, 75 of the 121 laundresses were Mexican origin women in 1917. Most of the women earned from $4 to $6 a week. A number of Tejanas testified about their low earnings during the Texas Industrial Welfare

Tejanas worked in the state's cigar industry. Here they pack cigars at the Kohl-berg Cigar Factory in El Paso in 1913. Aultman Collection, El Paso Public Library.

Commission's November 1919 hearings in El Paso. Guadalupe Espejo candidly described how she put her salary to use:

> I am getting $7 a week at the American Laundry in a collar machine. I have one dependent. My room rent is $5 a month; groceries cost $5.50 a week and I cannot buy a coat a year or one in two years. My clothing costs $10 to $12 a year and two pairs of shoes a year cost $4.50 a pair. The coat I have on I bought 10 years ago on the installment plan. I think $15 a week would be needed to live on comfortably.[37]

Eloise Alcalá, an employee of El Paso Manufacturing Company who earned $8 a week, also testified before the commission, informing its members that she needed to earn $25 a week in order to buy food for her family.[38]

El Paso Tejanas also worked in the cigar and garment industries. At Kohlberg Cigar Factory, they were 22 of the 113 employees. Bergman's Factory relied on a large number of Mexican women to produce its shirts and overalls in 1902. Reportedly, only three Anglo women worked for Bergman's. The company paid the Mexicanas approximately $9 a week, but offered the three white women $10 to $14 a week.[39]

Civic and labor officials came to the support of Tejana workers during the commission hearings, urging salary improvements. Henry Walker, with the city's employment bureau, recommended pay increases for household servants, noting that raising salaries would bring better workers. Julia Roldán, a Tejana teacher for the YMCA, also spoke up for increasing women's paychecks. She informed the officials, "Give the Mexican girl the same chance and she will show equal efficiency with the American girl." W. J. Moran of the *Labor Advocate,* the news organ of the Central Labor Union, also championed improved wages for Tejanas. All these pleas made little difference to employers, however, and the women's salaries remained quite low.[40]

TEJANA WORKERS: RIPENING FOR A STRIKE

Nationwide, between 1909 and 1915 the number of commercial laundry employees grew from 105,216 to 203,215. While hand laundries continued to exist, mostly employing women in Manhattan and Brooklyn, the new steam technology provided an opportunity to expand the industry.[41]

By 1919 El Paso was home to six commercial steam laundries, with Tejanas making up the majority of the more than 500 women who washed and ironed clothes for a living. A decade later, Mexican American women workers still dominated the laundry industry.[42]

When the Texas Industrial Welfare Commission carried out its investigation of laundry workers' wages in 1919, it discovered that laundresses in the state earned a weekly salary of $9.39, although the average cost of living was $13.78. In El Paso, where the cost of living was a reported $19.09 per week, the average laundry worker earned only $12.05. Tejanas testifying before the commission declared that they earned much less, from $4.00 to $5.75 per week. Studies carried out in Dallas in 1918 reported that local laundresses received salaries of $12.00 per week; in Del Rio, they earned 15 cents per hour and in Houston they earned $1.00 per day. Another study, completed eight months later, revealed that laundresses in El Paso, San Antonio, and Corpus Christi could count on an average salary of $6 a week.[43]

For these salaries, employees generally toiled long hours in bad conditions. In 1915 the Bureau of Labor Statistics reported that the women worked from ten to twelve and a half hours per day. Thus, during a reg-

Labor organizer Manuela Solis Sager (right) with her brother and sister in front of their South Texas family home at Cannel Coal Company, San José, Webb County, around 1910. Courtesy Roberto R. Calderón.

ular workday, the women spent many hours exposed to workplace hazards, including poor ventilation and lighting.[44]

In the 1930s Mexican origin women accounted for 103 employees at the Texas Steam Laundry in San Antonio, while Mexican males accounted for 49 workers. Together they made up more than half of the total of 221 workers. Like their fellow workers in El Paso, the San Antonio laundry employees' working conditions were harsh. In 1936 the Women's Bureau reported on fifty-two of the local laundries, finding that, among other problems, thirty plants had cement floors, a major health hazard for workers whose jobs required them to stand for long hours. Moreover, almost half of the fifty-two laundries did not have adequate safety standards.[45]

In 1932 the Women's Bureau reported that Mexican seamstresses in the state earned weekly wages of $5.45 for making dresses and $5.70 for sewing infants' clothing. Women home sewers earned less than half the amount that women factory employees made, averaging between $2.00 and $3.00 a week. Only one of more than 100 home workers who were surveyed earned as much as $5.00 per week. In 1936, a more thorough study by the Women's Bureau reported that home workers were usually older, from thirty to fifty years of age. Some of these workers also toiled ten and more hours a day under conditions that were not subject to safety regulations. In addition, the majority of these home-based employees made less than 5 cents an hour.[46]

For this minuscule amount of money, the women made hand-kerchiefs and children's clothing, producing finely constructed work that required "intricate embroidery, smocking and tucks." This highly skilled labor was "tedious and time-consuming." Most of the women, however, found themselves with little choice but to accept the employment they were offered because they had to contribute to their family's income. One typical home worker, for instance, reported that she had been paid 42 cents for the twelve hours it had taken her to make one dress. The outfit later sold for $8.[47]

Besides paying Tejanas such low wages, garment manufacturers in San Antonio failed to abide by national standards for maintaining a healthy and clean work environment. By 1940 a ban was imposed on industrial work in the home due to the city's failure to enforce safety guidelines.[48]

The International Ladies Garment Workers Union (ILGWU) attempted to unionize garment workers in San Antonio in response to the women's plight. However, ILGWU did not employ a Tejana labor organizer. The union relied instead on Rebecca Taylor, an Anglo from San Antonio who spoke Spanish. Further, the ILGWU was affiliated with the American Federation of Labor (AFL), which did not consider female employees good union prospects. This situation also proved detrimental to organizing Tejanas.[49] Years later, Rebecca Taylor noted that discrimination against Mexicana workers, coupled with the very large supply of individuals willing to toil for low wages, were the principal obstacles to establishing a solid union base among garment workers.[50]

Mechanization of the cigar and pecan shelling industries by the late 1930s also drastically affected Tejana workers. Between 1917 and 1938,

In 1933 workers at the Finck Cigar Factory in San Antonio picketed the plant while wearing banners reading "We are striking for better conditions." *San Antonio Light* Collection, University of Texas Institute of Texan Cultures.

for instance, cigar companies replaced manual labor with machines. This mechanization led to the closing of small companies, which threw many Tejanas out of work. From a nationwide workforce of 114,300 in 1919, employers cut back to a total of 56,000 in 1935. After 1938, mostly large mechanized factories operated, employing unskilled or semiskilled workers.[51]

The Finck Cigar Company, one of the companies whose conditions Tejanas would protest through strikes, opened its doors in San Antonio in 1893 with $1,000. By 1934, 90 percent of its 500 workers were Mexican. More than half were no older than twenty-five and a majority were single. Like their fellow workers in other industries, women at Finck Cigar Company also labored under terrible circumstances. Indeed, Finck had the reputation as the least sanitary of all businesses in the city. It also paid the worst salary of all the factories.[52]

The pecan-shelling industry, in whose filthy surroundings Tejanas also labored, had by the 1930s made San Antonio the pecan-shelling capital of the state and perhaps even of the country. About 20,000 Mexican Americans, mainly female, worked for more than one hundred shelling companies. The industry originally started on the city's west side, where most Mexicans lived. In time, it spread to other parts of the city, but Mexicans continued to comprise the bulk of pecan-shelling employees.[53] During the Great Depression, entire Tejano families turned to pecan shelling to subsist. Although the industry had thoroughly mechanized its operations in the late 1920s, many owners reversed this trend during the depression, largely due to the availability of workers who could be employed at "extremely low wages after 1929."[54]

Inside the plant "shacks," the pecan shellers sat on backless benches, with a box to deposit pecans placed in front of them. In 1936 the Women's Bureau found the crowded plants inappropriately ventilated, with dust from the pecan shells surrounding the workers with a continuous haze. Floors were dirty, oily, and slippery. Working conditions for home-based pecan shellers were no better. One study of Mexican American female workers in San Antonio during the Great Depression reported: "Thousands of human beings living in decrepit wooden shacks or in crowded corrals, breathlessly shelled pecans in a race with starvation." The women's hands also swelled and became infected from handling broken pecan shells.[55]

In the middle of the depression, the Women's Bureau reported that 477 female pecan shellers earned an average of $3.55 a week, which amounted to less than 5 cents per hour for the forty to forty-eight hours they regularly worked each week. In general, a woman who shelled eight pounds of pecans during an eight-hour workday took home an estimated $2.25 per week. The owner of Southern Pecan Shelling Company, Julius Seligmann, acknowledged to the Texas Industrial Welfare Commission that his employees earned about $2.50 a week.[56]

The women's extremely low salaries ensured severe deprivation. In 1938 a family could not manage on such wages. For instance, a family of 4.6 members, with two members working in pecan shelling, had an annual income of $251, although the cost of living in the southern United States was about $1,374 per annum. As a result, many families turned to the federal surplus center, churches, and other community agencies for additional support.[57]

¡YA BASTA! GOING OUT ON STRIKE

Laundry Workers Are Out: More Than 300 Girls and Women
Effected (sic) by Strike That Was Forced upon Them[58]
Labor Advocate headline, El Paso, October 31, 1919

Faced with abysmal working conditions, many Tejanas banded together
to fight their exploitation. In 1919 the laundry workers in El Paso used
the most potent tools in their power to challenge their bosses. They organized a union and went on strike.

The Tejana laundresses of El Paso established a local of the Laundry
Workers International Union on October 23, 1919, with the support of
J. L. Hausewald, vice president of the State Federation of Labor, and
other trade unionists. A week later, Acme Laundry fired two Tejana
union members for recruiting other women for the new union. When
management rejected demands by the other laundresses at Acme that
the two employees be reinstated, 200 workers went on strike. Women
at five other laundries in the city supported the Acme protesters and
walked off their jobs as well. In the succeeding days, nearly 500 more
women joined the effort and the strike commenced in earnest.[59]

On October 31, 1919, the *Labor Advocate,* the newspaper of the Central Labor Union (CLU), reported on the women's activities since the
formation of the union by the Acme Laundry workers on October 23.
Under the headline "More Than 300 Girls and Women Effected (sic) by
Strike That Was Forced upon Them," the paper stated that Acme's refusal to reinstate the fired workers had caused the walkout. The paper
also noted the ages of the workers, stating that some were "hardly in
their teens and some of them bent with age." It also decried the poor
wages that the workers earned—on average, $5.50 a week. The paper
asked, "What chance has a girl or woman to live a decent, respectable
life at the wages of this kind."[60]

Anglo labor leaders were determined to direct the strike. On the first
day of the walkout, the CLU called a meeting of several hundred
women, who voted unanimously to strike. The union leaders did not,
however, allow the women to represent themselves before the laundry owners. Instead, they sent a delegation of men to represent their
interests, and hired C. N. Idar, the brother of journalist and political
activist Jovita Idar, to organize the women. The *Labor Advocate* reported
that Idar would doubtless bring "much good" to the strikers' efforts because he was familiar with the "customs of the Mexican and will be able

More than 300 Tejana laundry workers went on strike in El Paso in 1919 to protest miserable wages and atrocious working conditions. Copied from El Paso City and County *Labor Advocate,* October 31, 1919. Print from Texas Newspaper Collection, Center for American History, University of Texas at Austin, CN 10505.

to help them in a great way." Idar, an organizer for the AFL, was a member of the prominent Idar family of Laredo, who as owners of *La Crónica* fought for Mexican Americans' civil rights. A supporter of women's rights, Idar would later ensure the inclusion of women's auxiliaries and youth in the Order of Sons of America.[61]

As the strike continued, the *Labor Advocate* upheld the workers' charges of unfair wages, contrasting the local women's $4 to $6 weekly salaries to the $14 weekly salaries that laundresses earned in Dallas, Fort Worth, and Galveston. The laundry owners countered the allegations, insisting that El Paso workers earned almost $9 for working a 54-hour week.[62]

On November 7, 1919, the *Labor Advocate* reported that 300 "girls" continued to strike and that large sums of money to support their efforts had been collected from other trade unionists, including railroad workers, plumbers, and ironworkers. In addition, nearly twenty organizations had donated money to the women's cause, and cab drivers had pledged their support. The newspaper also announced that the workers had opened their own laundry. Women at the temporary establishment were doing flat work and other tasks that did not require machinery. The *Advocate* claimed that the laundry was making $50 a day.[63]

Despite white male leaders' domination of the strike, Tejana strikers assumed some authority for creating a sense of solidarity. In one instance they stood on the international bridge between Mexico and the United States and intimidated women to keep them from crossing over to work in the laundries. Local civic organizations and the Spanish language press also came to the strikers' support, although they held different perspectives regarding the women's activism. While the press insisted that women use nonviolence in confronting their employers, the Círculo de Amigos, a mutual aid society, lent wholehearted support to all of the women's strike activities because they were "exhibiting character, strength, and racial solidarity in their actions." In the círculo's view, the Mexican American community had a responsibility to assist the women in their struggle.[64]

Ultimately the strike brought the laundresses neither wage increases nor other improvements. By December 1919 laundry owners had replaced the strikers, drawing from the immense pool of unemployed women residing on both sides of the border to fill jobs. Although their protests failed to gain them any concessions, Tejanas involved in the El Paso laundry strike of 1919 had initiated important actions against worker exploitation. In addition, from their limited base of power they had influenced the strike's direction in a male-dominated union environment.[65]

THE CIGAR STRIKE OF SAN ANTONIO, 1933

[W]e don't want to be treated like slaves.[66]

MRS. W. F. "REFUGIO" ERNST

By 1930, Mexicans accounted for more than 83,000 of the 230,000 inhabitants of San Antonio. Tejana workers continued to provide the majority of the labor force for the city's low-paying cigar-making, garment, and pecan-shelling companies during the 1930s. Indeed, they comprised 79 percent of the workers in these industries. During the Great Depression, they organized significant efforts to protest their working conditions, which placed them at the forefront of labor actions in San Antonio during the 1930s.[67]

Women workers walked out of the Finck Cigar Company on August 3, 1933. Protesting unfair wages, poor working conditions, and ill treatment, they organized a local union and engaged in a struggle with the company for two years. Early in the strike, they asked the mayor to persuade Ed Finck, the company owner, to come to terms with them. Seeking to negotiate a fair settlement, they also brought in the National Labor Relations Board (NLRB). When the government's efforts to bring the desired results failed, the strikers took up confrontational tactics and picketed Finck.[68]

Unlike the El Paso laundry strikers in 1919, Tejana cigar strikers were clearly in charge of their actions against Finck. They elected Mrs. W. H. "Refugio" Ernst, whom the company had fired for organizing workers, to direct strike activities and act as their spokesperson. Three other Tejanas—Adela Hernández, Modesta Herrera, and Mrs. E. J. Padilla—assisted her as advisors. Under their leaders' direction, the strikers picketed daily in groups of four. To support their cause, they raised funds by holding carnivals; they also fanned out across the city and sought donations for the strike. Ernst called on city leaders to inspect Finck for violations of the city's health code. The *San Antonio Weekly Dispatch* took note of their efforts and criticized the inability of the Cigarmakers' International Union to bring the workers into an ICU-led organization. Deplorably, the ICU had dispatched a staff member to organize a union only after the workers had gone out on strike. The women paid little heed to the ICU's overtures, relying instead on their own initiative. Throughout the strike they organized rallies and other events to raise awareness of their labor grievances.[69]

After the mayor convinced Finck to rehire strikers on a seniority basis and to improve conditions, workers returned to the plant. The truce, however, lasted only a short time. When Finck refused to rehire the four walkout leaders, disputes broke out again, with workers forcing Finck before the NLRB. The women testified that company managers regularly humiliated employees, with grievances ranging from being charged for the loan of towels to unnecessary physical examinations. In 1934 the Regional Labor Board found in favor of the women and ordered Finck to make changes in working conditions and to rehire 100 workers who had been fired for union activities. Finck ignored the order and the women returned to picketing, this time using force against strikebreakers—tearing their dresses and pulling their hair. In retaliation, the strikebreakers hired by Finck attacked the picketers, kicking them and engaging in fistfights. Police stepped in to arrest 21 strikers, including Ernst. Soon after, the police arrested another 25 women strikers and 36 male supporters.[70]

Finck never agreed to settle with the workers, and the company turned to nonunion women to fill its jobs, which eventually brought unionizing efforts to an end.[71] Though they failed to change working conditions at Finck, Tejana workers nonetheless showed their ability to organize themselves and lead their own union.

THE PECAN SHELLERS STRIKE OF 1938

What is a pecan sheller's life worth?
Emma Tenayuca asked herself/she looked
at the woman across the desk
who knew . . .

and Emma said
something had to be done . . . [72]

TERESA PALOMO ACOSTA,
"About Emma Tenayuca and the Pecan Shellers"

In the 1930s Texas produced 40 percent of the country's pecans. Moreover, 50 percent of the crop was grown within a 250-mile radius of San Antonio. At the time of the 1938 strike, one of the largest labor struggles in Texas history, approximately 400 pecan-shelling estab-

In 1938 San Antonio pecan shellers toiled in hot, dusty sheds, where they regularly endured fifty-four-hour work weeks, earning about 6 cents an hour. That same year they struck for higher wages and better working conditions. Courtesy Anita Pérez. Print from the Woman's Collection, Texas Woman's University.

lishments employed around 12,000 Tejanas, who earned from $1 to $4 a week, or $192 annually. Although the federal government had established federal wage codes during the 1930s to protect workers, the rules principally benefited women in the Northeast, and Texas did not adopt any codes for raising salaries that would compensate for this discrepancy.[73]

In 1933, five years before the strike, Magdaleno Rodríguez of the Pecan Shelling Workers' Union had organized pecan workers. Julius Seligmann, owner of a pecan plant and a leader in the industry, provided financial backing for Rodríguez, effectively making him the leader of a company-controlled union. Although Alberta Snid, a Tejana labor organizer, thought well of Rodríguez, others viewed him as a pawn of the pecan-shelling companies. After he disappeared from the labor scene in San Antonio, the union declined. Other pecan sheller organizations existed in the city: El Nogal and the Texas Pecan Shelling Workers' Union. Mrs. Lilia Caballero served as secretary for the independent El Nogal, which boasted 4,000 members, half of whom were too poor to afford the 5-cent monthly union dues.[74]

One event precipitated the pecan shellers' strike. When workers' rates dropped from 6 cents to 5 cents per pound for halves on January 31, 1938, an estimated 6,000 to 8,000 pecan shellers walked off their jobs the following day, February 1. The ensuing six-week-long strike became the "longest and bitterest" one of the decade, and its leaders were regarded as radical. When the Congress of Industrial Workers (CIO) could not immediately unite the existing unions into one front, the strikers exercised their own will, choosing as their leader a twenty-three-year-old fellow Tejana with a history of activism dating to her teens. Her name was Emma Tenayuca, but she became known as La Pasionaria (the Fervently Committed Woman) because of her commitment to the workers.[75]

A native of San Antonio, Emma Tenayuca was born in 1916 to a politically aware Mexican family proud of its Indian heritage. As a high school student, Tenayuca had participated in a reading group that discussed the economic issues of the Great Depression. Drawn to concerns expressed by workers, Tenayuca had joined the Workers Alliance, a Communist group, and she had supported the Finck cigar strikers in 1933.[76]

Tenayuca was highly regarded by poor and working-class Mexican Americans because of her commitment to protest the conditions of poverty and racism that they faced. For instance, as secretary for the West Side Unemployment Council, she held mass meetings in 1935 to object to the purging of thousands of Mexican families from the work relief programs of the Works Progress Administration. Her championing of worker rights earned her enemies within the Mexican American middle class and the Catholic Church. Concerned that her efforts to inculcate leadership skills in Mexican American workers would threaten their religious authority, Catholic religious leaders sought to discredit her.[77]

Both the pecan strikers and *La Prensa,* the most important local Spanish language newspaper, stood behind Tenayuca's leadership, but the CIO adamantly opposed her because of her socialist views. Tenayuca removed herself from public leadership of the strike in response to concerns that her Communist Party ties would harm the workers' efforts. She continued, however, to play an important advisory role. Other Tejana strike leaders—Minne Rendón, Mela Solis, and Juana Sánchez—remained on the five-member strike committee. Under their leadership, women walked the picket lines, even though the police verbally and physically harassed them and often arrested them. The police carried three-foot-long axe-handles to club picketers and they tear-gassed them on at least eight occasions. Many of the women were undaunted by these tactics and faced down opposition to their pickets and demands. For some women, involvement in the strike served to change their perception of themselves. It also gave them an increased understanding of labor issues, and they sought to extend this knowledge to others. As Zaragosa Vargas wrote of them: "The empowered women persuaded their husbands and children to come to the rallies, where they could be educated about the issues."[78]

A number of individuals and groups supported the strikers. Cassie Jean Winifree, representing the Women's International League for Peace and Freedom, provided food for the strikers. She and other women investigated conditions in the jails at the request of the Citizens Labor Aid Committee. The Pecan Workers Emergency Relief Committee called on U.S. Secretary of Labor Frances Perkins, the first female cabinet member, to look into the strikers' complaints during her visit to the city. Religious and civic leaders lent public support to the women's cause. An attorney offered his services to the women. Members of the Tejano community wrote letters to national officials, asking for their intervention. One Tejana contacted the U.S. Department of Labor and offered her services to help settle the walkout. A Tejano wrote to President Franklin D. Roosevelt, asking that he inquire into the strikers' charges against the pecan-shelling industry. Ernesto Galarza, who became a renowned Mexican American labor scholar, also sent a letter to the president.[79]

Amelia de la Rosa, Natalie Camareno, and Velia Quiñones participated in a meeting between the city government and industry officials in an effort to settle the strike through an arbitration board. The board, composed of three Anglo men, ruled that wages should be reinstated to 6 cents per pound, the same rate as before the strike. It also affirmed that salaries would later be renegotiated and increased. Industry leaders, however, had other plans in response to this proposal. They soon had their companies once again employing the 1920s innovation, mechanized shelling,[80] effectively throwing many Tejanas out of a job.

While the wage gains of the strike were a short-lived victory, the women had succeeded in creating a mass movement. Years later Alberta Snid, a notable labor leader, said:

[W]e learned that being united was power. A single person cannot do anything, alone we cannot do anything. People are power.

Indeed, when the strike started, only 50 Tejanas belonged to the pecan shellers' union. By the end of the strike, some 10,000 were members, inspired by such leaders as Snid and Tenayuca.[81]

A POSTSCRIPT TO TEJANA LABOR ACTIONS: BEYOND THE 1940S

The strikes of laundresses, cigar makers, and pecan shellers in 1919, 1933, and 1938, respectively, were not the only major labor actions that Tejanas created in the twentieth century. While this chapter covers their labor struggles only through 1940, it should be noted that Tejanas have continued to engage in labor activism. In May 1972, during the Chicano movement, 4,000 women in El Paso went on a two-year strike against Farah, a clothing manufacturer. Almost two decades later, in January 1990, Levi-Strauss suddenly announced that it was dismissing more than 1,000 of its San Antonio workers and moving its operations abroad. As a result, women created Fuerza Unida (United Force) on February 12, 1990. A movement to work for justice in the workplace both in the United States and abroad, and to press for corporate responsibility, Fuerza Unida celebrated its tenth anniversary in 2000. The organization's recent projects include the family wellness program, the Member Leadership Development Institute, and a workers' union training program. The women of Farah and of Fuerza Unida thus illustrate that Tejana workers in the state's major urban areas have continued to fight for workers' rights, based on the foundation that generations of women before them established.[82]

CHAPTER SEVEN

Education: Learning, Teaching, Leading

Estella Gómez graduated from Sam Houston High School in Houston in 1929. Melisio Gómez Family Collection, Houston Metropolitan Research Center, Houston Public Library.

Mexican Americans first entered the state's public education system during the late nineteenth century. Previously, during the colonial period, they learned reading, writing, and other skills informally from adults in the missions, presidios, *ranchos,* and towns. Children also gained knowledge from oral tradition, folklore, drama, and textbooks. Only the elite sent their children to study in Mexico or Spain. In 1802 Texas governor Juan Bautista Elguezabal ordered that all children up to age twelve attend school, but his order was not enforced.[1]

During the Mexican Texas period (1821–1836), the State of Coahuila y Texas approved a constitution that provided for a system of primary education. However, a variety of problems, including a lack of teachers and financial support and little interest in educating the ordinary population, were obstacles to its implementation. By the 1880s Mexican children began to attend rural schools and by the 1890s they entered city schools. In both cases, students often attended segregated Mexican schools. In San Angelo, for example, separate elementary schools were established in the barrios by the late 1920s. The San Angeleño students, like other Tejano children, rarely continued their education beyond the elementary grades, with only the children of the wealthy attending college. Some Tejano children attended Catholic parochial, Protestant, and private secular schools. The vast majority of Mexican children had limited opportunities to acquire an academically sound education well into the twentieth century. In addition, for many years they attended schools that promoted the heritage of Anglos and excluded the culture and language of Mexicans.[2] Indeed, many Mexican Americans have strong memories of being punished for speaking Spanish in school.

Throughout the decades, Texas Mexicans have brought significant lawsuits to rectify racial discrimination and poor educational opportunities in public schools. In *Del Rio ISD* v. *Salvatierra,* a case tried in 1930, the State Court of Civil Appeals found Texas in violation of the Fourteenth Amendment of the United States Constitution. In *Cisneros* v. *Corpus Christi ISD,* a federal case argued in 1970, the court recognized Mexican Americans as a minority group and extended to them the protection granted by the U.S. Supreme Court's famous *Brown* v. *Board of Education of Topeka, Kansas* in 1954. In the landmark 1984 *Edgewood ISD* v. *Kirby,* Mexican Americans sought to remedy inequities caused by the use of property taxes to fund schools, a practice that left property-poor districts unable to provide an adequate education to children.[3] Tejanos have also filed other cases in opposition to racial discrimination in the state's public schools.

SCHOOLS FOR TEJANAS: 1850–1940S

> No, she doesn't need to go to school. She is going to grow up and get married and have many *chamaquitos* (children). What does she need school for?[4]
>
> A TEJANA, reciting her father's rationale for not educating her

Despite the objections of some parents to schooling their daughters, many Mexican American females have, in fact, attended school. For

El Paso school girls around 1912. Aultman Collection, El Paso Public Library.

The graduation class of 1929 and other students at Our Lady of Guadalupe parochial school in Houston. María Casiano Collection, Houston Metropolitan Research Center, Houston Public Library.

many years, however, they attended in smaller numbers than Mexican males. Those in the rural areas were limited to poorly equipped ranch or Mexican schools. Others attended *escuelitas,* the schools that Mexican Americans founded to educate children. The daughters of the wealthy were enrolled in private schools run by Protestant denominations and the Catholic Church: the Ursuline Academy, founded in San Antonio in 1851; the Rio Grande Female Institute, established in Brownsville in 1854 by Melinda Rankin; the Holding Institute (originally Laredo Seminary), established in Laredo in 1880 by the Methodist Episcopal Church; and the Presbyterian School for Mexican Girls, established in Taft in 1924.[5]

The church-sponsored schools provided a variety of educational experiences. The Rio Grande Female Institute offered a regular academic curriculum and Bible studies that stressed Protestantism. It remained open until approximately 1874, although it was closed during the Civil War. At the Holding Institute, female students could acquire a bachelor's degree in teaching prior to 1913. Between 1913 and 1929, students took normal school training to become teachers. By 1945, an estimated 35 percent of the 11,000 students who attended Holding were from Mexico. By 1887, at Ursuline Academy, the second-oldest girls' school in the state, students came from West Texas and Mexico to study. Ursuline had room for 80 boarders and was considered a "first class" institution. Sister Magdalen de la Garza, a descendant of the original Canary Islanders, was an early director of the school. The Presbyterian School for Mexican Girls sought to provide Tejanas with basic literacy skills. It graduated two students in 1928 and another 100 by 1945. Upper-level students could also take classes at the local public school in Taft. In 1937 the school offered senior homemaking classes. In 1939 students operated a kindergarten in the Mexican section of Taft, and in 1941 they started a day nursery.[6]

TEACHING PIONEERS: 1860–EARLY 1950S

Sister teacher, you . . . have seen flashes of light budding in the eyes of some children and have felt the pleasure of understanding that you have opened the doors of knowledge for a human being.[7]
JOVITA IDAR

Public school teaching, usually considered a woman's occupation, provided Tejanas with the opportunity to become professional women and

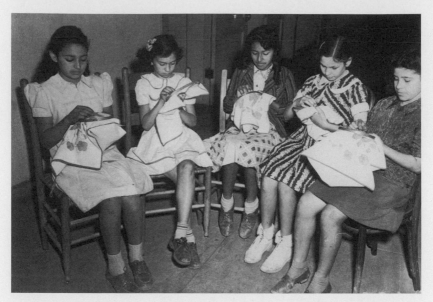

In 1941 fifth grade Tejanas at Johnson School in San Antonio work on their embroidery. Throughout much of the twentieth century, school officials regularly steered Tejanas away from studying academic subjects. *San Antonio Light* Collection, University of Texas Institute of Texan Cultures.

establish lifelong careers in education. Mexican origin women who joined the ranks of teachers and taught in El Paso County as early as 1860 included Carlota Valles, Josefa Valles, Eugenia Onofa, and Trancita Márques. A number of Tejanas were teachers all across South Texas by the 1880s and 1890s. The San Antonio public school faculty included Ada de la Torre, Florence de Zavala, Salistona Crail, Dorotea Coy, and Armanda Andrada. In 1879 Alta G. Garza was a faculty member of Laredo's Spanish–English high school. By 1900 other Laredo teachers were Felipa Saenz, Josefa Contreras, Rosa Sevallis, Adela Montemayor, and María Villareal. In Zapata County, Josefa Navarro, Gertrudis Ramírez, Sofía Peña, Lucinda Domínguez, and María Torres listed their occupation as teacher, while in Starr County, Ernestine Vela, Gabriela Saenz, and Eva Ramírez worked as teachers.[8]

The stories of specific women who pioneered the field provide some insights into Tejanas' entry into the state's public education system as teachers and leaders. Adina Emilia De Zavala, the granddaughter of Lorenzo de Zavala, the first vice president of the Republic of Texas, entered the Sam Houston Normal Institute at Huntsville in 1879 and graduated in 1881. She taught in Terrell from 1884 to 1886 and later also taught in San Antonio. Elvira Rodríguez de Gonzáles, born in 1883, in Mier, Tamaulipas, Mexico, on September 20, 1883, earned an A.B. from the Laredo Seminary (later the Holding Institute). She taught in Webb County from 1903 to 1908. She earned a teacher's certificate in 1920 and later taught in San Diego in 1931–1932. Élida García (later Élida García de Falcón) was reportedly one of the first to graduate from the Holding Institute, in 1900. She also attended normal schools in Corpus Christi and San Marcos. Beginning at age seventeen, she taught first in Springtown and later in San Diego, Hebbronville, and Rio Grande City. Josefina López de Ximenes, born to Mexican and Polish parents in Panna María, Texas, in 1865, was the first Mexican American teacher in Wilson County. López de Ximenes graduated from the Floresville Academy, where she taught until her marriage in 1893 to Manuel J. Ximenes, a deputy sheriff and United States deputy marshal in Wilson County. After she became a widow in 1911, she probably provided for her family as a farmer. Twenty-six of her descendants, including five of her seven children, followed in her footsteps and became teachers. In San Angelo, Ella Balencia taught sixty Mexican students from approximately 1902 to 1904.[9]

Educator Praxedis Torres Mata was a daughter in the respected pioneer family of Cirilo Mata and Aniceta Rodríguez of Uvalde. Born in 1889, Mata attended normal school around the turn of the century in San Antonio. After she graduated, she took a job teaching in Uvalde County public schools in approximately 1905, becoming the first Mexican American teacher in the county. She also taught in the "Mexican school" in Sabinal. Mata passed on her love of teaching to a number of her descendants, including her daughter, Anita Torres Smith, who holds a doctorate in education. Praxedis Mata Torres died in 1973.[10]

Jovita González (later Jovita González de Mireles), an educator, folklorist, and novelist, taught in the Rio Grande City schools, probably in the 1920s, after attaining a teacher's certificate. She acquired the job through the intercession of several people, including Encarnación Sabinas, the county and district clerk. While González worked as a teacher, she lived with relatives, saving money for college. She also taught in Encinal, functioning as the lead teacher at a two-teacher school. Following her graduation from Our Lady of the Lake University in San Antonio in 1927, González became a Spanish teacher at Saint Mary's Hall, an Episcopal school for girls in that city. She later obtained a Master of Arts degree from the University of Texas at Austin (1930) and had a twenty-one-year career as a teacher of Spanish and history at W. B. Ray High School and at Miller High School in Corpus Christi. In 1941 González collaborated with her husband, Edmundo Mireles, and R. B. Fisher, superintendent of Corpus Christi schools, on the first book of the series *Mi libro español*. Two years later, in 1943, the three authors completed the second and third books. The books were among the first that offered students lessons on such Mexican heroes as Father Miguel Hidalgo y Costilla, the martyred leader of the independence movement in Mexico. Later, in 1949, she and her husband coauthored *El español elemental*, a series of books for six grade levels. The books included the Mexican folksongs "Las mañanitas" and "Allá en el rancho grande." All of these books were used in Texas and elsewhere in the country.[11]

As a young student González had studied with at least one Mexican teacher, Élida García, who taught her in English at the San Román Ranch. González credited her educational progress to García's instruction. "Even though the English I learned was elemental," González recalled, "it helped me a great deal. This, together with my knowledge of Spanish, helped me to enter the fourth grade at the age of ten." She reported that she finished the equivalent of high school English by age eighteen.[12]

Emilia Wilhelmina Schunior Ramírez taught throughout the Rio Grande Valley, including Roma, Rio Grande City, Edinburg, and La Joya. She also became principal of the Roma schools after teaching there in 1935. School authorities offered Ramírez the post of superintendent of Starr County Schools, but she declined it. In 1950–1951 she taught at Pharr. Sometime in the 1950s she attained a master's degree from the University of Texas at Austin.[13]

TEJANAS AND THE *ESCUELITA* MOVEMENT

> Very shortly Srta. María Rentería, educator, will open the Nuevo Colegio de Párvulos [New School for Kindergartners]. . . . She has ample pedagogical knowledge and skills . . . [14]
>
> *La Crónica,* September 7, 1911

Throughout South Texas and South Central Texas, Mexican origin women helped establish and operate private *escuelitas* to offer Tejano children the opportunity to study academic subjects and to maintain their language and culture. Colegio Altamirano, one of these *escuelitas,* was founded in Hebbronville in 1897 by Dionicio Peña, Francisco Ba-

rrera Guerra, Tomás Barrera, José Ángel Garza, and Ascensión Martínez. The one-room school cost a family $2.10 per month to educate a
child. Two dollars went toward the teacher's salary and 10 cents toward
school maintenance. Women who taught at the *colegio* (school) included
Laura Ríos, Avelina Carmona, Ernestina Carmona, María Rivas, Emilia
Dávila, and Angelita Ramírez. Dávila taught for two different periods,
from 1910 to 1916 and from 1930 to 1955. Beatriz Vásquez, a graduate
of the school, recalled that Altamirano students entered professional careers in education, medicine, and law. The school apparently operated
until 1958.[15]

The Liga Femenil Mexicanista, established by women at El Primer
Congreso Mexicanista held in Laredo in 1911, committed itself to
teaching Mexican children and thus may have been one of the prime
supporters of the *escuelita* system of education.[16] Historian Emilio Zamora has noted that although men also taught in these schools, women
were clearly the chief teachers of the *escuelitas:*

> The personnel administering and teaching in *las escuelitas* were gen-
> erally single women, certified in teachers' schools from Mexico.
> Teachers advertised their skills in instructional methodology, mate-
> rial content, and diversity of curriculum.[17]

Teachers could set up an *escuelita* in a room in their homes. They
used simple equipment and supplies, making do with what they could
obtain. Some provided students with blackboards and benches. Others used blank newsprint glued together for students' tablets. *Escuelita*
teachers used a bilingual-bicultural curriculum in language, social studies, science, mathematics, geography, and physical education. They also
offered classes in music and drama. Students took their final examinations in a public forum, and the Tejano community attended the event
to hear students recite, sing, complete mathematical problems, and perform plays. One public examination in South Texas drew 300 persons
for a program that lasted from eight o'clock in the evening until four
o'clock the following morning.[18]

Advertisements offering teachers' services for the *escuelitas* regularly
appeared in Spanish language newspapers in the 1910s. *La Crónica* noted
on September 7, 1911, that María Rentería was soon to open Nuevo
Colegio de Párvulos. A graduate of the Normal de Señoritas in Mexico City, she was experienced in elementary and secondary instruction. Rentería's advertisement also promised special opportunities. "For

young girls whose instruction in Spanish is incomplete, she will offer individual instruction in grammar and composition." In addition, Rentería planned to provide instruction in the arts and crafts.[19]

On October 19, 1911, *La Crónica* ran a similar advertisement:

Principal: María de Jesús de León; Graduate, Teacher's College, State of Nuevo León. Elementary and secondary education. Also excellent courses in all handicrafts, under the competent direction of Srita. Benedicta de León. A school which achieves practical results through the moral and intellectual accomplishments of the students. Iturbide Street, No. 309.[20]

La Crónica also reported on the public examinations given by the *escuelita* at the Rancho de San Pedro in Zapata County. During the examinations, which lasted for two or three days, twenty-eight boys and girls under the direction of Hortensia Peña Barrera demonstrated their abilities. Students also displayed their talents in music by singing "beautiful" and "patriotic" songs and presenting a play. At the conclusion of the examinations, the students exhibited their work in sewing, drawing, and calligraphy. Beatriz Vásquez, a graduate of Colegio Altamirano, considered the examinations a "grueling" time for students, who had to pass every subject.[21]

While the *escuelitas* educated a number of Tejanos who entered the professions, they likewise provided the children of the poor the opportunity to learn. In Cotulla, María Romo taught farmworkers' children to read and write in Spanish in the late 1920s. She also supplied books to the mother of two of her students, Felipe and Juan González. In turn, Mrs. González, the boys' mother, taught neighborhood children English, mathematics, and spelling. Her daughter Manuela tutored the children for free. María Romo, who had reputedly fought in the Mexican Revolution, also organized student celebrations of Mexican patriotic days.[22] Like other *escuelita* teachers, she tried to help them retain their cultural heritage. Manuela González remembered: "When we were doing all this . . . it was just a matter of having to do something for somebody . . . but now it's history. It's something to be proud of."[23]

Tejana-led *escuelitas* such as María Romo's left a positive imprint on the children. As a youngster, Sabina Palomo Acosta attended both a ranch school in Loma Vista in southeastern Zavala County and an *escuelita* in Crystal City. She recalled that she learned almost nothing at the ranch school, where the students were predominantly Anglo and classes were conducted in English. In addition, Anglo students regularly harassed the Mexican students. One favorite method of intimidating the Tejanos included snatching tortillas and tacos from their hands and deliberately throwing the food to the ground. Acosta and her classmates were afraid to retaliate, and their teachers did not come to their assistance. In contrast, she recalled with relish her success during her brief attendance at the *escuelita* in Crystal City, where her family moved when they left Loma Vista. There, in the company of other Mexican children and under the tutelage of a Mexican teacher, she learned to read and write sufficient Spanish to serve her throughout her adulthood.[24]

The *escuelita* system served Tejanos in other areas of the state. Elia Martínez Gómez taught at the Barbarossa Specht School, an *escuelita,* between 1929 and 1936. The school was located in the rural community of Barbarossa, between Seguin and New Braunfels. As the only teacher for the school, Gómez taught all grades between first and seventh. She usually had at least fifty students enrolled in her *escuelita,* although at times as many as seventy attended.[25]

In addition to providing poor students the opportunity to acquire an education, the *escuelitas* provided a vital service to the community by preparing future leaders. Dan García, one of María Romo's students in Cotulla, remembered that she taught him enough Spanish grammar to allow him to advance rapidly in the Mexican school where Lyndon Baines Johnson taught in 1928. García later became a local leader during the 1960s, when he was the first Mexican American elected to the Cotulla City Council. He also served as director of the local Community Action Program of the Johnson administration's War on Poverty.[26]

TWO EARLY CAPITAL CITY EDUCATIONAL LEADERS

Two women who spent the bulk of their careers with the Austin Independent School District were at the forefront of Tejana educational leadership. One of them, Consuelo Herrera Méndez, was the first Mexican American female to teach in the public schools of the capital city; the other, Hermilinda Rodríguez, created a bilingual education program for her school years before state authorities embraced the concept.

Méndez became the first Tejana to teach in Austin's public schools only after the City Council of Parent-Teacher Associations convinced school superintendent Arthur N. McCallum to hire her in 1927. She taught first and second graders in the segregated four-room Comal

School on the city's east side in the midst of the Mexican American barrio. After 1937, when she was permanently certified, she taught at Zavala Elementary School. After serving at Comal, Brooke, and Zavala
Elementary Schools for forty-five years, she retired in 1972. In recognition of her service, the school district named Méndez Middle School
for her in 1987, two years after her death.[27]

Hermilinda Rodríguez championed bilingual education when she
became principal of Zavala Elementary School in the 1960s. Because
nearly one-third of the school's Mexican American students knew little
English, Rodríguez offered them instruction in Spanish. School officials
did not initially provide her any money for instruction in Spanish, so
Rodríguez obtained books from Puerto Rico and trained her teachers.
She later acquired a state grant to support her work. Her methods became nationally known, and educators traveled to Austin to learn from
her program. At her retirement in 1984, all but two of Austin's sixty-
one elementary schools offered bilingual education.[28]

LITTLE SCHOOL OF THE 400 AND HEAD START

In 1957 Felix Tijerina and the League of United Latin American Citizens (LULAC) set up an educational project known as the Little School
of the 400 to teach Spanish-dominant children a vocabulary of four
hundred basic words in English to help them successfully complete first
grade.[29]

Seventeen-year-old Isabel Verver of Ganado first learned of the Little
School of the 400 when she read a magazine article about Tijerina. The
LULAC leader later hired her to recruit teachers, as well as to teach a
class of preschool children. Verver's work impressed Tijerina, who then
organized additional classes for June 1958 in several other cities, in-
cluding Sugar Land, Aldine, Ganado, Edna, Brookshire, Rosenberg,
Vanderbilt, Wharton, and Fort Stockton. Tijerina hired local Mexican
American women to teach the classes.[30]

The Little School teachers successfully taught approximately 1,000
children. However, Tijerina could not raise sufficient cash to keep the
schools open. He and LULAC did, however, convince the Fifty-sixth
Texas Legislature to pass House Bill 51 in 1959, authorizing the Preschool Instructional Classes for Non-English Speaking Children Program, which used an expanded vocabulary of five hundred words. In
the summer of 1960, 614 teachers worked with more than 15,000 students in 135 school districts in eighty-one counties, mainly in South

Texas and along the border. Some programs were, however, organized in such northern or western locations as Waco, Abilene, and Dallas. The following summer, 772 teachers and 18,000 students participated in programs in 158 school districts.[31]

Many educators have credited the Little School of the 400 as the model for the Head Start preschool program that the Johnson administration implemented in the mid-1960s. Mexican American women also worked as teachers in this new program. María Carrizales of Weslaco was one of a number recruited to teach for Head Start. She also benefited personally from the experience, earning a scholarship to Texas Woman's University. She later returned to teach in the Weslaco school district. Carrizales, who was active in the Democratic Party, shared her experiences in Head Start with Louis Martin of the National Democratic Party in a letter:

> This summer I had the unique experience of being head teacher of our local Operation Head Start and . . . we were able to reach some of the most disadvantaged and culturally deprived children in our small town.

Carrizales also served as a supervisor at six elementary schools and observed Head Start programs in the course of her work. She reported that the children made great progress with the assistance of many community volunteers. Indeed, Texas led the nation in the number of children enrolled in Head Start, and nationally the program benefited many Mexican Americans.[32]

THE CONTINUING NEED FOR TEJANA PUBLIC SCHOOL EDUCATORS

In the contemporary period, Tejanas have continued to enter public school teaching, although they are still a minority of public school teachers. In 1999–2000 the Texas Education Agency reported that 16.6 percent of the state's public school teachers were Hispanic, 8.6 percent were African American, and 73.9 percent were Anglo. In addition, the TEA reported that 77.4 percent of all public school teachers were women, while only 22.5 percent were men.[33]

Tejanas have taken on major leadership roles within school districts. These include Dolores Muñoz, who has risen to the level of superintendent. In 1999 she headed the Edgewood Independent School District in San Antonio, historically a poor district. In 1999 Edgewood had an enrollment of 13,300 students, most of them Mexican American.[34] In Austin in the late 1990s Martha García was the principal of Ortega Elementary, another urban school that serves a large number of poor children. At the time she relied on assistance of The Austin Project, a program that had helped her students dramatically improve their scores on the state's mandated tests.[35] Both Muñoz and García are representative of Mexican American women with the administrative education and experience to head the inner-city schools, where Latinas are rapidly becoming the majority of students. In future years, more Tejana administrators will be needed to take on leadership roles both inside the classroom and in public school administration.

GOING TO COLLEGE: THE CASE OF YNÉS MEXÍA DE REYGADES

We must send forth the highest prepared individuals. That will be my guiding principle for the next six years.[36]

GUADALUPE RANGEL, first Tejana regent

Some Tejanas have pursued a college education, although doing so has often been a daunting challenge. Segregation, English-only rules in public schools, sexism, lack of academic counseling, and school authorities' insistence on placing them in vocational educational courses have kept many Tejanas from attending college.

Ynés Mexía de Reygades, the daughter of José Antonio Mexía, provides one early example of someone who led a singular life as an educated woman. Mexía de Reygades was born in Washington, D.C., in 1870 but spent her childhood in Limestone County, where the family settled on eleven leagues of land that eventually became Mexia, Texas. She eventually left Texas to be educated on the East Coast and in Canadian private schools. She later studied at Saint Joseph's College in Emmitsburg, Maryland, and at the University of California at Berkeley.[37]

Mexía de Reygades led an unusual life for a woman of her generation, becoming in her fifties a well-regarded botanist who undertook solo expeditions in North and South America in the 1920s. She ultimately collected 145,000 specimens, 500 of which were new. She was also credited with discovering two new species. She published her research in *Madroño,* the journal of the California Botanical Society (1929 and 1935) and in the *Sierra Club Bulletin* (1933, 1937). Her botanical collections have been preserved at various sites, including the Gray Herbarium at Harvard University and the Field Museum of Natural

History in Chicago. Mexía de Reygades donated her archives to the Bancroft Library at the University of California at Berkeley. They reveal many more aspects of her life as a botanist.[38]

TEJANAS AND THE UNIVERSITY OF TEXAS AT AUSTIN

No one is quite certain of the date that Tejanas first enrolled at the University of Texas, which was founded in 1883 in Austin as "a university of the first class," albeit for white students only until well into the twentieth century. While Mexican Americans were not banned from the university through the strict legal segregation that denied African Americans entry until *Sweatt* v. *Painter* (1950),[39] administrators certainly did not actively recruit them into the institution. Because the University of Texas is the flagship educational institution of the state, it is instructive to consider the history of Tejana students at its main campus in Austin.

As early as 1917–1918, the name of a Spanish-surnamed female student, Lucita Escajeda of San Elizario, appeared in the directory of the University of Texas. She is not mentioned in subsequent directories, making it difficult to determine her fate at the university. Several years later, Rachel Garza, born in Rio Grande City on November 30, 1902, received her bachelor's and master's degrees from the university, in 1922 and 1923, respectively, possibly making her the first Tejana graduate of the institution. According to the University of Texas's personnel records, she taught Romance languages at the university in 1924. Garza earned a salary of $1,800 for teaching.[40]

In the 1930s other Tejanas followed Escajeda and Garza to the University of Texas, among them Elena Farías Barrera. Born in Mier, Tamaulipas, Mexico, in 1910, she graduated from Mission High School in 1929 and earned a bachelor's degree in sociology from the university in 1932. She returned to the Rio Grande Valley and became a public school teacher in Roma and La Joya. As a member of the student body of the University of Texas in the early 1930s, Barrera would have been one of an estimated thirty students of Mexican descent enrolled there. Statewide, the Mexican American college population has been estimated at 250 students during this era. The noted educator, folklorist, and novelist Jovita González was one of this group and likely one of the first Texas Mexicans to receive a master's degree from the University of Texas, in 1930.[41]

By the end of the twentieth century, some notable changes in the accomplishments of Mexican American females at the University of Texas at Austin (UT Austin) had occurred since the Tejana pioneers had enrolled. The Texas Higher Education Coordinating Board reported that 510 Hispanic females earned bachelor's degrees at UT Austin in 1997. Statewide, a total of 5,161 Hispanic females earned bachelor's degrees in 1997. While these numbers seem impressive, they are quite small in comparison with the 2,498 white females who earned bachelor's degrees at UT Austin in 1997. Statewide, a total of 20,329 white females earned bachelor's degrees in the same year.[42]

In 1997, Hispanic females earned 96 master's degrees at UT Austin and 1,075 statewide, while white females earned 832 master's degrees at UT Austin and 6,262 statewide. At the doctoral level, 17 Hispanic females earned degrees at UT Austin and 44 did so statewide. White females earned 212 doctoral degrees at UT Austin and 629 statewide in the same year.[43]

TEJANA PROFESSORS, THE ACADEMY, AND THE COMMUNITY

The much smaller number of Mexican American women who received doctoral degrees near the end of the twentieth century at the state's principal doctoral-granting institution, UT Austin, indicates that few would assume positions as professors and university administrators in either Texas or other states as the new century began.

In the decades prior to the turn of the twentieth century, Tejanas had entered the professorial ranks in the state's colleges and universities in even smaller numbers. Two examples exist of women who taught at the University of Texas in the 1940s and early 1950s. Eva Ruissy García Currie, born in 1912 in Cuatro Ciénegas, Coahuila, Mexico, joined the faculty of the University of Texas in 1946–1947, after serving as an assistant to the dean of women and counselor for Mexican American students there. Currie was awarded her bachelor's and master's degrees at the university in 1933 and 1944, respectively. In 1972, after some twenty-six years of service, she earned tenure as an assistant professor of speech communication. Emilia Wilhelmina Schunior Ramírez, born in 1902 in Sam Fordyce (near Mission), became an assistant professor of Spanish at Pan American College (now the University of Texas–Pan American) in 1952. She had earlier been a teacher and principal in the Rio Grande Valley.[44]

Since the Chicano movement of the 1960s and 1970s, Tejanas have completed undergraduate degrees and gone on to attain doctoral degrees and faculty positions at various universities. As students, some

Eva García Currie became a member of the faculty at the University of Texas in 1946, after serving as a counselor for Mexican American students there. Courtesy Office of the Executive Vice President and Provost, University of Texas at Austin.

of these individuals were involved in the Chicano movement and Chicana feminist activities. The four Tejanas discussed below represent others who have combined research and teaching with community involvement.

Norma E. Cantú, a professor of English at UT San Antonio and a notable writer, earned her doctoral degree from the University of Nebraska. Prior to teaching at UT San Antonio, she had a long teaching and administrative career at Texas A&M International University in her hometown of Laredo. She has also been a leading member of Mujeres Activas en Letras y Cambios Sociales (MALCS; Women Active in the Arts and Social Change), a national organization of Mexican American women—university professors, students, and community activists—who are advocates of women's issues and studies.[45]

Cynthia E. Orozco, a native of Cuero, Texas, holds a Ph.D. in his-

Two notable Tejanas, Cynthia E. Orozco, historian, far right, and Sylvia Orozco, director of the Mexic-Arte Museum in Austin, center, with Governor George W. Bush at the Governor's Mansion in December 1999. Photo by Paula Cocke.

tory from the University of California at Los Angeles and is an authority on both LULAC and Mexican American women. In 1983 Orozco established the Chicana Caucus of the National Association of Chicana/Chicano Studies (NACCS) and helped organize the first NACCS conference on women. She has contributed greatly to the study of Mexican origin women's organizational history. She provided significant research direction for articles on Mexican Americans that appeared in the *New Handbook of Texas* (1996).[46]

Leticia Magda Garza-Falcón, a Rio Grande Valley native, earned a Ph.D. in comparative literature from UT Austin. She became an associate professor of English at Southwest Texas State University in 1993, where she also directed the Center for Multicultural and Gender Studies. In 2000 she became director of the Ethnic Studies program and an associate professor of English at the University of Colorado at Denver.[47]

Ángela Valenzuela, a native of San Angelo, earned a Ph.D. in sociology at Stanford University. An associate professor of curriculum and instruction at UT Austin since 1999, she was appointed associate direc-

Leticia M. Garza-Falcón. Garza-Falcón received a doctorate in comparative literature from the University of Texas at Austin in 1993. Her book *Gente Decente: A Borderlands Response to the Rhetoric of Dominance* was published by the University of Texas Press in 1998. Courtesy Leticia M. Garza-Falcón.

tor of the Center for Mexican American Studies there in 2000. She was awarded the Scholar Award from the Texas Association of Chicanos in Higher Education in 2000 for her distinguished research in education.[48]

These four women represent a fraction of a still small number of Mexican origin women from Texas who have attained doctoral degrees and positions as university professors. Indeed, in 1997 only 104 Hispanic females were tenured university faculty members in Texas. A little more than one-half of these tenured faculty taught at UT System schools in Arlington, Austin, Brownsville, Edinburg, El Paso, the Permian Basin, San Antonio, and Tyler. Another 114 Hispanic females held tenure-track positions in 1997. Approximately 43 percent of these women were at the same UT System schools, with UT El Paso and UT Pan American each having thirteen Hispanic female tenure-track faculty members.[49] The data make clear that Spanish-surnamed women professors are a distinct minority of the professional employees in the UT System schools.

Nationwide, Mexican American and other Latina professors also

Ángela Valenzuela, associate professor of curriculum and instruction and in 2000 associate director of the Center for Mexican American Studies, University of Texas at Austin. Courtesy Ángela Valenzuela.

remain a minority. In her article "Latinas in the Academy," Bárbara Robles, a Tejana who teaches at the Lyndon B. Johnson School of Public Affairs at UT Austin, reported that 519 women identified as Hispanic had earned doctoral degrees nationwide in 1995. This number had risen from 388 in 1990. While Robles notes that the increase was important, she also suggests that it was actually only a modest improvement, because the Latino population in the nation has also continued to grow significantly, thus diminishing the gains that Latinas have made in joining university faculties.[50]

ORGANIZING FOR EDUCATIONAL EQUITY AND WOMEN'S ISSUES

Tejanas have also been involved in efforts to establish Mexican American higher education organizations. In 1974 Teresa H. Escobedo, a professor of education at UT Austin, joined with Efraim Armendáriz and

Leonard A. Valverde, also UT Austin professors, to organize a statewide organization of Chicana and Chicano faculty members. After some initial planning, a conference in San Antonio brought together a group of 150 Mexican Americans who held postsecondary education positions. The conference participants drew up a constitution on August 9, 1975, establishing the Texas Association of Chicanos in Higher Education (TACHE). For the past twenty-five years, TACHE has focused on Mexican American issues in higher education by holding annual conferences, publishing a newsletter, and carrying out other activities regarding Mexican American educational concerns.[51] In addition to Escobedo, other women have held leadership positions with TACHE since its founding.

Some Tejanas have sought to focus more exclusively on women's accomplishments and concerns in higher education. Since 1983, the "Brindis a la mujer" (A Toast to Women) conference has been held in Laredo. The gathering has brought together women to discuss a wide array of topics. The 2000 conference, for instance, invited participants to discuss women's issues in art, culture, literature, history, science, the environment, community activism, and leadership. Norma Cantú, a UT San Antonio professor, has long been one of the organizers of "Brindis a la mujer."[52]

Whether more Tejanas will attain tenured faculty positions in the state depends on various factors. Several studies through the years have outlined recommendations to improve the situation. The Texas Higher Education Coordinating Board issued the final report of the Advisory Committee on Women and Minority Faculty and Professional Staff in 1997. The report included several recommendations, beginning with a proposal that all colleges and universities commit themselves to diversity. Both these and other recommendations echo what previous studies have suggested: increasing the funding for recruiting faculty, providing the spouses of new professors with employment in the community, and encouraging faculty members to write letters of reference for minority candidates.[53]

TEJANA POSTSECONDARY EDUCATIONAL LEADERS: A FEW EXAMPLES

Tejanas also entered the leadership ranks at high administrative levels in Texas higher education in the late twentieth century. Guadalupe Quintanilla, once branded as retarded by her Anglo teachers, acquired a doctoral degree in education in 1971 and was named the first director of

Juliet V. García was the first Mexican American woman to lead a major
university in the United States when she was named president of Texas Southmost College in 1986. García was appointed president of the University of Texas
at Brownsville–Southmost College in 1992. Courtesy office of Juliet V. García.

Mexican American Studies at the University of Houston. She also
served as an assistant vice president for academic affairs at the institution. By 2000 Quintanilla, semiretired, was honored as "one of the 100
Texas women who have made a difference in the last century" by the
Women's Chamber of Commerce of Texas.[54]

In 1986, when Juliet V. García, a native of Brownsville with a Ph.D.
from the University of Texas at Austin, was named president of Texas
Southmost College, she became the first Mexican American woman in
the nation's history to head a college. In 1992, when Southmost merged
with UT Brownsville, she was named to head the dual institution. By
2000 a small number of other Tejanas also held other significant ad-

ministrative positions at four-year institutions. One of them, Vickie Gómez, was promoted to assistant vice president for enrollment management at the University of Texas of the Permian Basin in Odessa, Texas. She had previously served as director of admissions there.[55]

At the community college level, Sylvia Ramos, another Tejana, was president of the Eastside campus of the Houston Community College System in 2000. In Laredo, Nora R. Garza was dean of general education at the Laredo Community College and president of the Texas branch of the American Association of University Women in 2000.[56]

A few Tejanas have also ascended to the governing boards of the state's four-year universities. In 1993 Governor Richards named Guada-

Vickie Gómez became director of admissions and later assistant vice president for enrollment management at the University of Texas of the Permian Basin in Odessa in the 1990s. Courtesy office of Vickie Gómez.

lupe Rangel of Corpus Christi to serve a six-year term on the Texas A&M University System Board of Regents. In 1999 Governor Bush appointed Patricia Díaz Dennis of San Antonio to the Texas State University System Board of Regents. Also, Delia Reyes was a member of the governing board for Texas Woman's University in 2000. In addition, thirteen other Mexican American women joined community college governing boards, and Amparo Cárdenas chaired the board of trustees for South Texas Community College.[57]

TEJANAS AND THE UNIVERSITY OF TEXAS AT AUSTIN: FUTURE DIRECTIONS

In the late 1990s, as Mexican American admissions at UT Austin and other public higher education institutions were declining even as the state's Mexican American population was increasing, Irma Rangel, an attorney and state representative from Kingsville, succeeded in passing legislation that ensured that the top 10 percent of the state's high school graduates could enroll in any Texas college. The law was passed in the hopes of countering some of the impact of *Hopwood* v. *State of Texas* (1996), which banned the use of race in college admissions. In 2001, after the U.S. Supreme Court refused to hear the university's appeal of *Hopwood,* the case was effectively closed.[58]

A year earlier, in 2000, UT Austin director of admissions Bruce Walker noted that minority student enrollments had indeed increased as a result of the 10 percent legislation. He admitted, however, that the addition of an affirmative action program would help bring even more minority students to the campus.[59]

Also in 2000, the University of Texas System's annual report sought to highlight its interest in educating more minority women. The report featured Mexican American females studying nontraditional fields or working with projects to improve minority student educational opportunity. For instance, a photograph of third-year student Ruby Torres was prominently displayed on one page, showing her taking advantage of the South Texas Engineering, Math, and Science Program at UT Brownsville. On another page, Priscilla Alejos was pictured attending an advanced biology camp sponsored by the UT Health Science Center at San Antonio. Susana Navarro was featured as the executive director of the El Paso Collaborative for Academic Excellence, which promotes education among Mexican American children in the border city. The initiative that Navarro directed had garnered praise from both the *New York Times* and then–U.S. secretary of education Richard Riley.[60]

While significant efforts such as the projects featured in the UT System's annual report will likely reach only a fraction of the many eligible Tejana public school students in the state; alone they will not achieve an equitable representation of Mexican origin women in professional fields in the coming decades. The problem remained at the end of the twentieth century that many Tejanas continued to attend inferior schools and continued to be tracked into vocational educational programs.

In her award-winning book *Subtractive Schooling: U.S.-Mexican Youth and the Politics of Caring,* UT Austin associate professor Ángela Valenzuela traced the experiences of a number of students at an almost completely Mexican American–populated high school in Houston's inner city. She found over a three-year period of study at the school that the mostly non-Mexican and non-Spanish-speaking staff have failed to effectively teach the students, in part because they have not invested time or interest in implementing a culturally affirming curriculum, one that would provide students with important resources to succeed academically.[61] Indeed, many Tejanas attended segregated schools at the twentieth century's end, enduring the same kinds of negative experiences that Valenzuela recounts in *Subtractive Schooling.*

In "Resegregation in American Schools," Harvard researchers Gary Orfield and John Yun report that Hispanics attended the most segregated schools in the nation in the 1990s. In the 1996–1997 school year, for instance, three-quarters of Hispanics were enrolled in schools with on average 50 percent non-Anglo students. The study concluded that Anglo students were the "most isolated," attending schools that were on average 81 percent Anglo.[62] Historically, segregated schools have been the least successful in graduating minority college-bound students, in part because they often lack a rigorous curriculum, sufficient financial resources, and a dedicated and culturally sensitive staff to meet the needs of the students. Thus, a large number of Tejana students, despite a host of lawsuits, ended the century enrolled in schools that are as segregated and as poorly equipped to educate them as the Mexican schools that their predecessors attended earlier in the twentieth century.

In addition to Valenzuela, other researchers have pointed out the necessity for having a "caring" professional staff of individuals from the students' background in public schools. Yet in the 1990s, Hispanic teachers nationwide accounted for only 80,046 (3.1 percent) of the total 2,546,167 teachers in the United States. (In Texas, as noted earlier, Hispanics were 16.6 percent of the total number of teachers.) The number of non-Hispanic white teachers was 2,188,975, or 86 percent of all teachers in the country. Moreover, the new entry-level tests required to enter a teacher preparation program in the five southwestern states have been judged a major barrier for potential minority teachers, who have a lower passing rate.[63]

Thus, how well Tejanas will fare in the increasingly standards-based educational world, with few Tejana teachers to guide them toward a high school diploma or the desire to pursue a university education, remains a troubling concern. Their predecessors' history suggests that Tejanas will continue to achieve greatly when given the opportunity.

CHAPTER EIGHT

Entering Business and the Professions

In 2000 Gloria Vásquez Brown was a vice president of the Federal Reserve Bank of Dallas. Courtesy Federal Reserve Bank of Dallas.

Female children need to be instructed about self-fulfillment and encouraged to succeed at whatever they attempt. . . . As we individually succeed, we need to bring other women along with us.[1]

DR. CATALINA E. "HOPE" GARCÍA

SELENA'S DREAM AND TEJANAS

Entertainer and businesswoman Selena Quintanilla Pérez, a star of Tejano music by her teens, acquired the financial independence and rewards of pursuing her dreams in her early twenties. Besides being a successful musician, she owned Selena Inc., a boutique-salon in Corpus Christi and San Antonio that featured her own designs. Not surprisingly, despite her death at an

Dr. Catalina García received her medical degree from Southwestern Medical
School in Dallas in 1969, reportedly the first Tejana to graduate from there.
Courtesy Vivian Castleberry.

early age in 1995, Selena has continued to represent in spirit what Mexican American women share in common: the desire to realize their
dreams of financial independence. Her achievements remain an inspiration to Tejanas.

In 1985, two years before Selena won the Tejano Music Association
Award for female entertainer of the year, *Woman's News,* a Dallas publication, featured twelve local Tejanas in careers in medicine, private industry, and government. Among the twelve were Dr. Catalina "Hope"
García, the first known Mexican American female graduate of the University of Texas Southwestern Medical School in Dallas; attorney Elena
Díaz, an honors graduate of the University of Texas at Austin; and
María Teresa García, a graphics designer at General Dynamics who
graduated with honors from Southwest Texas State University. Almost
a decade later, the March 1994 issue of *Texas Hispanic* featured more
than twenty-five women, including Judge Berta Alicia Mejía of the
315th Judicial District Court in Harris County, Judge Hilda Gloria
Tagle of the Nueces County Court at Law, no. 3, and Dolores "Lolita"

Guerrero, president and chief executive officer of Lolita's Mexican Restaurant.[2]

In 2000, six years later, the Laredo National Bank and the South Texas National Bank honored thirty-six female employees. "These women are trailblazers and role models, and we are delighted to celebrate their accomplishments and dedication," noted Gary O. Jacobs, president of Laredo National Bank. Among those honored were senior vice president Adelina Guzmán, a forty-four-year veteran; operations officer Hermina González, with twenty-seven years in banking; and collateral specialist Dolores Mares, with twenty-one years of experience.[3]

At the same time, Gloria Vásquez Brown, a mathematics graduate of Texas Woman's University, was a vice president with the Federal Reserve Bank of Dallas. At the southern tip of the state, Juanita González, a twenty-year veteran of the banking industry, was a vice president of Bank One International Corporation. In Central Texas sisters Cynthia and Lidia Pérez owned and operated the very popular Las Manitas restaurant in Austin, making them two of the more than 5,000 Latinos who owned their own businesses in Travis County by the early 1990s.[4]

Other women who had realized some of their dreams by 2000 included El Paso native Elisa Jiménez, a New York City fashion designer; Graciela Martínez, a senior vice president with the El Paso Energy Corporation; and Sylvia Aguilar, who in 1999 became the first woman to assume a position as city police captain in El Paso. In Central Texas the mother-daughter team Josephina and Gloria Rocha had owned and operated The Fabric Shop in South Austin for more than thirty years. Yolanda López Gómez worked as a tailor and operated Primo Tailors with her husband, also in Austin. María Rodríguez was senior vice president of broadcasting at KLRU, a public television station in the capital city.[5]

Thus, by 2000 numerous Tejanas were professional women. Yet, nationwide, they and other Latinos owned only 2 percent of all businesses. Seeking to increase their numbers, Latino Initiatives for the Next Century (LINC), a national organization of business and political leaders, sought at the turn of the twenty-first century to improve Latinos' standing. Bambina (Bambi) Cárdenas Ramírez, an educator and community leader from San Antonio, was the only female member of the LINC advisory board, which proposed to contribute $25 million to the effort. She was one of two individuals appointed to oversee LINC in Texas.[6]

Another Tejana, Janie Barrera of Corpus Christi, headed Acción

Texas, a promising initiative to assist low-income entrepreneurs. The nonprofit lending organization had been established in 1994 to help small business owners. By 2000 the agency had 600 clients, with more than 50 percent of them minority women. With initiatives in the major urban areas of Austin, Dallas, El Paso, Houston, San Antonio, and the Rio Grande Valley, Acción Texas had helped such clients as Patricia Alarcón, a single mother. She used her $1,000 loan to expand her Latino and Tejano tape sales business. Acción Texas had also provided several loans to Juana Pérez, another entrepreneur who had spent sixteen years as a migrant farm laborer. By 2000 she had expanded her business, Juana Pérez's Store, a food market located near her home in the Rio Grande Valley.[7]

The work of Acción Texas is only the latest of the efforts that Mexican American female leaders have made to improve the economic standing of women. An earlier successful venture occurred in the 1970s. Lupe Anguiano, a former nun, organized two important projects to help Tejanas become employable. In 1973 she set up Mujeres Unidas in San Antonio under the auspices of the National Council of Catholic Bishops. The program helped 500 female heads of household with job training and employment opportunities. In 1978 Anguiano set up National Women's Employment and Education (NWEE), another job preparation program for women. NWEE claimed a more than 90 percent success rate in placing women in jobs, in contrast to the 16 percent success rate of the government's Work Incentive Program. By 1988 Anguiano was named one of the 100 most important women in the country by *Ladies Home Journal*. Her program was also featured on CBS's *60 Minutes*. NWEE closed its Texas headquarters in 1988 and moved to Los Angeles to continue to work with poor women.[8]

THE LONG ROAD TO EQUAL CAREER OPPORTUNITY

Tejanas began working at clerical jobs after World War II, taking the first steps on their long road toward white collar employment. By 1950 some 24 percent of Spanish-surnamed females in Texas were office workers, while 22 percent worked in factories. Another 19 percent were household servants and 15 percent were service employees. Laborers accounted for 11 percent of Tejana workers, including agricultural and crafts employees. However, only 4 percent of Tejanas worked as managers and another 4 percent as professional and technical workers.[9]

In the 1930s a small number of Tejanas worked as clerks and secretaries. Russell Lee Photograph Collection, Center for American History, University of Texas at Austin.

In the next several decades, Tejanas continued to struggle to over-come inferior educational opportunities and employment discrimination that prevented them from entering professional careers. In 1970 statistics from the Women's Bureau of the U.S. Department of Labor revealed that only 7 percent of "Spanish origin" women in the state were professional and technical workers, a rise of only 3 percentage points over the twenty-year period from 1950.[10]

Approximately a decade later, in 1981, the National Commission on Working Women reported that nationwide Latinas comprised only 11 percent of professional and administrative employees. The figure included nurses and teachers. The report also noted that 31 percent of the group remained in clerical positions. According to the study, Latinas' median income was $8,331. In 1997, approximately sixteen years later, their income had risen to $10,260, according to the U.S. Census. It still lagged behind that of white women, whose median income was $14,389. In 1999 the average wage for Latinas in Texas was $10,113.[11]

THREE FIRSTS: FROM POLICEWOMAN TO WEST POINT GRADUATE
TO THE TEXAS WOMEN'S HALL OF FAME

When Enriqueta Rubio López was interviewed about her memories of her life in El Paso, she related that she was born on March 9, 1908, and later attended Franklin School on Overland Street. The seventy-one-year-old also recalled that Virginia Méndez, her mother, "was a police-woman; the first policewoman." Enriqueta continued, "Later she was a probation officer." Virginia Méndez was also involved in civic affairs, and her work to promote voting among the city's Spanish-speaking voters helped elect three mayors. "In those days . . . they all loved my mother. They would wait for mother to come and tell them how to vote. Everybody used to call my mother 'The little lawyer.'" [12]

When she was appointed to the United States Military Academy at West Point in 1977, Elgin native Debra López Fix became the first woman of Mexican origin to enter the renowned military academy. She graduated in 1981 and was commissioned a second lieutenant in the regular army. In 1998, as Lieutenant Colonel Debra López Fix, she returned to deliver the academy's Diez y Seis de Septiembre keynote address, "Women in Leadership." [13]

In the intervening years, Lieutenant Colonel Fix served her country in various capacities, including commanding the 203d Personnel Services Battalion, U.S. Army, in Alaska. By 2000, she was the commander of the 30th Adjutant General Battalion, the only female assigned to the United States Army Infantry Center and School. She was responsible for the basic training of more than 24,000 soldiers. Fix also earned the Meritorious Service Medal, the Army Commendation Medal, and the Air Assault Badge. In 2001 she was assigned to the Pentagon. Not long after beginning her new assignment, Lieutenant Colonel Fix saved the lives of three colleagues trapped in the Pentagon, after a hijacked commercial airplane struck it on September 11, 2001. The hijackers were presumably associated with the Al-Queda terrorist network headed by Osama bin Laden. [14]

When Dr. Clotilde P. García was honored by induction into the first Texas Women's Hall of Fame in 1984, she had spent decades as a physician to Mexican Americans, as an American G.I. Forum leader, and as a lay historian, with numerous publications on Tejano history to her credit. Since recognizing her accomplishments more than fifteen years ago, the Texas Women's Hall of Fame has recognized nine other Tejanas for their political leadership, business acumen, community building,

Lieutenant Colonel Debra López Fix was the first woman of Mexican origin to enter West Point, in 1977. In 1981 she was commissioned a second lieutenant in the regular army, and by 2000 she commanded the 30th Adjutant General Battalion (Reception), responsible for basic training of more than 24,000 soldiers. Courtesy Debra López Fix.

and musicianship. In 2000, Juliet V. García, president of the University of Texas–Southmost College, and Anna María Farías, an attorney and housing expert, were inducted into the Texas Women's Hall of Fame.[15]

JOVITA PÉREZ OF LAREDO: THE CUSTOMS HOUSE BROKER

> There were many men in this business. It was a man's world; yet [Jovita Pérez] was able to compete in this world because of her character, discipline, intelligence, force of will, and ability to protect her clients and the government.[16]   OFELIA SALINAS

In Laredo in 1939, Jovita Pérez opened the Jovita Pérez Customs House at 112 Convent Avenue, with a $2,000 loan from the Laredo National Bank. When World War II began, her firm obtained special permits to import war materials, including Mexican rubber. The company also rushed valuable raw materials to the Allied nations. In 1942, three years after opening her customs house, Pérez hired Lydia Garza, the first of a number of female employees. Eventually, Baudelia García, Juanita Durán, and Ofelia Salinas also went to work at the customs house. Salinas became a thirty-year employee.[17]

Pérez's rise to the ownership of her own customs house began in approximately 1918, when she convinced the A. Grimwood firm to hire her. She served the company first as a clerk and later as a dispatcher. After that she worked for ten years for Brennan and Corrigan, where she became a manager.[18]

By the time of her death in 1970, Doña Jovita's firm was grossing more than half a million dollars a year. Forty-nine years after Doña Jovita received her customs house brokerage license, María C. Longoria, another Tejana, was licensed in the business. Other women have also followed in Pérez's footsteps.[19]

FROM STORE CLERKS TO BUSINESS OWNERS TO WHITE HOUSE ADMINISTRATORS

Tejanas have held jobs as clerks in specialty and department stores for a number of decades. Prior to World War II, holding such a position was tantamount to being a member of the middle class. The case of sales clerk Petronila María Pereida Goodman is particularly compelling. In 1907 she became the first woman to work at Eli Hertzberg's jewelry store in San Antonio. Highly regarded for her business acumen, by the 1940s she had risen from her $5 weekly salary as a clerk to the position of president and sole proprietor of Hertzberg's, at the time the largest jewelry company in the city. In 1941 she hired Annie Laurie Ector, one of the first African Americans to work as a sales clerk in San Antonio.[20]

In McGregor, María Quiroz de León, an agricultural worker who married into a farm-owning family, also found a job in sales. Hired in the 1950s by Winn's, the local five-and-dime store, she was in charge of fabrics and women's lingerie; she placed orders and rang up sales.[21] Other Tejanas sought to improve their lives through store clerking. For these women, who lacked businesses of their own, undertaking such indoor work gave them a step up from the drudgery of factory and field work.

By the last quarter of the twentieth century, Tejana entrepreneurs in the food industry had a long record of accomplishment, with Faustina Porras Martínez of Dallas, María (Chata) Sada of the Big Bend area, and Señora Reyes Ibarra of Corpus Christi all having established restaurants much earlier in the century. In the following years, many other women also opened their own restaurants throughout the state, often in conjunction with their families.

In 1973 Ninfa Rodríguez Laurenzo, who was to become one of the most successful Tejana businesswomen of the twentieth century, entered the restaurant business in Houston. She already had some twenty-four years of experience in the food industry, having operated Rio Grande Food Products Company with her husband since 1948. In 1973 Laurenzo, by then a widow, set up an eatery consisting of ten tables in one section of the family's factory. The effort was a success, enabling her to open another restaurant in 1976. She eventually moved into related enterprises, such as the Bambolino Italian Drive-Thru and Joey Jack's Seafood. In time she presided over an 800-member workforce. In 1979 the Texas Restaurant Association selected Laurenzo as Woman Restaurateur of the Year. The National Hispanic Chamber of Commerce also honored her as Business Woman of the Year in 1981 and 1983. Her business suffered a downturn in the 1990s. It subsequently underwent bankruptcy and was sold to the Serranos restaurant chain. Nonetheless, her reputation as a talented restaurateur was already established. At her death in June 2001, she was recalled as a savvy businesswoman and thoughtful community leader.[22]

By the 1990s two sisters, Cynthia and Lidia Pérez, operated a well-known and successful downtown restaurant in Austin, Las Manitas. The Pérez sisters' operation has also become a showcase for Latino arts, with its walls usually filled with paintings. The restaurant regularly hosts

Ninfa Laurenzo, a highly successful restaurateur, opened Ninfa's Mexican restaurant in Houston in 1973. Courtesy Mama Ninfa's Restaurants, Houston.

events for La Peña, a notable arts organization that the Pérez sisters helped establish. They, like many other Tejana restaurateurs in the decades before, began their business as street vendors.[23]

Tejanas in small communities have also run successful restaurants. Ronnie and Michelle Rubio, a mother-daughter team, own and operate La Bahía in Goliad, Texas. Ronnie Rubio, a 1948 graduate of Goliad High School, opened for business in 1962. Active in the local Tejano community, she has served as president of the General Zaragoza Society, which her father helped found, and been on the board of the Private Industry Council. She has also seen another generation of Mexican American women in her family become successful. By 2000 one of her nieces was a student and a cheerleader at Harvard University.[24]

Tejanas began entering government service at the start of World War II. One of them, twenty-one-year-old Elsa Rodríguez, went to work for the government in 1943 at Blackland Army Airfield in Waco. She had earlier been rejected for a stenographer's position at a defense facility in McGregor, a small neighboring city, on the basis that if she were hired all the white secretaries would quit in protest. Rodríguez was the only Tejana employee at Blackland. She earned approximately $2,000 in annual wages. Rodríguez later moved to Austin and worked as a secretary and equal employment coordinator at Bergstrom Air Force Base.[25] Henrietta López–Rivas left her $1.50 weekly job cleaning houses and barns to work as an interpreter for the government during the war. As an employee of the Civil Service, she earned $90 a month. Later she held a job repairing airplane instruments at Kelly (formerly Duncan) Air Force Base in San Antonio. Apolonia Torres also worked at Kelly, helping build airplanes. Torres was the daughter of Uvalde County's first Mexican American teacher, Praxedis Torres Mata. Gloria Yzaguirre Stephen, a native of Rio Grande City and 1939 graduate

Esperanza Martínez and L. F. King overhaul an engine at Kelly Field in San Antonio in 1947. Few women kept their World War II jobs as mechanics after the war, although they had carried out their nontraditional work with great efficiency. *San Antonio Light* Collection, University of Texas Institute of Texan Cultures.

A woman identified only as Miss Placencia became the first Mexican American nurse to be commissioned as a navy nurse in San Antonio, around 1941. She was sworn in by Cleofas Calleros. Courtesy Cleofas Calleros Estate, University of Texas Institute of Texan Cultures.

of the University of Texas at Austin, served as a civilian counterespionage agent during World War II in Texas, California, and Mexico.[26]

In the 1960s Yolanda Garza Boozer, a San Antonio native and graduate of Incarnate Word College (now the University of the Incarnate Word), entered government service. While working as a secretary at CBS-TV in New York City, she met Senator Lyndon B. Johnson, who offered to find her a job if she ever moved to Washington, D.C. When she later relocated to the nation's capital, then–Vice President Johnson hired her. In 1963, when Johnson became president, she moved with him to the White House as his personal secretary, the only Mexican American woman to have ever held such a post. Boozer worked with President Johnson after his retirement as well, and later served as the executive assistant to the director of the LBJ Foundation.[27]

Three decades later, another Tejana entered government service in the White House. María Echaveste served as White House deputy chief of staff from 1998 to 2001, during the Clinton administration. Echaveste, a South Texas native and a Stanford-educated lawyer, was born into a family of migrant farmworkers. She went to the White House post following service at the Department of Labor, where she oversaw minimum wage and child labor issues and the Family and Medical Leave Act. In undertaking the White House position, Echaveste became one of the first Mexican American women to attain such a high rank in a president's administration.[28]

At the state level, Governor Ann Richards promoted Mexican American women's aspirations during her administration. Aurora Sánchez headed her Office of Human Resources. As director of the office, Sánchez was responsible for personnel, staff development, equal employment opportunity, and the job bank. Richards also appointed former state representative Lena Guerrero to the Railroad Commission, Betty Flores (later mayor of Laredo) to the board of the Department of Housing, and Sonia Hernández as director of educational projects for the Governor's Office. Sandra Martínez Tenorio served as the first director of the Governor's Commission for Women and later oversaw border issues for Governor Richards.[29]

Other Tejanas served on the Governor's Commission for Women:

Yolanda Garza Boozer of San Antonio was personal secretary to President Lyndon B. Johnson from 1963 to 1968, the only Mexican American woman to have held such a post. Photo by Yoichi Okamoto. Courtesy Lyndon Baines Johnson Library and Museum.

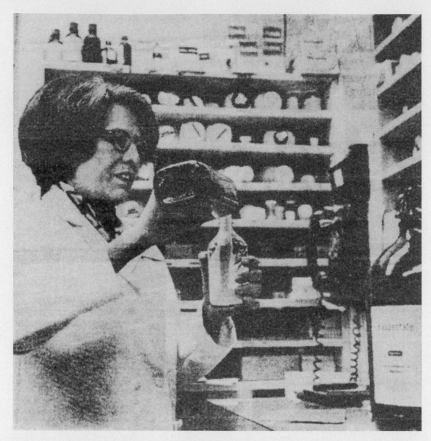

Martha X. García Rodríguez was one of the first Tejanas to become a registered pharmacist, in 1944. She graduated from the College of Pharmacy at the University of Texas and worked at Brackenridge Hospital in Austin for many years. Courtesy Martha X. García.

Dolores Briones of El Paso; Irene Cantú of Hereford; Choco Meza of San Antonio; Amalia Rodríguez-Mendoza of Austin (also commission chair); María Luisa Mercado of Lubbock; Judge Hilda Tagle of Corpus Christi; Jesusa Sánchez-Vera of Alice; Lucinda Montemayor Flores of Brownsville; Dolores Gómez Barzune of Dallas; Celia Morales of Midland; and Lolita Ramos of Beaumont.[30]

ENTERING THE HEALTH PROFESSIONS

Mary Headley Edgerton was the first native of Rio Grande City, and possibly the first Mexican origin woman in Texas, to become a medical doctor. She was born on October 28, 1887, to María de Pilar Treviño de Headley of Camargo, Mexico, and Dr. Alexander Manford Headley, a native of Rothbury, England. She attended the Incarnate Word Convent in Rio Grande City, where she lived, and graduated from Women's Medical College in Philadelphia, Pennsylvania, in 1910, when she was twenty-three. Edgerton returned to practice medicine in Rio Grande City and became famous for halting a smallpox epidemic in the city. Edgerton was also a feminist and a member of the National Women's Party, an organization that worked for women's rights.[31]

Clotilde P. García, another important pioneer in medicine, was born in 1917, seven years after Mary Headley Edgerton became a physician. García, who received her medical degree in 1954, completed her undergraduate degree at the University of Texas in 1938, making her one of the few Tejanas to earn a degree there prior to World War II. Before attending medical school, García earned $800 a year teaching for nu-

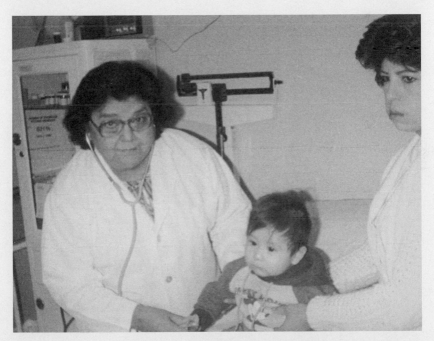

Dr. Clotilde García and her nurse, Isabel Móntes, with a young patient, Corpus Christi, 1985. In 1954 Dr. García earned a medical degree from the University of Texas Medical Branch at Galveston, making her one of the first known Tejana physicians. She practiced with Dr. Héctor García, her brother. Both were leaders of the American G.I. Forum of Texas. Courtesy Tony Canales, Corpus Christi.

merous years at a two-room ranch school, one of the few places where Mexican American women could find teaching jobs during the era.[32]

When she graduated from the University of Texas Medical Branch at Galveston in 1954 at age thirty-seven, Dr. García was near the top of her class despite setbacks and lack of encouragement from school officials. Afterward, she practiced medicine in Corpus Christi with Dr. Héctor García, her brother. She dedicated herself to bringing medical care to Mexican Americans, many of whom were quite poor.[33]

Dr. García once recalled the conditions under which she worked:

> People earned forty cents an hour: no Medicare, no Medicaid, no welfare, no Social Security. I would take care of his [Dr. Héctor García's] patients and my patients . . . I got so sick on my feet I couldn't walk. . . . I wore high heels because I didn't want . . . [it] said, 'She looks like a man'. . . . But I enjoyed working; people had confidence in me.[34]

During the 1960s, Dr. Clotilde García sought to improve Tejanas' opportunities to become nurses. She acquired funds from the Office of Equal Opportunity during the Johnson administration and established nurses' training programs. Her project grew quickly and branched out to include training for laboratory and X-ray technicians.[35]

Tejanas have continued to struggle to acquire medical degrees. Two examples exist of contemporary women who, like García, also waited until they were older to study medicine. Eva Carrizales, born in 1952, around the time that García was a medical student, enrolled in the Texas College of Osteopathic Medicine in Fort Worth while she was the mother of three small daughters. Her youngest child was three months old. Earlier, she had obtained a bachelor's degree in biology and chemistry and acquired training as a laboratory assistant. While she waited to be admitted to medical school, Carrizales taught school in the Rio Grande Valley. She later completed a residency in surgery in Dallas. Likewise, Linda Sagarnaga Magill longed to become a physician. Attending school part-time, she took seven years to complete college. She enrolled at the University of Texas School of Medicine in Houston at the age of twenty-nine and ultimately became an anesthesiologist.[36]

Even by the late 1990s few Tejanas were physicians. In fact, in the 1998–1999 school year, only 42 Hispanic females earned a degree at the four medical schools of the University of Texas System, and another 3 graduated from the Texas A&M University System College of Medicine. During the same year, 194 white females earned degrees at UT medical schools and 16 white females earned degrees from the Texas A&M medical program. White males continued to attain more medical degrees than any other group, earning 282 degrees at UT medical schools and another 29 at A&M's medical college during the same period.[37]

An unusual moment occurred in spring 2001, when Elisa Cuéllar, Adriana Juárez, and Daniella Ochoa, students at Texas A&M International University in Laredo, were all admitted to medical school for fall 2001. Cuéllar and Juárez planned to enroll at the University of Texas Medical Branch at Galveston and Ochoa at the Texas A&M University Health Science Center in College Station. Their acceptance to medical school made the news in Laredo, where they all grew up and graduated from high school.[38]

Tejanas have also pursued careers in nursing. In 1906 Eva Carrillo de

Eva Carrillo de García, seated right, was a nurse and social worker. She and Dr. Alberto García, her husband, seated left, published *El Vanguardia,* the first known Spanish language newspaper in Austin, in 1920. Their children, left to right, back row standing: John Albert García, Alicia Ella García, Ruissy Eva García, and Esperanza María García; front row, in parents' laps: Martha X. García and Nicanor García. (See pages 161 and 184 for photos of two daughters as adults.) Courtesy Martha X. García.

Esther Díaz, as a nursing student, and José Luis Zacarías, her future husband, in front of Brackenridge School of Nursing dormitory, University of Texas, in Austin in 1953. Courtesy Esther Díaz and José Luis Zacarías.

García was one of the earliest to enter the field. De García graduated from the nursing program at Bethany Hospital in Kansas. She put her training to work among the Mexican American needy in Austin, where she moved in 1915 with Dr. Alberto García, her physician husband. In El Paso, Dorothea Muñoz worked as a nurse at Newark Hospital, which was located next door to Houchen Settlement House. Esther Díaz of Brownsville received her nursing degree from the University of Texas at Austin in 1953. She later became the first Mexican American head nurse at Brackenridge Hospital in Austin. Díaz's nursing career spanned thirty-four years. A number of years later, Irma Aguilar combined nursing with university teaching. Aguilar grew up in Marfa. She completed nursing school in El Paso and earned a bachelor's degree in nursing at West Texas State University in Canyon. She later earned two master's degrees, one in counseling and the other in nursing. She taught at the Texas Tech University Health Sciences Center School of Nursing in Odessa, received a doctorate in nursing, and also became a certified nurse practitioner.[39]

Nationwide, the number of Spanish-surnamed nurses has remained low, comprising less than 1.6 percent of all nurses in 1996. At the Canseco School of Nursing at Texas A&M International University in Laredo—the same school that produced the three women accepted to medical school in 2001—officials have sought to increase the number of minority nurses. In 2000 the institution's South Texas Access to RN Education (STAT-RN) program, a new effort, attracted 114 applicants, 70 percent of whom were female, for 35 available slots.[40]

ENTERING THE COURTROOM: TEJANA LAWYERS AND JUDGES

Adelfa Callejo, born in South Texas in 1923, saved enough money over five years to afford one semester's tuition at the Southern Methodist University School of Law. After ten years of night school, she earned her law degree in 1961, when she was thirty-seven years old. Unable to

Adelfa Callejo of Dallas was one of the first Tejanas to earn a law degree in Texas, in 1961 from Southern Methodist University School of Law. She is a founder and former president of the Mexican American Bar Association of Texas. Courtesy Vivian Castleberry.

find employment as an attorney, she offered to do pro bono work for $1 a year for the Dallas Bar Association's Legal Aid Society. The bar turned her down.[41] Approximately three decades later, Callejo recalled her determination to overcome the obstacles placed in her way:

> Many people handle discrimination in different ways—I handled mine with anger. I opened up my own practice and learned very quickly that the key to success was money. If I was going to be an effective advocate of human rights, then I had to become a millionaire . . . so that is what I proceeded to do. . . . The representation of minority lawyers is lacking. We still do not have enough Hispanic attorneys, much less Hispanic women attorneys.[42]

Another Tejana, Irma Rangel, born in 1931 in Kingsville, graduated from Saint Mary's University School of Law in San Antonio in 1969. She had previously taught school for fourteen years. In 1973, after serving as a law clerk and later as an assistant district attorney in Corpus Christi, she went into private practice in her hometown. Years later, Rangel recalled that she went into law because she wanted to have a greater impact on her community by working in civil rights. In 1976 Rangel was elected to the Texas legislature, becoming the first Mexican American woman in the Texas House of Representatives.[43]

Since the time that Callejo and Rangel earned their law licenses, other women have entered the profession and made notable contributions to their communities. Graciela Guzmán Saenz of Houston has served as a city council member at large in Houston. Sylvia R. García of San Diego, Texas, has served as presiding judge of the City of Houston Municipal Courts and as city controller for Houston. San Antonio native and UT law school alumna Norma Martínez has worked for Rural Legal Aid since passing the State Bar in 1979. She managed the Bexar County Rural Legal Aid office for thirteen years. Martínez also argued before the U.S. Supreme Court in *Lyng* v. *Castillo, et al.* (1986), a case involving citizens' rights to food stamps. Mary Helen Berlanga, an attorney in private practice in Corpus Christi, has served on the State Board of Education. In Austin, Susana Alemán has served for many years as the assistant dean for student affairs at the University of Texas School of Law. Marta Rosas of Lubbock has practiced with Sim, Kid, Hubbert, and Wilson and served as a member of the Board of Law Examiners, Supreme Court of Texas. Hilda Gloria Tagle of Corpus Christi was named a federal judge in 1998 during the Clinton administration.[44]

Perhaps Vilma Martínez, born in San Antonio in 1944, is the best-known Tejana attorney. In 1973, when she was twenty-nine, Martínez became the president of the Mexican American Legal Defense and Education Fund (MALDEF), leading it until 1982. Under her leadership, MALDEF ensured that Mexican Americans were included in the protections guaranteed under the Voting Rights Act of 1965. In *Plyler* v. *Doe* she helped protect the rights of undocumented children to a public education. In addition, during her tenure with MALDEF, the organization initiated the Chicana Rights Project. In private practice in California since 1982, Martínez has also served with the Southwest Voter Registration and Education Project and on the Advisory Committee for the U.S. Commission on Civil Rights. She has also been a member and chairperson of the Board of Regents of the University of California.[45]

At the start of the 1990s, some 2,400 lawyers of Hispanic descent were in practice in Texas, according to the Mexican American Bar Association of Texas, with the majority working in the Rio Grande Valley. Approximately 500 of the 2,400 were women. Around a decade later, the State Bar of Texas reported that 1,151 Spanish-surnamed women practiced law in the state.[46]

Still, the numbers of Tejanas entering the legal profession lag behind those of white women. For instance, in 1997 a total of 52 Hispanic females received law degrees from the state's four public law schools, with 29 earning their degrees at the University of Texas at Austin. In comparison, a total of 343 white females earned law degrees, with 157 earning their degrees at UT Austin. Moreover, the entering class in fall 2000 at the UT Austin law school was composed of 477 students, only 34 of whom were Mexican Americans. Eleven, less than half of this number, were women.[47] Further, in 2000 no Tejanas were tenured professors at the University of Texas School of Law, the state's top law degree-granting institution. By fall 2001, however, Brownsville native Norma Cantú, former assistant secretary for civil rights at the U.S. Department of Education in the Clinton administration, became a visiting professor at the UT law school. Cantú, who graduated at age twenty-two from the law school at Harvard, served as regional counsel for MALDEF, where she worked on *Edgewood ISD* v. *Kirby* (1984), a landmark case that changed the public finance system of the state's public education system.[48]

REPORTING THE NEWS: ENTERING BROADCAST AND PRINT MEDIA

Serving the Mexican American community has often motivated Tejanas to work with the print or broadcast media. Civic leader María L.

Aida Barrera created *Carrascolendas,* the first national children's bilingual educational television program. Her memoir, *Looking for Carrascolendas: From a Child's World to Award-Winning Television,* was published in 2001. Photo by Carlos Miranda. Courtesy Aida Barrera.

de Hernández was the first Tejana radio announcer in San Antonio in 1932. Later, in the 1960s, she gave bimonthly speeches on Mexican American educational and social issues on a San Antonio television program sponsored by El Círculo Social Damas de América. Also in 1932, Carolina Malpica Munguía became the first Tejana to host her own program, *La estrella* (The Star), on KONO in San Antonio. Her program featured the music, literature, geography, and culture of Mexico. Angie Morales, who produced *Que Dios se lo pague* (May God Reward You) on KLVL-AM in Pasadena, the first Spanish language radio station to serve the Gulf Coast region, was another early Tejana radio personality. KLVL, which received its license in 1950, broadcast news from throughout the Americas and provided entertainment through its *radionovelas* (radio dramas). The station, owned by Felix Hessbrook Morales, her spouse, was considered "la madre de los Mexicanos" (the mother of Mexicans) because it emphasized community needs. Angie Morales's program, for instance, successfully solicited assistance for poor families. On another KLVL program, *Yo necesito trabajo* (I Need a Job), individuals received job referrals.[49]

In the 1970s Rio Grande Valley native Aida Barrera created, wrote, hosted, and produced *Carrascolendas,* the nation's first award-winning bilingual educational television program for Spanish-speaking children. The program was produced in Austin at KLRN (now KLRU), the public television station on the UT Austin campus. It was eventually broadcast on about 200 out of 243, or 82 percent, of public television stations in the country. Barrera went on to win more than ten awards for her work as the program's producer, including the UNICEF Prize in 1973 and the Gold and Bronze Awards from the New York International Film Festival in 1981 and 1983, respectively. She later produced many other television programs and published a memoir in 2000, *Looking for Carrascolendas: From a Child's World to Award-Winning Television.*[50]

Contemporary Tejana independent newspaper publishers include Cathy Vásquez-Revilla of Austin, who began publishing *La Prensa,* a bilingual newspaper, in the mid-1980s. An activist who has worked to improve the quality of life in East Austin, traditionally a Mexican American barrio, Vásquez-Revilla created *La Prensa* to serve as a voice

Aida Barrera and Austin public school students rehearsing for *Carrascolendas* in 1970. Also pictured is Fred Williams, University of Texas at Austin. Courtesy Aida Barrera.

for Mexican Americans. In Laredo Meg Guerra has been the sole owner and publisher of *LareDOS* since the late 1990s. Under Guerra's direction, the newspaper has published stories of cover-ups and corruption in the Laredo area.[51]

Tejanas have also held positions as newspaper columnists and television personalities. Mercedes Olivera has enjoyed a long tenure as a writer who covers Mexican American issues for the *Dallas Morning News*. Veronica Salazar has held a similar role at the *San Antonio Express-News*. In addition, by the 1980s Martha Tijerina was considered the most influential media representative among Mexican Americans in San Antonio for her long-running interview show on KWEX-TV. In Houston, Evangelina (Vangie) Vigil-Piñon, a notable poet, was in 2000 the public affairs director for ABC-KTRK television, where she also served as producer and host of *Community Close-up: Viva Houston,* a program on the Latino community.[52]

Nationally, the best-known Tejana publisher is Christy Haubegger, who founded *Latina,* a glossy monthly magazine, in 1996. Haubegger, who holds a law degree from Stanford University, took four years to launch the periodical. To ascertain the content Latinas would prefer in a national magazine, she organized focus groups with Latinas around the country. The result of her work was a bilingual lifestyle publication.[53]

The first issue of *Latina* featured a story on Jennifer Peña, then a preteen singer; a piece on Dolores Huerta, a cofounder of the United Farm Workers Union; and an article on the impact on Latinas of Henry Cisneros's affair with an Anglo woman. The first edition, like succeeding ones, also included a host of materials on makeup, beauty, and fashion aimed at Latinas. The publication has thrived and by 2000 boasted a circulation of approximately 250,000.[54] Haubegger is considered an astute businesswoman who took advantage of the large, virtually untapped market of Latina readers interested in a glossy magazine aimed at them.

These women's successes notwithstanding, Spanish-surnamed individuals remained in the mid-1990s less than 3 percent of the total number of professional journalists in the nation. A unique class and a unique publication at the University of Texas at Austin have drawn attention to the need to train more well-prepared minority journalists, including women. Mercedes Lynn de Uriarte, an associate professor of journalism with international experience as a reporter, established *Tejas* to provide students the opportunity to learn how to report with greater insight and depth on minority communities. In the years that she and instructor Chuck Halloran oversaw *Tejas,* the newspaper was cited for its excellent coverage of minority news and students won national awards for reporting. In 1994 the Association for Educators in Journalism and Mass Communication ranked *Tejas* among the top three college magazines in the country. Elizabeth Salinas, Tanya Garza, and David Trinidad, all reporters for the publication, won the prestigious Robert F. Kennedy Journalism Award for their work on "From Fields to Campus," published in the spring 1995 edition of *Tejas.*[55]

ORGANIZING TO SERVE TEJANA BUSINESSWOMEN AND PROFESSIONALS AND THE COMMUNITY

By the early 1970s, Tejanas had organized the Mexican American Business and Professional Women's Association (MABPWA) in Austin, Dallas, and San Antonio. MABPWA was the first major contemporary association for Tejana businesswomen in the state. The Dallas and San Antonio groups affiliated themselves with the National Federation of Business Women's Clubs.[56]

MABPWA emphasized three goals: women's career development, involvement in civic issues, and attention to cultural heritage. Veronica Salazar, María Rodríguez Berriozábal, and Luz M. Escamilla were early MABPWA leaders in San Antonio. Martha P. Cotera and Mary Helen Alvarado were other important early leaders.[57]

Each group carried out different activities to support women's advancement and influence within the Tejano community. In Austin MABPWA supported the establishment of a Mexican American Studies library at the Nettie Lee Benson Latin American Collection at the University of Texas. In Houston MABPWA pressed for protection of civil rights. In Dallas the organization focused on personal development, rape prevention, and employment workshops for women. Some affiliates provided a mentorship program for young Tejanas and established "Semana de la Mujer Chicana" (Chicana Week) to recognize the Tejanas' achievements.[58]

In 1987, more than a decade later, Tejanas established the Hispanic Women's Network of Texas (HWNT) in Dallas. Founded as a statewide organization for business and professional women, HWNT sought to improve the situation of women in public, corporate, and civic life. Its first officers included María Luisa Mercado, president; Amalia Rodríguez-Mendoza, first vice president—issues; Dianna Mendoza Freeman, second vice president—development; and Olga Cookie Mapula, third vice president—membership. HWNT also set up a board of directors composed of two women representing twelve regions in the state. In 1988 some 500 women were members.[59]

Tejanas involved in HWNT represent an array of businesses and professions, signaling the expansion of Tejanas' interests over time. The network's 1994 membership directory provides clues to the kinds of jobs that the middle-class members of HWNT held near the end of the twentieth century. Some owned dance and photography studios; others were educators, lawyers, and social workers. Some members worked in marketing and sales, while others were computer software developers, fashion designers, artists, advertisers, politicians, and health care providers.[60]

ROUTES TO FUTURE BUSINESSES

Bárbara Robles's study "Latina Entrepreneurial Activity in the 1990s: Lessons for the Twenty-first Century" provides insights into the future of Tejana businesswomen. She notes that, nationwide, the number of self-employed Latinas doubled between 1975 and 1990. By 2000 the growth of Latina-owned businesses outpaced that of "Latino [male] business owners and exceed[ed] the rates of new business growth for all other women and women of color business owners."[61]

Moreover, Latina entrepreneurs, 49 percent of whom are first- or second-generation business owners, share several distinguishing features that suggest a path for their success. Robles found that 62 percent of Latinas enter business to become their own boss and 61 percent to improve their lives and their family's income. In contrast, 58 percent of Anglo businesswomen pursue business ownership to be their own boss, while 50 percent do so to improve their lives and their family's income. A greater percentage of Latinas also turn for support in building their business to fathers (13 percent) and spouses (10 percent) than is found among Anglo women, who rely on fathers' and spouses' assistance at a rate of 4 percent.[62]

Robles further suggests that minority businesswomen have employed their traditional roles as "family mediator, nurturer, cultural-social transmitter" to transfer to a whole new generation of female entrepreneurs the desire to continue to give back to their community while also creating successful companies.[63] Projects such as Acción Texas may be a corporate model that can provide both capital and guidance for new female business leaders in the Tejano community.

HIGHER EDUCATION AND PROFESSIONAL ADVANCEMENT

Whether or not Tejanas gain a stronger foothold in business and professional life at a future date, when Latinos comprise some 46 percent of the state's population, is still in question. Gloria Rodríguez, a founder of Avance, a Texas-based program that focuses on Latino educational issues, has warned of negative future trends if the Tejano population in the state is not educated. She observed, "We don't want another South Africa, where the largest group [is] at the bottom."[64]

Indeed, Rodríguez has the data to bolster her concern. Nationwide, in 1997 only 55 percent of Latinos twenty-five years and older held a high school diploma, and only 7.4 percent had completed a bachelor's degree. In 1999 the *Austin American-Statesman* reported, "The educational success of black and Hispanic residents will likely continue to lag behind that of Anglos, causing income disparities to continue." The newspaper also noted that Anglos will continue to dominate higher-income brackets. In 1990, for instance, Anglos made up 92 percent of Texas households with incomes greater than $100,000, and they were forecast to lead this income bracket through 2030. The College Board, one of the nation's most influential educational organizations, also reported in 1999 that the number of Hispanic children raised in high-income families was not expected to increase in the first decade and a half of the twenty-first century.[65] Because income level and educational attainment have historically been linked, the education of Mexican American children will likely continue to lag behind other groups in the coming decades, thus making it more difficult for Tejanas to enter business and professional careers.

Near the end of the twentieth century, Mexican American legislators and business leaders were sounding a call to provide long overdue opportunities for their people in the business and professional world. On the second day of the 1999 session of the state legislature, Marilou Martínez Stevens, chairwoman of the Texas Association of Mexican American Chambers of Commerce (TAMACC), let legislators know that her organization expected fairness in the granting of state contracts and business. In a front page story of the *Austin American-Statesman,* she said, "We demand accountability. TAMACC will not stand by and let state agencies ignore minorities and their businesses."[66]

On the same day that she called on the state legislature to address minority business concerns, Mexican American members of the State Board of Education castigated their chairperson for failing to appoint a

Mexican American to any of the six available leadership slots on the fifteen-member board that determines policy for the state's public schools. The fact that Mexican Americans and other Latinos are slated to become 54 percent of the public school population by 2030 provided the board members with a more than sufficient rationale for insisting on equitable representation.[67]

In the twenty-first century, Tejanas' notable "first" accomplishments —the first physician, the first West Point graduate, the first federal judge—may, with sufficient opportunities, grow to a more representative number. Doubtless, future educational, economic, and political policies will affect Tejanas' prospects for achieving the dreams that were attained by Selena, the young woman who made her way in the world as a successful businesswoman.

CHAPTER NINE

Faith and Community

Members of Ladies LULAC Council no. 22 of Houston hold a poster announcing their annual charity ball to be held at the Shamrock Hotel in the 1930s. Women raised crucial funds to maintain Tejano organizations by organizing a variety of events. Courtesy Houston Metropolitan Research Center, Houston Public Library.

The mother is the one who shapes the values of her children. . . . Just as my mother did, I bring my children here to pray with me. . . . If you instill in the children all the good and teach them to feel good about the world, not to feel bad toward anybody . . . [t]hey will grow up with that thought. True? All the good. All the best. In order for them to live well.[1]

A MEXICAN AMERICAN
altarcista (home altar maker)

Mexican origin women have always played important roles within the Tejano spiritual and community life. They have practiced *comadrazgo* to provide godparenting and share a relationship of mutual support with their godchild's mother, and they have maintained the tradition of home altars. They have organized *sociedades guadalupanas* (Guadalupe societies) to practice devotion to Nuestra Señora de Guadalupe (Our Lady of Guadalupe) and led celebrations of her significance.

As the main interpreters and transmitters of moral values and faith within the culture, Mexican American women have played an important role in maintaining the Catholic faith among their people. Indeed, many Tejanos often recall that their "early faith journey" was shaped by a female elder, whether a mother, an aunt, a grandmother, or a godmother.[2]

Thus, at home or as teachers in catechism classes, Tejanas have taught children the practice of the Catholic faith. They have served as lectors and cantors during mass, reading from the Bible and leading the congregation in liturgical music. They have raised funds to build and maintain parishes and have lent their organizing and leadership skills to parish councils. Some women have served as nuns in the Catholic Church. Others have put their faith into practice in such grassroots organizations as Communities Organized for Public Service (COPS) and Valley Interfaith. Tejanas have also actively participated in Protestant denominations, providing their leadership, fund-raising, and teaching skills to the faithful of their denominations.

Mexican American women have likewise established organizations devoted to cultural heritage, self-help, health, education, and community building. In numerous cases, they have worked in female-male organizations, such as the *sociedades mutualistas* (mutual aid societies), the American G.I. Forum of Texas, and the League of United Latin American Citizens (LULAC).[3]

HONORING NUESTRA SEÑORA DE GUADALUPE

Our Lady of Guadalupe represents everything we as a people should strive to be: strong yet humble, warm and compassionate, yet courageous enough to stand up for what we believe in.[4]

JULIA, a follower of Guadalupe

The sixteenth-century appearance of the Indian Virgin to Juan Diego, an Indian peasant, early in the morning on December 9, 1531, on the hill of Tepeyac outside of Mexico City, instilled a strong, lasting devotion to her among the Mexican people. Her appearance occurred

Nuestra Señora de Guadalupe (Our Lady of Guadalupe), the Patroness of the
Americas, holds a special significance for Mexican Americans. Courtesy Our
Lady of Guadalupe Church, San Antonio. Print from Texas Council for the
Humanities.

approximately a decade after the Spanish conquest of Mexico in 1519–
1521. The native people interpreted her appearance to one of them at
the site reserved for Tonantzín, the Indian mother goddess they revered, as a sign of divine protection against the brutality of Spanish colonial oppression. Officially accepted in 1754 by the Church as a true
sign of the Virgin Mary, the Indian Virgin came to be known as Nuestra Señora de Guadalupe, the mestiza Madonna. In Catholic tradition
she is considered the patroness of North and South America, and she
has a special significance for Mexican Americans, for whom she represents faith, identity, hope, and liberation—ideals they have drawn upon
for both personal and group survival in the sometimes hostile environment they have faced in Texas. So important is she in the Tejano community that she is also simply referred to as "Guadalupe," indicating the
strong affection in which she is held.[5]

Nuestra Señora de Guadalupe is especially important to Mexican
American women, who must contend with racial prejudice, poverty,
and sexism. For them, she represents a sympathetic mother who hears
their requests for assistance in daily life. She is thus the mediator of their
entreaties to God for help in overcoming difficult circumstances. Moreover, many Mexican American women consider Guadalupe a woman
whose unqualified love of human beings all people should emulate.
Perhaps even more importantly, Nuestra Señora provides them the opportunity to have intimate contact with the divine through prayer.[6]

From the time of her appearance to Juan Diego, Mexicans have recognized that the love of Nuestra Señora for them is boundless. In eighteenth-century New Spain they revered her as a protectress who ensured a bountiful harvest of food. Indeed, her December 12 feast day
fell during a critical period—between the end of the fall *maíz* (corn)
harvest and the preparation for new planting in the spring. Tejano settlers on the northern frontier of New Spain also used the occasion of
her feast to rejoice in their survival of harsh living conditions.[7]

Both women and men have participated in honoring Nuestra Señora
de Guadalupe. By 1750 public expressions of devotion to her were
common in San Antonio. Women assembled jewelry and other ornaments for adorning the church and the image of Guadalupe, while men
assembled the equipment for fire salutes. During the community processions that were part of the festivities, women were the immediate at-
tendants of the image of Nuestra Señora. Their prominent place in this
annual display of *guadalupanismo* (a strong devotion to Guadalupe) reflected Tejanas' leadership in the community's spiritual practices.[8]

Cuca Borrego and her home altar, San Antonio, 1986. Tejanas have followed the spiritual practice of altar making since their earliest days in the state. Courtesy Kay Turner.

HOME ALTARS AND *SOCIEDADES GUADALUPANAS:*
PRIVATE AND PUBLIC EXPRESSIONS OF FAITH

Tejanas have created home altars as private sites for prayer and reflection since their settlement in the American Southwest. *Altarcistas* have traditionally placed an image of a major religious figure at the center of their altars. Those so honored include Nuestra Señora de Guadalupe, El Niño Jesús (the Child Jesus), or La Virgen de San Juan de los Lagos. Sometimes they honor favorite saints such as Saint Anthony and Saint Jerome with this central role. *Altarcistas* surround the central icon with an array of saints, family photographs, personal gifts, and other items that are special to them. They light votive candles on the altar to convey the sacredness of the site. The *altarcistas* usually offer formal prayers in front of their altars on a daily basis. They may also prayerfully submit informal and intimate petitions for divine intervention in personal and social concerns, issues, and causes.[9]

Older women have often been the principal keepers of home altars, but younger women also build them, bringing new perspectives to the tradition. Writer Gloria Anzaldúa, for instance, has said that altar making has permitted her to "bare" her soul, while also allowing her to communicate with her mestiza heritage. The *ofrenda* (offering) is a related form of a home altar. Painter Carmen Lomas Garza has created a famous one—*Ofrenda para Antonio Lomas*—to pay tribute to her grandfather, who taught her important cultural values.[10] Museum exhibitions have brought public attention to altar making. In 1980 the Texas Memorial Museum at the University of Texas at Austin offered the exhibition "La vela prendida" (The Ever-Burning Candle) to coincide with the December 12 feast day of Nuestra Señora de Guadalupe. The exhibition title echoed the light of faith that the lit candles placed on home altars symbolize for *altarcistas*. At the Mexic-Arte Museum in Austin, the annual celebration of *Día de los Muertos* (Day of the Dead) has also brought the home altar tradition into a public space, with exhibitions offered annually.[11] Nonetheless, the practice of maintaining home altars has remained principally a private female practice for women to express their spirituality in a culturally relevant way.[12]

Altarcistas may not necessarily participate in the formal rituals of the Catholic faith. However, women involved in the *sociedades guadalupanas* are generally dedicated parish members who may combine the private altar-making tradition with public church-sanctioned expressions of women's dedication to Nuestra Señora de Guadalupe. Calling themselves simply Guadalupanas, women are traditionally the leaders of the *sociedades,* although José Navarro reportedly headed the first known *sociedad guadalupana* in San Antonio, which was established in 1912. Female members have also dominated membership of the *sociedades,* although men also participate.[13]

Sociedades guadalupanas carry out their devotion to Nuestra Señora de Guadalupe in a variety of ways. They pray together and receive Holy Communion as a group. Members practice other acts of devotion, such as carrying Guadalupe's image in a public pilgrimage through a neighborhood to extend the protection of the Virgin to the area. Following the tradition of Tejanas in earlier periods, they continue to organize the annual December 12 feast to honor Guadalupe.[14]

The Guadalupanas also perform charitable acts and involve themselves in the community to represent the "all-encompassing" love of Nuestra Señora de Guadalupe. Thus, in her name, the Guadalupanas have set up diabetes detection campaigns, ministered to prisoners, assisted at battered women's homes, organized social activities for youth, offered religious education, and taught English to Mexican Americans.[15]

Lupe Medina of Mexico was reportedly sent to a convent in San Antonio by her uncle to prevent her from marrying her sweetheart. Here she is pictured as a novice. Courtesy Teresa Palomo Acosta.

CATHOLICISM, RELIGIOUS ORDERS, AND LAS HERMANAS

Most Mexican Americans have historically been Catholic. The Mexican Revolution, which brought thousands of Mexicans into the state to join family members, heralded the entry of a large number of Mexican nuns into the state to provide parochial education to the Tejano popu-

In 2000 Sister Joseph Moreno was the last active member of the Order of the Catechist Missionary Sisters of Saint John Bosco, which was established in Roma in 1938 to serve Mexican public school children. Reprinted from *Catholic Spirit,* June 2000, Austin. Courtesy Sister Joseph Moreno.

lace. In 1930 the Missionary Catechists of Divine Providence, an order composed of Mexican American women, was established specifically to minister to Mexican Catholics in Houston. Tejanas also served their community as members of the Catechist Missionary Sisters of Saint John Bosco, established in 1938 in Roma, Texas. The Missionary Sisters often worked with Mexican public school children. They "rode trains and buses, slept in sacristies, and brought their own wash tubs to scrub off the dust of the journey" as they carried out their work in South and Central Texas. By 2000 Sister Joseph Moreno was the last remaining active member of the order. She was stationed in Taylor, where she continued her work in the local parish.[16]

Other women in religious life have combined their faith with community involvement. In April 1971 Sisters Gloria Gallardo and Gregoria Ortega organized a meeting in Houston of fifty women who came from a variety of religious communities. Under the two nuns' leadership, the group established the national organization Las Hermanas and invited both lay and religious women to join it. Chartered by the state in February 1972, Las Hermanas opened membership in the organization to Catholic women from any country. The national office was initially established in Houston but was later moved to Our Lady of the Lake University in San Antonio.[17]

The organization carried out various activities to promote social change and improve women's roles. Women served on the staff and board of the Mexican American Cultural Center in San Antonio, influencing the training of leaders in Tejano parishes. Through Proyecto Mexico, the group sought to ensure that Mexican-born religious women worked in parish ministries rather than in the kitchens of American seminaries. Las Hermanas also supported the United Farm Workers Union through boycotts and demonstrations for workers' rights, and they devoted themselves to act on issues affecting women in the church. To spread word of their mission, the group published a newsletter, *Informes,* which was distributed nationally to 1,000 subscribers.[18]

PROTESTANTISM

Texas Mexicans have been members of Methodist, Presbyterian, and Baptist denominations since the nineteenth century, in effect becoming pioneers of "Tejano Protestantism" at a time when Anglo Protestant missionaries were focusing their attention on Mexicans in Mexico. In 1871 Alejo Hernández, a one-time Catholic seminary student, was ordained a Methodist minister. Others have followed him into pastoral leadership in other denominations.[19]

The arrival of large numbers of Mexicans in the state during the Mexican Revolution caused Protestant missionaries working in Mexico to shift their attention to the Tejano population and oversee their religious direction. The Tejanos, however, eager to shape their own Protestantism, established their churches in the early twentieth century without Anglos' supervision. To bolster their efforts, the Tejanos organized the Texas-Mexican Presbytery (1908), the Baptist-Mexican Convention (1910), and the (Methodist) Texas-Mexican Mission (1914).[20]

Women have long been leaders in the Tejano Protestant community. Eva Carrillo de García, a missionary nurse and community leader in Austin, was an elder at the University Methodist Church as well as a founder of the second Mexican Methodist Church in the city. Jovita

Children at the Presbyterian Sunday School in Corpus Christi. Russell Lee Photograph Collection, CN #09189, Center for American History, University of Texas at Austin.

Idar, a journalist and political activist, was an editor for *El Heraldo Cristiano,* published by the Methodist Church's Rio Grande Conference. Élida García de Falcón, a teacher and a member of the family of one of the first Mexican American Methodist ministers, spent twenty years as a translator for the Methodist women's division. De Falcón translated the official *Methodist Hymnbook* (*Himnario metodista*) and the *Methodist Book of Rituals* (*Ritual metodista*). Both documents greatly aided the Methodists' expansion into the Tejano community. By 1979 Tejanas' involvement in Protestant churches as leaders was reinforced when Rebecca Reyes became the first Mexican American woman ordained a minister in the Presbyterian faith.[21]

TEJANA VOLUNTEER ORGANIZATIONS

Mexican origin women have organized female voluntary organizations throughout the twentieth century to serve several major purposes: to champion women's causes, to fight racial discrimination and economic and social exploitation, and to celebrate cultural heritage. Thus, each generation's efforts share historic links. Women who participated in Ladies LULAC, founded in 1933, or who worked with Communities Organized for Public Service (COPS), founded in 1974, are linked by similar purposes to the women of the first known twentieth century Tejana voluntary organization, the Liga Femenil Mexicanista, founded in 1911. A group that promoted the education of women and children, organized theatrical and literary activities, and contributed charitable relief to poor Tejanos, the Liga is the earliest known model for many of the organizations that Tejanas have since established. Martha P. Cotera has observed that the Liga was also a feminist organization because only females belonged to it and because it endorsed women's education.[22]

WOMEN AND *SOCIEDADES MUTUALISTAS*

As they participated in mutual aid ladies auxiliaries, Mexican American women developed leadership skills by planning the "banquets, dances,

Annual meeting of the Methodist Women's Missionary Society at El Mesías Methodist Church, Houston, 1938. Rachel Lucas Collection, Houston Metropolitan Research Center, Houston Public Library.

Members of El Campo Laurel, Mutualista Benito Juárez, and Pasadena's Mutualista Miguel Hidalgo meet in 1925 at Magnolia Park in Houston. Mary Beltrán Collection, Houston Metropolitan Research Center, Houston Public Library.

and other social events" needed to maintain the organizations. Indeed, their efforts provided Tejano groups with much sought after "money, food, service, and entertainment."[23] In general, the women's work supported projects in community uplift, cultural maintenance, and resistance to racism. Moreover, the women kept organizations solvent and helped shape Texas Mexican community service.

Indeed, beyond sustaining *sociedades mutualistas* in the 1920s and 1930s, women contributed to specific projects of the Comité Patriótico Mexicano, the Hijos de Texas (a splinter group of Hijos de America), and the Club Cultural Recreativo México Bello. Working with the Hijos de Texas, they provided Christmas gifts to Mexican children. Women also cooperated on social and legal issues with the Comisión Honorífica Mexicana, a mutual aid, protection, and charitable organization established across the nation by the Mexican Consulate in 1920–1921 to aid citizens of Mexican descent.[24]

CRUZ AZUL MEXICANA

In 1920 women in San Antonio established the Texas branch of Cruz Azul Mexicana (Mexican Blue Cross), one of the most significant organizations of Mexican origin women. Cruz Azul Mexicana worked independently as well as hand in hand with male groups. The group functioned under the umbrella of the Comisión Honorífica Mexicana

Members of the Cruz Azul Mexicana in Granger in 1929. Women established the Texas branch of the organization in San Antonio in 1920 and later expanded it to serve other parts of the state. Photograph by John P. Trlica. Courtesy Photography Collection, Harry Ransom Humanities Research Center, University of Texas at Austin.

and was especially interested in assisting female pecan shellers, laborers, and laundresses. Two of its leaders were María Luisa Garza, a journalist who served as president, and Delfina Tafolla, who was a vice president.[25]

Each one of the *comisiones honoríficas* (honorific commissions), which were often located in rural areas, was under the jurisdiction of the closest Mexican Consulate. The San Antonio office of the consulate oversaw the *comisiones* in East, Central, and South Texas, as well as in Oklahoma. While the *comisiones* were made up of men, their inclusion of Cruz Azul, a women's charitable organization, made them in essence a female-male entity, with women working within their own organizational structure.[26]

In the 1920s, Cruz Azul contributed to the Tejano community in major ways. With $4,000 gathered through public fund-raising, the group established a free public clinic in San Antonio. Patients could obtain food at the clinic, and mothers were provided with circulars on infant care. Cruz Azul also established a library, supplying it with materials obtained from Coahuila, Mexico. With the Comisión Honorífica Mexicana, Cruz Azul wrote sample contracts to help Tejano workers obtain fair employment; provided for a legal defense fund; and established a Mexican industrial school. With the *comisión* and the local Mexican Consulate, Cruz Azul also planned a census of Mexicans in San Antonio to ascertain their needs.[27]

The organization operated in other cities in South Central Texas, including Asherton, Castroville, Charlotte, Mackay, Luling, and Phelan, and in Malakoff in East Texas. Like many other Tejana organizations, it raised money for its projects through a variety of events, including dances and theatrical productions. The organization also published a news magazine, *Revista Azul* (Blue Magazine), later renamed *Revista Nacional* (National Magazine).[28]

Cruz Azul and the Comisión Honorífica worked together to assist families subjected to forced repatriation during the Great Depression. In Houston the two groups raised money for fifty such families in 1931. In addition, Cruz Azul helped approximately 1,500 unemployed individuals in Houston during that same year.[29]

Cruz Azul Mexicana belonged to the Confederación de Organizaciones Mexicanas y Latino Americanas (COMLA), a coalition composed of Tejano voluntary groups. COMLA was founded at a state gathering of *mutualistas* in Port Arthur on November 27, 1938. To ensure the moral, economic, and cultural betterment of Mexicans, it established libraries and cultural enrichment programs. In Wharton,

COMLA temporarily succeeded in getting "Mexicans Not Allowed" signs in public places removed. In 1941, at what might have been its final state convention, COMLA focused on the need to fight segregation.[30]

SPANISH-SPEAKING PTA

Assigned to poor and segregated schools, the vast majority of Tejano children received an inadequate education in the 1920s. Anglo school officials contended that Mexican children were better served in separate schools due to their inability to speak English. However, the officials also placed English-speaking Mexican students in these separate schools solely on the basis of their Spanish surnames, clearly segregating them on the basis of ethnicity.[31]

Tejanas' concern with the treatment of Mexican children in the state's public school system led them to form the Spanish-Speaking PTA as local groups in 1923. The group focused exclusively on the educational and health needs of Mexican American schoolchildren. The Texas Congress of Parents and Teachers recognized the Spanish-Speaking PTA four years later, in 1927. Operating into the 1950s, the organization maintained branches in Kingsville, Corpus Christi, Robstown, San Antonio, and other cities. Mexican American men and a few female Anglo teachers supported the SSPTA's efforts. Historian Cynthia Orozco has noted that the organization may have been one of the first voluntary organizations in which Mexican origin women "interacted with mainstream society" to accomplish their goals.[32]

In 1933 Mrs. A. G. Treviño headed the thirty-member Spanish-Speaking PTA in Kingsville. The group carried out a number of school improvement projects. Members planted trees and set up gardens, provided encyclopedias, and purchased a piano and victrola. They also operated a free cafeteria. At the David Crockett School in San Antonio, the group had seventy-six members in the late 1930s. When Carolina Malpica Munguía, a notable community leader, headed the Crockett chapter, members sponsored a soup kitchen to provide free lunches to Mexican children. The Crockett chapter also set up bathing facilities to maintain children's hygiene and organized a sewing circle to furnish children with clothing for school. In San Diego, Elvira Rodríguez de González started a chapter of the Spanish-Speaking PTA and was the district chairwoman for the organization from 1927 through 1936. Her area included nineteen South Texas counties. A graduate of the Holding Institute in Laredo and a certified teacher, she wrote *A Year*

Book for Spanish-Speaking Parent Teacher Associations to assist the group's efforts.[33]

The work of the Spanish-Speaking PTA was considered of vital importance in educational circles by 1939, when the Texas Parent Teacher Association hired Mrs. T. J. Martin, an Anglo committed to educational opportunities for all children, to coordinate the organization's work. In addition, the Texas PTA began to translate its materials into Spanish and engaged Consuelo E. Herrera, a Zavala Elementary School teacher in Austin, to translate articles from *Texas Parent-Teacher,* the Texas PTA's publication. In 1941, the magazine added a new column for Texas Mexican parents and students, "El hogar creativo" (The Creative Home).[34]

The efforts of the Spanish-Speaking PTA foreshadowed the implementation of bilingual education, which the state instituted on June 3, 1973, when Governor Dolph Briscoe signed into law the Bilingual Education and Training Act. With the advent of integration and bilingual education, the group apparently went into decline.[35]

SOCIEDAD DE LA BENEFICENCIA MEXICANA

Alicia Guadalupe Elizondo de Lozano, a businesswoman and philanthropist, started the Sociedad de la Beneficencia Mexicana de San Antonio, a middle-class women's voluntary association, to provide poor members of the Tejano community with medical care. The Beneficencia Mexicana, founded probably in the 1930s, operated under the motto "charity, order, and efficiency." Genoveva González, a civic leader and lay social worker, belonged to the Beneficencia Mexicana. Her son, Henry B. González, who learned firsthand from her the value of public service, was the first Tejano elected to the U.S. House of Representatives, in 1961.[36]

Ignacio Lozano, the publisher of *La Prensa* and Alicia de Lozano's husband, initiated a fund-raising campaign to help the organization construct a health clinic to serve poor Mexicans. Money for the clinic came from various sources. The Club Femenino Orquidia and the Club de Jóvenes Católicos provided $286 to the effort. Some Anglo businessmen, including the Finck Cigar Company owners, also contributed money.[37]

La Prensa collected $27,000 by 1930, allowing the Clínica Mexicana to be constructed at 623 South San Saba. Matilde Elizondo, a Tejana who owned La Gloria Grocery and Meat Market, provided medical supplies and equipment. Clients paid 25 cents for the first visit only. Both Mexican and Anglo volunteer doctors attended patients. The Junta de Beneficencia, a group eventually composed primarily of women, oversaw the clinic. Alicia de Lozano served as president of the clinic's board of directors from 1930 to 1938. María de los Angeles G. de Velasco assumed the presidency in 1939.[38]

WOMEN'S CLUBS IN HOUSTON AND SAN ANTONIO

Our commission has worked for more than a month achieving the distribution of 28 food baskets, 30 big bags, 40 small bags, 40 medium bags, 18 bundles of clothes, 180 toys, 20 half pints of milk, and 4 boxes of bread from Jalisco bakery. . . . Also distributed were baskets of fruit donated by Sr. Rómulo Munguía, one box of candy blow pops, 16 candy flowers from Sr. Ramírez, 2 boxes of cookies and seven toys.[39]   CAROLINA MALPICA MUNGUÍA

Women's clubs complemented the work of voluntary and charitable organizations in the Tejano community. In Houston two notable ones were El Club Femenino Arco Iris and El Club Femenino Chapultepec. Founded in the 1930s, these women's groups held dances and other

Members of the Círculo Femenino México Bello, around 1936. Mr. and Mrs. Félix Tijerina Collection, Houston Metropolitan Research Center, Houston Public Library.

Lorraine Castro reigned as queen of the Taylor Diez y Seis de Septiembre celebration in 1935. Photograph by Studio of Alf H. Otto. Print from University of
Texas Institute of Texan Cultures.

social events in Tejano neighborhoods, including Magnolia Park. In
1937 María Medrano, Edelia Cantú, Catalina and Virginia Gómez, and
Hortensia and Lupe Quintanilla established another women's group,
Club Terpsicore, which took its name from Terpsichore, the mytho-
logical muse of dance. Besides providing for the social life of the community, the club raised money to aid the Salvation Army in combating
tuberculosis. By 1940 other clubs sprang up in Houston—Club Selva,
Cielito Lindo, Club Orquidia, and Club Femenino Dalia. All of these

groups attracted to the ranks "aspiring young women" of the Mexican barrios. Women from different generations joined the clubs, thus maintaining continuity in the groups' work.[40]

Women's clubs emerged in San Antonio as well. Círculo Cultural Isabel la Católica, originally known as Círculo Social Femenino Mexicana, functioned from the late 1930s through the early 1940s, mainly to assist needy Mexican origin females. Círculo members were often between ages twenty-one to forty-six. Carolina Malpica Munguía, credited as principal founder of the Círculo Social, served as its first president, and civic leader María L. de Hernández was its first board member. Munguía firmly believed that women were the "guardians of society's moral fabric," with a responsibility to uplift the entire Tejano populace economically, culturally, and socially. Thus, in addition to assisting the poor and elevating women's status, the club was concerned with improving "morality and order." The Círculo also donated its time and skills to the *fiestas patrias* (Cinco de Mayo and Diez y Seis de Septiembre) and assisted the Tejano community with food and toys during the Christmas holiday.

Club members also worked with Cruz Azul Mexicana by sending delegates to its convention. In 1939 the club sponsored an exhibition of Mexican art at the Witte Museum.[41]

AMERICAN G.I. FORUM WOMEN'S AUXILIARY

Tejanas were involved from the outset in the American G.I. Forum of Texas, founded in 1948 by World War II veterans under the leadership of Dr. Héctor García. Beatriz Tagle Pérez was one of the most prominent leaders of the Forum. Beginning in 1959, for thirty years she was in charge of the local chapter in Corpus Christi, assisting in its efforts to end the segregation of Mexican American public school students. In 1976 she was elected state treasurer of the Forum. She was also involved in Ladies LULAC Council no. 26 in Corpus Christi. Pérez was honored with a recognition banquet in 1988 for her contributions. Isabelle Tellez, Dominga Coronado, Molly Galván, and Dr. Clotilde García also played significant roles in the veterans' organization.[42]

As the Forum evolved from dealing strictly with veterans' issues to focus on civil rights matters, women participated in efforts to register more Tejano voters and to lobby for equal opportunities for all members of the Mexican American community. In 1956, at the Forum's first annual conference, women led the effort to formalize their roles in the organization and succeeded in gaining recognition for a women's auxiliary.[43]

After establishing the auxiliary, women took on more responsibility in defining the Forum's goals. In addition, in 1957, a year after the auxiliary was founded, the group sponsored a women's leadership conference to promote women's roles. The auxiliary also supported the education of women and was concerned with the rights of both Tejana workers and Mexican female immigrants. Moreover, the fact that the group was a women-only organization suggested a level of "feminist consciousness" in its efforts, according to historian Cynthia Orozco. In a number of ways, then, the auxiliary's work in women's and civil rights foreshadowed Tejanas' contributions to the Chicano movement and their involvement in the Democratic and Republican Parties.[44]

WOMEN AND LULAC: POST-1930S

Throughout the 1940s and on to the end of the twentieth century, women LULAC members have continued to work on civil rights issues that concerned the organization from its beginnings. In 1948 they were involved in fund-raising for the *Delgado* v. *Bastrop Independent School District* lawsuit. In the 1950s Ladies LULAC registered voters and collected poll taxes. In El Paso Lucy Acosta and her council established Project Amistad, a protective services program for the elderly funded by the Texas Department of Human Services. In 1987 the McAllen chapter established the LULAC Information and Referral Center to help immigrants establish residency in the United States. Ladies LULAC also began a successful scholarship program, thus promoting college education for Mexican American youth.[45]

Reflecting new visions and trends, a feminist council was established in Houston in the 1970s and women in El Paso named one of their councils "Las Comadres" in the 1980s. By 1991 women's participation in LULAC had grown dramatically and they constituted half of the membership. Three years later, in 1994, Belén Robles, a chief U.S. Customs inspector and member of Ladies LULAC no. 9 in El Paso, won election as the first female national president of LULAC after twice running unsuccessfully for the post. She won by a slim margin of six votes against Rosa Rosales, the Texas state LULAC director from San Antonio. Under Robles's four-year presidency from 1994–1998, LULAC held its first educational summit and first civil rights symposium, and it also supported court challenges to Proposition 187, an anti-immigrant law in California.[46]

Besides assuming national leadership roles in LULAC in the contemporary period, women have convened their own national gatherings. In March 2001, 400 women from across the country met in San Antonio at the annual National LULAC Women's Conference. Their agenda at the turn of the twenty-first century included familiar issues: education, employment, health, and domestic violence. Rosa Rosales, LULAC national vice president for women, told the delegates, "We ourselves as a community have to take on these issues and make them a priority."[47]

TEJANAS AND COMMUNITIES ORGANIZED FOR PUBLIC SERVICE (COPS)

We are here to demand action. We don't want excuses.[48]

MRS. HÉCTOR ALEMÁN

Communities Organized for Public Service (COPS) became a powerful local organization in San Antonio during the 1970s, forcing public officials to improve the city's long-neglected west side. Female members of COPS, always a central core of the group, advanced to leadership in the organization due to their hard work and tenacity. Beatrice Gallego, Carmen Badillo, Beatrice Cortes, Sonia Hernández, Helen Ayala, and Rachel Salazar were six of the first seven presidents of COPS; Andrés Sarabia was the first president of the organization.[49]

Ernesto Cortes, the community organizer who helped establish COPS in 1974 under the Industrial Areas Foundation banner (IAF), sought to attract to the organization natural leaders: people who were comfortable working with their PTAs; people who liked to organize fiestas for their churches; people who could motivate others to complete a project. He also wanted to attract individuals who could draw crowds to their events. When Cortes solicited help from local parishes to find natural leaders, he learned that women in the Catholic parishes on the west side possessed the commitment, experience, and qualities that COPS members and leaders needed.[50]

Indeed, women had acquired leadership experience in the Mexican Catholic parishes through their *sociedades guadalupanas* and their work as catechists, lectors, and lay leaders. Moreover, hardly a parish existed that did not rely on women's countless tamale sales and other fundrais-

Beatrice Gallego, one of the many female leaders of Communities Organized for Public Service (COPS) in San Antonio, speaks at a meeting. *San Antonio Light* Collection, University of Texas Institute of Texan Cultures.

ers to support a host of projects. The women had for years upheld the vitality of their parishes through their volunteerism. In them, Cortes found some of the best natural leaders available. Moreover, they were dedicated to the hard work of community organizing, and proved themselves by showing up for meetings and studying the issues that affected their neighborhoods. As a result of the women's commitment to improving their neighborhoods, COPS became a model for using the people's power to transform poor neighborhoods.[51]

The challenges that the COPS women faced were daunting. One of these stood out for its egregious visibility. Much of the west side of San Antonio still lacked curbs and storm drains in 1974. After each gale that hit the city, the canals on the west side often became filled with tall grass, discarded mattresses and tires, and other garbage. These trash-laden canals then overflowed into the streets, causing major damage to residents' homes. In addition, many families lived in abysmal housing, and they had few recreation centers or parks for their children. Although the COPS women knew firsthand the existence of bad conditions in their neighborhoods, they took classes in community training and diligently studied official documents to learn how to make expert presentations before city officials.[52]

In public hearings COPS women, asking pertinent and detailed questions about neighborhood problems they wanted resolved, grilled city authorities. They also did their homework in the barrio, setting up meetings, calling on people to join their efforts, and putting together projects. They became adept at producing results. Thus, it was through such hard work that women like Beatrice Gallego, Carmen Badillo, Sonia Hernández, and others rose to lead COPS.[53]

The organization's members knew that confronting leaders publicly placed their concerns in the public's mind, so they attended city council meetings regularly to put their agenda before officials. At one 1977 public hearing called to hear testimony on the west side's flooding problems, Mrs. Héctor Alemán, a COPS spokeswoman, declared, "We are here to demand action. We don't want excuses." Forced to address the group's demands, the city staff immediately developed a plan to finance a solution. As a result, the following November voters approved a $46 million bond issue to solve the decades-long flooding problem.[54]

By relying on well-developed research and leadership skills, and by adopting confrontational tactics, COPS became one of the ten most powerful groups in the city in 1976, only two years after it was founded. The group won $100 million in city funds to improve the west side. It was also victorious in the election to create ten single-member districts, with the mayor elected at large. Afterward, five Mexican Americans won seats on the city council. The election of Henry Cisneros, grandson of civic leader and businesswoman Carolina Malpica Munguía, as mayor was also directly tied to the work of COPS. Membership dues and fund-raising provided the group the stability to continue its work well past 1974. In 1999 the organization celebrated its twenty-fifth anniversary, still actively involved in projects dealing with issues of educational reform, affordable housing, infrastructure improvements, economic development, and a living wage.[55]

Organizations similar to COPS have also been established in other regions of the state under the leadership of the Industrial Areas Foundation. By 2000 IAF had set up twelve community organizations to improve education in one hundred public schools in Texas. One successful venture occurred in the Rio Grande Valley, where poor homeowners in Las Milpas colonia have often had no equity in their property or access to public utilities. Rosario Bustos and Sylvia Morales, both with children enrolled at Las Milpas Palmer Elementary School, have been local leaders. Bustos helped negotiate program funds for Palmer with the Texas education commissioner. Yolanda Castillo, the school's parent liaison, once picked strawberries and cotton for a living. In 1999 she traveled to the White House to accept a $600,000 grant to assist Palmer in providing computer literacy and graduate equivalency diploma (GED) classes, as well as other services, to its students and families.[56]

A ROSTER OF TEJANA COMMUNITY LEADERS:
NINETEENTH TO TWENTIETH CENTURY

Women like Rosario Bustos, Sylvia Morales, and Yolanda Castillo, who worked to improve their children's education in an obscure and poor colonia at the end of the twentieth century, share much in common with the many other women, famous and ordinary, who have provided for the faith and community life of Mexican origin people throughout the state since they settled in the U.S. Southwest.

After moving to South Texas in the 1860s, Paula Losoya Taylor was a principal benefactor of the fledgling city of Del Rio, contributing to its cultural life and helping build churches and schools in the area. Early in the twentieth century, Adina Emilia De Zavala worked to preserve San Antonio de Valero Mission (the Alamo). Barricading herself for three days inside the structure, she helped save the mission's historic long barracks from destruction. María (Mary) Torres Reyna, a successful Houston businesswoman and a founding member of Ladies LULAC Council no. 22, became a philanthropist who tirelessly promoted Tejano culture and used her wealth to assist orphans. In 1975 the City of Houston honored her with Mary T. Reyna Day. In El Paso, María Guillermina Valdes Villalva became a scholar and activist. She worked for the rights of workers in the maquiladoras along the border. She was especially concerned with working women's rights and cofounded the Centro de Orientación para la Mujer Obrera. Villalva also mentored several generations of labor and border studies scholars.[57]

In Fort Worth, Tejanas have served their people in a variety of ways. Their efforts from the mid-1980s to the mid-1990s were documented in *Outstanding Women of Fort Worth*. Leaders included Maggie Cagigal, a federal employee and member of the Fort Worth Commission on the Status of Women, and Christina M. Contreras, a bilingual elementary schoolteacher and organizer of Parents in Education and Amistades, a support group for the Fort Worth Ballet Folklórico Azteca. Lucy Gasca

Coronado, owner of Coronado's Fashions for twenty-five years, raised funds for scholarships, and Bertha García directed the Ballet Folklórico Azteca. In the 1990s Eva Herrera was the first Tejana elected to the Fort Worth School Board. She ensured that a health center and library were established in her neighborhood. Hortensia Laguna, the Fort Worth Health Department's only Mexican American nurse in 1978, was a charter member of the Hispanic Women's Network of Texas, Fort Worth chapter. Rosa Linda Navejar, a banker for eighteen years, was the host of *Hispanics Today* on the Fort Worth city cable channel. Juanita Martínez cared for nine foster children and provided free holiday meals for poor children. Pauline G. Valenciano was a thirty-year volunteer, managing a community action center. She also helped homeowners fight building code violations.[58]

Other Tejanas continued to be cited for their community work in the 1990s. Gloria Rodríguez was inducted into the Texas Women's Hall of Fame in 1993 for civic and volunteer leadership. Rodríguez earned a Ph.D. in early childhood education from the University of Texas at Austin and established AVANCE, a highly successful parenting education program in San Antonio, in 1973 when she was twenty-five years old.[59] Rodríguez's organization, the first of its kind, was nonetheless built on decades of work by earlier Tejana community advocates who championed the Spanish-Speaking PTA and similar organizations to help children gain access to an equal education.

AVANCE, the program Rodríguez created, is a model for reducing the number of school dropouts and preventing child abuse. The program, still in operation in 2000, garnered attention from national television networks and was recognized with numerous awards, ranging from the National Award for the Prevention of Child Abuse to the Barbara Bush Foundation for Family Literacy Award. Rodríguez served on the Harvard University Family Research Project and headed the Texas Governor's Head Start State Collaboration Task Force.[60]

In Austin in the late 1990s, Susana Almanza, founder and executive director of People Organized in Defense of Earth and her Resources (PODER), was recognized nationally for her work to protect the predominantly Mexican American neighborhood in East Austin. PODER had been established several years before under her leadership to promote economic and environmental justice for minority residents in the city. Among PODER's notable achievements was the closing of gasoline terminals that had contaminated barrio residents' land.[61]

Also in the 1990s, San Antonio community leader Graciela Sánchez was the executive director of the Esperanza Peace and Justice Center, which has been in operation since January 1987. The center has been a unifying force for activists, artists, workers, and others committed to social change. It publishes a monthly publication called *La Voz de Esperanza*. In Houston María Jimenez, a longtime activist, worked internationally on immigration and related human rights issues with the American Friends Service Committee.[62]

Thus, Tejanas at the end of the twentieth century were as involved in an array of local, regional, national, and international activities and organizations as their grandmothers and mothers before them, working to provide services to other women and to their community. In doing so, they have continued to nurture the spiritual and community life of their people.

CHAPTER TEN

Politics, the Chicano Movement, and Tejana Feminism

Martha P. Cotera, a noted feminist, was the first Tejana to write a survey of Chicana history. In 1972 she was a candidate for the State Board of Education on the Raza Unida Party ticket. Courtesy Martha P. Cotera.

We have a rich legacy of heroines and activists in social movements and armed rebellions from which we can draw models to emulate.[1]

MARTHA P. COTERA

We have practiced a different kind of leadership, a leadership that empowers others, not a hierarchical kind of leadership.[2]

ROSIE CASTRO

Martha P. Cotera and Rosie Castro, like many other Tejana feminists who joined the Chicano movement of the 1960s and 1970s, grounded their ideas in the legacy of their political great-grandmothers, grandmothers, and mothers: the women of the Liga Femenil Mexicanista, Partido Liberal Mexicano, Cruz Azul Mexicana, and many other voluntary and community groups that working- and middle-class Tejanas shaped prior to the 1940s. Thus, during the Mexican American quest for civil rights in the 1960s and 1970s, Tejana feminists pursued a political vision they believed would empower women and their community. As Cotera wrote in 1977, Chicana feminists created an agenda that included special concerns, such as improving education and child care, protesting rape, and calling for nonsexist ethnic studies in public schools and universities.[3] Feminists in the Tejano community did not always agree with Anglo feminists, whom Tejanas viewed as too narrowly focused on women's oppression. Tejana feminists were certainly concerned with challenging women's oppression, but they were equally committed to fighting racial discrimination.[4]

TEJANAS AND THE CIVIL RIGHTS LANDSCAPE

By the time the American G.I. Forum Women's Auxiliary held its important, groundbreaking women's leadership conference in 1957, the United States was three years into the new civil rights law of the land. In 1954 the U.S. Supreme Court, in *Brown* v. *Board of Education,* had ruled that the separation of the races in public schools was unconstitutional. In Texas, however, Governor Shivers, a staunch opponent of integration, had sent the Texas Rangers to Mansfield, Texas, in 1956 to prohibit black students from attending public school. Under the administration of his successor, Governor Daniel, Texas slowly began to integrate.[5] Because the women in the auxiliary were concerned with Tejano educational needs, the new civil rights era bolstered their lobbying for equal opportunity.

In the years leading up to and immediately following the 1954 high court decision, the Tejano community was engaged in pursuing several civil rights cases. The 1948 *Delgado* v. *Del Rio ISD* banned public schools from segregating Mexican American students in separate buildings on a school campus. In 1954, the same year that the *Brown* decision was handed down, *Hernandez* v. *State of Texas* found that Mexican Americans had been subjected to Jim Crow rules, thus violating their civil rights. Although Jim Crow laws were not aimed at Mexican Americans, Anglos had, in fact, subjected them to Jim Crow on the basis that they were "an inferior and unhygienic people."[6] In 1957 in *Hernandez* v. *Driscoll Consolidated ISD,* the court ruled that public schools had discriminated against Mexican American students by placing them in segregated classes in the first and second grades. The schools had argued

The Robstown Ladies Auxiliary of the American G.I. Forum of Texas. Women maintained the Forum's viability through their organizational and leadership skills. Courtesy Dr. Héctor P. García Papers, Special Collections and Archives, Bell Library, Texas A&M University–Corpus Christi.

that the separate classes were designated to assist non-English-speaking children, but they could not explain why students whose dominant language was English were also sent to separate classrooms.[7]

TOWARD THE CHICANO MOVEMENT

The lawsuits of the 1940s and 1950s were a major part of the Tejano community's quest to gain full participation in the economic, social, cultural, and political life of the state.[8] The school cases exemplified major concerns of Tejanas associated with such organizations as La Liga de Defensa Pro-Escolar and LULAC, both founded before 1940.[9]

During World War II, Mexican Americans continued to be involved in associations and conferences that addressed civil rights issues. The U.S. Office of the Coordinator of Inter-American Affairs (CIAA) attempted in 1941 to deal with anti-Tejano sentiment embodied by public school inequities and general discrimination. In 1943 the Spanish-Speaking People's Division of the CIAA and the National Catholic Welfare Conference sponsored the first of two meetings on Mexican

Americans in San Antonio. The second, held in 1945, brought attention to segregation and the need for bilingual education.[10]

Beyond the fight over equality in the classroom and public places, the Tejano community also defended the right of Felix Longoria, a soldier who had been killed in World War II, to a burial service at the funeral chapel in Three Rivers, his hometown. In particular, women in the American G.I. Forum helped organize a grassroots campaign to treat the remains of Longoria, which were returned to the family several years after his death, with dignity. After Senator Lyndon B. Johnson offered assistance in the matter, Longoria was buried in Arlington National Cemetery on February 16, 1949.[11]

Tejanas also worked along more traditional political lines to support the struggle for civil rights. Ladies LULAC Council no. 9 in El Paso successfully collected 4,378 poll tax receipts, winning the poll tax contest among civic clubs in the city. "We have been getting out the vote every year," reported Mrs. Joseph Rey, chairwoman of the council, "but it has been a telephone campaign in the past. This is the first time we actually sold poll tax receipts. Most of the women in our club work days but get on the phone in the evening. Friday night we will take poll lists and begin calling to get the voters to the polls."[12] At the time of the mayoral campaign of Raymond L. Telles of El Paso in 1957, LULAC joined hands with Los Compadres, a community group at Our Lady of Light Church whose lay leaders included Mrs. Frank Maldonado.[13] The efforts of the LULAC women increased the number of registered Mexican American voters, thus contributing to Telles's victory.

Three years later, Mexican American women worked in the 1960 campaign to elect a Democrat to the United States presidency. Manuela Contreras González, an old friend of Lyndon B. Johnson from his days as a teacher in Cotulla, was one of many women in the Tejano community who worked in the Viva Kennedy Clubs established at the time. Women in Hidalgo County were also part of the Viva Kennedy movement. Estela Lone Treviño of Edinburg was named vice-chairwoman of the county's Viva Kennedy Club, and women generally took part in all the group's activities. In Corpus Christi, Dr. Clotilde García ensured that women in the American G.I. Forum campaigned actively on behalf of the Democratic presidential ticket. She also hosted social gatherings for important candidates who traveled to South Texas seeking Mexican American votes. The Viva Kennedy Clubs ultimately led to the formation of the Political Association of Spanish-Speaking Organi-

Women in El Paso practice casting their ballots in a facsimile of an electronic
voting booth devised by Raymond L. Telles, El Paso mayoral candidate, in
1957. Courtesy Mario T. García and personal collection of Ambassador
Raymond L. Telles.

zations (PASSO), which called for measures to improve educational opportunities and to pay farmworkers a minimum wage. In 1963 PASSO
formed a coalition with Mexican American migrant farmworkers and
Del Monte employees in Crystal City and overthrew the Anglo faction
at city hall. Mexican Americans won all five city council seats. This action, considered the first uprising of the Chicano movement in Texas,
ended the decades-long political stranglehold of Anglos on the South
Texas community. Although the coalition fractured two years later, the
1963 election of Mexican Americans in Crystal City was a major turning point in the quest for Tejano civil rights in Texas.[14]

THE CHICANO MOVEMENT

In essence, the Chicano movement consisted of working-class adults and youth from the barrios, farmworkers, the Mexican American Youth Organization, the Raza Unida Party, and the middle class. Ignacio García has written that many Chicano activists were interested in establishing a movement that merged all classes and social groups within the Mexican American community. According to García, the activists hoped that "a small progressive middle class not yet removed from its working-class origins" could strengthen the movement, thus allowing the community to wage a more successful struggle against racism and class oppression. Guadalupe San Miguel Jr. has likewise noted that in 1969 and 1970 Tejano moderates and middle-class members in Houston became involved with activists in the fight for public school equity. Middle-class leaders, however, lost their influence with the Chicano movement because they clung to integrationist politics and accommodation to the Anglo establishment as a way to achieve equality. The more radical members of the Chicano movement were, on the other hand, committed to directly confronting Anglo society on a variety of issues that affected the vast majority of Mexican Americans: the need for fair pay and better working conditions for farmworkers, long overdue educational opportunities for youth, economic and political self-determination, and their right to maintain their cultural heritage. Indeed, movement activists considered the Mexican American barrio, with its base in the working class of the community, a rich source of cultural and political strength that only needed to be mobilized to struggle for Chicano empowerment. But even the activists were divided, with some supporting a reformist agenda and others a radical one that would bring down capitalism and replace it with socialism.[15]

Movement members called themselves Chicanas and Chicanos as a way of affirming their distinctive mestizo identity. The designation was likely drawn from the pre-Columbian peoples in Mexico, who called themselves Meshicas, later changed to Mexicas by the Spaniards. Moreover, because the "ch" sound in Spanish may express community fellowship, in the civil rights era the term Chicano affirmed Mexican Americans' identity as part of a people who shared a history and culture grounded in the pre-Columbian Americas. While some individuals in the Mexican American community viewed the term as pejorative, those in the *movimiento* (movement) turned it into a symbol of pride, one that also implied a commitment to social justice.[16]

Support The Valley Farm Workers and a State $1.25 Minimum Wage Law For All Workers

Join The March and Rally in Austin Labor Day, Sept. 5

9:30 a.m.   Leave from St. Edward's University on South Congress and March to the Capitol

11:00 a.m.   Rally at Capitol Grounds

1:30 p.m.   Picnic and Speakers at Zilker Park
BRING YOUR LUNCH

For More Information:
Robert Canino   GL 3-6394
Cristo Rey Church   GR 8-5913

This flyer was circulated in 1966 to advertise a Labor Day march by farmworkers, who were demanding a $1.25 minimum wage. Tejana activists in the Chicano movement were involved in helping agricultural workers gain economic rights. Acosta–Winegarten Collection (provisional title), Benson Latin American Collection, University of Texas at Austin.

The farmworkers' strike of June 1, 1966, against Starr County melon farmers became one of the defining moments of the Chicano movement. The strikers demanded a minimum wage of $1.25 an hour and recognition of the Independent Workers' Association as a collective bargaining negotiator. The ensuing dispute between the mostly Tejano farmworkers and Anglo farmers mobilized Mexican American youth

Dr. Clotilde García, far left walking, and other members of the American G.I.
Forum of Texas take part in the June 1966 march from the Rio Grande Valley
to the capitol in Austin in support of the United Farm Workers and minimum
wage legislation for farmworkers. Also pictured are an unidentified farmworker
(holding sign), the Reverend James Navarro, and Dr. Héctor P. García. Courtesy
Dr. Héctor P. García Papers, Special Collections and Archives, Bell Library,
Texas A&M University–Corpus Christi.

in South Texas into walkouts, pickets, marches, and boycotts to protest dismal economic, educational, and political conditions beyond the
fields.[17]

The strike by the farmworkers of the Rio Grande Valley, who organized under the banner of the United Farm Workers Union (UFW)
in 1966, thus helped shape the issue of social justice within the *movimiento*. American G.I. Forum members, including women, participated
in the famous farmworkers' June 1966 march to the state capitol to
protest the deplorable conditions under which agricultural workers
lived. Dr. Clotilde García, a prominent Forum member, walked at the
front of the organization's contingent alongside a female farmworker
who carried a sign that read "All We Want is Justice." Reverend James
Navarro and Dr. Héctor García also walked at the front of the Forum's
delegation. The march brought farmworkers attention from the press,

the scrutiny of a congressional subcommittee on agricultural labor, and the involvement of U.S. Senator Ralph Yarborough (D-Texas), who joined the marchers as they neared the capitol.[18]

Subsequent news accounts of farmworkers laboring in the fields and protesting to gain better working and housing conditions served as a catalyst for the *movimiento*. The UFW garnered more attention for *la causa* when it set up offices for its lettuce boycott in Corpus Christi, Fort Worth, Houston, and San Antonio. The 1972 state Democratic convention also endorsed the boycott, thus bolstering the workers' cause.[19]

Rebecca Flores was for many years the state director of the United Farm Workers, before she became a regional director of the AFL-CIO. During her UFW service, more legislation to protect agricultural workers was passed by the Texas legislature than at any other time in the state's history. Courtesy Rebecca Flores.

FEMINISM AND THE CHICANO MOVEMENT

As women examined their place within the movement, they began to question traditional female roles and male dominance of the leadership. This experience gave rise to Chicana feminist thought and action in the 1970s and 1980s. For Chicana feminists, gaining social equality meant ending both sexist and racist oppression.[20]

In 1971 Francisca Flores, a major contributor to Chicana feminist thought, challenged women to move forward to support other women:

> The issue of equality, freedom and self-determination of the Chicana—like the right of self-determination, equality, and liberation of the Mexican [Chicano] community—is not negotiable. Anyone opposing the right of women to organize into their own form of organization has no place in the leadership of the movement.[21]

Martha P. Cotera, a leading Tejana feminist, declared:

> The aggregate cultural values we [Chicanas] share can also work to our benefit if we choose to scrutinize our cultural traditions, isolate the positive attributes and interpret them for the benefit of women. . . . To do this, we must become both conversant with our history and philosophical evolution, and analytical about the institutional and behavioral manifestations of the same.[22]

Women who shared the views of Flores and Cotera were often castigated as a threat to the political unity of the Chicano movement. They were identified as both anti-male and lesbian since, in some individuals' views, lesbianism was an extreme outcome of feminism. Thus, Chicana feminists and Chicana lesbians were considered *vendidas* (sellouts) bent on assimilating into "the feminist ideology of an alien [white] culture."[23] Chicana lesbians in particular were attacked virulently for not conforming to stereotypical images of Mexican origin women as good wives and mothers.[24] Despite these accusations, prominent female leaders in the Chicano movement embraced feminism.

MARTHA P. COTERA: A TEJANA FEMINIST LEADER

During the 1970s Martha P. Cotera, a feminist and activist associated with the Raza Unida Party, wrote and delivered a number of speeches that were collected in *The Chicana Feminist,* which she published in 1977 through Information Systems Development, her research and publications company. In topics ranging from Mexican American women's feminist heritage to women's political power and cultural identity to class and race issues, she laid out many of the concerns that Chicana feminists in Texas and elsewhere in the country addressed during the *movimiento.* In *Diosa y Hembra: The History and Heritage of Chicanas in the U.S.* (1976), she explored Mexican American women's heritage from the pre-Columbian period to the Chicano movement in an effort to educate women about the legacy they had inherited from their female predecessors.[25]

Through her books and in many speeches, panels, and conference presentations, Cotera had a strong hand in developing the direction of Tejana feminist actions in the 1970s. Notably, she put her ideas to use with Mujeres Por La Raza, the women's caucus within the Raza Unida Party, and with the Mexican American Business and Professional Women's Association, which she also helped lead in the early 1970s.

Cotera's writings were based on her knowledge and celebration of Mexican women's history of activism. Through her writings, speeches, and activism, she excited women about their history and challenged them to continue to defend their community, much as their predecessors had done. Cotera viewed the Chicana feminists' precursors— women such as Jovita Idar and Sara Estela Ramírez—as the political and spiritual guides for the present generation, and she denounced the idea that Chicana feminists took their cues from Anglo feminists. For instance, in the first chapter of *The Chicana Feminist,* entitled "Our Feminist Heritage," she lists women's political and social activism carried out by previous generations of women affiliated with the Liga Femenil Mexicanista, Hijas de Cuauhtémoc, and the newspapers *Vesper* and *La Mujer Moderna.* She recalls women like Soledad Peña and María L. de Hernández.[26] Thus, Cotera's writings in *The Chicana Feminist* provided an important intellectual and historical foundation for the direction of Tejana feminism during the *movimiento. Diosa y Hembra,* on the other hand, afforded tools for all individuals—female and male—in the *movimiento* to reflect on the meaning of Mexican American women's history. Because Cotera wrote both books while she was participating in the *movimiento,* they in essence formed a casebook of contemporary Tejana activism as well as a history of the political ideology that guided Chicana feminists during the 1970s.

City council candidates who ran on the Raza Unida Party ticket in San Antonio on February 20, 1971, included (left to right) William Benavides, Gloria Cabrerra, Rosie Castro, and Mario Compean. Courtesy *San Antonio Light* Collection, University of Texas Institute of Texan Cultures.

PUTTING FEMINISM INTO PRACTICE IN THE CHICANO MOVEMENT

Educated middle-class women, working-class women, and women from different generations became involved in the *movimiento*. Luz Gutiérrez, María L. de Hernández, Evey Chapa, Irma Mireles, Martha P. Cotera, Alma Canales, Severita Lara, Virginia Múzquiz, María Elena Martínez, Juana Bustamante y Luera, and Rosie Castro were prominent *movimiento* women who represented at least three generations. Hernández and Músquiz symbolized two earlier generations. Hernández, for instance, had a history of involvement in Mexican American equity issues for approximately forty years, beginning with her leadership in the 1929 founding of Orden Caballeros de América. Múzquiz was a pioneer in seeking public office, having run a campaign for the Texas legislature in 1964. Both of the women and their younger colleagues became important local, state, and national leaders in the Raza Unida Party.[27]

Luz Gutiérrez and Virginia Múzquiz helped to found the Raza Unida Party (RUP), which was officially established on January 17, 1970. In

1969 they and other women participated in the RUP organizational meetings of the Zavala County Ciudadanos Unidos (United Citizens). Gutiérrez recalled that the women had to be clear about their intention to be fully vested members of the party: "We actually had to walk in to one of the meetings . . . and [say], 'Hey, we don't want to be tamale makers and . . . the busy bees. We really want to be part of the decision-making process.'"[28]

Soon Tejanas led by Ino Álvarez, Evey Chapa, and Martha P. Cotera organized a female caucus within RUP, Mujeres Por La Raza, to advance the cause of women within the *movimiento* in Texas. Mujeres Por La Raza immediately went to work, electing Luz Gutiérrez as the first Zavala County chair in January 1970. When RUP held its first state convention in San Antonio in October 1971, women comprised 31 of the 104 delegates, likely a result of the caucus's actions. Moreover, Evey Chapa of the Mujeres caucus helped draft the RUP party platform, ensuring that it included sections on the importance of women (especially equality for women) and the family. The platform also made certain that the RUP state executive committee included a woman. Two members of Mujeres Por La Raza, Virginia Múzquiz and María Elena Martínez, rose to other leadership positions. Múzquiz led the Raza Unida Party as national chair from 1972 to 1974, and Martínez headed the Texas RUP as state chair from 1976 to 1978.[29]

The women's caucus conducted much of its business at Conferencias de Mujeres por la Raza Unida (Raza Unida women's conferences). Evey Chapa, Martha P. Cotera, Chelo Ávila, Irma Mireles, and Juana Bustamante y Luera arranged a number of the gatherings. The caucus held the first such meeting on August 4, 1973, in San Antonio. Cotera prepared "A Reading List for Chicanas" to guide the women's discussions on that occasion.[30] The group met again in Corpus Christi on September 19, 1973, and in Crystal City on December 1, 1973. At the first meeting the participants focused on the political education of women. Sessions emphasized strategies to organize rural and urban areas and provided women with lessons on the structure of state and local politics. The Corpus Christi gathering also educated local Mexican American women in ways to become involved in their community's educational and social needs. María L. de Hernández, a longtime community civic leader and orator, was one of the featured speakers at the San Antonio meeting. Virginia Múzquiz was a featured speaker at the Corpus Christi conference.[31]

Mujeres Por La Raza had members in Austin, Corpus Christi, Dallas,

Houston, Laredo, and smaller communities such as Mercedes and Crystal City, the latter considered the heart of the Chicano movement in the state. Female high school and college students also contributed to the caucus's work. The Delegación de Mujeres del Colegio Jacinto Trevino, a Chicano college that opened in September 1970 in Mercedes during the *movimiento,* called for Mujeres Por La Raza to support the Farah garment workers' strike in El Paso. The caucus also battled racism and classism among Anglo women. For instance, the group withdrew from the Texas Women's Political Caucus when it refused to endorse Alma Canales, the Raza Unida Party candidate for lieutenant governor in 1972.[32]

After approximately eight years of organizing women's political activism in the Chicano community, the caucus ended its work, due to the demise of the Raza Unida Party, which failed to garner 2 percent of the state vote in the 1978 election, thus losing its position as a state party.[33]

CHICANA RIGHTS ON THE NATIONAL STAGE:
LA CONFERENCIA DE MUJERES POR LA RAZA

The Mujeres Por La Raza caucus was only one of the channels through which Tejana feminists gained a political voice. On May 28–30, 1971, the Conferencia de Mujeres por la Raza, also known as the National Chicana Conference, was held in Houston. The conference, probably the first interstate gathering of women in the *movimiento,* brought together about 600 women at the Young Women's Christian Association (YWCA) in the Tejano barrio of Magnolia Park. During the three-day meeting the women discussed and debated several areas of concern: education and employment; sex and birth control; marriage and children; and religion.[34]

They also passed resolutions calling for free abortions, free birth control, free sex education, and twenty-four-hour child care centers for Mexican American families. Another resolution urged men to take greater responsibility in child rearing. Although participants reached agreement on major issues, disharmony plagued the gathering. Disagreements raged over the YWCA Anglo staff's possible influence on the event. In addition, Elizabeth (Betita) Martínez, an activist with roots in the national civil rights movement, criticized the conference for failing to deal with poor and working-class women. The women also disagreed over the conference's emphasis on the problems caused by sex-

LA CONFERENCIA
De Mujeres
Por La Raza

UNDER THE AUSPICES OF THE

YWCA

Young Women's Christian Association

May 28 - 30, 1971

Houston, Texas

Program cover for "Conferencia de Mujeres por la Raza." The meeting, also
known as the National Chicana Conference, was the first interstate gathering
of Chicana feminists. It was held on May 28-30, 1971, at the Magnolia Park
YWCA, Houston. Courtesy Houston Metropolitan Research Center, Houston
Public Library.

ism. An estimated half of the participants walked out of the meeting on
the basis that the conference was not focusing sufficiently on racism.[35]

OTHER CHICANA CONFERENCES: 1970–1975

For a five-year period, from 1970 to 1975, Mexican American women
sponsored a host of meetings to deal with specific issues. In July 1970

an informal Chicana caucus met in Austin under the leadership of Martha P. Cotera. The group worked on its presentation of a women's agenda at the upcoming RUP state meeting. In winter 1970, when the RUP met in Houston, Yolanda Birdwell, Carmen Lomas Garza, Gloria Guardiola, Alma Canales, and Martha P. Cotera again gathered to discuss women's roles and to protest the lack of female speakers and workshop leaders at the RUP meeting.[36]

Tejanas also held numerous other meetings during these five years. The Texas Women's Political Caucus meeting in Mesquite, Texas, on March 11, 1972, was attended by 100 "very politicized" Chicanas who vowed to work on Chicana issues within the structure of the National Women's Political Caucus (NWPC). Cotera was a keynote speaker at the event. At the February 9–11, 1973, NWPC meeting in Houston, more than 100 Chicanas from across the country gathered to strategize and pass resolutions favorable to Chicanas. One year later, on February 23, 1974, women met at the Chicana Educational Conference at Saint Edward's University in Austin. The participants discussed bilingual education, employment, day care, welfare, rape, and revenue sharing.[37]

In June 1974 the Mexican American Business and Professional Women of Austin held their first annual meeting to discuss local Chicana issues. Martha P. Cotera, Amalia Rodríguez-Mendoza, and Annabelle Valle were the principal conveners. Women gathered at the Chicana Symposium on the campus of Texas Southern University on April 22, 1974, and at a symposium on October 4, 1974, at the University of Texas at El Paso. They also met during Chicana Week in May 1975 on the University of Texas at Austin campus. Mujeres Unidas of Houston organized the statewide Chicana Identity Conference at the University of Houston on November 15, 1975. At this event women made presentations on history, education, labor, and politics. Two nationally known Chicana feminists, Anna Nieto-Gómez of California and Martha P. Cotera of Texas, delivered keynote addresses.[38]

Including the conferences that Mujeres Por La Raza held in the early 1970s, Tejana feminists organized approximately a third of some thirty-two known Chicana conferences and meetings held nationwide in the five-year period from 1970 to 1975. Tejana feminists also led workshops at national Chicana meetings outside the state during this period. For instance, at the Chicana Seminar at the University of Notre Dame in spring 1975, Evey Chapa, Lydia Espinosa, and Gloria Gutiérrez Roland led workshops. Some of the gatherings that the feminists attended involved women in older established groups founded in Texas, such as LULAC and the American G.I. Forum's Women's Auxiliary.[39]

WOMEN AND THE MEXICAN AMERICAN YOUTH ORGANIZATION

The Mexican American Youth Organization (MAYO) was founded in 1967 in San Antonio by José Ángel Gutiérrez, Willie (William) C. Velásquez, Mario Compean, Ignacio Pérez, and Juan Patlán. The five Tejanos incorporated MAYO as a nonprofit organization with local chapters and a state-level board of directors. Drawing its members mainly from high school and college students, MAYO reached its greatest strength in 1969 when more than forty chapters were operating in cities around the state. Members committed themselves to the protection and advancement of Tejanos through economic independence, schools that met their needs, and a third political party to provide strength and unity to the community.[40]

During its major period of activity, from 1967 through 1970, MAYO was considered the "avant garde organization of social change and empowerment for Chicanos in Texas."[41] MAYO apparently diminished in size in 1971–1972 because the Raza Unida Party, which grew out of the organization, drew MAYO members to its ranks. The MAYO chapters operating after 1972 often focused on educational and social issues.[42]

MAYO rejected the more diplomatic stance of traditional Mexican American civil rights organizations, but it nonetheless gained the support of those groups. In San Antonio, for instance, the American G.I. Forum and LULAC admired MAYO's "aggressive style." Local Mexican American businessmen lent financial assistance. Prominent scholars also backed the group. For instance, at the University of Texas at Austin, Américo Paredes, the renowned anthropologist and folklorist, and George I. Sánchez, a highly regarded educator, gave their support to the university-based MAYO chapter.[43]

Women who joined MAYO were, like the men, often attracted to it by its strategy of "militant direct action" and by the vision that inspired Rosie Castro—the desire to attain "a leadership that empowers others." However, she and other women in MAYO soon found that gaining respect for this ideal was a struggle. Yet, despite the sexism of some male members and leaders of MAYO, women played important roles in the organization, working on policy and helping carry out its goals. After the formation of the Raza Unida Party in 1970, women took on greater leadership roles within MAYO and the *movimiento,* often acting as spokespersons. Women were especially important to the success of the group in several regions of the state. Choco Meza worked toward its goals in Eagle Pass, while Yolanda Birdwell did so in Houston. Evey Chapa was stationed in Fort Worth, Rebecca Flores in West Texas, and Severita Lara in San Antonio. Vivian Santiago played a significant role as an organizer and was involved in the transition of MAYO to the Raza Unida Party in the early 1970s.[44] Many other unnamed and unknown women also contributed to the grassroots efforts of the group.

At the University of Texas at Austin, women participated actively in MAYO. They worked as leaders and as writers, editors, and advertising saleswomen for the UT Austin MAYO newspaper, *El Despertador de Tejas.* In 1972 Beatriz Gonzáles served as president of the chapter. At this critical time, she guided the organization through significant talks with the UT Austin administration regarding the establishment of an undergraduate degree in Mexican American Studies. Gonzáles led countless strategizing sessions during this period, often sacrificing her own studies and her health to battle with an administration reluctant to establish the program. (Indeed, in later years MAYO leaders and members have been recognized for their contributions to the creation of the bachelor's degree in Mexican American Studies at the university.) In 1973–1974 Teresa Palomo Acosta served as editor of *El Despertador.* She worked with Sonia Díaz de León, another MAYO member, to sell advertising to merchants on Austin's east side to pay for the newspaper. In the mid-1970s Angélica Martínez and Alicia López were coeditors of *El Despertador.* Irma Orozco and Angelita Mendoza were reporters. Martínez and López were also officers and sat on the MAYO executive committee. A "Chicana Comments" column that featured women also appeared in *El Despertador* in the mid-1970s.[45]

SEVERITA LARA AND THE CRYSTAL CITY SCHOOL BOYCOTT

Brown Legs are Beautiful Too
We Demand Chicana Cheerleaders[46]
  —POSTER RECALLING THE CRYSTAL CITY SCHOOL WALKOUT

In fall 1969 Severita Lara, a high school junior, was joined by Diana Serna, Mario Treviño, and other Chicano students in leading the Crystal City public school walkout. In the spring of that year, students had organized to protest unfair tactics in the selection of the school's cheerleaders. The cheering squad had traditionally been chosen through student elections. However, as the Chicano school population grew, the

Severita Lara and other student activists led Mexican American students in a walkout from Crystal City public schools from December 9, 1969, to January 6, 1970, to protest discrimination against them by school authorities. Courtesy *San Antonio Express-News* Collection, University of Texas Institute of Texan Cultures.

school administration changed the selection process, placing a teachers' committee in charge. The committee's choices always resulted in the selection of three Anglo females and one Mexican American female. In spring 1969 two Anglo cheerleaders graduated from Crystal City High School. Chicano students endorsed Diana Palacios to fill one of the two vacancies created by the students' graduation. Palacios' ascension would ensure that the cheering squad was equally divided, with two Anglos and two Chicanas. The teachers' committee, however, chose two Anglo females to fill the vacancies, leaving the Chicanos with their one traditional place, a position that Diana Pérez already held.[47]

The conflict over the teachers' decision escalated when Severita Lara and the other leaders, supported by MAYO, presented the superintendent with a list of seven demands from Chicano students. Among other issues, the students asked for the addition of bilingual-bicultural education, and they sought protection for students who protested poor educational opportunities. They also requested that band members elect their own baton twirlers and that student elections determine such school favorites as most beautiful girl or most handsome boy. The students won some concessions, including a quota system to equalize the number of Anglo and Chicana cheerleaders. This change made it possible for Palacios to later try out successfully for a place on the cheering team. The school authorities also agreed to study the students' demands for bilingual and bicultural education. These victories were undercut, however, when the school board overturned the school officials' decisions in June 1969.[48]

The following October, the Ex-Students Association of Crystal City High School insisted that the homecoming queen be selected from students with at least one parent who was a local high school graduate. When Severita Lara protested the ex-students' dictate on the grounds that it excluded many Mexican American students whose parents had not completed high school, Crystal City school administrators suspended her for two days. MALDEF attorney Gerald López intervened on Lara's behalf, and she was allowed to return to school. She and the other students then increased their demands to a list of eighteen. Women in particular, including Luz Gutiérrez and Virginia Múzquiz of the Raza Unida Party, backed the students' protests. The expanded list of demands called for hiring more Mexican American teachers, reducing class sizes, involving parents as teacher's aides, and protecting the free speech of teachers who challenged school administration policies. On December 8, 1969, the board rejected the eighteen demands. The following day, after staying up all night making preparations to protest the decision, approximately 200 students walked out and gathered in front of the high school. By afternoon the group had swelled to 500, and the Crystal City walkout commenced.[49]

On December 19 state officials arrived to investigate the students' charges of discrimination. Meanwhile, the boycott had spread to the middle and elementary schools, and it expanded to the Minimax, a major Anglo-owned store in Crystal City. With officials from the U.S. Department of Justice acting as mediators, the school board agreed to enact most of the eighteen demands, and the boycott ended on January 6, 1970. The walkout that Severita Lara had helped lead was judged a success. Lara later studied in Mexico City and earned a bachelor's degree in 1976 from Incarnate Word College (now the University of the Incarnate Word) in San Antonio. She returned to work at Crystal City High School, first as a biology teacher and later as a resource teacher and school librarian. From May 1995 to May 1996, Lara also served as mayor of Crystal City.[50]

THE MEXICAN AMERICAN LEGAL DEFENSE AND EDUCATIONAL FUND AND THE CHICANA RIGHTS PROJECT

The incorporation of the Mexican American Legal Defense and Educational Fund (MALDEF) in 1968 allowed the Tejano community to use the courts to defend its interests during the period of the Chicano movement. With the assistance of the National Association for the Advancement of Colored People (NAACP), MALDEF received a $2.2 million five-year start-up grant from the Ford Foundation. The organization initially established its headquarters in San Antonio but later moved to San Francisco.[51] However, it retained a regional office in San Antonio.

Tejana attorney Vilma Martínez, who had helped write the Ford Foundation grant to fund MALDEF, took over as president and general counsel of MALDEF in December 1973. Under her direction, the organization implemented a Chicana Rights Project (CRP) the following year. Operating from offices in San Antonio and San Francisco, the CRP pursued cases involving discrimination, employment, health, housing, and credit. Patricia M. Vásquez headed the Texas effort, and Carmen A. Estrada was in charge of the San Francisco operation.[52]

In 1975, with three of MALDEF's divisions—litigation, research, and community education—at its disposal, the CRP began to monitor the impact of the Comprehensive Employment and Training Act (CETA) on Mexican American women in San Antonio. The CRP's

Guadalupe Luna (center) and Norma Cantú (right) were leading Tejana attorneys for the Mexican American Legal Defense and Education Fund (MALDEF). To the left is Judith Sanders Castro, also an attorney for the organization in the 1990s. Courtesy *La Prensa,* San Antonio.

work resulted in a victory in an administrative complaint case against the city, *Hernández, et al.* v. *Cockrell, et al.* After the issue was settled in the CRP's favor, participation of women and minorities in CETA programs jumped from 20 to 50 percent.[53]

The Chicana Rights Project challenged other forms of discrimination against Mexican American women. For example, in one instance the CRP filed lawsuits against mandatory sterilization of women. The project also forced the five major banks in San Antonio to undergo compliance reviews and demanded that they provide employment opportunities to women.[54]

In addition, the CRP sought to educate Mexican American women about their rights in economic, health, immigration, and legal issues by publishing materials on these areas, including *Chicanas: Women's Health Issues, Hispanic/Women's Employment Rights,* and *Texas Women's Legal Rights Handbook.* Further, by organizing women's rights panels and workshops, as well as by providing testimony to state and federal agencies, the Chicana Rights Project became a national resource used in defending Mexican American women. The status of the project was tenuous, however, because it relied on outside funding. Thus, in March

1983, when MALDEF ran out of money to support the CRP, the project was abandoned.[55]

TEJANA FEMINIST RESEARCH: EMPOWERING CHICANAS

> With the inception of the Chicana Research and Learning Center in 1973, the attempt began to fill in the information void concerning Chicanas and to rectify the stereotypes developed about Chicanas.[56]
> —EVEY CHAPA

In 1973 Tejanas set up the Chicana Research and Learning Center (CRLC) in Austin, reportedly the first such program in the United States run by and for Mexican American women. Its first office was in the Methodist Student Center on Guadalupe Street near the University of Texas at Austin.[57] *Movimiento* female leaders took charge of the CRLC. To signify its commitment to issues affecting *la raza* women, the CRLC adopted a logo that incorporated the universal symbol for female with an Aztec eagle. Evey Chapa, a Raza Unida Party leader, served as executive director. The board of directors was composed of women.[58]

The CRLC sought to deal with the social and educational barriers to Chicanas' progress.[59] The center's concern with the situation of Mexican American women workers was based on the continuing struggles that both rural and urban Mexican female laborers endured. Although the farmworkers' 1966 Starr County strike against melon farmers and the workers' subsequent march to the capitol had provided momentum for the *movimiento,* agricultural workers in Texas continued to face low pay and appalling conditions in the fields in the 1970s. For example, farmworkers had no sanitary toilets or clean drinking water in the fields, and they continued to suffer health hazards resulting from pesticide spraying of the fields.

Women factory workers also continued to suffer difficult circumstances. In May 1972 El Paso workers at the Farah Manufacturing Company, 85 percent of them Tejanas, went on strike for better wages and decent working conditions. The strike was a rallying point for the Chicano movement, with women especially concerned about the need to improve the situation at Farah. Strike materials pointed out the links between the farmworker movement, Farah strike, *movimiento,* and women's rights: "Like the Farmworkers, the Farah strike is an important step forward in the continuing struggle of the Chicano people. . . . Most of the 4,000 strikers at the Farah plants are Chicanas."[60]

The Chicana Research and Learning Center sought to create proj-

ects that countered the exploitation faced by both agricultural and urban workers. With the volunteer assistance of Chicana students at the
University of Texas at Austin, the center's small staff developed and implemented bilingual-bicultural demonstration projects to assist Tejanas.
Some women planned curriculum and training programs, while others
worked in teams to research Chicana history. State and federal agencies
took note of the CRLC's work, enabling the center to establish links to
the Civil Rights Commission and the Texas Manpower Commission.[61]

Several publication projects and one particular training program best
demonstrate the CRLC's dual mission of research and service. In 1976
the CRLC published two important documents. *La Mujer Chicana: An
Annotated Bibliography* was an effort to publicize Chicanas' abilities and
achievements as well as their needs and concerns. *La Mujer* listed 320
documents that covered twelve areas of interest to women, among them
feminism, labor history, the movement, culture, machismo, and the
family. The publication also contained material on other Third World
women to underscore the fact that "the Chicana experience is inter-
twined with the history and culture of these *mujeres*." In her introduction to the bibliography, CRLC director Evey Chapa notes the value of
the publication:

> Chicanas must continue to research and document the realities of
> their experience. Until Chicanas begin to document and publish
> these realities from a Chicana perspective, historians will continue
> to ignore the contributions of Chicanas and other social scientists
> will continue to distort the image of la mujer Chicana.[62]

The other significant CRLC publication was *La Mujer Chicana: A Texas
Anthology,* an effort to document Chicana history. The center also contributed to the development of an anthology on Chicanas published by
Notre Dame University Press and to a handbook on women's legal
rights compiled by the Women's Law Caucus at the University of Texas
at Austin School of Law. Moreover, the CRLC helped develop the first
course on Chicanas in Texas offered at UT Austin. Evey Chapa, CRLC
director, taught the course in spring 1975.[63] Thereafter, a course entitled "Ethnicity and Gender: La Chicana" was usually offered for both
the fall and spring semesters by the Center for Mexican American Studies at the university throughout most of the 1990s. With one exception,
Mexican American women have taught the course.[64]

One of the CRLC's most important projects was its unique "con-
cientización y desarollo de la mujer" (women's consciousness raising
and personal growth). Consisting of training sessions on Chicana his-

tory and values, the project ultimately served some 500 women.[65] The CRLC was also in communication with Chicanas in other states and sought to inspire all Chicanas to study their history, to join the *movimiento,* and to awaken in others the value of Chicana studies. Like many other enterprises dependent on outside funding, the CRLC struggled to survive. Although it likely closed its office at the Methodist Student Center in 1976 due to a lack of funding, it was still functioning in 1984. That year it cosponsored with the Mexican American Business and Professional Women of Austin a panel entitled "Las Fundadoras: Heritage of Mexican American Women in the U.S."[66]

TEJANAS AND TWO-PARTY POLITICS

While a number of Tejanas joined the Chicano movement, championed Chicana feminism, or worked with the Raza Unida Party in the 1970s, others joined the established two-party system of politics. In 1972 Mexican Americans organized Mexican American Republicans of Texas (MART). In 1965, prior to establishing MART, they had worked through the Mexican-American Advisory Committee within the Republican Party of Texas.[67] With the support of Senator John Tower (R-Texas), the group won funds and grants that benefited LULAC, the American G.I. Forum of Texas, and SER–Jobs for Progress. Indeed, a SER grant obtained through MART helped establish the Mexican American Chambers of Commerce.[68]

Women also joined the Mexican American Democrats (MAD), which was initially organized as a caucus at the state Democratic Party convention in 1975. Permanent officers for the organization were in place by 1977, and women eventually assumed positions of leadership. Nora Linares of San Antonio served as chairwoman of MAD from 1989 to 1991. Other female leaders include Mary Castillo of Houston, Adelfa Callejo of Dallas, Minnie García and Sylvia Hernández of San Antonio, Alicia Chacón of El Paso, Judith Zaffirini of Laredo, and Margaret Gómez of Austin.[69]

Doubtless, Tejana leaders—well-known Chicana feminists, unknown and unnamed women from every generation living in the state's many barrios, and student activists—all came of political age as a result of their involvement in the issues that the Chicano movement sought to address. All of these women likewise presented their community with much-needed female political leadership. Just as important, they provided the impetus for more Mexican origin women to seek public office in the last decades of the twentieth century.

Winning and Holding Public Office

Alicia Chacón of El Paso has served on the El Paso City Council and the Ysleta School Board, and as regional director of the Small Business Administration. In 1990 she was elected county judge in El Paso, becoming the first woman and first Mexican American in one hundred years to win that office. Courtesy office of Alicia Chacón.

Our people have to get used to voting for . . . Mexicanas that appear on the ballot.[1]

VIRGINIA MÚZQUIZ

PRECURSORS TO CONTEMPORARY POLITICAL EMPOWERMENT

The participation of Mexican American women in political life as elected public officers grew steadily in the last quarter of the twentieth century, evolving from their history of involvement in Tejano politics. The women who ran for public office in the last two decades of the twentieth century had many predecessors to emulate. For instance, between 1900 and 1920 Mexican origin women worked with the Partido Liberal Mexicano (PLM) during the Mexican Revolution and organized the

Liga Femenil Mexicanista at El Primer Congreso Mexicanista. In the succeeding decades, they participated in the League of United Latin American Citizens (LULAC), Ladies LULAC, and the American G.I. Forum of Texas, including the American G.I. Forum Women's Auxiliary. Women also made inroads into the Democratic Party through the Viva Kennedy Clubs in 1960. Many other women organized and helped lead the Raza Unida Party to its electoral victories in the 1970s. Other women became involved in the Mexican American Democrats (MAD) and the Mexican American Republicans of Texas (MART). Undoubtedly, the women associated with these organizations helped launch Tejanas' ascension to public office.

Mexican origin women have served in public office for more than forty years, winning races to serve on city councils, school boards, and county commissions. With the election of Irma Rangel (D-Kingsville) in 1976, Tejanas entered state public service as members of the Texas legislature. A decade later, in 1986, Judith Zaffirini (D-Laredo) won election to the Texas Senate. Leticia Van de Putte (D-San Antonio) joined her in that chamber in 1999. By 2000 thirteen Mexican origin women, including one Republican, Elvira Reyna (R-Mesquite), had served in the Texas legislature.

All of these women have benefited from the experiences of the women who preceded them, who ran for office at a time when few women in the state could seriously consider becoming politicians. In 1951, six years before the American G.I. Forum Women's Auxiliary held its historic leadership conference and almost twenty years before the founding of the Raza Unida Party and Mujeres Por La Raza, Consuelo Herrera Méndez was one of the few daring enough to seek public office. Méndez, the first Mexican American woman to teach in the Austin public schools, ran for a seat on the Austin City Council. She lost the race. Despite her defeat, she remained committed to political participation. She headed Ladies LULAC Council no. 202 and was state chair of the group in 1961. With Patricio J. Méndez, an attorney and her husband, she continued to work in campaigns and register voters in the Tejano community for many years.[2]

WINNING PUBLIC OFFICE IN LAREDO AND WEBB COUNTY: FROM SCHOOL BOARD TO STATE SENATE TO MAYOR

In the 1940s along the U.S.–Mexico border, Josefina Dodier attained a place on the Webb County School Board. She apparently acquired her position in a contest in which she faced little competition.[3] Norma

Elizabeth G. "Betty" Flores was elected mayor of Laredo in a special election in 1998, making her the first Tejana to head a major city in the state. Later that year Flores won a four-year term. Courtesy office of Betty Flores.

Zúñiga Benavides was the first Mexican American woman who won a political contest outright, when she was elected to the Laredo Independent School District Board in 1959.

HOW THE LAREDO WOMEN WON:
FROM NORMA ZÚÑIGA BENAVIDES TO BETTY FLORES

Between the 1940s and 1990s slightly more than 30 Webb County Tejanas entered public office. They held both appointive and elective offices as members of school boards, the community college board, the city council and city government, the commissioners court, one state district court, the Texas legislature, and the mayor's office (see Table 2). While they have not, by any means, dominated regional politics, they have made important gains for women in electoral politics.

Historian Lucy Cárdenas, who surveyed the candidates' backgrounds and political strategies, found that the women who won this impressive

TABLE 2. *Mexican Origin Women in Public Office in Webb County, 1940s–1990s*

Year	Name	Seat
1940s	Josefina Dodier	Webb County School Board
1950s	Matilde V. Germain	Nye Common School Board
1956	Amparo Gutiérrez	Nye Common School Board
1959	Norma Z. Benavides	Laredo Independent School District Board of Trustees
1977	Lydia S. Linares[a]	Laredo Independent School District Board of Trustees
1980	Raquel González[a]	Laredo Municipal Junior College Board of Trustees
1981	María G. Zúñiga	Laredo Independent School District Board of Trustees
1982	Hortencia C. González	City of Laredo secretary
1982	Lilia Pérez	Webb County Commissioners' Court
1983	Elma S. Ender[a]	State district judge
1984	Alma B. Martínez	Laredo Municipal Junior College Board of Trustees
1984	Virginia M. Pérez[b]	Webb County Commissioners' Court
1986	Judith G. Gutiérrez	Webb County Commissioners' Court
1986	Judith P. Zaffirini	Texas Senate
1987	Roberta Martínez	United Independent School District Board of Trustees, Laredo
1988	Rosie C. Hinojosa	Webb County Commissioners' Court
1988	Consuelo G. Montalvo	Laredo City Council
1988	Anna C. Ramírez	County attorney for Webb County
1990	Arlene R. Aldridge	Laredo City Council
1990	Cecilia M. Moreno	Laredo City Council
1991	Berta Domínguez	United Independent School District Board of Trustees, Laredo
1992	Cynthia M. Jackson	Laredo Municipal Junior College Board of Trustees
1992	Patricia Barrera	Webb County tax assessor
1992	Sharon Cruz	United Independent School District Board of Trustees, Laredo
1994	Alma Ochoa	United Independent School District Board of Trustees, Laredo
1996	Bebe Zúñiga	Laredo Independent School District Board of Trustees

(continued)

TABLE 2. *(continued)*

Year	Name	Seat
1996	Virginia P. Muller	United Independent School District Board of Trustees, Laredo
1996	Christine Treviño	United Independent School District Board of Trustees, Laredo
1996	Consuelo G. Montalvo	Laredo City Council
1996	Cecilia M. Moreno	Laredo City Council
1998	Christine Treviño	United Independent School District Board of Trustees, Laredo
1998	Judith G. Gutiérrez	Webb County Commissioners' Court
1998	Elizabeth Flores	Laredo city mayor

[a] Elected to office after appointment.
[b] Served an appointive term.
SOURCE: Adapted from María de la Luz Rodríguez Cárdenas, "Laredo Women in Politics: Fearless Voices in a Common Struggle."
NOTE: All women who were not elected to office after appointment or who did not serve an appointive term came to office through a general election.

string of public positions shared important characteristics. For instance, the candidates were by and large professional women and economically self-sufficient. They had been reared in politically active families which were involved in the civic life of the community. The candidates had worked in Laredo as members of charitable organizations and as lay leaders in their churches prior to running for office. This kind of involvement had provided them with opportunities to gain leadership skills. Many of the candidates also considered themselves reform-minded and guided by an "intense sense of moral responsibility."[4]

In campaigning for office, the candidates were efficient and organized and able to create coalitions by drawing from various groups. The candidates acquired adequate financial backing and learned to work with the area's "political chieftains"—female and male. They welcomed all campaign volunteers who presented themselves, making sure to include "fence menders [and] peacemakers" in approaching campaign issues and voters. The candidates also adhered to a focused and simple platform and learned to adapt their tactics as their campaigns warranted.[5]

Norma Zúñiga Benavides, the first of the Webb County women to run a successful campaign in a contested race, represents the educated professional women who have run for and won public office in Laredo. Born in that city in 1926, Benavides was, at sixteen, the valedictorian of her graduating class at the Ursuline Academy in Laredo. After she earned a degree in mathematics and chemistry, summa cum laude, from Incarnate Word College in San Antonio (now the University of the Incarnate Word), she taught at the Ursuline Academy for twenty-three years. In 1959 Benavides won a place on the Laredo Independent School District Board of Trustees in a highly contested election. Running on the Reform Party ticket, she wrested power away from the Independent Party, which had controlled politics in the region for nearly a century. Benavides had lost a campaign for the board earlier in the 1950s, when she ran against Pepe Martin. After her election in 1959, she was secretary of the school board during her three-year term. In her role she brought a new openness to the board and helped to raise the level of professionalism of educators in Laredo's schools.[6]

In 1998, almost forty years after Benavides won a place on the Laredo school board, Elizabeth "Betty" García Flores won the mayorship of the city in a special election. With her election, she became the first Tejana to head both a major city in the state and the second-fastest-growing city in the nation. She won reelection in May of that same year for a four-year term. Like Benavides, Flores, a banker for many years, came from the middle class. Her father, Eloy García Sr., who is credited with influencing her entry into politics, served as a trustee of Laredo Community College. Before her ascension to the position of mayor of Laredo, Flores did community work in the city, focusing on the issues of food, shelter, and child care. She also served as a Webb County affordable housing officer and as a consumer advocate for the Federal Reserve Board.[7]

Benavides and Flores, whose elections occurred in a four-decade time frame, illustrate that Mexican origin women in Laredo and Webb County politics could win elective office several years before the Chicano movement and continue to muster the voters' support many years after the demise of the movement. Moreover, the Laredo women, in ways that they themselves may not have realized, were following the steps of such women as Jovita Idar, Leonor Villegas de Magnón, and Sara Estela Ramírez, all active participants in Tejano political life in Laredo in the early 1900s.

CHICANO MOVEMENT WOMEN: RUNNING FOR OFFICE IN ZAVALA COUNTY

[The] Raza Unida Party knows where Chicano voting strength and organization comes from and because of this, it is supporting women candidates.[8]   MARTHA P. COTERA

In 1964, five years after Benavides's ascension to the Laredo School Board and one year after Chicanos won all five city council seats in Crystal City, Virginia Múzquiz ran and lost a campaign for the Texas legislature from her district, which included Zavala, Uvalde, and Medina Counties. José Ángel Gutiérrez, a cofounder of the Raza Unida Party, served as her campaign manager. He traveled the entire district with her, covering Sabinal, D'Hanis, Hondo, Devine, Uvalde, Carrizo Springs, La Pryor, Batesville, and Crystal City. Gutiérrez later admitted that before he worked on the Múzquiz campaign, he had given no thought to public office beyond the confines of Crystal City. He recalled, "Mrs. Múzquiz showed me the obvious, that Mexican voters were everywhere and Chicanos had to contest all types of elections."[9]

The Múzquiz campaign was also a lesson in registering voters and convincing Mexican Americans that a woman was a worthy choice. Gutiérrez, writing about the experience years later, remembered the struggle to convince both women and men to vote for her. That single fact, he wrote, was the "last obstacle to overcome."[10]

Múzquiz's bid for the Texas legislature served as an opening for Tejanas who ran for state office later, calling themselves by various labels—Chicanas, Mexican Americans, Hispanics, and Latinas. The 1964 defeat did not end Múzquiz's political career. In 1972, eight years after her defeat in the contest, she won election as county clerk of Zavala County under the banner of the Raza Unida Party that she helped found.[11]

In addition to Múzquiz, two other women won public office in Zavala County in the 1972 election. Elena Díaz was elected county commissioner and Gregoria Delgado won the race for justice of the peace in Precinct 3. With their victories, the women helped crack open "the door for *raza* power in Zavala County." In 1974, when the Raza Unida Party swept to victory in local and county elections, Múzquiz won the office of county clerk again. Other Tejanas were also elected to public office in the 1974 election in Crystal City and surrounding areas. Carmen Flores won the office of county treasurer. Two women were elected justices of the peace, Irene Ojeda in Batesville and Rosa Quijano in La Pryor.[12]

RAZA UNIDA PARTY WOMEN AS STRATEGISTS AND POLITICAL LEADERS

Women affiliated with Mujeres Por La Raza, the women's caucus within the Raza Unida Party, demanded a significant role in the party. To underscore their seriousness in this endeavor, women participated in major RUP events in large numbers. For instance, they represented approximately one-half of the participants at the party's first national convention, held in El Paso on September 1–4, 1972. The Mujeres Por La Raza caucus also took on the vital grassroots work at the local level, overseeing RUP offices and organizing support among voters to garner success for the party at the polls.[13]

More importantly, RUP women broke new ground through their candidacy for public office at the state level. In 1972, running under the RUP banner, Tejanas mounted their first campaigns to capture two statewide offices. Alma Canales ran for lieutenant governor, and Martha P. Cotera was a candidate for the State Board of Education. In 1974 María Jiménez and Orelia Hisbrook Cole ran for state representative. Cole's campaign platform called for improved child care, equal civil rights, and environmental protection. She also supported a progressive corporate income tax.[14]

While all four women lost their contests, they exhibited determination and tenacity as pioneers in the contemporary political era. Although RUP disbanded in the late 1970s, these women nonetheless achieved a measure of political success by promoting women's leadership abilities within RUP and by advancing the cause of electing Mexican American women to political office.

BEYOND SOUTH TEXAS: TEJANAS ASCEND TO LOCAL OFFICE AROUND THE STATE

In 1969, the same year that the Crystal City students staged their successful walkout in South Texas, far to the north of the state Anita Nañez Martínez was elected to the Dallas City Council. A native of Dallas who grew up in the Little Mexico barrio there, she was the daughter of one of the first female members of the city's Mexican American business community—Anita Mongoras Nañez, who operated a beauty salon. Martínez, a long-time volunteer in her community, ran as the candi-

In 1969 Anita Martínez, running as a candidate for the white establishment's Citizen's Charter Association, won a race for the Dallas City Council, becoming the first Mexican American elected to a city government post there. She served two terms, until 1973. Courtesy Vivian Castleberry.

date of the white male establishment's Citizen's Charter Association, a group that had long controlled city government. She won the race with 52 percent of the vote, making her the first Mexican American to hold an elected city government position in Dallas. She served two terms, until 1973.[15]

Martínez was a political moderate, and her views sometimes put her at odds with local Mexican American activists. Her agenda, nonetheless, reflected some of the Chicano movement's concerns for serving the Tejano community: better health clinics, libraries, and recreation centers for the barrios. As a member of the council, Martínez responded to these needs by successfully championing an $8 million allocation for improving West Dallas, where many Mexican Americans lived. After she left the council, Martínez served on President Nixon's National Voluntary Service Advisory Council and was one of six Americans named to evaluate the Peace Corps.[16]

In 1978 María Cárdenas, who had earlier been affiliated with the Raza Unida Party, won a seat on the City Commission of San Angelo, District 3. Her election followed the creation of single-member districts, a process that has allowed for more minority representation in public office. Cárdenas defeated two opponents in her first race. She was reelected unopposed in 1980 and was ranked among the most powerful women in the city that same year. In 1982 and 1983, after being reelected for yet another term, she served as mayor pro-tem.[17]

The election of Anita Nañez Martínez and María Cárdenas made both women a rarity in the 1960s and 1970s, when few Mexican Americans held public office in the state. In 1984, when the National Association of Latino Elected and Appointed Officials (NALEO) first published its annual report, the *Roster of Hispanic Elected Officials,* it noted that nationwide Latinas voted more often than Latino men but comprised only 376 or 12 percent of all Latino elected officials, mostly members of school boards (152) or municipal officials (113). NALEO also reported that six Latinas in the country had been elected to a state office, but none held an elected federal position. NALEO noted that 1,427 Latinos held office in Texas, nearly half of the 3,128 Latino officeholders in the country. The fact that the state had more than 1,200 elective offices for its 254 counties and nearly 1,000 city governments was one reason Texas had such a high number of Latinos holding public office.[18]

In 1984 NALEO also reported on the election of Tejanas to various offices around the state. For instance, two served as county treasurer, one as a county commissioner, and one as a county tax assessor. By 1986, two years later, eight Mexican origin women had been elected county treasurer. In Alton, a small community in the Rio Grande Valley, San Juanita Zamora was the mayor in 1985. The Tejanas who were elected to office from 1984 to 1990 were spread over more than twenty-five counties and included rural and urban sites: Floresville in Wilson County and Edcouch in Hidalgo County; Laredo in Webb County and El Paso in El Paso County. In Zavala County, the site of significant Tejana political activity during the Chicano movement, Tejanas continued to hold local public office in the 1980s, with women winning races for county tax assessor, county clerk, district clerk, and county treasurer—all in Crystal City.[19]

Mexican American women also continued to be elected to local boards of education in the 1980s. Most of the women represented areas with dense Mexican American populations in locations such as Ysleta,

Anthony, Brownsville, Pearsall, Lyford, Harlingen, and Mercedes. A notable election was that of Augustina Reyes, who earned a seat on the board of trustees of the Houston Independent School District in 1981 and again in 1983. She assumed the presidency of the board in 1984. Olga Gallegos joined her on the board in 1987. In addition to the more than fifty Mexican origin women and other Latinas elected to school boards, several were elected as community college trustees in the 1980s, probably beginning with Della May Moore, who won a place on the Austin Community College board of trustees in 1982. In 2001 she was still serving in this role. Other women elected to community college boards included Delia Acosta, who won a place on the Alamo Community College board in San Antonio in 1986. Lucy Acosta, a prominent Ladies LULAC leader, and Mary Rose Cárdenas were elected to the boards of El Paso Community College and Texas Southmost College in Brownsville, respectively, in 1990.[20] Attorney Mary Helen Berlanga of Corpus Christi also won a notable race in 1982, when she was elected to the State Board of Education. By 1999 she was the most senior member of the board, as well as a leader of its progressive faction.[21]

Tejanas also held judicial and law enforcement positions in the 1980s. For instance, Irene Canales-Janssen, Joanne Lara, Pilar Martínez, Rosa Quijano, Precilla Rodríguez, Becky Sierra, and Maggie Trujillo were justices of the peace in San Antonio, Fort Davis, Cotulla, La Pryor, Balmorhea, San Marcos, and Channing, respectively. Edna Cisneros was county attorney for Willacy County in 1985.[22]

By 1993, Spanish-surnamed women accounted for 404 officials in the state. Of this total, 166 served mainly as members of school boards and 110 served as municipal officials. In 1996 their total number dropped to 343, but it rose again in 1997 to 360. By 2000 women comprised 455, almost one-fourth, of the 1,855 elected Latino officials in the state. The women continued to serve principally on boards of education (190) and as municipal officers (119).[23]

SUCCESSFUL LOCAL CANDIDATES: SOME FIRSTS IN THE CITIES

In 1980 Margaret Gómez of Austin, a long-time administrative assistant to Travis County commissioner Richard Moya, won the race for constable of Precinct 4. With her win, she became the first Mexican American woman elected to office in Travis County. She was also the first female constable in Travis County. In 1995, after serving in that posi-

San Antonio City Council member María Antonietta Berriozábal introduces her parents during her mayoral campaign, around 1991. On far left is Manuel Berriozábal, her husband. Courtesy *La Prensa,* San Antonio.

tion for more than ten years, Gómez won election as county commissioner for Precinct 4.[24]

In 1981, a year after Gómez first won the constable race in Travis County, the Mexican American Business and Professional Women's Association (MABPWA) campaigned for María Antonietta Berriozábal, one of its members who was running for city council in San Antonio. MABPWA, which had been organized in the early 1970s to elevate the status of Tejanas both as workers and as members of the Tejano community, was in the forefront in promoting her successful candidacy for the city council.[25]

Berriozábal had not initially sought the position. She was, however, working with a coalition of Chicanas who wanted to endorse a woman for the vacancy created on the council when Henry Cisneros decided to run for mayor. After the group failed to find a suitable female candidate, it recruited Berriozábal to run for the seat, opposite a male candidate. Women's support netted a victory for Berriozábal, who became the first Tejana council member in the city's history. She was reelected several times, ultimately serving for ten years.[26]

During her decade-long tenure, Berriozábal used her role to empower her constituents, encouraging them to speak for themselves on matters they brought before the council, including neighborhood issues and child care concerns. In 1991, after a long career representing Mexican American interests, Berriozábal ran for mayor, narrowly losing. Had she won, she would have become the first woman of Mexican descent to head a major city in the United States.[27]

In El Paso Alicia Chacón became the first Mexican American female member on the city council, winning a seat in 1983. By then she had gained experience in two public offices. Her 1970 victory in a local school board election had made her the first Mexican American to serve as a trustee on the school board of Ysleta, a community situated in the lower valley of El Paso where she had grown up. Then in 1974 Chacón won election as county clerk of El Paso, making her the first woman to hold that office as well. She resigned the post in 1978 when President Jimmy Carter named her regional director of the Small Business Administration (SBA). In her new job with the SBA, she oversaw a five-state area that included Texas, New Mexico, Oklahoma, Louisiana, and Arkansas.[28]

In 1990 Chacón returned to public office in El Paso when she became a county judge, the first woman elected to that post and the first Mexican American to gain that distinction in one hundred years. After losing her 1994 reelection campaign, she became president of the United Way of El Paso County.[29]

In Houston, Sylvia García was elected city controller in 1998 after ten years as presiding judge of the city's municipal court system. García, an attorney, grew up in Palito Blanco and graduated from Texas Woman's University, where she served as student body president.[30]

THE COURTS: TEJANAS ON THE BENCH

When I lobbied for my appointment as a judge, one of the commissioners tried to discourage me. He said the job of a judge was too stressful for a woman. (I was still appointed by a margin of three to two.)[31]   HILDA TAGLE, first Tejana named a federal judge

Elma Teresa Salinas Ender, judge of the 341st District Court in Laredo, was the first Mexican American woman appointed to a district court bench in the United States. Governor Mark White appointed her to the position in 1983. A 1978 graduate of Saint Mary's University School of Law, by 2000 she had won reelection to the position many times.[32]

In 1985 Hilda Tagle of Corpus Christi was named to the bench of the Nueces County Court-at-Law no. 3. A decade later, President Bill

Sylvia García was elected city controller of Houston in 1998 after ten years as presiding judge of the city's municipal court system. Photograph by Kaye Marvins. Courtesy office of Sylvia García.

In 1983 Elma Salinas Ender of Laredo became the first Mexican American woman in the United States to serve on the bench of a district court, when Governor Mark White (D) appointed her. She was elected to a full term in 1984. Courtesy office of Elma Salinas Ender.

In 1998 Hilda Tagle won confirmation to a federal district judgeship in the Southern District of Texas in Brownsville. She is the first Mexican American woman to hold such a position in the nation's history. Courtesy Governor Bill and Vara Daniel Center for Legal History, State Bar of Texas.

Clinton nominated the graduate of the University of Texas School of Law for a federal judgeship in the Southern District of Texas, in Brownsville. The United States Senate confirmed her nomination in 1998, making her the first Tejana federal judge in the state and nation's history.[33]

Leticia Hinojosa, a native of Brownsville, became the first judge of the newly created Hidalgo County Court at Law no. 4 in 1989, making her the third Tejana judge of record in the state. She won election to the position the following year with 68 percent of the vote. The election was apparently a hotly contested race. She later recalled that her victory illustrated that "the public was ready for a Hispanic woman judge."[34]

Two other Tejanas, Linda Reyna Yañez of McAllen and Nelda Rodríguez of Corpus Christi, sit on the 13th Court of Appeals, which has jurisdiction over both criminal and civil cases. Governor Ann Richards appointed Yañez, making her the first Tejana to serve on an appeals court in the state. Yañez and Rodríguez are two of the four Mexican American judges on this court. When the 13th Court of Appeals was established in 1963, most of the judges were white men. By 1999 four of the six judges were Mexican Americans.[35]

TAKING A SEAT AND PASSING LAWS: TEJANAS IN THE LEGISLATURE

Yes, sir, that is exactly what I'm doing. I dusted off in May, I swept up in June, and I'm going to mop up in November.[36]

STATE SENATOR JUDITH ZAFFIRINI, speaking to a man
who thought women should be home, cleaning house

By 2000 Mexican origin women had served in the Texas legislature for almost a quarter of a century. Table 3 contains pertinent information on each of the thirteen women elected to the state legislature.

From 1923 to 2001, some 92 women had served or were serving in the Texas legislature: 13 Tejanas, 12 African Americans, and 67 white women. This diversity in female legislators greatly contrasted with the period between 1922 and 1966, when the first 20 women elected to the Texas legislature were all white and all Democrats. The female composition of the legislature began to change in 1967, when Barbara Jordan,

Judith Zaffirini of Laredo was the first Tejana elected to the Texas Senate, in 1986. A Democrat, she has served continuously since then. Courtesy Senate Media Services.

TABLE 3. *Tejana Legislators, 1977–2001*

Year Assumed Office	Name	Chamber of Texas Legislature	Town, County	Occupation
1977–	Irma Rangel (D)	House of Representatives	Kingsville, Kleberg	Attorney
1985–1991	Lena Guerrero (D)	House of Representatives	Austin, Travis	Communications business owner
1987–	Judith Zaffirini (D)	Senate	Laredo, Webb	Educator
1991–1999	Christine Hernández (D)	House of Representatives	San Antonio, Bexar	Educator
1991–1999*	Leticia Van de Putte (D)	House of Representatives	San Antonio, Bexar	Pharmacist
1993–1995	Yolanda Flores (D)	House of Representatives	Houston, Harris	Attorney
1993–1996	Sylvia Romo (D)	House of Representatives	San Antonio, Bexar	CPA
1993–1999	Diana Dávila (D)	House of Representatives	Houston, Harris	Legislative aide
1993–	Vilma Luna (D)	House of Representatives	Corpus Christi, Nueces	Attorney
1993–	Elvira Reyna (R)	House of Representatives	Mesquite, Dallas	Private sector work
1995–	Jessica Farrar (D)	House of Representatives	Houston, Harris	Architect
1997–	Norma Chávez (D)	House of Representatives	El Paso, El Paso	Business manager
1997–	Dora Olivo (D)	House of Representatives	Stafford, Fort Bend	Attorney, teacher

*In 1999, Van de Putte won a special election to fill a Senate seat, and won a race for a regular term in November 2000.
SOURCE: Nancy Baker Jones and Ruthe Winegarten, *Capitol Women: Texas Female Legislators, 1923–1990*.
NOTE: (D) = Democrat; (R) = Republican.

Irma Rangel (D) of Kingsville won a seat in the Texas House in 1976, making her the first Tejana elected to the Texas legislature. She has served continuously since then, and in 2000 became chair of the House Higher Education Committee. Courtesy office of Irma Rangel.

an African American attorney from Houston, took her seat in the Texas Senate. The end of the white primary, redistricting, urbanization, the women's and civil rights movements, and the rise of the Republican Party have all contributed to the election of women. For Tejana legislators, the growth of the Mexican American population, the Chicano movement, the increase in the number of educated Tejanas, and their participation in traditional two-party politics have been particularly important factors in making their election possible.

Irma Rangel is the dean of Tejana legislators, having served since 1977. A Kingsville attorney, she was the first Tejana elected to the Texas House, in 1976. Rangel had worked as a teacher in Venezuela and California, written a Spanish textbook, and graduated from law school before she realized the importance of Tejano participation in public life.[37]

After serving as an assistant district attorney in Corpus Christi, a job she accepted after insisting that she earn the same salary as her male counterparts, Rangel opened her own law office in Kingsville and became interested in local politics. When she attended a conference on women in public life in 1975, members of the Mexican American Women's Caucus and the Texas Women's Political Caucus (TWPC) encouraged her to run for the legislature. The TWPC provided her with seed money, but the bulk of her first campaign funds came from female migrant farmworkers, who donated to her campaign before they headed north to work in the fields. "They knew I had been involved with the farmworkers' march in 1966 and that I was compassionate toward their problems," she recalled. Members of the League of United Latin American Citizens and the American G.I. Forum also worked in her campaign.[38]

Although Rangel was unaware until she arrived in Austin that she was the first Tejana member of the Texas House, she was determined to "show them that a Mexican American woman could do as well as or better than any other legislator." Throughout her long tenure, Rangel has focused on legislation that helps women, children, and the poor. For instance, she has passed laws that have provided educational and employment programs for mothers on welfare, created centers for victims of domestic violence, facilitated donations of food to the elderly poor, and increased funding for South Texas colleges by more than $400 million. Although she is a Catholic, Rangel supports women's reproductive rights and helped defeat an effort to criminalize abortion. In 1993 Rangel became the first female to chair the Mexican American Legislative Caucus. In 1994 she was elected to the Texas Women's Hall of Fame. In 1995 she became chair of the Higher Education Committee in the Texas House. Two years later, in 1997, Texas House speaker Pete Laney assigned her committee the responsibility of studying the effects of the *Hopwood* decision, which banned the consideration of race in university admissions. During the same year Rangel became the first female or Mexican American to receive the G. J. Sutton Award from the Legislative Black Caucus for passing a bill ensuring that students in the top 10 percent of their high school classes be guaranteed admission to Texas colleges. As of 2001, she was completing her eleventh term in the Texas House of Representatives.[39]

Lena Guerrero was the first Tejana to be elected to the legislature from Austin. She served three terms (1985–1991). As a youth, Guerrero worked with her family in the fields in the summer. In the 1970s, she was active in student politics at the University of Texas at Austin and in the Democratic Party. She also served as president of the Texas

Lena Guerrero (D) was elected to the Texas House of Representatives in 1984 and served until 1991, when Governor Ann Richards (D) appointed her chair of the Texas Railroad Commission. Photograph by Lucia Uhl. Courtesy Lena Guerrero.

Young Democrats and as executive director of the Texas Women's Political Caucus.[40]

Guerrero won a Travis County seat in the Texas House in 1984 at the age of twenty-six, one of the youngest women and the second Tejana ever elected. She was pregnant during her second session and often brought her son to the floor during her third. "Sometimes that was the only time I could see him," she recalled. Interested in civil rights and women's issues, Guerrero supported, sponsored, and passed bills to strengthen child abuse enforcement, retirement benefits for state employees, and mass transit, as well as to provide a minimum wage for agricultural workers. She also supported a law prohibiting discrimination against AIDS patients, and another establishing a child care system for capitol employees. Governor Bill Clements vetoed her bill endorsing long handle tools for field workers. She also worked with Representative Debra Danburg on legislation that recognized rape as a reality within marriage. The two women succeeded in getting their bill passed in part because they educated the wives of their male colleagues about the issue, and the women then convinced their husbands of the bill's merits.[41]

When Guerrero entered the legislature, she was known as an uncompromising firebrand, but she changed her approach in order to succeed. She became skilled in the art of compromise and in writing bills that would pass. Guerrero also chose Pete Laney, who was later Speaker of the House, as her mentor. She began playing golf, hunting, fishing, and telling jokes with her male colleagues in an effort to gain their support. Reflecting on the sexist attitudes and behavior that she encountered, Guerrero has said, "That male-dominated system often made us [the female legislators] fly off to lunch with each other just to have some sense of 'Is it me, or what?'"[42]

In 1989 *Texas Monthly* recognized Guerrero as one of the ten best legislators in the Texas House. In 1990 she was named by *Newsweek* as a promising Hispanic leader and in 1991 by *USA Today* as one of several women with the potential to become the first female president of the United States. In 1991 Governor Ann Richards appointed Guerrero to the Texas Railroad Commission (TRC), which regulates oil and gas and other industries, making her the first female and first minority member of the commission. Guerrero served as chair for two years. When she ran for reelection to the TRC in 1992, she was accused of lying on her resume about having graduated with honors from the University of Texas at Austin. In truth, she had left the university several hours short of a diploma. Guerrero maintained that she did not know she had not graduated, but voters did not believe her and she lost the election. She later opened her own lobbying firm, Lena Guerrero and Associates, and completed her university degree in 1993. She has said that she looks forward to the day when "there are so many women on the floor of the Texas House and Senate that we're not counting any more . . . we're looking at substance and character and personalities."[43]

In 1986, Judith Lee Pappas Zaffirini became the first Tejana elected to the Texas Senate and the first woman elected to the legislature from Laredo. In her first campaign, a male voter told her that he thought women belonged at home cleaning house instead of running for office. She responded, "Yes, sir, that is exactly what I'm doing. I dusted off in May, I swept up in June, and I'm going to mop up in November." With her election, Zaffirini joined Cyndi Taylor Krier and Eddie Bernice

Johnson in the Texas Senate, making the 70th Legislature the first in
Texas history to have more than one female senator.[44]

Zaffirini has earned a reputation as one of the hardest-working sen-
ators in the chamber. She arrives at her office before five o'clock in the
morning and rarely socializes. In 1997, at the end of the 74th Legislature, she was the only senator with 100 percent attendance and voting
records. During the next session, she cast her 15,000th consecutive
vote, a record not likely to be broken. In 1995 she said, "It doesn't matter to me that I was the first Mexican American woman elected to the
Texas Senate. What matters to me is that since 1987, I have passed 215
bills." Two pieces of her legislation have ensured that all Texas children
are immunized and that drunk drivers have their licenses suspended.
She has also passed legislation banning the operation of radioactive
waste dumps in her district. Her other important legislation has helped
stop the spread of colonias (substandard housing areas inhabited primarily by low-income Tejanos) and helped reform the Medicaid and
the welfare systems. Zaffirini has supported programs to prevent school
dropouts, to provide drug abuse education programs, to increase compensation to crime victims, and to establish Texas A&M International
University at Laredo. She has also worked to pass bills that restrict mi-
nors' access to tobacco, that require the reporting of child abuse, and
that strengthen laws against stalking and domestic violence.[45]

Zaffirini has often used humor to deal with her male colleagues' sexist remarks. In 1993 she laughed off a comment by Lieutenant Governor Bob Bullock, who said that if she "cut her skirt off about six inches
and put on some high heels she could pass anything she wanted." A fellow senator congratulated her for getting her bill on radioactive waste
passed by a 28 to 2 vote, saying, "You have to understand what that
means coming from me, because . . . for me, the only purpose for
women is to entertain men between wars." Zaffirini's response to this
backhand compliment was simple: "Twenty-eight to two—who cares
what he thinks?"[46]

In 1997 Zaffirini was elected president pro tempore of the Texas
Senate and served as governor for a day. She has received numerous
awards, including being named by *Texas Monthly* as one of the ten best
legislators in the Texas legislature in 1997 and 2001. Zaffirini has credited part of her success to her upbringing in Laredo, where Tejanos are
not a minority but "the dominant population. We are bilingual, bicultural, binational . . . and proud of it."[47]

In the 1990s, ten Tejanas won election to the Texas legislature. Sylvia Romo, a San Antonio CPA, won a race for the Texas House. Afterward, she rejected the advice of a male senior member who told her to use her first year in the legislature to "just sit back and learn" and not expect to "do anything great this session." Romo did not heed his advice. She recalled, "During my first session, I passed a major constitutional amendment, and I filed twenty-seven bills and passed a third of them." She also had to contend with sexism from male members of the House. One such experience occurred during a debate over a program designed to help women start their own businesses. A male colleague, who hoped to enact similar legislation for veterans, argued, "Veterans have done a lot for this country. You tell me, what have women done for this country?" Romo did quite a bit during her two terms, sponsoring more than ninety pieces of legislation, including a successful one against child labor.[48]

In 1994, Romo was selected by the National Federation of Women Legislators to chair the Texas celebration of the one-hundredth anniversary of the election of the first woman to a state legislature (Colorado, 1895). Working with the Center for the Study of Women and Gender at the University of Texas at San Antonio, she raised private funds to produce *Getting Where We've Got to Be,* a video history of women in the Texas legislature, which premiered in 1995. Although Romo had planned to run for a third term, she resigned her House seat in 1996 to run for Bexar County tax assessor-collector instead. She won that position, and in 1997 became the first female tax assessor-collector in Bexar County history.[49]

Christine Hernández was elected to the Texas House in 1990. Before her election, she taught elementary school for ten years and served as president of the San Antonio Federation of Teachers. The Mexican American Democrats named her Hispanic Woman of the Year in 1984. In 1985 she was selected as one of "100 Young Women of Promise" by *Good Housekeeping* magazine. She served on the Governor's Commission for Women from 1991 to 1993. Hernández recalled that during her legislative service, her male colleagues, who were unaccustomed to the presence of female lawmakers, tended to pay attention to the women's appearance and to their behavior as "good girls." Hernández credits Irma Rangel with serving as a role model for her and the other Tejana legislators. In 1998 Hernández resigned from the legislature to run for the U.S. Congress. She lost an expensive campaign to replace U.S. Rep. Henry B. González in Congress.[50]

Leticia Van de Putte (D) from San Antonio, Bexar County, was elected to the Texas House of Representatives in 1990 and served until 1999, when she won a special election to the Texas Senate, becoming the second Tejana there. In 2000 she won a race for a regular Texas Senate term. Photograph by Zavells, Inc. Courtesy office of Leticia Van de Putte.

Leticia Van de Putte, a San Antonio pharmacist, was also elected to the Texas House in 1990. In 1999, she won a special election to fill the San Antonio Senate seat vacated by Greg Luna, joining Judith Zaffirini as the second Tejana in that chamber. Van de Putte won her race for a regular term in the November 2000 election. In 2001 the Texas Women's Political Caucus honored Van de Putte for her service in both chambers of the Texas legislature, including her efforts to acquire $200 million for the Children's Cancer Center in San Antonio.[51]

Tejanas from other parts of the state also won legislative seats during the 1990s. They include Jessica Farrar, Diana Dávila, and Yolanda Flores of Houston; Vilma Luna of Corpus Christi; Norma Chávez of El Paso; Dora Olivo of Fort Bend County; and Elvira Reyna of Mesquite, the only Republican Tejana legislator. For them and their previously

State Representative Elvira Reyna (R) was elected to the Texas House of Representatives in 1992 from Mesquite, Dallas County, and has been reelected four times. Courtesy office of Elvira Reyna.

elected Mexican American female colleagues, the state legislature has remained a male terrain. Farrar has said, "This is still very much . . . an Anglo gentlemen's world, which is so different, and sometimes it's hard to get my perspective across. At the same time, it gives me an opportunity because I don't have a very conservative constituency [and] I can go after some issues like hate crimes or domestic violence. . . . I've been real active on the civil rights band[wagon]. That includes not just people of color, but people of different religions and sexual preference." Farrar, who won election at age twenty-seven, has also been successful in passing legislation for affordable housing.[52]

Diana Dávila first ran for the legislature in 1992, a year known as the "Year of the Woman," and served three terms, from 1993 to 1999. Dávila has acknowledged that her experience as a legislative aide in the previous two sessions helped prepare her for a career in public office. As an aide, she worked on redistricting, which led to the creation of many new urban districts designed to provide greater opportunities to elect minority candidates. When the redistricting process created a new seat in her area, she decided to run for it and won. As a legislator, one of her priorities was a child abuse and neglect prevention program.[53]

Yolanda Flores, an attorney from Houston, served one term, from 1993 to 1995. Four years later, in the 76th Legislature (1999–2001), eight Tejanas—Leticia Van de Putte and Judith Zaffirini in the Senate, and Norma Chávez, Jessica Farrar, Vilma Luna, Dora Olivo, Irma Rangel, and Elvira Reyna in the House—were members of the legislature.[54]

The possibility of increasing the numbers of Mexican origin women in the legislature depends, in part, on the willingness of women to run and on voters to elect them. "We need more women to run and more women to win," Senator Judith Zaffirini has said. "Cumulatively, women comprise half of the population and, cumulatively, we are mothers of the other half. . . . We need a population in the Legislature that reflects the population in the state. . . . We must be as diverse as the population we represent."[55]

State Representative Jessica Farrar (D) was elected to the Texas House of Representatives from Houston, Harris County, in 1994, and has been re-elected three times. Courtesy office of Jessica Farrar.

In 1990 Amalia Rodríguez-Mendoza won election as district clerk of Travis County, and was reelected in 1994 and 1998. She served as chair of the Governor's Commission for Women from 1991 to 1993, appointed by Governor Ann Richards (D).

TEJANA POLITICAL AMBITIONS: FUTURE DIRECTIONS

Throughout the state Tejanas continued to be actively involved in running for office during the 1990s. In 1997 María Elena Torralva became the second Tejana within the decade to run for the mayor's position in San Antonio. An educator, corporate executive, and member of many civic organizations, she lost her bid for the office. In 1998 Travis County Tejanas Amalia Rodríguez-Mendoza and Dolores Ortega-Carter won reelection and continued to carry out their roles as district clerk and county treasurer, respectively, in the capital city. Both women received an endorsement from the *Austin American-Statesman*. In Round Rock, a city just north of Austin whose population had exploded in recent years, Martha Chávez, a high school teacher, continued to serve as a member of the city council, a position she first won in 1993. In 1999 immigration attorney Margaret Donnelly placed second in the Dallas City Council election for District 1.[56]

In 2000 Texas-born Mexican American women were not the only Latinas aspiring to public office. In Dallas, New Mexican-born Regina Montoya Coggins ran as a Democrat for the 5th Congressional District but lost the race. A Harvard-educated attorney and former member of the Clinton administration, Coggins's campaign platform included support for abortion rights, the Prescription Drug Fairness Act, and use of the budget surplus to pay down the national debt. She also opposed the privatization of social security.[57]

As the new century and new millennium began, Lydia Camarillo, a native of El Paso and head of the Southwest Voter Registration Education Project, was named chief executive officer of the Democratic National Convention. Her ascension to the $136,700 Los Angeles-based position came as the result of her work with the country's largest voter registration project. Her selection was also very important to the future of the Democratic Party, which hopes to maintain its dominance among Latino voters around the country.[58]

Camarillo's new role may result in the election of Tejanas to more

In 1998 Dolores Briones was elected county judge in El Paso County, making her the highest elected official there. Courtesy Judge Dolores Briones.

influential public offices. Nonetheless, Christine Hernández, a former state representative from San Antonio, has maintained that in the new century "Latinas will begin their careers at the local level," much as they have in the past, serving on school boards and in other similar posts. In 1997, eager to encourage more women to run for office, Hernández joined with former state representative Lena Guerrero, Travis County district clerk Amalia Rodríguez-Mendoza, former director of the Texas Lottery Nora Linares, and other women in founding the Latina Foundation to encourage more Tejanas to consider a public service career.[59]

CHAPTER TWELVE

Arts and Culture

Miss Eco's Fountain, by Consuelo (Chelo) González Amezcua (1903–1975) of Del Rio, was drawn with ballpoint pens. Amezcua supported herself as a store clerk while perfecting her Texas filigree art. She achieved national recognition in her later years. Courtesy Margaret Nunley and Frieda Werden Collection, Texas Woman's University.

I can sing songs from memory for hours. I don't have to be looking at them. I have them here in my head. . . . Mamá remembered a lot of songs—she carried them around in her head. I inherited some of that from her: her voice, her talent, her comprehension.[1]

LYDIA MENDOZA

Called "La Alondra de la Frontera" (the Border Lark), singer and guitarist Lydia Mendoza had a career that stretched from the 1920s through the rest of the twentieth century, becoming one of the most highly regarded Tejana singers ever. Pat Mora has had a notable career as a poet and children's book author. Leonor Villegas de Magnón, who was a supporter of the Mexican Revolution, recounted her experiences during the conflict in *La rebelde* (The Rebel). These women are only three of the many Tejanas who have performed on the stage; written poems, novels, and stories; painted canvases and murals; collected folklore; and maintained cultural traditions for the Mexican origin community in the state.

INVOKING WORDS ACROSS THE GENERATIONS

The 1970s marked the beginning of what has become a fruitful contemporary era for Tejana writers. In 1975, during the Chicano Literary Renaissance, Ángela de Hoyos of San Antonio published *Arise Chicano! And Other Poems* through M&A Editions, a publishing house she owned with her husband. In 1976, one year later, Carmen Tafolla collaborated with Reyes Cárdenas and Cecilio García-Camarillo on *Get Your Tortillas Together,* another important collection of poetry. Tejana writers also found venues for their work in *Tejidos,* a quarterly published in Austin between 1973 and 1978, and *Caracol,* a journal edited by Cecilio García-Camarillo and published in San Antonio between 1974 and 1977.[2]

The works of poets Ángela de Hoyos, Carmen Tafolla, Evangelina (Vangie) Vigil-Piñon, and Rosemary Catacalos appeared in the anthologies of literary gatherings known as Flor y Canto Festivals (also called Cantos al Pueblo) held in the Southwest in 1977, 1978, and 1980.[3] Arte Público Press, based at the University of Houston and one of the nation's best known Latino publishing houses, brought out Vigil-Piñon's *Thirty an' Seen a Lot* in 1982 and Pat Mora's *Chants* in 1984. Poet Rosemary Catacalos's *As Long as It Takes,* a chapbook, appeared in 1984. Her book *Again for the First Time* (1984) won a Texas Institute of Letters Award. In 1986 the poet was awarded a Dobie-Paisano fellowship, which permitted her to devote time to writing at the ranch that had been owned by the late folklorist J. Frank Dobie.[4]

Because the Tejana writers who emerged in the 1970s were among the first to receive attention from literary critics outside the Mexican American community, an unfortunate tendency to view Mexican origin women as emerging writers has persisted. This label belies the fact that Tejanas had set words down on paper decades before the 1970s.

Ángela de Hoyos, Carmen Tafolla, Evangelina Vigil-Piñon, and Rosemary Catacalos, four of the leading poets of the contemporary period, belong to a deeply rooted flowering tree of Tejana literary creation. While little is yet known about the literary creations of women

Evangelina Vigil-Piñon is a well-regarded Chicana poet whose first collection, *Nade y Nade,* was brought out in 1978. Courtesy Evangelina Vigil-Piñon.

between 1700 and 1900, recent scholars have brought to light the works of some early twentieth century Tejana writers, thus providing a window to their work and their contributions to Tejano literature. More work remains to be done on many unknown writers from 1700–2000.

TWENTIETH CENTURY WRITERS: THE EARLY PERIOD

> Do you know, Angela, I often wonder if there isn't a part of us that is completely ours given to us at birth which cannot possibly belong to anyone else. How can we completely belong to papá, if we have separate souls?[5]
>
> JOVITA GONZÁLEZ AND EVE RALEIGH, *Caballero: A Historical Novel*

Sara Estela Ramírez was both a poet and a political figure in Laredo. A prominent member of the Partido Liberal Mexicano, the major opposition party of the Mexican Revolution, Ramírez published poems and essays in at least two Tejano newspapers, *El Demócrata Fronterizo* and *La Crónica*. She also likely published her work in two feminist newspapers that she founded or edited, *Aurora* and *Vésper: Justicia y Libertad*.[6]

Twenty-one of her known poems and essays, all appearing between January 8, 1908, and April 9, 1910, have survived. These works, written in Spanish, focus on philosophy, politics, male-female relationships, and sisterhood. "Diamantes negros," "A Juárez," "Huye," and "Surge" are some of her best known works, with the last considered an anthem for women's liberation.[7]

Leonor Villegas de Magnón, a political activist and a founder of La Cruz Blanca, set down an autobiographical account of her life during the Mexican Revolution, *La rebelde* (The Rebel). The last three-quarters of the book focus on her work with La Cruz Blanca. She initially wrote a Spanish language version, sometime in the late 1910s or early 1920s. During the 1940s she wrote an English version. Villegas de Magnón failed to find a publisher for either manuscript in Mexico or in the United States. In 1994 Clara Lomas collaborated with Leonor Smith, Villegas de Magnón's granddaughter, in bringing the manuscript to the public in Arte Público's English edition, *The Rebel*.[8]

Josefina María Niggli, born in 1910, the year that Sara Estela Ramírez died in Laredo, arrived in Texas in 1913 as a child of some three years. In 1928, when she was eighteen, she published her first book, *Mexican Silhouettes,* a collection of poetry that her father financed. Later, some of her stories were printed in *Mexican Life* and *Ladies Home Journal*. At the University of North Carolina at Chapel Hill, where she obtained a master's degree, she wrote the play *Singing Valley,* which was produced in North Carolina. Her other known plays are *The Fair God, The Cry of Dolores,* and *Azteca*. One of her plays, *Soldadera,* depicts the women of the Mexican Revolution. The University of North Carolina published Niggli's *Mexican Folk Plays* in 1945. One of her novels, *Mexican Village* (1945) was made into the film *Sombrero*. *Step Down Elder Brother,* her second novel, appeared in 1947. She completed her last novel, *A Miracle for Mexico,* in 1964.[9]

THE WRITERS OF MÉXICO DE AFUERA

Beatriz Blanco was a journalist affiliated with the group of exiles known collectively as "el México de Afuera" (Mexico Abroad). Determinedly nationalistic in their loyalty to their home country, they saw their stay in Texas as temporary, one that would end at the conclusion of the revolution. Blanco was one of the few women who worked at *La Prensa,* the newspaper that Ignacio E. Lozano, also a member of el México de Afuera, founded in San Antonio in 1913. She edited the *Página del hogar y de las damas* (Home and Ladies Page) for the newspaper. She also composed short stories and essays, many influenced by her strong Catholicism. She returned to Mexico in 1940. Rosario Sansores and Hortensia Elizondo were also Mexican journalists associated with *La Prensa.*[10]

In 1917 Adina Emilia De Zavala, who was principally concerned with preservation of San Antonio de Valero Mission (the Alamo), wrote *History and Legends of the Alamo and Other Missions in and around San Antonio.* Earlier, in 1911, she wrote a pamphlet, *The Story of the Siege and Fall of the Alamo: A Résumé.* De Zavala also contributed to the *Handbook of Texas* (1952), possibly the only Tejana to work on the first edition of the publication.[11]

In 1918 Olga Beatriz Torres published *Memorias de mi viaje* (Recollections of My Trip). In 1994 San Antonio College professor Juanita Luna Lawhn's translation of Torres's book was published in the bilingual edition *Memorias de mi viaje/Recollections of My Trip.* Luna Lawhn notes that the book is an epistolary memoir which charts the impact of leaving one culture and entering another.[12]

FIVE TEJANA FOLKLORISTS

Other Tejanas have collected and published folklore. One of them, María Elena Zamora O'Shea, was born on Rancho La Noria Cardenena, near Peñitas, Hidalgo County, on July 21, 1880. She was a descendant of a Spanish land grant family. In 1935 she set down her fictionalized history of Mexicans living between the Nueces River and the Rio Grande in *El mesquite.*[13] The book recounts the daily lives and traditions of the early settlers of El Ranchito on land that is now part of Corpus Christi. In 2000 Texas A&M University Press published a new version of the book. Fellow folklorist Emilia Schunior Ramirez's *Ranch Life in Hidalgo County after 1850,* published in 1971, was another effort to depict the life of Mexican women in the late nineteenth century.[14]

Three other Tejanas—all born within approximately ten years of one another—were important folklorists, and one was also a novelist. Josefina Escajeda, born to a prominent El Paso County family in 1893, collected stories for the Texas Folklore Society's *Puro Mexicano* (1935). Among her works are "The Witch of Cenecu," "Doña Carolina Learns

Jovita González, a folklorist, historian, writer, teacher, and the first and only Mexican American woman to be president of the Texas Folklore Society (1931–1932). Courtesy E. E. Mireles and Jovita González de Mireles Papers, Special Collections and Archives Department, Bell Library, Texas A&M University–Corpus Christi.

a Lesson," and "A Hanged Man Sends Rain." Writer Fermina Guerra was born in 1897 on the 3,000-acre Buena Vista Ranch, northeast of Laredo. Her 1941 master's thesis, "Mexican and Spanish Folklore and Incidents in Southwest Texas," covers many aspects of folklore along the border. The text also includes information on women's domestic activities, drawn from her interviews with women, including her mother. In 1941 her work "Rancho Buena Vista: Its Ways of Life and Traditions" was published by the Texas Folklore Society in *Texian Stomping Grounds*. "Mexican Animal Tales" appeared in *Backwoods to Border* in 1943. The fifth and most prominent member of this group of women folklorists was Jovita González, who was born in 1904 on a family ranch located near Roma, Texas.[15]

Jovita González's 1930 master's thesis, "Social Life in Cameron, Starr, and Zapata Counties," has been widely quoted by contemporary scholars of Texas Mexican culture. The work is considered one of only a handful of documents from the period "that did not view Mexicans as a social problem." One of the first Texas Mexicans to receive a master's degree, González became a notable pioneer in collecting Mexican folklore and was the first Tejana president of the Texas Folklore Society in 1931–1932. She produced an array of other work, including a series of textbooks for use in the classroom, *El español elemental,* with Edmundo Mireles, her husband. Her early folklore publications included "Folklore of the Texas-Mexican Vaquero," "America Invades the Border Towns," "Among My People," and "With the Coming of the Barbed Wire Came Hunger."[16]

She also wrote two novels, both discovered in her papers after her death in 1983. She coauthored one of the books, *Caballero: A Historical Novel* (1996), with Eve Raleigh. The novel explores racism and male dominance in nineteenth-century South Texas. In 1997 Arte Público Press published González's *Dew on the Thorn,* the first of her two novels. In the book she creates the altered lives of Texas Mexicans as Anglos begin their invasion of Tejano land.[17]

THE CHICANA GENERATION AND BEYOND

In the 1970s, Estela Portillo Trambley of El Paso became one of the prominent contemporary writers in the Tejano community. Like others in the new era, she continued her predecessors' tradition of writing about the Tejano community from a woman's perspective. Among Trambley's important works are *Day of the Swallows,* a play (1971); *Rain of Scorpions and Other Stories,* a collection of short stories (1975; reprint, 1992); *Woman of the Earth,* a novel (1981); and *Sor Juana and Other Plays,* a collection of dramas (1983). In 1973 Trambley also edited the first all-women's edition of *El Grito,* a notable Chicano publication. She won the Quinto Sol Award for writing in 1972.[18]

In the mid-1970s Inés Hernández Tovar, a Chicana poet from Galveston, edited *Hembra,* a publication brought out by the Center for Mexican American Studies at the University of Texas at Austin, with assistance from the Chicana Research and Learning Center. *Hembra* featured the work of poet Carmen Tafolla and less well known contemporary writers Janis Palma Castroman and Angelita R. Mendoza. *Hembra* also included Josefina Fraga's "Año que te vas" (The Year That You Leave), a poem that first appeared in *La Prensa* on January 15, 1934. The inclusion of this earlier poet's work and an essay on the early twentieth century poet Sara Estela Ramírez demonstrated that contemporary Tejana authors were aware of some of their literary predecessors. Visual artists Santa Barraza and Nora Gonzáles Dodson were also represented in the anthology.[19]

In San Antonio, poet and publisher Ángela de Hoyos contributed to the dissemination of the works of the Chicana generation by bringing out the first collections of two leading poets of the group. In 1978 her M&A publishing house brought out Evangelina Vigil-Piñon's *Nade y nade*. Five years later, in 1983, M&A Editions issued Carmen Tafolla's *Curandera*. Both writers went on to create other significant works. Vigil-Piñon's second chapbook, *Thirty an' Seen a Lot* (1982), won an American Book Award from the Before Columbus Foundation. In 1983 and 1987, Vigil-Piñon edited "Woman of her Word: Hispanic Women Write" for *Revista Chicano-Riqueña,* a journal published by Arte Público Press. In *Curandera* (1983), Carmen Tafolla established herself as a master of code-switching, skillfully combining English and Spanish. Another important collection of Tafolla's work is *Sonnets to Human Beings and Other Selected Works* (1992), for which she won the 1987 National Chicano Literary Competition.[20]

El Paso native Pat Mora is one of a group of Tejana writers who published books beginning in the 1980s. Arte Público brought out her collection *Chants* (1984). Since then, she has published several other poetry collections, children's stories, and a memoir, *House of Houses* (1997). Poet Teresa Palomo Acosta of McGregor was one of a small group of women writers who participated in Flor y Canto, the first national Chicano literary festival, held in Los Angeles in fall 1973. She self-published *Passing Time* in 1984. Acosta's *Nile Notebooks* (also self-published) and *Nile & Other Poems* followed in 1994 and 1999, respectively. Rio Grande Valley native Gloria Anzaldúa's groundbreaking *Borderlands: La Frontera = the New Mestiza* was published in 1987 and reissued in 1999. The author has drawn critical praise for her book's incisive exploration of the United States–Mexico border region, which she has compared to "*una herida abierta* [an open wound] where the Third World grates against the first and bleeds." In *Borderlands* Anzaldúa also explores the issues surrounding her lesbianism and other critical frontiers that all Chicanas traverse, including spiritual and political boundaries.[21]

Irene Beltrán Hernández has written two works for young adults, *Across the Great River* (1989) and *Heartbeat, Drumbeat* (1992). E. D. Santos, who left Texas at the age of seventeen but returned to live in the state later in life, wrote *On the Road, Too* (1988), an account of a Tejana heroine amid the San Francisco scene of "drugs/sex/rock'n'roll." Tina

Norma Cantú is a professor, activist, feminist, and author of *Canícula: Snapshots of a Girlhood en la Frontera*. Courtesy office of Norma Cantú.

Juárez published *Call No Man Master* (1995) and a sequel, *South Wind Come* (1998). Both are historical novels that trace the life of Carmen Rangel during the Mexican War of Independence and the U.S. Civil War. In 1999 Elva Treviño Hart's autobiography, *Barefoot Heart: Stories of a Migrant Child,* was published by the Bilingual Press. The book deals with Hart's childhood days as a migrant worker in the 1950s, traveling with her family from Pearsall, Texas, to Minnesota and Wisconsin to harvest the fields.[22]

Other Tejanas who have published fiction and nonfiction in recent times include Roberta Fernández, who brought out *Intaglio: A Novel in Six Stories* (1990). Beatriz de la Garza published *The Candy Vendor's Boy and Other Stories* (1994) and *Pillars of Gold and Silver* (1997). Norma Cantú also published her fictional autobioethnography, *Canícula: Snapshots of a Girlhood en la Frontera* (1995). Aida Barrera's memoir, *Looking for Carrascolendas: From a Child's World to Award-Winning Television* (2001), is a recent addition to the nonfiction genre.

Chicago native Sandra Cisneros has lived in San Antonio for many years and has become identified with the state's Chicano literary world.

Celeste Guzmán, a poet from San Antonio. Her work has appeared in *¡Floricanto Sí! Contemporary U.S. Latina Poetry.* Courtesy Celeste Guzmán.

Her works are not, however, the product of growing up in Texas or of being shaped by the unique Texas Mexican experience. Cisneros has held the Dobie-Paisano Fellowship and the coveted MacArthur Fellowship. Her publications include *The House on Mango Street* (1984), *My Wicked, Wicked Ways* (1987), and *Woman Hollering Creek and Other Stories* (1991).

NEW POETS FOR THE 1990S AND THE FUTURE

Poets Victoria García-Zapata, Celeste Guzmán, Elvia Padilla, and Nicole Pollentier all appear in *¡Floricanto Sí! A Collection of Latina Poetry* (1998), an anthology that demonstrates a wide array of styles and themes of Latina poets from around the country. Wings Press of San Antonio has published Guzmán's chapbook *Cande te estoy llamando,* García-Zapata's *Peace in the Corazón,* and Mary Grace Rodríguez's *Long Story Short* as part of its Poesía Tejana publishing project, an effort to provide a new generation of writers an audience.[23]

Tammy Gómez, born in Stamford, has toured the Southwest with her band La Palabra (The Word). A notable performance poet, she edited *Yoniverse: In a Loud Kitchen,* an anthology of women writers from Austin. In 1994 the *Austin Chronicle* called her the "Best In-Your-Face

Poet (in two languages, no less)." Some of her performance works include *Piso on Earth* and *Inculcated Con Fusion*. Gómez combines dance, poetry, race, gender, and sexual politics in her work. Another new Tejana voice in the 1990s is that of Sarah Cortez of Houston, a Harris County deputy constable. Her work has appeared in the *Texas Observer* and other venues. In 2000 Arte Público Press published her collection *How to Undress a Cop: Poems*. The book was awarded the Pen Texas Literary Award.[24]

IN ANOTHER VEIN: LEONORA RIVES-DÍAZ, PIONEER COMPOSER, AND MARÍA BELÉN ORTEGA, EARLY CLASSICAL SINGER

Leonora Rives-Díaz is one of the few known early Tejana composers. The Hauschild Music Company of Victoria and the Thomas Goggan and Brothers Company of Galveston and San Antonio, the two oldest sheet music publishers in the state, published several of Rives-Díaz's works: "The Twentieth Century Waltz" (1901), "No puedo menos que pensar en ti" (I Cannot Help but Think of You; 1904), and "Sin ti no vivo" (Without Thee I Cannot Live; 1904). Thomas Goggan and Brothers published "New Administration Grand March" (1885) and "Texas State Capitol Grand Waltz" (1888). The latter was written for

Tammy Gómez, a noted performance poet, is the director of the poetry tent at the annual Texas Book Festival in Austin. Courtesy Tammy Gómez.

Sheet music for "Sin ti no vivo" (Without Thee I Cannot Live), composed by Leonora Rives-Díaz in 1904. She is one of the few known early Tejana composers. Courtesy Henry J. Hauschild, Victoria.

the dedication of the state capitol and in honor of Governor Lawrence Sullivan Ross, the first governor to occupy the new capitol.[25]

Luis Díaz, Leonora's husband, was also a composer whose work the Hauschild Company likewise published. He also directed a small dance orchestra consisting of himself and his sisters Clara, Lucy, and Mary Díaz. The group was apparently in popular demand for dances at the turn of the twentieth century.[26]

The Díaz Sisters Orchestra of San Antonio was in popular demand for dances around 1900. Left to right: Clara, Lucy, and Mary. Their brother and sister-in-law, Luis Díaz and Leonora Rives-Díaz, were early Mexican American composers. Courtesy Henry J. Hauschild, Victoria.

María Belén Ortega, who was born in Mexico but reared in Dallas, pursued a classical career as a soprano. She studied voice with Feodore Gontzoff at Southern Methodist University following her high school graduation in 1932. Ortega made her debut at the 1936 Texas Centennial, which led to performances with major orchestras. In 1937 Governor James Allred nicknamed her the "Nightingale of the Americas," and she went on a goodwill tour of Mexico. In later years she sang in New York City and entertained Eleanor Roosevelt. An opportunity to sing in Spain earned her a contract to record *A Serenade by Belén Ortega, Nightingale of the Americas.* In 1989 the Meadows School of the Arts at Southern Methodist University established a $50,000 endowed scholarship in her name. Robin Martínez was awarded the first Belén Ortega Scholarship in 1990.[27]

LA ONDA TEJANA: IMPORTANT EARLY SINGERS

Lydia Mendoza is considered the most significant of the early female interpreters of Texas Mexican music. She sang on the earliest recordings produced in the state. Mendoza made her first recording in 1928 as a member of her family's Cuarteto Carta Blanca (Carte Blanche Quartet), when the group responded to an advertisement in *La Prensa* seeking musicians. The *cuarteto,* which Leonora Mendoza, Lydia's mother, managed, recorded twenty pieces for the Okeh label, thus becoming part of the "race" recordings that Victor Talking Machine made when it ventured to San Antonio in the 1920s to record Spanish-speaking musicians.[28]

Mendoza, whose life has been related in several accounts, including *Lydia Mendoza: A Family Autobiography* (1993), went on to have a long and illustrious recording and performing career as a soloist. Usually accompanying herself on a twelve-string guitar, she earned a reputation for her uniquely artful and dramatic interpretation of songs. Two of her most famous recordings are "Mal hombre," a song she reportedly found on a chewing gum wrapper, and "Delgadina," a work critical of a father's "questionable intentions toward his daughter."[29]

Mendoza has remained the most honored pioneer among twentieth-century Tejana singers. She received the National Heritage Award from the National Endowment for the Humanities in 1982, and she was inducted into the Texas Women's Hall of Fame in 1985. In 1991 she became the first Tejana singer named to the Conjunto Hall of Fame.[30]

LYDIA MENDOZA
"La Alondra de la
Frontera"

•Tres Puñaladas
•Tu Recompensa
•Sin Fe
•Dos Caminos
•Cuando El Destino
•Besando La Cruz
•No Se Ha Perdido Nada
•Viejos Amigos

Lydia Mendoza, one of Texas's most outstanding singers, guitarists, and recording stars, began her career as part of her family group, Cuarteto Carta Blanca. In 1985 Mendoza was inducted into the Texas Women's Hall of Fame. Courtesy Houston Metropolitan Research Center, Houston Public Library.

Other singers in her generation also had solo careers: Chelo Silva, Rosita Fernández, Delia Gutiérrez, Juanita García, and Beatriz Llamaz. Silva first recorded for the Texas Mexican border music project of William A. Owen, and began to make records for the Falcón label in 1954. In the late 1950s, she became the most popular recording artist along the border and was known as "La Reina de los Boleros" (the Queen of Boleros). Rosita Fernández began to sing professionally in the 1920s

Rosa Domínguez was a popular San Antonio singer on radio station WCAR in 1925. *San Antonio Light* Collection, University of Texas Institute of Texan Cultures.

when she worked with her uncles, the Trío San Miguel of San Antonio. She won a local singing competition in 1932, which launched her successful career as a soloist, interpreting boleros and *rancheras* (country "ranch" songs). For more than fifty years she worked with orchestras headed by Beto Villa and Eduardo Martínez. In Texas she became famous for her twenty-six years as the star performer with the Fiesta Noche del Río in San Antonio.[31] Delia Gutiérrez began singing as a girl of eight with the orchestra of Eugenio Gutiérrez, her father. She also recorded for the Ideal and Falcón labels. Juanita García won a talent show in 1950, which earned her a recording contract with Falcón Records. Beatriz Llamaz, who recorded approximately one hundred songs, was also a popular entertainer throughout the Southwest.[32] Ventura Alonzo was likewise a vocalist. Further, she was a rarity among Tejana musicians of her era, working as a composer and professional accordionist. Alonzo also led her own group, Alonzo y Sus Rancheros.[33]

Many other singers worked as duets. Juanita and María Mendoza, Lydia Mendoza's sisters, performed as a duet for a number of years. Carmen Hernández Marroquín and Laura Hernández Cantú recorded many songs as the duet Carmen y Laura for Ideal Records, which was founded in the 1940s by Armando Marroquín, Carmen's husband, and Paco Betancourt. The duet was among the first to introduce blues and swing to Tejana singers' repertoire.[34]

Many other women were a part of duets and trios that began performing in the 1940s: Las Hermanas Segovia, Las Hermanas Guerrero, Las Hermanas Cantú, Las Hermanas Góngora, Las Rancheritas, Hermanitas Parra, "Las Preferidas" Hermanas Sánchez, Hermanas Peralta, Marcela y Aurelia, and many more. These singers recorded for various Tejano companies, including Falcón, Azteca, Globe, Río, and Corona.[35]

In recent years early Tejana musicians have received renewed attention in various venues. Arhoolie Records has released two CDs drawn from the Falcón catalog, *The Women* and *The Soulful Women Duets of South Texas*. In addition, the Texas Music Museum has made efforts to bring these musicians and their music before the public in conferences and exhibitions. The museum has also archived Tejana musicians' biographies, performing histories, and accomplishments at its Austin headquarters. In 2000 the organization's symposium "First Ladies: Texas Women in Music" featured singers Beatriz Llamaz and Rita Vidaurri.[36]

LA ONDA TEJANA: TEJANO MUSIC IN THE CONTEMPORARY ERA

Just as Lydia Mendoza was considered the most significant Tejana singer of her generation, by the 1990s the same was said of Selena Quintanilla Pérez, who became a success while still a teenager. Selena was a beneficiary of both the legendary Mendoza and of musicians whose careers started in the 1970s while Selena, who was born in 1971, was still a child.

Vikki Carr, one of Selena's more recent predecessors, pursued the bolero style of such artists as Chelo Silva and Rosita Fernández. Born in El Paso in 1942, Carr began her career singing in English. By 1972, however, she had recorded her first Spanish language album, *Vikki Carr en español*. In 1985 she won a Grammy for *Simplemente mujer* and another in 1992 for *Cosas de amor*.[37]

Laura Canales, another of Selena's recent predecessors, was born in 1954. She made her debut in 1973 at age nineteen with the group Los

Selena Quintanilla Pérez (1971–1995) in 1991. Selena rose from her start as
an eleven-year-old member of her family's band to stardom as the top Tejana
vocalist and the winner of a Grammy. *San Antonio Light* Collection, University
of Texas Institute of Texan Cultures.

Únicos. Canales became well known in the mid-1970s, and in the following decade her popularity soared, earning her the designation "La
Reina de la Onda Tejana" (The Queen of Tejano Music). Starting in
1983, she received the Tejano Music Association (TMA) Award both as
a vocalist and entertainer for four years in a row. Her record number of
consecutive awards remained intact until the late 1980s, when Selena
began her own winning streak.[38]

Corpus Christi native Lisa López, the niece of Tejano musician
Isidro "El Indio" López, initially recorded in English but moved into
Spanish language recording in 1981. That year she recorded her larg-
est career hit, "Si quieres verme llorar" (If You Want to See Me Cry),

which reached the number one spot on the *Billboard* Latin Tracks chart. In 1982 she also won top honors from the TMA for the song. In 1986 López became the first Tejana to debut on the *Billboard* Latin 50 chart.[39]

"LAS SUPER TEJANAS" [40]

By the end of the twentieth century, Tejana singers and musicians appealed to a broad and growing audience. As artists, they represented a variety of backgrounds, interests, and styles.

Individually, the best known among them had created their own unique sounds. Tish Hinojosa, who was reared on San Antonio's west side, was notable for infusing her work with folk music. Shelly Lares, a contemporary of Selena (they were both born in 1971), was influenced by both Gloria Estefan's Cuban music style and Wynonna Judd's country music. Accordionist Eva Ybarra played traditional Tejano conjunto

Tish Hinojosa, born and reared on the west side of San Antonio, is a noted contemporary singer living in Austin. Photo by Peter Nash. Courtesy Tish Hinojosa.

music and headed her own band. Rosie Flores, a rock and rockabilly singer, had added a Tex-Mex aspect to her sound. Mary Stansel, Mary Wells, and Rosalinda Peña, the three members of Las Madrugadoras (The Early Risers), performed traditional Mexican songs.[41]

On the evening of January 29, 2000, these seven Tejana musicians—who had never met and did not know one another's music—came together at Austin's Paramount Theatre in a one-time-only concert organized by Texas Folklife Resources. The concert was called "Las Super Tejanas" to denote the breadth and range of the musicians.[42]

BEYOND SELENA: THE FUTURE OF THE TEJANA SOUND

Selena's popularity as a singer was drawn at least in part from her ability to reinvent the basic Mexican cumbia, adding "catchy hooks, sing-along choruses, [and] . . . *salsa*." From her beginnings as an eleven-year-old member of her family's band, Selena y Los Dinos, to her tragic death from a gunshot in 1995, Selena created a repertoire that made her the top contemporary vocalist of La Onda Tejana. Also famous in Mexico, she won all the major TMA Awards year after year, beginning in 1987. In 1993 she also won a Grammy for *Selena Live.* At the time of her death, she had been recording *Dreaming of You,* her crossover debut into the English record market.[43] A feature film about her life, *Selena,* produced after her death, brought national attention both to her and to Mexican American music.

Several singers have emerged as potential successors to Selena's stature in La Onda Tejana. In 2000 the *Texas Monthly* declared that Élida Reyna, who has been recording music since 1994, was the reigning queen of Tejano music, based on her TMA Awards and twelve hit singles. Other important singers in the 1990s included Stephanie Lynn, Amber Rose, and Margarita. In the late 1990s, teenager Jennifer Peña was the most prominent of the new generation of singers. In 1997, 1998, and 1999 she won Tejano Music Association Awards, including best vocalist in 1999. Her band, Los Jetz, was recognized with the TMA Award for most promising band in 1998. In 2001 Peña won two more TMA Awards, for best vocalist and female entertainer of the year.[44]

MEXICAN AMERICAN THEATER: THE BEGINNINGS

The earliest known Spanish language theater in Texas premiered in Laredo in early December 1884, when Mexican actors performed at the Salón Teatro del Mercado. Little is known about the occasion. Francisco Solórzano, one of the actors who performed at the event, went on to help develop Mexican American theater in the state. By 1900 the number of Spanish language theatrical companies in Texas had grown, due in part to Mexico's interest in providing a training ground for actors in the provinces. Between 1900 and 1910, Tejano audiences were entertained by at least twenty-five companies composed of touring companies based in Mexico, resident companies, and a combination of the two. The Mexican Revolution also forced some troupes across the border into Texas. By 1917 larger and more sophisticated companies entertained audiences in San Antonio and Laredo. The Compañía Dramática Mercedes Navarro and the Gran Compañía Dramática Mexicana of Rosita Arraiga performed in El Paso in 1919 and 1920, respectively.[45]

Mexican theater companies regularly performed in Mercedes, Pharr, and Mission and occasionally appeared in Hebbronville, Benavides, and San Diego. A regular theatrical circuit extending from Rio Grande City to Brownsville was instituted. The Great Depression and the advent of Spanish language vaudeville and films brought an end to the companies' extensive performing schedules in the state.[46]

EARLY TEJANA STAGE PERFORMERS

Concepción Hernández was one of the most prominent female members of the Mexican American stage in the early twentieth century. Born in Mexico, she made her home in San Antonio after 1911. Antonia Piñeda de Hernández, her mother, was the leading actress with the Compañía Hernández, founded by Encarnación Hernández, her husband. After his death, Señora Hernández managed the company from 1888 until 1904. Compañía Hernández subsequently became the Compañía Villalongín, renamed after her son-in-law Carlos Villalongín, who took over its direction upon her retirement.[47]

The Compañía Villalongín grew to have at least ten actors and six to eight actresses. Technical staff members included prompters, a property master, and a costumer. The company's repertoire covered a large number of tragedies, dramas, melodramas, and comedies. Its popularity was based in great part on the reputations of Concepción Hernández and Carlos Villalongín.[48]

Hernández performed mainly in Texas, in San Antonio, Dallas, Houston, and Victoria. As the leading actress in the Compañía Villalongín, she played María in *Tierra baja* (*The Lowlands*), María Antonietta

Women were stars in numerous traveling theaters that were popular in Texas from the late 1800s through the early 1930s. This flyer advertises a performance by Houston actors in Baytown in 1929. Chairez Family Collection, Houston Metropolitan Research Center, Houston Public Library.

in *La llorona* (*The Weeping Woman*), and Doña Inés in *Don Juan Tenorio*. María Luisa Villalongín, her niece, trained with her and took over the role as the company's leading lady when Concepción Hernández retired in the early 1920s.[49]

The Solsona Dramatic Company, a resident theater based in San Antonio in the 1890s, featured family member Carmen Velasco Solsona in leading roles. María Solsona, also a family member, was another featured actress. The company was popular due to its ability to satisfy a wide array of community interests and values.[50]

CARPAS: THE WORKING CLASS'S THEATER

Carpas (tent circuses or theaters), which relied on such traditional circus routines as acrobatics, clowning, comedy routines, dancing, dramatic monologues, pantomime, and singing, were a highly popular form of entertainment among the working class, beginning in the nineteenth century. Indeed, the *San Antonio Ledger* reported on the presence of *carpas* in the state as early as 1852. The *pelado* (the underdog), one of the most important stock characters in the *carpas,* made audiences roar with laughter in sketches about treacherous political schemes, where he used his wits to survive. *Pelado* characters were distinctly drawn. Two of the well-received ones were Don Slico (Mr. Slick) and El Bato Suave (the Smooth Guy). Beatriz Escalona Pérez, the female equivalent of the *pelado* character, was the best known female *carpa* performer. However, three other San Antonio residents, María del Carmen, María P. de Sampers, and Amelia Solsona, predated her, working in the tent theaters during the 1910s.[51]

BEATRIZ ESCALONA PÉREZ

Comedienne Beatriz Escalona Pérez, a native of San Antonio, was known by her stage name, La Chata (Button-nosed). Her career crossed through several periods of Mexican American theater in the state, from the 1920s to the 1970s.[52] Pérez first performed at the age of eighteen at El Paso's Teatro Colón, in approximately 1921. She later toured with Los Hermanos Areu in Mexico and in the southwestern United States. In 1930 she left Los Hermanos Areu and formed her first production company, which she called Atracciones Noloesca.[53]

Pérez developed the comic figure La Chata sometime between 1925 and 1935. Created from her impressions of Mexican and Mexican

American maids, La Chata was a combination of an "innocent and savvy, sweet and strong-willed" woman. She became a hugely popular character. In 1938 Pérez created a second company, called Beatriz Noloesca "La Chata" Compañía Mexicana. From the 1930s through the 1950s she toured extensively in the United States. She continued to perform on radio and in person throughout the 1970s.[54]

TEJANAS ON THE STAGE IN THE CONTEMPORARY PERIOD

The revival of Mexican American theater after World War II began with the farmworker movement in California, where Luis Valdez organized the Teatro Campesino in the 1960s. In Texas, acting troupes, inspired by Valdez, came together around the political activism of the Chicano movement. Acting groups were active in various regions of the state, and they often presented their work through *actos,* highly stylized and satirically comic renditions of the social and political conditions of Mexican Americans.[55]

While some Tejanas became involved in theater through these regional acting troupes, others undertook formal training in the drama departments of universities. For instance, in Kingsville Tejanas joined the Texas A&I University Teatro Bilingüe. Elizabeth C. Ramírez, a member of the group, later earned a doctoral degree in theater and founded the Chicano theater program at California State University in Sacramento. She also wrote *Footlights across the Border: A History of Spanish-Language Professional Theatre on the Texas Stage.* Tina C. Navarro, another Teatro Bilingüe member, became a costumer on both coasts and later taught at Trinity University in San Antonio.[56]

Cora Cardona, who obtained a drama degree from the National Institute of Fine Arts in Mexico City, cofounded Teatro Dallas in 1985 with Jeffrey Hurst, her husband. The theater emphasizes Latin American drama. Cardona has directed most of the theater's productions and won awards for best acting and best directing from regional arts critics. Teatro Dallas hosts an annual Día de los Muertos project, and began an International Theater Festival in the 1990s.[57]

Amparo García-Crow has written and directed a number of works in Texas, California, and New York. Her play *Under a Western Sky* has been performed in New York City. García-Crow, a member of the theater faculty at the University of Texas at Austin, also founded Prism Works, a company dedicated to producing new multicultural works.[58]

Ruby Nelda Pérez of San Antonio and Irene Gonzáles of Austin have had long careers in their respective cities. González has performed in a vast array of productions for many years. In the 1990s she became the unofficial diva of Chicana actresses in the state capital. Her acting in the comedy *Petra's Pecado* (Petra's Sin) has been especially noted. Ruby Nelda Pérez has toured with *A Woman's Work,* a one-woman stage show based on a series of works by Chicana writers. Her other one-woman shows, *Doña Rosita's Jalapeño Kitchen* and *Rosita's Day of the Dead,* were written by playwright Rodrigo Duarte Clark, with Pérez providing ideas for the character of Rosita.[59] Pérez has also performed with Teatro Bilingüe in Houston and continued working with Los Actores de San Antonio, a theater group affiliated with the Guadalupe Cultural Arts Center (GCAC) there. Indeed, the GCAC, among the best-known Mexican American arts centers in the Southwest, has provided Tejana actresses many opportunities to act on the stage. Since the mid-1980s, numerous women have performed there in more than twenty different productions.[60]

MEXICAN AMERICAN WOMEN AND TEXTILE ARTS

stretched out they lay
armed/ready/shouting/celebrating

knotted with love
the quilts sing on.[61]

TERESA PALOMO ACOSTA, "My Mother Pieced Quilts"

Tejanas have a long tradition of making quilts, embroidering, crocheting, and creating *deshilado* (drawn work). They have, for instance, practiced quilting since their earliest settlements in Zapata and Webb Counties in the late 1700s and early 1800s.[62]

Tejanas' needlework has remained mainly a private artistic expression, with much of it going unnoticed by the general public. However, the 1984 book *Texas Quilts, Texas Women* took note of their quilting tradition. In addition, the 1986 exhibition "Arte entre nosotros/Art among Us" at the San Antonio Museum of Art featured Tejana needlework artists.[63] Many countless unknown textile artists have produced work for private use in their homes and as gifts. Research on, and preservation of, their work has yet to be carried out.

 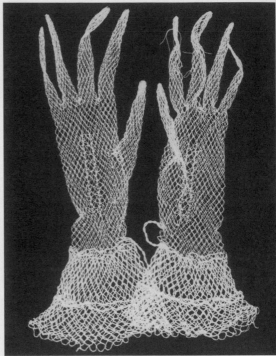

In approximately 1940 Juanita Palomo created these gloves, probably for a wedding in which she served as an attendant. She is pictured in 1936, at approximately age fifteen. Courtesy Juanita Palomo Campos.

THREE FOLK ARTISTS: CHELO, ADMONTY, AND BEATRICE

Consuelo (Chelo) González Amezcua was born in Piedras Negras, Coahuila, Mexico, in 1903. She immigrated with her family to Del Rio in 1913 and spent the rest of her life there. Alice (Admonty) Dickerson Montemayor was born in Laredo in 1902, where she lived all of her life. Beatrice Valdez Ximénez was born in Graytown in 1904. Although they were contemporaries, each of these women created uniquely different art, beginning at distinctly different periods of their lives. Amezcua started in her youth, Montemayor in old age, and Ximénes while working in her family's business. Amezcua became a self-described filigree painter of complex illustrations, Montemayor a self-taught folk artist, and Ximénez a sculptor of large cement works.[64]

Amezcua incorporated poetry into some of her work, which celebrates both women and her Mexican American heritage. In 1968, when she was in her sixties, she began to garner public attention and to participate in invited exhibitions, including a solo exhibition at the McNay Art Museum in San Antonio. Her work has also been shown at the Bronx Museum of Art and at galleries in New York City.[65]

Alice Dickerson Montemayor often signed her work "Admonty." She had earlier in life been a well-known leader and proponent of women's rights both in LULAC and Ladies LULAC. She began her career as a painter in old age, creating canvases that depicted women, nature, and the family. She enjoyed numerous successes, including several solo exhibitions in Mission and Laredo, as well as in Chicago, Mexico, and Riverside, California.[66]

Beatrice Valdez Ximénez created cement sculptures she called *animales feos* (ugly animals) that were inspired by her interest in children's books and television nature programs. Ximénez learned to shape cement pieces by working in her husband's cement furniture business.

El comedor de María (María's Dining Room), by Alice Dickerson Montemayor, 1979. Montemayor was one of the first female leaders of the League of United Latin American Citizens. She later became a well-known folk artist. Courtesy Aurelio Montemayor, San Antonio.

During more than twenty-two years of sculpting, she completed approximately fifty life-size figures. Ximénez's *animales feos* were both realistic and imaginary. Her work was included in "Handmade and Heartfelt," an exhibition that toured the state in 1986. The following year she presented a workshop on cement sculpture at the Guadalupe Cultural Arts Center. Her works have remained in private collections.[67]

SANTA AND CARMEN OF KINGSVILLE: TWO ARTISTS FROM THE CHICANA GENERATION

> The art I was creating functioned in the same way as the zabila (aloe vera) plant when its cool liquid is applied to a burn or an abrasion. It helped to heal the wounds inflicted by discrimination and racism.[68]
>
> CARMEN LOMAS GARZA

Santa Barraza and Carmen Lomas Garza began their careers during the Chicano movement. Both have had major careers, creating important works in the post–Chicano movement period and achieving recognition in the world of art.

Barraza, who returned to her hometown in the 1990s to lead the Department of Art at Texas A&M University–Kingsville, has been recognized for working in such traditional forms as the Mexican *retablo* (tableau) and Mayan and Aztec codices. Titles of her work often reflect her strong connection to her mestiza heritage. *Lydia Mendoza's canto a la Virgen* (Lydia Mendoza's Song to the Virgin), *Mayahuel, diosa del maguey* (Mayahuel, Goddess of the Maguey), *Emma Tenayuca,* and *La diosa del maíz con la lluvia* (The Goddess of Corn with the Rain), all part of a 2000 exhibition at Mexic-Arte Museum, illustrate her interest in representing Chicanas as cultural icons or heroines. Barraza has also created important public art. A notable piece is *Ollin,* a 43-foot-diameter mural at the Burton Grossman Rotunda in the Biosciences building on the campus of the University of Texas at San Antonio.[69]

Carmen Lomas Garza is well known for images that celebrate everyday life among Mexican Americans. One of her major exhibitions, "Pedacito de mi corazón" (Little Piece of My Heart), featured forty-eight works that reflect important values in Tejano life: family celebrations, faith healing, storytelling, and *tamaladas* (tamale-making feasts).[70]

Garza has been outspoken about the struggles she endured as a child in Kingsville and as a college art student. No classes were offered in pre-Columbian or Mexican art when she was a student at Texas A&I University in Kingsville (now Texas A&M University–Kingsville), al-

Curandera II, by Carmen Lomas Garza, the noted artist born in Kingsville. Color-etching print, 10½ × 13⅜ inches. Copyright 1979 Carmen Lomas Garza. www.carmenlomasgarza.com. Photograph by Wolfgang Dietze. Print courtesy Texas Woman's University.

though more than half of the art students there were Chicanos. Thus, she drew her inspiration from talking with other Chicano art students. Major art institutions have increasingly recognized her work. Lomas Garza has also written and illustrated children's books, including *Family Pictures/Cuadros de familia* (1990).[71]

CONTEMPORARY VISUAL ARTISTS AROUND THE STATE

Tejana artists working in the late twentieth century include conceptual artist Celia Muñoz of El Paso, who has lived in Dallas for many years. In 1999 Muñoz created critically acclaimed works to memorialize the more than fifty young women raped and killed along the El Paso–Juárez border. The pieces are both a critique of the North American Free Trade Agreement and "a commentary on the fashion industry, feminism, and women in Juárez." One work that evokes the theme is *Fibra y Furia: Exploitation Is in Vogue.*[72]

In Austin, Connie Arismendi has rooted her work in the folk art of

Marsha Gómez (1951–1998) of Austin, a noted sculptor and peace worker, is pictured here around 1995 with her work *Madre del mundo* (Mother of the World). Print copied from *Foundation for a Compassionate Society Herstory Report*. Print courtesy of Genevieve Vaughan.

her heritage, incorporating mixed media, paintings, and prints to explore various topics. In the late 1990s, her exhibition of twenty-eight works, "The Ascent of Memory: New Work by Connie Arismendi," was the final presentation of the well-regarded Galería Sin Frónteras in the city. Photographer Kathy Vargas, who has directed the Guadalupe Cultural Arts Center visual arts program, has shown her work in solo exhibitions in Rome and Mexico City. Vargas has also participated in several group exhibitions, including "From Media to Metaphor: Art about AIDS" in New York City and "Hospice: A Photographic Inquiry" at the Corcoran Gallery in Washington, D.C. In 1998 Vargas was awarded an Artist of the Year exhibit at the San Antonio Art League. She also had her first retrospective exhibition at San Antonio's McNay Art Museum in December 2000. *Kathy Vargas: Photographs, 1971–2000,* the official exhibit catalog, was published in conjunction with the event.[73]

The late Marsha A. Gómez, of Mexican American and Choctaw heritage, was also a significant contemporary artist. Although not born in Texas, her work and life became identified with the state during her more than twenty-five years of residence in Austin. Working primarily as a sculptor and potter, Gómez created pieces influenced by traditional artists Doña Rosa of Oaxaca, Mexico, and María Martínez of the San Ildefonso pueblo in New Mexico. A year before her death in 1998, Gómez was awarded a $15,000 grant to study traditional pottery in San Miguel de Allende, Guanajuato, Mexico. A peace activist most of her life, she created numerous commissioned works for public spaces. One of a series of sculptures created under the rubric *Madre del mundo* (Mother of the World) was placed at a peace encampment on western Shoshone land opposite a missile test site in Nevada. When federal agents closed down the encampment, they confiscated the work. It was ultimately returned and placed at the Alma de Mujer Center for Social Change outside of Austin, where Gómez served as director. Two other *madre* sculptures were also placed in Texas, one at the Peace Farm in Amarillo, directly across from the Pantex nuclear warhead facility, and another at Casa de Colores, a resource center on indigenous heritage, in Brownsville.[74]

CHICANAS AND THE MURAL MOVEMENT

The 1960s heralded the revival of an important Mexican art form—mural painting—in Mexican American barrios throughout the Southwest. Many unknown artists, male and female, filled the walls of business buildings, recreation centers, housing projects, and schools with murals, often depicting themes that reflected an array of pre-Columbian art, revolutionary heroes, and the political messages of the Chicano movement. Muralists around the state worked on solo or group projects. Some muralists were formally trained, others self-taught. In El Paso more than 100 murals have been painted since the mid-1960s. Likewise, in San Antonio and Houston the muralist movement flourished, with Chicano artists drawing on a heritage handed down by famous Mexican muralists José Clemente Orozco, Diego Rivera, and David Alfaros Siquieros, known collectively as *los tres grandes* (the three great ones). In San Antonio, by the early 1990s several teams of artists had completed more than 130 murals.[75]

Women have been involved in these efforts to continue one of Mexico's most significant art traditions. Sylvia Orozco worked with Pío Púlido to paint a mural for the Chicano Culture Room, *La educación y evolución chicana,* at the Texas Union, the University of Texas at Austin.

Irene Martínez and Monika Acevedo were on the team that created *Myths of Maturity* at the library of the University of Texas at El Paso in 1991. Mago Orona Gándara, a muralist in El Paso, created works as a solo artist, including *Señor Sol* and *Time and Sand*.[76]

Since the reinvigoration of mural painting by the artists of the Chicano movement, the tradition has continued among a younger generation of Tejanas. In 1998, for instance, seventeen-year-old Valerie Ramírez, encouraged by her grandparents, created a mural at San Angelo Central High School. Her Spanish teacher, Teresa Pérez, lent a classroom wall for the project. Ramírez's efforts generated a strong interest and awareness of mural painting among the students at her school.[77]

MUJERES ARTISTAS DEL SUROESTE

Tejana visual artists created an array of opportunities for women to exhibit their work and create a network of support and communication during the late 1970s. Their efforts also helped establish a strong female presence in the Mexican American art world.

In 1977 Santa Barraza and Nora González Dodson cofounded Mujeres Artistas del Suroeste (MAS). The idea for the group grew out of the Encuentro Artístico Femenil (Women's Artistic Workshop) held at Juárez-Lincoln University, a Chicano college housed for a time at Saint Edward's University in Austin. MAS initially served both literary and visual artists and worked in collaboration with the League of United Chicano Artists (LUCHA) in Austin. The women later severed their LUCHA affiliation, set up their own gallery and studio in Austin, and devoted themselves to supporting Tejana visual artists.[78]

On September 13–16, 1979, MAS and LUCHA sponsored the international Plástica Chicana Conference in Austin. The gathering brought together artists from various disciplines as well as art critics to discuss the historical importance of Chicano art.[79] MAS also organized its own exhibitions, including *Voces mexicanas* (Mexican Voices) at Juárez-Lincoln University in 1978; *MAS y MAS* (More and More) at García's Art Gallery in San Antonio in 1978; and *"Bésame MAS"* (Kiss Me Again) at the Xochil Art and Culture Center in Mission in 1978 and 1979. Women who exhibited their work through MAS forums presented a variety of themes and styles, from realism to expressionism. Santa Barraza, Carolina Flores, María Flores, Alice Dickerson Montemayor, Sylvia Orozco, Modesta Treviño, and Carmen Rodríguez were some of the artists who showed their work through MAS.[80]

MAINTAINING A CULTURAL LEGACY

Women in the Tejano community have always kept cultural traditions alive. Through their work with the Comité Patriótico Mexicano, which began in El Paso in the late 1890s, and later through such women's clubs as the Círculo Cultural Isabel la Católica, Tejanas have promoted the celebration of such *fiestas patrias* as Cinco de Mayo and Diez y Seis de Septiembre, dates that recall important moments in Mexican history. Women's charitable groups such as Cruz Azul Mexicana joined with other Tejano organizations to promote their cultural heritage by erecting a statue to honor the Goliad-born general Ignacio Seguín Zaragoza, who successfully led the Mexican forces against the French in Puebla, Mexico, on May 5, 1862.[81]

Women have continued to have an active role in maintaining their cultural heritage in the contemporary era, initiating ventures that benefit the entire Tejano community. For instance, artist Carmen Lomas Garza helped establish the Xochil Art and Culture Center, which operated in Mission from 1977 to 1989.[82]

Women have founded and cofounded other cultural organizations. Cynthia Pérez, Lidia Pérez, María Elena Martínez, and other women established La Peña in Austin in 1982. By the early 1990s, La Peña was known as a major arts organization, supported by the Texas Commission on the Arts and the City of Austin as well as by foundations, memberships, and concession sales.[83] It has thrived throughout the almost two decades since its founding, hosting exhibitions, concerts, literary gatherings, films, and other cultural events. Many of its events are held at Las Manitas, the restaurant that Cynthia and Lidia Pérez own in downtown Austin.

Artists Sylvia Orozco, Pío Púlido, and Sam Coronado cofounded Mexic-Arte Museum in Austin in 1984. Púlido and Coronado ultimately left the museum to pursue their own work. Except for a brief sabbatical, Orozco has since served as executive director of Mexic-Arte, leading it to prominence as a major cultural institution in the city and state. With grants from private and public agencies, Mexic-Arte has grown from its original location of 300 square feet in the city's former arts warehouse district to a 24,000 square-foot location downtown.[84]

The museum's offerings have been innovative and varied. In addition to exhibiting the works of visual artists, including children from the local community, it has promoted Spanish language theater and other venues for Latino cultural expression. Each year it hosts Día de

Dolores Gómez Barzune of Dallas won the prestigious Linz Award in 2001 for her many years of support for the arts in that city. Courtesy Dolores Gómez Barzune.

los Muertos events and *fiestas patrias* celebrations. In 2000 Mexic-Arte won major local support when the city council provided $2 million to keep the museum at its downtown location.[85]

Women-led cultural projects can be found in other cities as well. In El Paso Rosa Ramírez Guerrero created the International Folklórico Dance Group and has long been considered the principal force behind the preservation of Mexican cultural heritage in El Paso County. Known for both her community involvement and artistic achievement, Guerrero has won numerous awards, including an Adelante Mujer Hispana V Award. In 1994 she was inducted into the Texas Women's Hall of Fame.[86]

In the Rio Grande Valley, Helga García-Garza directed the Casa de Colores, a museum and resource center in Brownsville, from the 1990s through 2001. Under her direction, Casa de Colores focused on indigenous heritage, youth programs, native medicine and plants, and environmental issues. In Dallas Dolores Gómez Barzune, a longtime arts patron, was awarded the prestigious Linz Award in 2001. Barzune chaired the fund-raising campaign that acquired $7.7 million for the city's Latino Cultural Center, for which construction began in December 2000. She has also worked with the Dallas Symphony and with ArtsPartners, a school district and city government venture to increase children's participation in the arts. At the start of the twenty-first century, Barzune was appointed chair of the Dallas Cultural Affairs Commission and served on the board of the Women's Museum there. In Central Texas, Lupita Norma Barrera has been an independent curator, focusing on Mexican American heritage. In 1997 she organized a major yearlong exhibition on Tejanos at the Lyndon Baines Johnson Library and Museum: *Los tejanos: Sus huellas en esta tierra* (The Texas Mexicans: Their Footprints on the Land). In 1999, when Barrera assumed the position of mission manager at Goliad State Park, she became responsible for interpretative programming at Mission Espíritu Santo, Mission Rosario, the Zaragoza birthplace, and the Fannin Battleground.[87]

Tejana composers, poets, singers, novelists, muralists and sculptors, and other artists have, in each period of their history in the state, created a very specific cultural legacy. Just as important, other women working as administrators, curators, and arts patrons have established and supported organizations and projects to maintain the Mexican American community's artistic vision and cultural heritage.

Grinding Corn

They kneel—grinding corn.
And, oh, how hard kneeling is on the soul.
It's like bearing a cross on your shoulders
Sun up to sun down.

But then I hear them
Rattle around in the cupboards
and magic happens in the kitchen. Chiles
Pop open.
They perfume the air. Garlic and comino
Hit the skillet with a crackle,
Harmonizing with the rice.
It turns earth brown in aceite.

Who are they anyway? These women grinding corn
On metates. Do you merely call them
Aunts and mothers and sisters?

And why bother with them,
With the songs they sing

As they form corn dough,
As they shape tortillas in their palms.

Is theirs any history to collect?

This is what I ask.
But this much I already know:
They stand up when they must. They speak
Other truths—grinding corn.

About real power.
About real beauty.

TERESA PALOMO ACOSTA, *Nile & Other Poems*

Fifty Notable Tejanas

1. Francisca Alavez (or Álvarez) (b. 18–). Goliad. Known as Angel of Goliad for saving lives of Texians imprisoned by Mexican Army after Goliad executions on March 27, 1836.

2. Consuelo (Chelo) González Amezcua (1903–1975). Del Rio. Worked as dime store clerk while perfecting her Texas filigree art, which she produced with ballpoint pens and for which she received national recognition.

3. Angelina (b. 16–). East Texas, Mission San Juan Bautista. A leader of Caddo Nation who was educated by Spanish missionaries. Translated for Spanish, French, and native peoples from 1716 to 1721.

4. Rosa María Hinojosa de Ballí (1760–1801). Reynosa, Mexico; La Feria, Texas. Pioneer rancher and landowner who owned one-third of present-day Lower Rio Grande Valley.

5. Juana Josefina Cavasos Barnard (1822–1906). Somervell County. Ran trading post with her husband.

6. María Belén Ortega (b. 1914). Dallas. Internationally known opera singer.

7. María Betancour (1703–1779). San Antonio. One of the Canary Islanders who settled in San Antonio in 1731. Prosperous landowner and social leader.

8. Beatriz Blanco (b. 18–). San Antonio. Member of el México de Afuera, the exile community of Mexicans living in Texas during the Mexican Revolution. Journalist with *La Prensa*.

9. Yolanda Garza Boozer (d. 1998). San Antonio. Worked in programs division of CBS-TV before joining staff of Vice President Lyndon Baines Johnson in 1961. Became the first Mexican American personal secretary to a U.S. president—Lyndon Johnson—in 1963.

10. María del Carmen Calvillo (1765–1856). Floresville. Successful rancher who supervised her crews on horseback. Built sugar mill, granary, and irrigation system.

11. María Pérez Cassiano (1790–1832). San Antonio. Wife of Spanish governor of Texas; ran affairs of state in his absence.

12. María Josefa Esparza (b. 18–). San Antonio. One of first women in San Antonio area to be invested in Sisters of Charity of Incarnate Word; became Sister Claude.

13. Élida García de Falcón (1879–1968). Laredo, Corpus Christi, Rio Grande Valley. Methodist writer, teacher, and translator.

14. Eva Carrillo de García (1883–1979). Austin. Community leader, nurse, and copublisher of *El Vanguardia* with Dr. Alberto García, her husband.

15. María Gertrudis de la Garza Falcón (1734–1789). Brownsville. Owner of a large South Texas land grant, Espíritu Santo, on which Brownsville is located.

16. María Josefa Granados (b. 17–). San Antonio. Owner of largest store in town, selling pins, saddles, diapers, dresses, and chamber pots. Wife of Fernando Veramendi, merchant and public figure.

17. Fermina Guerra (1897–1988). Kingsville, Laredo. Folklorist, oral historian, and teacher.

18. María L. de Hernández (1896–1986). Lytle. Civil rights, educational, and political leader for more than forty years. Founder with husband of *Orden Caballeros de América*. Organized *Protectora de Madres*. Author of *México y los cuatro poderes que dirigen al pueblo*.

19. Jovita Idar (1885–1946). Laredo, San Antonio. Journalist, teacher, and feminist. President of the *Liga Femenil Mexicanista* in 1911.

20. Petra Vela de Vidal Kenedy (1825–1885). Brownsville, Kenedy County, Corpus Christi. Rancher and philanthropist.

21. Patricia de la Garza de León (1777–1849). Victoria. Cofounder, with her husband, Martín de León, of Victoria; pioneer landowner and community builder.

22. Alicia Guadalupe Elizondo de Lozano (1899–1984). San Antonio. Philanthropist, clubwoman, founder of Sociedad de la Beneficencia Mexicana, and publisher of *La Prensa* after husband's death.

23. María Luna (b. 18–). Dallas. One of Dallas's first Tejana entrepreneurs, who founded Luna's Tortilla Factory in 1924 in her home.

24. Esther Nieto Machuca (1895–1980). El Paso. National organizer for women in LULAC.

25. Leonor Villegas de Magnón (1876–1955). Laredo. Teacher, writer, and founder of La Cruz Blanca with Jovita Idar; they nursed wounded soldiers during the Mexican Revolution. Author of *La rebelde* (The Rebel).

26. Faustina Porras Martínez (1900–1990). Dallas. Established one of the first Mexican restaurants in that city; founder of El Fenix restaurant chain.

27. Consuelo Herrera Méndez (1904–1985). Austin. First Mexican American woman hired by Austin public schools; taught for forty-five years. Later, a middle school was named for her. State chair of Ladies LULAC.

28. Lydia Mendoza (b. 1916). San Antonio, Houston. Singer known as "La Alondra de la Frontera" (the Border Lark); winner of National Heritage Award from National Endowment for Humanities in 1982. Inducted into the Texas Women's Hall of Fame in 1985. Inducted into the Conjunto Hall of Fame in 1991, the first Tejana so honored.

29. Jovita González de Mireles (1904–1983). Roma. Folklorist, novelist, educator. First and only Mexican American woman to head the Texas Folklore Society, in 1931–1932. Author of *Dew on the Thorn* and, with Eve Raleigh, *Caballero: A Historical Novel.*

30. Alice Dickerson Montemayor (1902–1989). Laredo. LULAC leader. Nationally recognized folk artist.

31. Carolina Malpica Munguía (1891–1977). San Antonio. Teacher, host of radio show; founder of Círculo Cultural Isabel la Católica. Grandmother of Henry Cisneros.

32. Anita Mongaras Nañez (d. 1950). Dallas. Opened one of first woman-owned businesses in Little Mexico—a beauty shop—in her home in 1924.

33. Josefina María Niggli (1910–1983). San Antonio. Writer, poet, playwright, novelist.

34. María Elena Zamora O'Shea (1880–1951). South Texas, Alice. Teacher, lay historian, author.

35. Beatriz Escalona Pérez (1903–1979). San Antonio. Created and played famous comic character La Chata (Button-nosed). Founded two theatrical companies.

36. Jovita Pérez (1897–1970). Laredo. First known Tejana owner of a customs house. Community leader.

37. Selena Quintanilla Pérez (1971–1995). Corpus Christi. Popular contemporary singer who won all major Tejano Music Awards. In 1980s crossed over into national Latino and Latin American markets; Grammy Award winner.

38. Ynés Mexía de Reygades (1870–1938). Mexia. International collector of botanical specimens from 1922 to 1937. Credited with 145,000 specimens, which she found in travels to Mexico, Alaska, and South America.

39. Paula Losoya Taylor Rivers (d. 1902). Del Rio. Businesswoman. Cofounder of Del Rio who introduced irrigation and grape farming to area. Contributed land for school, cemetery, churches, and fort.

40. Leonora Rives-Díaz (b. 1860s). Victoria? Composer whose music was used for dedication of new Texas state capitol in 1888.

41. Herlinda Morales Rodríguez (b. 1903). San Antonio. Took over management of Rodríguez and Son Bottling Company after her husband's death in 1929. Became sole owner and president in 1933 and in 1934 renamed her business the Dragon Bottling Company; it was one of the most prosperous Mexican American-owned businesses in Texas by 1939.

42. María (Chata) Sada (1884–1973). Boquillas Canyon. Businesswoman who operated one of the first stores and cafes in Big Bend area, with her husband. Opened her home to community needs.

43. Margarita Muñoz Simon (ca. 1908–1998). Austin. Pioneer in Spanish language radio. Operated newspaper, *El Demócrata,* in 1940s and organized Diez y Seis celebrations. Leader in American G.I. Forum.

44. Emma Tenayuca (1916–1999). San Antonio. Political and labor leader. In 1938 led an estimated 6,000–8,000 pecan shellers out on strike in what was possibly the largest labor walkout in the state.

45. Teresa Urrea (1872–1905). Sinaloa, Mexico; Arizona; El Paso. Faith healer and symbol of Indian resistance to Porfirio Díaz.

46. Andrea Castañón Villanueva (Madam Candelaria) (1785–1899). San Antonio. Helped nurse Jim Bowie during Battle of Alamo (1836), for which she later received a pension.

47. Andrea Villarreal (b. 18–). San Antonio. Advocate of women's rights and supporter of the Partido Liberal Mexicano in early 1900s.

48. Teresa Villarreal (b. 18–). San Antonio. Copublisher with Andrea Villarreal, her sister, of *La Mujer Moderna,* a feminist newspaper, in early 1900s.

49. Salomé Ballí Young (b. 1831). Cameron County. Descendant of one of early owners of Santa Anita land grant. Expanded her holdings with John Young, her husband; became one of wealthiest Texans after his death.

50. Adina Emilia De Zavala (1861–1955). San Antonio. Teacher. Helped save Alamo from destruction through her chapter of Daughters of Republic of Texas. Creator of Texas Historical and Landmarks Association.

Time Line

1716–1721   Angelina, a member of the Caddo Nation, serves as a guide, translator, and interpreter for Spanish, French, and native peoples.

1716   Spanish-Mexican women enter present-day Texas as part of an expedition to establish permanent settlements in East Texas.

1717   The wealthy Mexican heiress Ignacia Xaviera de Echevers furnishes cattle to help her husband launch Texas's cattle industry.

1718   The first settlers of San Antonio de Béxar (present-day San Antonio) include six Spanish-Mexican women married to soldiers.

1720s   Four widows marry military men in San Antonio.

1731   Women are among the fifty-six Canary Islanders who establish the first permanent civilian settlement in San Antonio.

1745   Tomasa de la Garza requests a town lot in San Fernando.

1749   José de Escandón begins establishing settlements along the Rio Grande, between Laredo and Brownsville.

1752   Miguel de Castro of San Antonio leaves his widow considerable land, a house, livestock, and tools.

1767   South Texas Tejanas receive Spanish land grants. The Treviño family owns Circle T Ranch near Zapata.

1770s–1790s   María Egeciaca Rodríguez brings a case against Domingo Delgado for land possession.

Rosalia Rodríguez petitions for a town lot in San Antonio.

Ventura Garza requests a license to round up unbranded cattle.

A priest in Goliad arrests a girl for participating in a horse race on Saint Anne's Day.

1782   Antonia Rosalia de Armas sues Pedro Granados for a division of the family estate.

1783   Nacogdoches passes an ordinance outlining punishments for husbands who "shall assent to the prostitution" of their wives. Manuel Padrón is fined for beating his wife.

San Antonio passes an ordinance requiring "both honorable men and honorable women" to remain at home at night.

A census of population in centers of Spanish power includes 1,577 Spaniards, 677 Indians, 125 mestizos, 404 mulattoes, and 36 slaves.

1787   María Josefa Granados owns the largest general store in San Antonio.

1788   The Laredo lieutenant chief justice issues an ordinance against the mingling of the sexes at the Rio Grande.

1790s   Gertrudis de los Santos and Antonio Leal, her husband, own a 10-league grant on which San Augustine is built.

1790   Doña Rosa María Hinojosa de Ballí inherits land grants from her husband and father and soon owns one-third of the present-day Lower Rio Grande Valley.

1791   The Spanish census of Texas records 186 *mulatas* and Negro women as "free citizens."

1797   María Ignacia de Urrutia requests a license to round up unbranded stock.

1800   María de la Concepción Losoyo sues José María Martínez for raping her.

1805–1835   A number of women request military pensions and military allotments for their husbands' military service.

1810   Mexico declares independence from Spain.

Ana Luisa Jiménez demands child support from José Hidalgo.

1812   María Antonia Ibarvo petitions for rent due on buildings occupied by troops.

1813   María Antonia Rodríguez petitions to assume responsibility for the education of her nieces.

1814   María Pérez Cassiano, wife of the governor of Texas, runs affairs of state in his absence, including the review of troops in front of Spanish Governor's Palace in San Antonio.

María del Carmen Calvillo inherits a Wilson County ranch from her father and runs a successful operation with 1,500 cattle, 500 goats, sheep, horses, an irrigation system, sugar mill, and granary.

1816   The *alcalde* of Laredo denounces common-law unions as a "menace to the community's well-being."

1821   The Spanish government grants Moses Austin permission to settle 300 families in Texas. After his death, Stephen F. Austin renegotiates the contract with the newly independent Mexico.

Anglo Americans begin moving into Texas, bringing their slaves and some free people of color with them.

Mexico wins independence from Spain and promises citizenship and equal rights to all Mexicans.

1823 The Colonization Law of 1823 promises single men an additional one-quarter league of land if they marry a Tejana.

1824 Doña Patricia de la Garza de León stakes her inheritance to cofound the town of Victoria with Martín de León, her husband.

Teresa Arreola pays taxes for dances and grocery stores. María Guerra pays custom duties.

1827 The Constitution of Coahuila y Texas requires a uniform system of public instruction. Its new constitution states that slaves can be brought in for six months after adoption of the state's fundamental law.

1829 María Josefa Ríos accuses Francisco Gutiérrez de la Lama of statutory rape.

After Mexico abolishes slavery, slave owners bring slaves in as lifetime indentured servants.

1830s Almost sixty land grants are awarded to Mexican women.

1831 Ursula de Veramendi marries James Bowie.

1832 Doña Gertrudis Pérez donates 100 pesos to the San Antonio schools.

1833 Josefa Flores de Barker donates 200 acres of land to establish the town of Floresville.

1835–1836 Anglos and some Tejanos begin the war for independence from Mexico.

1836 Doña Patricia de la Garza de León and some of her family support the Texians in their war for independence from Mexico; nonetheless, they and other Tejanos become victims of anti-Mexican violence.

1840s The home of María Josefa Menchaca and her husband serves as a church, school, and community center in Bexar County.

1840s–60s A number of wealthy Tejanas in San Antonio marry Anglo men.

1840 The Texas Congress prohibits immigration of free people of color and requires free blacks to remove themselves or be sold into slavery, unless exempted by acts of Congress.

1842 The Mexican Army attacks and occupies San Antonio twice. Juan Seguín, the mayor of San Antonio and a supporter of the Texian cause, arouses Texian suspicions because he is corresponding with Mexican businessmen. Fearing for his life, he flees to Mexico.

1845 The U.S. annexes Texas, which becomes a state. The Texas legislature makes it illegal for any free black to remain without its consent.

1845–1848 The U.S.-Mexican War ends with the Treaty of Guadalupe Hidalgo. The Rio Grande becomes U.S.-Mexico boundary.

1848 The first women's rights convention is held in Seneca Falls, New York.

1849 Family members of Gertrudis de la Garza Falcón file suit to recover the land on which Brownsville is located. They win their case in 1852 but sell their land the next year.

1850s Tejanas like Salomé Vela in Hidalgo County acquire land through dowries and marriages.

1850 Girls attend school in Laredo in same proportion as boys.

1851 The Ursuline Academy is founded in San Antonio.

1853 The widow of Juan Mendiola sells her 15,500-acre land grant in Nueces County to Captain Richard King for $300. It becomes the basis for the King Ranch.

1854 Citizens of Austin expel all transient Mexicans, whom they fear will encourage runaway slaves.

ca 1854 Petra Vela de Vidal, a wealthy widow, marries Mifflin Kenedy, and they prosper in ranching and business.

1857 Francisca Ramírez and her husband move from Mexico to establish a large ranch in Presidio County.

1859 Juan Cortina leads a border uprising against Anglo mistreatment of Tejanos.

1860 Salomé Ballí Young, the widow of John Young, is one of Texas's wealthiest citizens, owning $100,000 in real property and $25,000 in personal property.

Paula Losoya Taylor and her sister found Del Rio.

1861 Mexican American abolitionists renounce allegiance to the Confederacy (*Corpus Christi Ranchero,* datelined Carrizo, April 12).

1861–1865 Texas secedes from the Union and joins the Confederacy. Tejanos serve in both the Confederate and Union armies during the Civil War.

1863 President Abraham Lincoln issues the Emancipation Proclamation.

1863 Chipita Rodríguez is legally hanged for murder. More than a century later, in 1985, Governor Mark White (D) signs legislation absolving her of murder.

1865 On June 19 Texas slaves learn they are free under Abraham Lincoln's Emancipation Proclamation of 1863. The date becomes known as Juneteenth.

The Thirteenth Amendment to U.S. Constitution abolishes slavery.

1867–1869 Tejanas register cattle brands in Nueces County.

1868 The Fourteenth Amendment to U.S. Constitution is ratified, extending citizenship to blacks.

1870s Tejanos begin to organize *sociedades mutualistas* (mutual aid societies).

1870 Petra Vela de Vidal Kenedy and Mifflin Kenedy, her husband, have assets of $139,000 and real estate valued at $21,000.

Texas is readmitted to the Union.

The Fifteenth Amendment to U.S. Constitution gives black males the vote but excludes women.

1871 María Josefa Esparza is invested in the Sisters of Charity of the Incarnate Word and takes the name Sister Claude.

1874   The Comanche Nation endures its final defeat at the Battle of Palo
Duro Canyon, followed by exile to reservations in Oklahoma.

The inauguration of a Democratic governor in Texas marks the end of
Reconstruction.

1875   The U.S. Civil Rights Act of 1875 provides for equal access to public
accommodations without regard to race.

1876   The present Texas Constitution is adopted, mandating a system of
free but segregated public schools.

1878   Rafaela Hinojosa and her husband move from Mexico to work a
19,000-acre ranch near Falfurrias.

The Holding Institute is founded in Laredo by Methodists to educate
Mexican boys and girls.

1880s   Tejanos are prosperous sheep owners in the Panhandle.

1881   Adina Emilia De Zavala earns a degree in education from the Sam
Houston Normal Institute at Huntsville.

1883   Classes begin for white students at the University of Texas in Austin.

Mexicanos protest the decision of the lessee of San Pedro Park in San
Antonio to deny them access to the dance platform.

1885–1942   Texas is the third in nation in the numbers of people lynched.

1887   "Mrs. Fernández is acting as inspectress at the ferry on the river"
(*San Antonio Express,* dateline Laredo).

Tula Borunda Gutiérrez opens one of the earliest Texas Mexican restaurants, in Marfa.

1888   Antonia Piñeda de Hernández takes over the management of the Carlos Villalongín Dramatic Company; her daughter Concepción becomes the
most prominent female member of the Mexican American stage.

The El Paso School Board opens a school to teach English to Mexican
children.

"Miss Zulema García [is] going to Paris, France to study music" (*San
Antonio Express,* May 23).

1890s   Four Tejanas in Brownsville own property worth more than $5,000.

The arrival of railroads results in increased Tejano settlement in cities such
as El Paso, Dallas, and Houston.

1891–1892   The Garza War attempts to launch a Texas-based revolt against
Mexican president Porfirio Díaz.

1893   The Texas Equal Rights Association of Anglo women and men is
founded in Dallas to work for women's suffrage.

1896   The U.S. Supreme Court rules in *Plessy* v. *Ferguson* that "separate but
equal" public facilities are constitutional.

In re Ricardo Rodríguez is the first federal civil rights case involving a Mexican's request for approval of his application for U.S. citizenship and gives him
the right to vote.

1901   Juana Gutiérrez de Mendoza begins publishing the newspaper *Vésper:
Justicia y Libertad.*

1902   State law requires the payment of a poll tax to vote.

1904   The Partido Liberal Mexicano (PLM), the major political party opposing Díaz, begins operating in Texas. Poet Sara Estela Ramírez is a major spokesperson for it.

ca 1905   Eciquia Castro opens a cafe in Houston.

1906   The Alianza Hispano-Americana spreads from Arizona to Texas.

1907   María Elena Zamora O'Shea becomes a school principal in Alice.

Petronila María Pereida Goodman becomes the first female employee at Hertzberg's, a jewelry company in San Antonio; she becomes the owner of the business in the 1940s.

1908   Adina Emilia De Zavala helps save San Antonio de Valero Mission (The Alamo) from commercial exploitation.

1910   Andrea and Teresa Villarreal found the feminist newspaper *La Mujer Moderna*.

The Mexican Revolution, which begins in 1910, results in one of the largest waves of Mexican immigration to the United States.

1911   Jovita Idar is elected president of the Liga Femenil Mexicanista in Laredo, organized at El Primer Congreso Mexicanista, the first statewide Mexican American civil rights meeting. The Liga supports the education of women.

1913   Leonor Villegas de Magnón recruits Jovita Idar to form La Cruz Blanca for the purpose of nursing soldiers wounded in the Mexican Revolution.

1914   Journalist Jovita Idar bars the doors to the Texas Rangers, who attempt to close down *El Progreso,* a newspaper for which she writes.

1914   *Soldaderas* (female soldiers) in the Mexican Revolution engage in fighting, providing medical assistance, and cooking. Hundreds of *soldaderas* traveling with the *federales* are incarcerated at Presidio and Marfa.

1914–1918   World War I takes place, with the U.S. entering in 1917.

1915   The Plan de San Diego, a revolutionary manifesto calling for armed struggle by Tejanos, African Americans, and Japanese Americans against Anglo exploitation, is issued.

Eva García is a nurse, social welfare volunteer, and a cofounder of the second Mexican Methodist church in Austin.

1917   The Immigration Act of 1917 closes U.S. doors on European laborers and bars immigrants deemed "undesirable."

1917–1918   The name of Tejana student Lucita Escajeda of San Elizario, Texas, appears in the directory of the University of Texas at Austin.

1918   Olga Beatriz Torres publishes *Memorias de mi viaje,* a memoir about her experiences as an immigrant.

Texas women win the right to vote in Democratic Party primaries.

1919   El Paso laundry workers go on strike, protesting dismal wages and atrocious working conditions.

1920s   The number of *mutualistas* in Texas cities increases.

The Ku Klux Klan is active in Texas.

1920   Tejanas establish Cruz Azul Mexicana in San Antonio to help women and the poor.

The Nineteenth Amendment to U.S. Constitution grants women the right to vote.

1921   Beatriz Escalona Pérez begins her theatrical career at the Teatro Colón in El Paso.

1922   Ynés Mexía de Reygades, a naturalist and botanist, makes her first expedition as part of a group. By the 1930s, she collects approximately 145,000 specimens in Mexico, Alaska, and South America.

1923   Rachel Garza earns a master's degree at the University of Texas, possibly the first Tejana to do so.

The Texas legislature passes the White Primary Act.

1924   Two Tejanas establish businesses in Dallas: Anita Nañez opens a beauty parlor in her home and María Luna opens the Luna Tortilla Factory.

The U.S. Congress creates the Border Patrol.

1926   Adelaida Cuellar begins a homemade tamale business in Dallas and later expands it into El Chico restaurant chain.

1927   Consuelo Herrera Méndez is hired to teach in Austin schools, one of the first Tejanas to teach in a major school system in the state. Later, a local school is named for her.

1928   Josefina María Niggli publishes her first book, *Mexican Silhouettes*.

Lydia Mendoza makes her first recording as part of La Familia Mendoza.

1929   The New York stock market crashes and the Great Depression begins.

Mexican Americans establish the League of United Latin American Citizens (LULAC) in Corpus Christi. LULAC becomes the longest active civil rights organization for Mexican descent citizens in the United States. Tejanas later organize LULAC women's auxiliaries.

The *Salvatierra* v. *Del Rio ISD* school desegregation suit is LULAC's first official court challenge to the segregation of Mexican descent students in public schools.

1930s   Alicia de Lozano founds Sociedad de la Beneficencia Mexicana in San Antonio, which establishes a medical clinic for Tejanos.

Thousands of Mexicanos are repatriated without due process.

Women in Houston and San Antonio found numerous social clubs to assist women and the Tejano community.

Manuela Gonzales obtains a job as a library aide in Cotulla under the National Youth Administration, a New Deal program.

1931   Jovita González becomes the first Mexican American woman to serve as president of the Texas Folklore Society.

1932   A Women's Bureau survey notes that in San Antonio Tejanas earn far less than Anglo working women. Tejana pecan shellers earn $2.65 a week, compared with Anglo women's wages of $4.15 per week.

Carolina Malpica Munguía hosts a San Antonio radio program, *La estrella*. She also helps run her family's printing business, Munguía Printers.

1933   Women organize Ladies LULAC. LULAC establishes the position of ladies organizer general.

The Finck Cigar Company workers in San Antonio go on strike.

1934   María L. de Hernández and her husband establish La Liga de Defensa Pro-Escolar to focus attention on the inferior education offered to Mexican origin children.

1935   María Elena Zamora O'Shea publishes *El mesquite,* a fictionalized history of Mexicans in South Texas.

Manuela Solis Sager organizes Tejano field workers.

1936   María Belén Ortega, an opera singer, appears at the Texas Centennial.

1937   Carolina Malpica Munguía helps found the Círculo Cultural Isabel la Católica.

Alice Dickerson Montemayor of Laredo becomes the first woman elected to the office of second vice president general of LULAC.

1938   Emma Tenayuca helps direct the efforts of an estimated 6,000–8,000 San Antonio pecan shellers, who go out on strike to protest meager earnings and sweatshop conditions.

The Order of the Catechist Missionary Sisters of Saint John Bosco is established in Roma to serve Mexican public school children.

ca 1938   Señora Reyes Ibarra owns The Little Mexican Inn in Corpus Christi.

1939   Esther Machuca produces an all-women edition of the May 1939 *LULAC News.*

1940s   Consuelo Herrera Méndez and her husband found the Zavala PTA in Austin. She translates the state PTA newsletter into Spanish and writes articles for it.

1940   María Luna is the only female charter member of Dallas's Little Mexico Chamber of Commerce.

1941   Fermina Guerra earns a master's degree from the University of Texas at Austin; her thesis is about Mexican and Spanish folklore in Southwest Texas.

1942   The bracero program begins, bringing an estimated 4.5 million Mexican workers to the United States between 1942 and 1964 to harvest crops on U.S. farms.

1943   Elsa Rodríguez works as a clerk at Blackland Army Airfield in Waco.

1944   The U.S. Supreme Court outlaws the state's White Primaries in *Smith* v. *Allright.*

1945   María L. de Hernández publishes *México y los cuatro poderes que dirigen al pueblo.*

1946   Eve García Currie is an instructor in Spanish and speech at the University of Texas at Austin.

1947   The federal Taft-Hartley Act curtails efforts to organize industrial and farm workers.

1948   Dr. Héctor García of Corpus Christi founds the American G.I. Forum of Texas.

Ninfa Rodríguez Laurenzo and her husband start the Rio Grande Food Products Company in Houston.

1949   Jovita González and Edmundo Mireles publish *El español elemental.*

The refusal of a funeral home to provide burial services to Felix Longoria in Three Rivers arouses national outrage.

1950   The U.S. Supreme Court rules in *Sweatt* v. *Painter* that segregation in higher education is unconstitutional; the court orders racial integration of the School of Law at the University of Texas at Austin.

1951   Consuelo Herrera Méndez is defeated in a race for the Austin City Council.

1953   Alicia de Lozano, the widow of Ignacio Lozano, assisted by Leonides González, takes over management of *La Prensa* in San Antonio.

1954   Clotilde García of Corpus Christi becomes a medical doctor.

In *Brown* v. *Board of Education,* the U.S. Supreme Court rules that "separate but equal" public schools are unconstitutional.

1957   The American G.I. Forum Women's Auxiliary, founded in 1956, holds an important women's leadership conference.

LULAC organizes the Little School of the 400 to teach children basic English words.

1959   Norma Zúñiga Benavides wins a seat on the Laredo School Board, becoming probably the first Mexican American woman in Laredo (and Texas) elected to public office.

late 1950s   Chelo Silva is the most popular recording artist along the border.

1960   Women are active in the Viva Kennedy Clubs in the presidential election. The clubs lead to the formation of the Political Association of Spanish-Speaking Organizations (PASSO).

1961   Adelfa Callejo receives a law degree from Southern Methodist University, likely making her the first Tejana attorney in Dallas.

1963   Yolanda Garza Boozer is personal secretary to President Lyndon B. Johnson, the first Mexican American woman to hold such a post.

1964   Virginia Múzquiz of Crystal City becomes the first Tejana to run for state representative but loses. In 1972 she is elected as the Zavala county clerk on the Raza Unida Party ticket.

The U.S. Civil Rights Act outlaws racial discrimination in public accommodations and employment.

The Twenty-fourth Amendment to U.S. Constitution outlaws the poll tax as a requirement for voting in federal elections.

1965   Margarita Huantes is the director of the San Antonio Literacy Council and publishes *First Lessons in English.*

1966   Farmworkers march from the Rio Grande Valley to Austin to protest working conditions and to demand increased salaries. The march is a catalyst for the Chicano movement in Texas.

The U.S. Supreme Court upholds the ban on the poll tax as a requirement for voting.

1967   The Marital Property Act is passed in Texas.

The Mexican American Youth Organization (MAYO) is founded in San Antonio.

The Mexican American Legal Defense and Educational Fund (MALDEF) is founded in Texas.

1968   Consuelo (Chelo) González Amezcua gains recognition for her filigree art.

1969   Severita Lara is a major leader of the Crystal City high school students' walkout to protest discrimination against Mexican Americans in the city's schools.

late 1960s–early 1970s   A new generation of Tejana feminists publish women's work, including poetry and political analysis.

1970s   Aida Barrera creates and produces *Carrascolendas,* the nation's first notable bilingual educational television program for Spanish-speaking children. Her work on the series brings her international awards.

1970   Women help establish the Raza Unida Party, as well as a women's caucus (Mujeres Por La Raza) within the party.

1971   La Conferencia de Mujeres por la Raza, the first national Chicana conference, is held in Houston.

The National Women's Political Caucus and Texas Women's Political Caucus are founded.

1972   Las Hermanas, an organization for lay and religious Catholic women, is founded in Houston.

Virginia Múzquiz serves as the national chair of the Raza Unida Party. Alma Canales runs for lieutenant governor on the Raza Unida Party ticket.

The Mexican American Republicans of Texas (MART) is founded.

Texas voters approve an equal rights amendment to the state constitution by a four to one majority.

The Texas legislature ratifies the federal Equal Rights Amendment.

1972–1974   A lengthy strike of 4,000 Farah garment workers, most of them Tejanas, takes place in El Paso. The women are supported by a national boycott.

Mexican American Business and Professional Women's Association (MABPWA), the first major business organization for Tejanas, is organized.

1973   In *Roe* v. *Wade,* the U.S. Supreme Court establishes a woman's constitutional right to an abortion.

1974   Vilma Martínez becomes the president and general counsel of MALDEF.

Tejanas establish the Chicana Research and Learning Center in Austin to sponsor bilingual–bicultural projects, including publications and conscious-ness-raising workshops for women.

Vilma Martínez wins a case before U.S. Circuit Court of Appeals that guar-antees the right of non–English-speaking children to a bilingual education.

MALDEF's Chicana Rights Project begins.

Communities Organized for Public Service (COPS) is founded in San Antonio by Ernesto Cortes, Beatrice Gallego, and others.

1975   Under the leadership of Barbara Jordan, Congress expands the Voting Rights Act to include Spanish speakers in the Southwest, including Texas.

Mexican American Democrats (MAD) is founded.

1976   MALDEF's Chicana Rights Project begins monitoring the impact of the Comprehensive Employment and Training Act (CETA) on Mexican American women in San Antonio.

Lucía Madrid opens a library in her family's store in Redford, along the Rio Grande, to serve the local community.

Irma Rangel of Kingsville becomes the first Tejana elected to the Texas House of Representatives.

1977   Debra López Fix, a native of Elgin, is the first woman of Mexican origin to enter West Point. In 1998, she becomes a lieutenant colonel.

Rosie Jiménez dies in McAllen from an illegal abortion, the first victim of the Hyde Amendment, which cut off funding for abortions in the federal Medicaid program.

1979   Rebecca Reyes is the first Tejana ordained as a minister of the Presby-terian faith.

The Plástica Chicana Conference, an international meeting on Latino arts, is held in Austin.

1980s   Artist Carmen Lomas Garza begins receiving national recognition.

1981   María Berriozábal wins a race for the San Antonio City Council.

1982   Mary Helen Berlanga, a Corpus Christi attorney, is elected to the State Board of Education.

1983   Elma Salinas Ender is the first Mexican American female appointed to a state court bench in the United States. She is later elected to a full term.

1984   Dr. Clotilde P. García is inducted into the first Texas Women's Hall of Fame.

Lena Guerrero becomes the second Tejana to win a seat in the Texas House of Representatives.

1985   Cora Cardona cofounds Teatro Dallas.

Lydia Mendoza and María Elena Flood are inducted into the Texas Wom-en's Hall of Fame.

1986   Judith Zaffirini of Laredo becomes the first Tejana elected to the Texas Senate.

Juliet García becomes the first Mexican American woman in the United States to head a college—Texas Southmost in Brownsville.

1987   Women organize the Hispanic Women's Network of Texas to improve the status of Latinas.

Sarah Leal Tatum is elected mayor of Rio Hondo.

1988   More than 600 women attend third biannual conference of Hispanas Unidas.

1990   Following the closing of the Levi-Strauss garment plant in San Antonio, Tejanas who are laid off by the company organize Fuerza Unida, a group committed to improving the conditions of laborers worldwide.

Leticia Hinojosa of Edinburg is appointed a judge for the Hidalgo County Court at Law; she wins election to the post in 1990.

An estimated 500 of 2,400 Texas Hispanic attorneys are women.

Alicia Chacón is the first female elected as a county judge in El Paso County.

Christine Hernández and Leticia Van de Putte are elected to the Texas House.

1991   Governor Ann Richards appoints a record number of Tejanas and African American women to her staff and to state boards and commissions. She names Lena Guerrero as chair of the Texas Railroad Commission.

1992   Yolanda Flores, Sylvia Romo, Diana Dávila, Vilma Luna, and Elvira Reyna are elected to the Texas House.

1993   Guadalupe Rangel becomes the first Tejana member of the Texas A&M University Board of Regents.

Spanish-surnamed women hold 404 public offices in Texas.

1994   State Representative Sylvia Romo represents Texas in the National Federation of Women Legislators.

Jessica Farrar is elected to the Texas House.

1995   Meg Guerra cofounds *LareDOS,* a newspaper, in Laredo.

Linda Chávez-Thompson is the executive vice president of the national AFL-CIO.

1996   *Hopwood* v. *State of Texas* bans consideration of race in Texas college admissions.

Christy Haubegger founds *Latina,* a nationally distributed magazine.

1997   Sylvia Romo is elected as Bexar County tax assessor-collector.

Sylvia Garcia is elected city controller of Houston.

1998   Elizabeth "Betty" García Flores is elected mayor of Laredo.

Hilda Tagle becomes the first Tejana federal judge in Texas and the United States, appointed by President Bill Clinton.

1998–2001   María Echaveste serves as the White House deputy chief of staff during the administration of President Bill Clinton.

1999   In a special election, Leticia Van de Putte, a San Antonio pharmacist, becomes the second Tejana elected to the Texas Senate. She is elected to a full term in 2000.

2000   Lydia Camarillo, a native of El Paso, is named the chief executive of the Democratic National Convention.

Notes

CHAPTER ONE

1. *Women in Texas History 1976 Calendar.*

2. Cynthia E. Orozco, "Mexican-American Women," *New Handbook of Texas,* 4:680–682 (hereafter *NHOT*).

3. La Bahia (Goliad) and Nacogdoches were outcroppings of presidios; San Antonio and Laredo were founded by royal ordinances regulating the creation of towns. Arnoldo De León, *Mexican Americans in Texas: A Brief History,* pp. 10–14.

4. Ibid.

5. Fray Espinosa's diary, cited in William C. Foster, *Spanish Expeditions into Texas, 1689–1768,* p. 120.

6. Diane Lu Hughes, "Angelina," *NHOT,* 1:179–180; Diane H. Corbin, "Angelina," in *Legendary Ladies of Texas,* ed. Francis E. Abernethy, p. 3. The definitive work on San Juan Bautista is Robert S. Weddle, *San Juan Bautista: Gateway to Spanish Texas.*

7. W. W. Newcomb Jr., *The Indians of Texas,* p. 304.

8. Cited in Timothy K. Perttula, *The Caddo Nation: Archaeological and Ethnohistoric Perspectives,* p. 11.

9. David La Vere, *Life among the Texas Indians: The WPA Narratives,* p. 14.

10. Newcomb, *Indians of Texas,* pp. 279–283, 296–297; La Vere, *Life among the Texas Indians,* pp. 92–93. La Vere does not mention women's roles in the pottery and beadwork art of the Caddos.

11. Foster, *Spanish Expeditions,* pp. 120, 153, 187, 210; Perttula, *The Caddo*

Nation, p. xxiii; Newcomb, *Indians of Texas,* pp. 279—298; La Vere, *Life among the Texas Indians,* pp. 80—81.

12. Donald E. Chipman and Patricia R. Lemée, "St. Denis, Louis Juchereau de," *NHOT,* 5:755—756; Patricia R. Lemée, "St. Denis, Manuela Sánchez Navarro de," *NHOT,* 5:756.

13. Hughes, "Angelina," *NHOT,* 1:179—180.

14. Hughes, "Angelina," *NHOT,* 1:179—180; Chipman and Lemée, "St. Denis, Louis Juchereau de," *NHOT,* 5:755—756; Lemée, "St. Denis, Manuela Sánchez Navarro de," *NHOT,* 5:756; Foster, *Spanish Expeditions,* p. 153; Donald E. Chipman, *Spanish Texas, 1519—1821,* pp. 105—112, 116, 281 n. 30; Elizabeth A. H. John, *Storms Brewed in Other Men's Worlds: The Confrontation of Indians, Spanish, and French in the Southwest, 1540—1795,* pp. 207—210. Spain was eager to provide a buffer to French advances from Louisiana into New Spain.

15. Hughes, "Angelina," *NHOT,* 1:179; Corbin, "Angelina," p. 16.

16. Perttula, *The Caddo Nation,* p. 85.

17. Nicolas de Laflora, cited in Foster, *Spanish Expeditions,* p. 193; La Vere, *Life among the Texas Indians,* p. 18.

18. Adrian N. Anderson and Ralph A. Wooster, *Texas and Texans,* p. 32; La Vere, *Life among the Texas Indians,* p. 40. Indian agent Robert S. Neighbors apparently led the Caddos across the Red River into Indian Territory after realizing that they would likely be massacred if they remained in Texas.

19. Carol A. Lipscomb, "Karankawa Indians," *NHOT,* 3:1031—1033. For more about the Karankawas, see Robert A. Ricklis, *The Karankawa Indians of Texas: An Ecological Study of Cultural Tradition and Change.*

20. "Coahuiltecan Indians," *NHOT,* 2:171—174.

21. Carol A. Lipscomb, "Comanche Indians," *NHOT,* 2:242—245; Newcomb, *Indians of Texas,* pp. 155—191.

22. Donald E. Chipman, "Agreda, María de Jesús de," *NHOT,* 1:56; Nancy P. Hickerson, "Jumano Indians," *NHOT,* 3:1016—1018; Carlos A. Castañeda, *Our Catholic Heritage* 1:196—215, 216—217, 339. María de Jesús de Agreda also wrote a controversial work, *The Mystical City of God and the Divine History of the Virgin Mary of God.* David J. Weber, *The Spanish Frontier in North America,* pp. 99—100.

23. Charles Gibson, *The Aztecs under Spanish Rule,* p. 398.

24. Thomas N. Campbell, "Muruam Indians," *NHOT,* 4:897—898; *Women in Texas History 1976 Calendar.*

25. Benedict Leutenegger, O.F.M., *Inventory of the Mission San Antonio de Valero: 1772,* p. 15.

26. Ibid., p. 21.

27. Ibid., p. 16.

28. Ibid., pp. 17, 19.

29. *San Antonio Express-News,* December 6, 1994.

30. Orozco, "Mexican-American Women," *NHOT,* 4:680.

31. Vicki Ruiz, *From out of the Shadows: Mexican Women in Twentieth-Century America,* p. 4.

32. Leutenegger, *Inventory,* p. 18.

33. Mrs. George Plunkett Red, *The Medicine Man in Texas,* pp. 23–24.

34. Leutenegger, *Inventory,* p. 19.

35. Orozco, "Mexican-American Women," *NHOT,* 4:680; Jesús F. de la Teja, "Forgotten Founders: The Military Settlers of Eighteenth-Century San Antonio de Béxar," in *Tejano Origins in Eighteenth-Century San Antonio,* ed. Gerald E. Poyo and Gilberto M. Hinojosa, p. 30.

36. Chipman, *Spanish Texas,* p. 112; Foster, *Spanish Expeditions,* pp. 109, 115.

37. By 1730, there were about forty married couples in San Antonio, at least half of whom were wed there. De la Teja, "Forgotten Founders," in *Tejano Origins,* ed. Poyo and Hinojosa, p. 32; San Antonio Bicentennial Heritage Committee, *San Antonio in the Eighteenth Century,* pp. 47, 49, 52.

38. San Antonio Bicentennial Heritage Committee, *San Antonio in the Eighteenth Century,* pp. 29, 36, 47, 49, 52.

39. Randell G. Tarín, "Leal Goraz, Juan," *NHOT,* 4:133–134; Gerald E. Poyo, "The Canary Islands Immigrants of San Antonio: From Ethnic Exclusivity to Community in Eighteenth-Century Béxar," in *Tejano Origins,* ed. Poyo and Hinojosa, pp. 41–58.

40. San Antonio Bicentennial Heritage Committee, *San Antonio in the Eighteenth Century,* pp. 96, 134. María Betancour's will is in the Bexar County Courthouse; a transcript is in the library of the San Antonio Conservation Society; Jack Jackson, *Los Mesteños: Spanish Ranching in Texas, 1721–1821,* pp. 93–94.

41. Papers of the Canary Islanders, 14th family, Box 2Q233, pp. 27, 58, Center for American History, University of Texas at Austin.

42. Mattie Alice Austin, "The Municipal Government of San Fernando de Bexar, 1730–1800," *Quarterly of the Texas State Historical Association* 8, no. 4 (April 1905): 336.

43. Teresa Palomo Acosta, "Cassiano, María Gertrudis Pérez," *NHOT,* 1:1016. The Spanish Governor's Palace was in María Cassiano's family for 125 years.

44. Jesús F. de la Teja, "Veramendi, Fernando," *NHOT,* 6:722; Edward S. Sears, "The Low Down on Jim Bowie," in *From Hell to Breakfast,* ed. Mody Boatright, p. 176.

45. Jesús F. de la Teja and John Wheat, "Bexar: Profile of a Tejano Community, 1820–1832," *Southwestern Historical Quarterly* 89, no. 1 (July 1985): 10–11; Jane Dysart, "Mexican Women in San Antonio, 1830–1860: The Assimilation Process," *Western Historical Quarterly,* October 1976, p. 366; Adán Benavides Jr., comp. and ed., *The Béxar Archives (1717–1836): A Name Guide,* p. 100.

46. Margaret Swett Henson, "Hispanic Texas, 1519–1836," in *Texas: A Sesquicentennial Celebration,* ed. Donald W. Whisenhunt, p. 40.

47. David J. Weber, *La frontera norte de México, 1821–1846: El sudoeste norte-americano en su época mexicana,* p. 94.

48. Leutenegger, *Inventory,* p. 30; Gilberto M. Hinojosa, "Religious-Indian Communities," in *Tejano Origins,* ed. Poyo and Hinojosa, p. 74.

49. Benavides, *Béxar Archives,* pp. 100, 341, 363, 393.

50. De la Teja, "Forgotten Founders," in *Tejano Origins,* ed. Poyo and Hinojosa, p. 30; San Antonio Bicentennial Heritage Committee, *San Antonio in the Eighteenth Century,* pp. 79–80, 82 n. 12. De Castro's will was dated May 16, 1752, and is in the Bexar Archives, Office of the County Clerk, Bexar County, San Antonio; Gerald E. Poyo, "Immigrants and Integration in Late Eighteenth-Century Bexar," in *Tejano Origins,* ed. Poyo and Hinojosa, p. 88.

51. Joseph W. McKnight, "Community Property Law," *NHOT,* 2:252; De León, *Mexican Americans in Texas,* p. 23; Jean Stuntz, "Spanish Laws for Texas Women: The Development of Marital Property Laws to 1850," *Southwestern Historical Quarterly* 104, no. 4 (April 2001): 543–559.

52. Alicia A. Garza, "Treviño Circle T Ranch," *NHOT,* 6:562–563; María de la Garza Falcón's ranch was situated on the site of present-day Brownsville. In 1849 some of her family filed suit to recover the land on which the town of Brownsville was located, claiming that holders of faulty titles had improperly conveyed the land to new owners. The Garza heirs won their case in 1852, but soon sold the Brownsville tract for one-sixth of its appraised value to the lawyers who had represented their opponents. Clotilde P. García, "Garza Falcón, Maria Gertrudis de la," *NHOT,* 3:111. In 1984 the Texas Department of Agriculture honored Antonio and Evangelina Treviño as the descendants of families who had kept their land in agricultural production for more than one hundred years. Jackson, *Los Mesteños,* pp. 385, 419; Malcolm D. McLean, *Papers Concerning Robertson's Colony in Texas,* vols. 4–12 (1977–1986), see especially vol. 8, p. 155.

53. Gertrudis de los Santos and her husband, Antonio Leal, were later arrested and prosecuted for selling contraband in one of the most famous trials in Texas history. Jackson, *Los Mesteños,* pp. 454–458. Robert Bruce Blake, "Leal, Antonio," *NHOT,* 4:133.

54. Letter to Louise Langardner, Texas Women's History Project, from Matilda Rosales-McLemore, Spanish archivist, Texas General Land Office, August 7, 1980, "Land Grants" file, Acosta-Winegarten Collection, Benson Latin American Collection, University of Texas at Austin.

55. Orozco, "Mexican-American Women," *NHOT,* 4:680; De León, *Mexican Americans in Texas,* p. 12; Abel Rubio, *Stolen Heritage: A Mexican-American's Rediscovery of His Family's Lost Land Grant,* p. 232.

56. Clotilde P. García, "Hinojosa de Ballí, Rosa María," *NHOT,* 3:629.

57. *Guide to Spanish and Mexican Land Grants,* no. 9.

58. Minnie Gilbert, "Texas's First Cattle Queen," in *Roots by the River,* ed. Valley By-Liners, p. 18.

59. García, "Hinojosa de Ballí, Rosa María," *NHOT,* 3:629; Gilbert, "Texas's First Cattle Queen," pp. 15–25.

60. Typed copy of the certified copy of the will executed by Rosa María de Hinojosa de Ballí in 1798, Reynosa, Tamaulipas, Mexico, Cameron County Deed Record Book X, p. 113.

61. Martin Bryan Glasscock, "Rancho Santa María," *NHOT,* 5:435; Texas Mother Committee, *Worthy Mothers of Texas, 1776–1976,* p. 5; Tom Lea, *King Ranch,* map showing Hinojosa-Ballí grants; Joe Graham, *El Rancho in South Texas: Continuity and Change from 1750,* p. 23; various materials in "San Patricia File I-697" and "Partial copy of original grantee map, Cameron County, 1976," located at the Texas General Land Office, Austin; Gilbert, "Texas's First Cattle Queen," pp. 15–25. De Ballí's will is in Cameron County Deed Record Book X. For articles about the trial, see Megan K. Stack, "Hundreds of [de Ballí] Descendants Sue for Rights to Padre Island," Associated Press wire service story, May 21, 2000; Megan K. Stack, "Jury Rules in Family's Favor in Padre Suit," *Austin American-Statesman,* August 3, 2000, p. B1; Megan K. Stack, "Jury: Millionaire Doesn't Need to Pay Damages," *Austin American-Statesman,* August 10, 2000, p. B7; Carlos Guerra, "Vindication for the 'Lost Lands,'" *Austin American-Statesman,* August 11, 2000, p. A15; and Dave Harmon, "The Fight for a Historic Birthright," *Austin American-Statesman,* October 1, 2000, pp. A1, A19. Kerlin appealed the decision of the jury and the case was still in litigation in 2001.

62. I. Waynne Cox, "Calvillo, María del Carmen," *NHOT,* 1:912; Benavides, *Béxar Archives,* p. 149; D. Jeanne Callihan, *Our Mexican Ancestors,* vol. 1 of *Stories for Young Readers,* pp. 49–54.

63. Paula Stewart, "De León, Patricia de la Garza," *NHOT,* 2:571–572; A. Carolina Castillo Crimm, "The Economic Impact of Hispanic Family Structure: The Families of Petra Vela de Vidal Kenedy and Patricia de la Garza de León," p. 2.

64. Craig H. Roell, "De León, Martín," *NHOT,* 2:571; Stewart, "De León, Patricia de la Garza," *NHOT,* 2:571–572.

65. A. B. J. Hammett, *The Empresario Don Martín de León: The Richest Man in Texas,* pp. 3, 4, 9; Paula Stewart, "De León, Patricia de la Garza," *NHOT,* 2:571–572; Janelle Scott, "Patricia de la Garza de León," January 8, 1982, manuscript, pp. 2–3, Special Collections, Texas Woman's University Library.

66. Hammett, *The Empresario,* pp. 6, 7, 26; Stewart, "De León, Patricia de la Garza," *NHOT,* 2:571–572; Scott, "Patricia de la Garza de León," p. 7.

67. Hammett, *The Empresario,* pp. 22–23; Scott, "Patricia de la Garza de León," p. 4.

68. Hammett, *The Empresario,* p. 7; Scott, "Patricia de la Garza de León," p. 4A.

69. Craig H. Roell, "De León's Colony," *NHOT,* 2:573–574; Stewart, "De León, Patricia de la Garza," *NHOT,* 2:571–572.

70. Roell, "De León's Colony," *NHOT,* 2:573–574; Scott, "Patricia de la Garza de León," p. 5; Victor Rose, *History of Victoria,* p. 11; Crimm, "Economic Impact of Hispanic Family Structure," pp. 3–4.

71. Roell, "De León's Colony," *NHOT,* 2:573–574; Stewart, "De León, Patricia de la Garza," *NHOT,* 2:571; Scott, "Patricia de la Garza de León," p. 6; *Victoria Sesquicentennial Scrapbook,* p. 5.

72. Scott, "Patricia de la Garza de León," pp. 6–8.

73. Ibid., pp. 6–7.

74. Roell, "De León's Colony," *NHOT,* 2:573; Roell, "De León, Martín," *NHOT,* 2:571.

75. Crimm, "Economic Impact of Hispanic Family Structure," p. 5. Crimm clarified the position of the de León family in a communication to the authors based on her research for her manuscript.

76. Hammett, *The Empresario,* pp. 54–55; 63–64; 66, 70; Crimm, "Economic Impact of Hispanic Family Structure," chap. 6, pp. 1–2.

CHAPTER TWO

1. Andrés Tijerina, *Tejanos and Texas under the Mexican Flag, 1821–1836,* p. 13.

2. Gilberto M. Hinojosa, *A Borderlands Town in Transition: Laredo, 1755–1870,* p. 19.

3. Abel G. Rubio, *Stolen Heritage: A Mexican-American's Rediscovery of His Family's Lost Land Grant,* pp. 232, 238. A. Carolina Castillo Crimm, work in progress (untitled), chap. 2, pp. 21, 25.

4. Jesús F. de la Teja and John Wheat, "Béxar: Profile of a Tejano Community, 1820–1832," in *Tejano Origins in Eighteenth-Century San Antonio,* ed. Gerald E. Poyo and Gilberto M. Hinojosa, p. 17.

5. Vicki Ruiz, *From out of the Shadows: Mexican Women in Twentieth-Century America,* p. 4; Cynthia E. Orozco, "Mexican-American Women," *New Handbook of Texas,* 4:680 (hereafter *NHOT*).

6. Ruiz, *From out of the Shadows,* p. 4; Orozco, "Mexican-American Women," *NHOT,* 4:680; Joe S. Graham, *El Rancho in South Texas: Continuity and Change from 1750,* pp. 25–26.

7. Graham, *El Rancho in South Texas,* p. 27.

8. Charles Ramsdell, *San Antonio: A Historical and Pictorial Guide,* rev. by Carmen Perry, p. 25.

9. Adán Benavides Jr., comp. and ed., *The Béxar Archives, 1717–1836: A Name Guide,* pp. xi–xiv. These documents reveal many instances of women's independent actions, including cases involving property and inheritance; marriage, divorce, and infidelity; physical assaults against women; enslaved women

of all ethnic groups; and requests for military pensions and for the return of property taken by the military.

10. Ibid., pp. 50, 64, 420, 447, 461, 865, 872, 901, 1030, 1056.

11. Orozco, "Mexican-American Women," *NHOT,* 4:680.

12. Hinojosa, *A Borderlands Town,* pp. 20–21, 35–36, 110.

13. Ibid.; Arnoldo De León, *Mexican Americans in Texas: A Brief History,* pp. 17, 26–27.

14. Jesús F. de la Teja, "Forgotten Founders: The Military Settlers of Eighteenth-Century San Antonio de Béxar," in *Tejano Origins,* ed. Poyo and Hinojosa, p. 32.

15. Hinojosa, *A Borderlands Town,* pp. 34–35, 46.

16. Ibid., p. 110.

17. The Criminal Code of Nacogdoches, 1783, cited in Francis E. Abernethy, "The Spanish on the Moral," *The Folklore of Texan Cultures,* ed. Francis E. Abernethy, p. 35.

18. Letter, "Cabildo to Governor Cabello," February 28, 1783, Bexar Archives.

19. Benavides, *Béxar Archives,* pp. 1080, 938, 417, 308, 2, 740, 927, 865, 184.

20. Teresa Palomo Acosta, excerpt from "In the territory of Bexar," typescript in the possession of the author.

21. Typed copy of the certified copy of the will executed by Rosa María de Hinojosa de Ballí in 1798, Reynosa, Tamaulipas, Mexico, in *Cameron County Deed Book X,* p. 113; Minnie Gilbert, "Texas's First Cattle Queen," in *Roots by the River,* ed. Valley By-Liners, p. 19.

22. Paula Stewart, "De León, Patricia de la Garza," *NHOT,* 2:571–572; Graham, *El Rancho in South Texas,* pp. 25, 28; Tijerina, *Tejanos and Texas under the Mexican Flag,* p. 121; De León, *Mexican Americans in Texas,* pp. 14–15; de la Teja and John Wheat, "Béxar," pp. 14–17; Timothy M. Matovina, *Tejano Religion and Ethnicity: San Antonio, 1821–1860,* p. 21. See Jeanette Rodríguez, *Our Lady of Guadalupe: Faith and Empowerment among Mexican-American Women,* for a discussion of the most important religious symbol of Mexico and the role that Our Lady of Guadalupe has played in the lives of Mexican origin women in the United States.

23. Stewart, "De León, Patricia de la Garza," *NHOT,* 2:571–572; De León, *Mexican Americans in Texas,* pp. 14–15; A. Carolina Castillo Crimm, "Economic Impact of Hispanic Family Structure," p. 13.

24. J. J. Cox, "Educational Efforts in San Fernando," *Texas Historical Association Quarterly* 6 (July 1902): 36–37, 43, 49.

25. Arnoldo De León, *The Tejano Community, 1836–1900,* pp. 6–7.

26. Jack Jackson, *Los Mesteños: Spanish Ranching in Texas, 1721–1821,* p. 225.

27. Orozco, "Mexican-American Women," *NHOT,* 4:680.

28. Donald E. Chipman, *Spanish Texas, 1519–1821,* pp. 155–156; Joan E.

Supplee, "San Xavier Missions," *NHOT,* 5:893–894; Ray Zirkel, "Zambrano, Juan José Manuel Vicente," *NHOT,* 6:1141; Elizabeth A. H. John, *Storms Brewed in Other Men's Worlds,* p. 291; Donald E. Chipman, "Rábago y Terán, Felipe de," *NHOT,* 5:399–400.

29. Benavides, *Béxar Archives,* pp. 383, 600; de la Teja and Wheat, "Bexar," p. 9; Jackson, *Los Mesteños,* pp. 131–133.

30. Benavides, *Béxar Archives,* pp. 244, 502, 599, 675, 844, 1078.

31. William C. Foster, *Spanish Expeditions into Texas, 1689–1768,* pp. 192–193; Chipman, *Spanish Texas,* p. 152.

32. Foster, *Spanish Expeditions,* p. 172.

33. Harold Schoen, "The Free Negro in the Republic of Texas, I," *Southwestern Historical Quarterly* 39, no. 4 (April 1936): 292, 298. Mary Ortero is an example of a free black mulatto with a Spanish surname.

34. Benavides, *Béxar Archives,* pp. 321, 440, 939, 881, 774, 202.

35. Tijerina, *Tejanos and Texas under the Mexican Flag,* p. 107; Ruthe Winegarten, *Black Texas Women: 150 Years of Trial and Triumph,* p. 3.

36. Doris E. Perlin, *Eight Bright Candles: Courageous Women of Mexico,* pp. 55–90. In her novel *Call No Man Master,* Tina Juárez writes of a mestiza, Carmen Rangel, who first supports the Spanish Crown but who, after witnessing the injustices endured by Indians, mestizos, and other people of color, first at the hands of the Spanish, then by whites in control of the newly independent Mexico, flees north to Texas with a young Anglo.

37. Jesús F. de la Teja, "Rebellion on the Frontier," in *Tejano Journey, 1770–1850,* ed. Gerald E. Poyo, pp. 24–25.

38. For Andrea Castañon Villanueva (Madam Candelaria) see Lisa Waller Rogers, *Angel of the Alamo: A True Story of Texas,* pp. 21–22; Matovina, *Tejano Religion,* p. 9; Crystal S. Ragsdale, *Women and Children of the Alamo,* p. 43; Donald Everett, *San Antonio: The Flavor of Its Past,* p. 26.

39. Jackson, *Los Mesteños,* pp. 544–555; Robert H. Thonhoff, "Arredondo, Joaquín de," *NHOT,* 1:255.

40. Benavides, *Béxar Archives,* pp. 413, 667, 1030, 1032.

41. Ibid., pp. 881, 520, 1001.

42. Andrés Tijerina, "Under the Mexican Flag," in *Tejano Journey,* ed. Poyo, pp. 33, 46–47.

43. Ruthe Winegarten telephone conversation with Gaylen Greaser, Texas General Land Office, Austin, June 12, 2000; Tijerina, *Tejanos and Texas under the Mexican Flag,* p. 107.

44. "Veramendi, Juan Martin de," *NHOT,* 6:722; Jane Dysart, "Mexican Women in San Antonio, 1830–1860: The Assimilation Process," *Western Historical Quarterly* 7, no. 4 (October 1976): 370.

45. De la Teja and Wheat, "Béxar," p. 20; *Women in Texas History 1976 Calendar.*

46. Paul D. Lack, *The Texas Revolutionary Experience: A Political and Social History, 1835–1836,* pp. 168, 185.

47. Orozco, "Mexican-American Women," *NHOT,* 4:680.

48. Adrian N. Anderson and Ralph A. Wooster, *Texas and Texans,* pp. 159–160. The only native-born Texans elected to the convention were five Tejanos. Two attended the convention (José Antonio Navarro and José Francisco Ruiz); the other three did not.

49. Stephen L. Hardin, "Efficient in the Cause," in *Tejano Journey,* ed. Poyo, p. 54.

50. Stewart, "De León, Patricia de la Garza," *NHOT,* 2:572; Crimm, "Economic Impact of Hispanic Family Structure," pp. 5–6; Crimm, work in progress (untitled), chap. 6, pp. 1–2.

51. Stewart, "De León, Patricia de la Garza," *NHOT,* 2:572. Crimm, "Economic Impact of Hispanic Family Structure." Crimm, work in progress (untitled), chap. 7, p. 33. Crimm notes that Fernando de León, one of Doña Patricia's sons, gave that land over to the church instead of to his sisters.

52. Craig H. Roell, "Benavides, Plácido," *NHOT,* 1:484; Hardin, "Efficient in the Cause," p. 55.

53. Lack, *The Texas Revolutionary Experience,* p. 205; Rubio, *Stolen Heritage,* pp. 242–243.

54. Crystal Sasse Ragsdale, "Alsbury, Juana Gertrudis Navarro," *NHOT,* 1:131–132; Rogers, *Angel of the Alamo,* pp. 43–45; George O. Coalson, "Villanueva, Andrea Castañón," *NHOT,* 6:752.

55. Cynthia E. Orozco, "Salazar de Esparza, Ana," *NHOT,* 5:774–775; George O. Coalson, "Alavez, Francita," *NHOT,* 1:91; Perlin, *Eight Bright Candles,* pp. 111, 121. In her chapter on Francisca Alavez, Perlin notes that the correct spelling of Alavez's last name has not been definitely determined. Surnames she has been given include Alinez, Alavez, Alevesco, and Alvárez.

56. Hedda Garza, *Latinas: Hispanic Women in the United States,* p. 23.

CHAPTER THREE

1. Teresa Palomo Acosta, *Nile & Other Poems,* pp. 90–92.

2. Yolanda Chávez Leyva, "Crossing Bridges/Burning Bridges," *La Voz de Esperanza,* February 2000, p. 3.

3. Jovita González de Mireles, "Memoirs," pp. 8–9, Mireles Papers, Bell Library, Texas A&M University–Corpus Christi, as cited in Leticia M. Garza-Falcón, *Gente Decente: A Borderlands Response to the Rhetoric of Dominance,* p. 107.

4. Neil Foley, *The White Scourge: Mexicans, Blacks, and Poor Whites in Texas Cotton Culture,* p. 21, citing *New York Herald,* January 30, 1848.

5. Arnoldo De León, *Mexican Americans in Texas: A Brief History,* p. 37.

6. Armando Alonzo, *Tejano Legacy: Rancheros and Settlers in South Texas, 1734–1900,* pp. 128–129, 132.

7. Rena Maverick Green, ed., *Memoirs of Mary A. Maverick,* p. 55; Timothy M. Matovina, *Tejano Religion and Ethnicity: San Antonio, 1821–1860,* pp. 33–

35, 51; David Montejano, *Anglos and Mexicans in the Making of Texas, 1836–1986,* pp. 27, 29; Stephen L. Hardin, "Efficient in the Cause," in *Tejano Journey, 1770–1850,* ed. Gerald E. Poyo, p. 55.

8. Joe S. Graham, *El Rancho in South Texas,* p. 37; De León, *Mexican Americans in Texas,* p. 39; Andrés Tijerina, *Tejano Empire: Life on the South Texas Ranchos,* p. 122. Tijerina states that most historians agree that after the 1880s Tejano families had lost most of "their ancestral lands."

9. Clotilde P. García, "Garza Falcón, María Gertrudis de la," *New Handbook of Texas,* 3:111 (hereafter *NHOT*).

10. John Ashton and Edgar P. Sneed, "King Ranch," *NHOT,* 3:1111–1112; Graham, *El Rancho in South Texas,* p. 39; Montejano, *Anglos and Mexicans,* pp. 60–61, 65–66, 79–81; Tom Lea, *The King Ranch,* vol. 1, pp. 99–105, 123; Ruthe Winegarten, *Governor Ann Richards & Other Texas Women: From Indians to Astronauts,* p. 35.

11. Helen Simons and Cathryn A. Hoyt, *A Guide to Hispanic Texas,* p. 170. Fort Davis was established in 1854. Ramírez and Faver probably supplied the U.S. soldiers with food after the Civil War.

12. Manuel Guerra, "Alberca de Arriba Ranch," *NHOT,* 1:93–94; Agnes G. Grimm, "Pérez, Pablo," *NHOT,* 5:150.

13. Alonzo, *Tejano Legacy,* pp. 114, 186.

14. De León, *Mexican Americans in Texas,* p. 40.

15. Alicia A. Garza, "Young, Salomé Ballí," *NHOT,* 6:1128.

16. Cynthia E. Orozco, "Kenedy, Petra Vela de Vidal," *NHOT,* 3:1065; A. Carolina Castillo Crimm, "The Economic Impact of Hispanic Family Structure: The Families of Petra Vela de Vidal Kenedy and Patricia de la Garza de León," pp. 8–10.

17. Orozco, "Kenedy, Petra Vela de Vidal," *NHOT,* 3:1065; Crimm, "Economic Impact of Hispanic Family Structure," p. 10.

18. Jane Clements Monday and Betty Bailey Colley, *Voices from the Wild Horse Desert: The Vaquero Families of the King and Kenedy Ranches,* p. 10; Crimm, "Economic Impact of Hispanic Family Structure," p. 13.

19. Crimm, "Economic Impact of Hispanic Family Structure," pp. 13–14; Orozco, "Kenedy, Petra Vela de Vidal," *NHOT,* 3:1065. Today Los Laureles is part of the King Ranch.

20. Crimm, "Economic Impact of Hispanic Family Structure," p. 14; Orozco, "Kenedy, Petra Vela de Vidal," *NHOT,* 3:1065.

21. Crimm, "Economic Impact of Hispanic Family Structure," p. 14; Orozco, "Kenedy, Petra Vela de Vidal," *NHOT,* 3:1065.

22. Cynthia E. Orozco, "Barnard, Juana Josefina Cavasos," *NHOT,* 1:385. Juana Cavasos's grandfather received the largest Spanish land grant in Texas. Pearl Andrus, *Juana, A Spanish Girl in Central Texas,* p. vii.

23. Montejano, *Anglos and Mexicans,* pp. 34–35.

24. Timothy M. Matovina, "Between Two Worlds," in *Tejano Journey,* ed.

Poyo, p. 80; Jane Dysart, "Mexican Women in San Antonio, 1830–1860: The Assimilation Process," *Western Historical Quarterly* 7, no. 4 (October 1976): 369–371; De León, *Mexican Americans in Texas,* p. 40.

25. Kenneth Wheeler, *To Wear a City's Crown: The Beginnings of Urban Growth in Texas, 1836–1865,* p. 41.

26. Matovina, "Between Two Worlds," in *Tejano Journey,* ed. Poyo, p. 80; Dysart, "Mexican Women in San Antonio," pp. 369–371; Matovina, *Tejano Religion and Ethnicity,* pp. 38, 50.

27. Dysart, "Mexican Women in San Antonio," pp. 372–374, 374 nn. 40, 41.

28. Matovina, *Tejano Religion and Ethnicity,* p. 62.

29. Green, ed., *Memoirs of Mary A. Maverick,* p. 54.

30. Teresa Griffin Vielé, *Following the Drum: A Glimpse of Frontier Life,* p. 111.

31. Frederick Law Olmsted, *Journey through Texas,* p. 79.

32. Antonia I. Castañeda, "The Political Economy of Nineteenth Century Stereotypes of Californianas," in *Regions of La Raza,* ed. Antonio Ríos-Bustamante, p. 189.

33. Vicki Ruiz, *From out of the Shadows: Mexican Women in Twentieth-Century America,* p. 5; Arnoldo De León, *The Tejano Community, 1836–1900,* p. 22.

34. Dysart, "Mexican Women in San Antonio," p. 367; Wheeler, *To Wear a City's Crown,* p. 42, citing Ferdinand Roemer's quotation on nude bathing in Texas, pp. 124–125.

35. Dysart, "Mexican Women in San Antonio," p. 367; Wheeler, *To Wear A City's Crown,* pp. 40–41; De León, *The Tejano Community,* p. 13.

36. Castañeda, "The Political Economy of Nineteenth Century Stereotypes," pp. 189–204; Arnoldo De León, *They Called Them Greasers: Anglo Attitudes toward Mexicans in Texas, 1821–1900,* pp. x, 9–10, 39–44.

37. Jovita González and Eve Raleigh, *Caballero: A Historical Novel,* p. 22.

38. David M. Pletcher, "Treaty of Guadalupe Hidalgo," *NHOT,* 6:558–559; Armando C. Alonzo, "Mexican-American Land Grant Adjudication," *NHOT,* 4:656–659.

39. Leyva, "Crossing Bridges/Burning Bridges," *La Voz de Esperanza,* March 2000, pp. 10–11; Kelly M. Stott, "The Intent and Effect of the [1848] Texas Married Women's Separate Property Law." From the 1930s to the 1950s Francisca Esparza, heir to a land grant in Webb County, organized the Alliance of Land Grants to help get land rights restored to original owners who were supposed to have been protected under the Treaty of Guadalupe Hidalgo. See Carlos M. Larralde, "Esparza, Francisca Reyes," *NHOT,* 2:893.

40. De León, *The Tejano Community,* pp. 17, 64, 77.

41. Gilberto M. Hinojosa, *A Borderlands Town in Transition: Laredo, 1755–1870,* pp. 75–76, 78.

42. The article was in the April 20, 1861 "*Corpus Christi Ranchero,*" as 'Let-

ter from Carrizo, April 12,' 1861,'" cited in Arnoldo De León, *Apuntes Tejanos,* vol. 2, p. 114.

43. Miguel González Quiroga, "Mexicanos in Texas during the Civil War," in *Mexican Americans in Texas History,* ed. Emilio Zamora Jr., Cynthia Orozco, and Rodolfo Rocha, pp. 54–55; Robert A. Calvert and Arnoldo De León, *The History of Texas,* p. 125; Jerry Thompson, "Cortina, Juan Nepomuceno," *NHOT,* 2:343–344; Jerry Thompson, "Benavides, Santos," *NHOT,* 1:485.

44. Orozco, "Kenedy, Petra Vela de Vidal," *NHOT,* 3:1065; Quiroga, "Mexicanos in Texas during the Civil War," pp. 57–61.

45. Rachel Bluntzer Hebert, *The Forgotten Colony: San Patricio de Hibernia,* p. 425.

46. Marylyn Underwood, "Rodríguez, Josefa [Chipita]," *NHOT,* 5:654–655; Marylyn Underwood, "The Ghost of Chipita," in *Legendary Ladies of Texas,* ed. Francis Edward Abernethy, p. 52.

47. Underwood, "The Ghost of Chipita," in *Legendary Ladies of Texas,* ed. Abernethy, p. 52.

48. Ibid., pp. 51–56; Underwood, "Rodríguez, Josefa [Chipita]," *NHOT,* 5:654–655; Hebert, *The Forgotten Colony,* pp. 425–426; Rachel Bluntzer Hebert, *Shadows on the Nueces: The Saga of Chipita Rodriguez;* De León, *They Called Them Greasers,* pp. 80–81. De León says that as a young woman, Chipita Rodríguez took up with a passing cowboy and bore a son (possibly Juan Silvera). The father deserted her, taking the infant with him. In 1863, when a young man looking like the father stayed in her inn with John Savage, later killed, Chipita thought the murderer was her son. To protect him, she wrapped the body in burlap and carried it to the river with the help of Juan Silvera.

49. Underwood, "Rodríguez, Josefa [Chipita]," *NHOT,* 5:654–655; Ruel McDaniel, "The Day They Hanged Chipita," *Texas Parade,* September 1962, pp. 18–19.

50. Underwood, "Rodríguez, Josefa [Chipita]," *NHOT,* 5:654–655. Jane Elkins, a Dallas slave, was the first woman legally hanged in Texas, executed on May 27, 1853, for having murdered Mr. Wisdom, her employer. Some historians think he had sexually assaulted her. She retaliated by splitting his head open with an ax while he slept. Charged with murder, she pleaded not guilty, was convicted by an all-white male jury, and was hanged. Winegarten, *Black Texas Women: 150 Years of Trial and Triumph,* p. 32. In 1998, Karla Faye Tucker, an Anglo, became the third Texas woman legally executed for a murder. She was convicted of the 1983 pickax murder of Jerry Lynn Dean.

51. Leyva, "Crossing Bridges/Burning Bridges," *La Voz de Esperanza,* February 2000, p. 6.

52. De León, *They Called Them Greasers,* pp. 80–81.

53. De León, *Mexican Americans in Texas,* p. 39.

54. Gloria Candelaria Marsh, "Moya, Juan," *NHOT,* 4:873–874.

55. Abel Rubio, *Stolen Heritage: A Mexican-American's Rediscovery of His Family's Lost Land Grant,* p. 72.

56. Rubio, *Stolen Heritage,* pp. 143–147. Other women, notably Lucy González Parsons of Johnson County, became radicalized as a result of witnessing extreme cases of racist behavior in Texas. Parsons's racial heritage remains a mystery. Some have claimed that she was of black slave origin, while others have noted that she may have been of Mexican and African American heritage. Parsons moved to Chicago in 1873 after she apparently married Albert Parsons, a white Radical Republican who supported black suffrage. Associated with the anarchists of Haymarket Square, Albert Parsons was hanged in 1886 on charges of conspiracy to commit murder during the Haymarket Square demonstrations for the eight-hour workday. His guilt has been widely disputed. Lucy González Parsons later became a highly regarded labor leader. She was a founder of the Industrial Workers of America. For an insightful account of Parsons's life, see Carolyn Ashbaugh's *Lucy Parsons, American Revolutionary.*

57. *Corpus Christi Weekly Caller,* May 26, 1899, cited in De León, *Apuntes Tejanos,* vol. 2, p. 97.

58. Teresa Palomo Acosta, "*In re Ricardo Rodríguez,*" *NHOT,* 3:856.

59. Arnoldo De León, *San Angelenos: Mexican Americans in San Angelo, Texas,* pp. 14–16, 23.

60. Hortense Warner Ward, "Ear Marks," in *From Hell to Breakfast,* ed. Mody Boatright, pp. 115–116.

61. Florence C. Gould and Patricia N. Pando, *Claiming Their Land: Women Homesteaders in Texas,* pp. 17, 56, 59, 63, 68, 72, 73, 75, 77, 81–84, 87–88, 91–92, 94, 97–98. Five Spanish-surnamed women also filed claims from 1845 to 1869. Gould and Pando obtained their information from the General Land Office in Austin.

62. Simons and Hoyt, *A Guide to Hispanic Texas,* p. 47.

63. De León, *The Tejano Community,* p. 82.

64. H. Allen Anderson, "Pastores," *NHOT,* 5:84–86; Myra Hargrave McIlvain, *Shadows on the Land: An Anthology of Texas Historical Marker Stories,* p. 34; H. Allen Anderson, "Romero, Casimero," *NHOT,* 5:671–672; De León, *Mexican Americans in Texas,* p. 59.

65. Foley, *The White Scourge,* p. 28; Rubio, *Stolen Heritage,* pp. 243–244.

66. Alonzo, *Tejano Legacy,* pp. 158–159; Alonzo, "Mexican-American Land Grant Adjudication," *NHOT,* 4:656–658.

67. The editor of *La Crónica,* as cited in Julie Leininger Pycior, *LBJ and Mexican Americans: The Paradox of Power,* p. 8. The editor that Pycior quotes is likely Nicasio Idar, who was publisher and editor of *La Crónica* from 1910 until his death in 1914.

68. Alonzo, *Tejano Legacy,* p. 12.

69. De León, *The Tejano Community,* p. 233.

70. Montejano, *Anglos and Mexicans,* pp. 56–57, 73–74, 79, 82.

71. De León, *Mexican Americans in Texas,* p. 61; Cynthia Orozco, "Mexican-American Women," *NHOT,* 4:681; photo caption for goat camp at La Mota Ranch, no. 82-416, Institute of Texan Cultures, University of Texas at San Antonio.

72. De León, *The Tejano Community,* p. 65.

73. Ibid., pp. 65–66, 77.

74. Leyva, "Crossing Bridges/Burning Bridges," *La Voz de Esperanza,* March 2000, p. 11.

75. Arnoldo De León, *Ethnicity in the Sunbelt: A History of Mexican Americans in Houston,* p. 6.

76. *San Antonio Express,* February 4, 1883, dateline El Paso, January 31, cited in De León, *Apuntes Tejanos,* vol. 1, p. 48.

77. Mario T. García, *Desert Immigrants: The Mexicans of El Paso, 1880–1920,* pp. 4, 38, 74–79; Winegarten, *Black Texas Women,* p. 48.

78. De León, *The Tejano Community,* pp. 84–85, 96; also see Teresa Palomo Acosta, "Losoya Taylor, Paula," *NHOT,* 4:297.

79. Alonzo, *Tejano Legacy,* p. 102.

80. Information sheet on Caterina Flores de Guerrero from the Institute of Texan Cultures, University of Texas at San Antonio, undated; Reynaldo J. Esparza, "Esparza, Enrique," *NHOT,* 2:893; Sister Josephine Kennelly, C.C.V.I., "Sisters of Charity of the Incarnate Word, San Antonio," *NHOT,* 5:1065.

81. Orozco, "Kenedy, Petra Vela de Vidal," *NHOT,* 3:1065.

82. Teresa Palomo Acosta, "Flores de Barker, Josefa Augustina," *NHOT,* 2:1038; Cynthia E. Orozco, "Garza, José Antonio de la," *NHOT,* 3:107.

83. Orozco, "Kenedy, Petra Vela de Vidal," *NHOT,* 3:1065.

84. Simons and Hoyt, *A Guide to Hispanic Texas,* p. 144; E. E. Mireles, "Doña Paula Losoya, Great Pioneer of Del Rio," *LULAC News,* March 1939, pp. 13–14.

85. L. Robert Ables, "The Second Battle for the Alamo," *Southwestern Historical Quarterly* 70, no. 3 (January 1967): 372–413. Ables describes in great detail the struggle in which Adina De Zavala engaged to protect the historically most significant portion of the Alamo. Ables also notes that, unlike her grandfather, the early statesman Lorenzo de Zavala, Adina De Zavala and the rest of the family eventually capitalized their surname.

86. De León, *Apuntes Tejanos,* vol. 2, p. 65.

87. De León, *The Tejano Community,* pp. 195–196; Roberto R. Calderón, "Unión, Paz y Trabajo: Laredo's Mexican Mutual Aid Societies, 1890s," in *Mexican Americans in Texas History,* ed. Zamora, Orozco, and Rocha, p. 68; Cynthia E. Orozco, "Beyond Machismo, La Familia, and Ladies Auxiliaries: A Historiography of Mexican-Origin Women's Participation in Voluntary Associations and Politics in the United States, 1870–1990," in *Renato Rosaldo Lec-*

ture Series Monograph, ed. Thomas Gelsinon, vol. 10, pp. 37–77; Orozco, "Mexican-American Women," *NHOT,* 4:681.

CHAPTER FOUR

1. Arnoldo De León, *The Tejano Community, 1836–1900,* pp. 36, 37, 43, 51, 88.

2. Joe R. Baulch, "Garza War," *New Handbook of Texas,* 3:113 (hereafter *NHOT*).

3. Frances Mayhugh Holden, "Urrea, Teresa," *NHOT,* 6:678–679; Alfredo Mirandé and Evangelina Enríquez, *La Chicana: The Mexican-American Woman,* p. 79.

4. Holden, "Urrea, Teresa," *NHOT,* 6:678–679.

5. Ibid.

6. *La Crónica,* April 9, 1910, p. 3. *La Crónica* notes that "Surge" was reprinted from *Aurora,* a publication that Sara Estela Ramírez published.

7. Emma Pérez, *The Decolonial Imaginary: Writing Chicanas into History,* pp. 59, 65. Teresa Palomo Acosta, "Partido Liberal Mexicano," *NHOT,* 5:77–78.

8. Acosta, "Partido Liberal Mexicano," *NHOT,* 5:78.

9. Emilio Zamora, "Sara Estela Ramírez: Una Rosa Roja en el Movimiento," in *Mexican American Women in the United States: Struggles Past and Present,* ed. Magdalena Mora and Adelaida R. Del Castillo, pp. 163–166. Emilio Zamora was one of the first historians to write about Sara Estela Ramírez's role with the PLM, and about her work as an essayist and poet.

10. Ibid.

11. Ibid., p. 165.

12. Mirandé and Enríquez, *La Chicana,* p. 204. Mirandé and Enríquez do not state whether or not Ramírez's colleagues lived, as she did, in Laredo. Like many others affiliated with the Mexican Revolution, these women probably lived in, or at least passed through, a variety of Tejano communities in South Texas.

13. Ibid., pp. 204–206.

14. Ibid.

15. Ibid.

16. Zamora, "Sara Estela Ramírez," p. 165.

17. Leonor Villegas de Magnón, *The Rebel: Leonor Villegas de Magnón,* ed. Clara Lomas, p. 118.

18. Claire Keefe in conversation with Ruthe Winegarten, June 24, 1981.

19. Clara Lomas, ed., Introduction to *The Rebel: Leonor Villegas de Magnón,* p. xvii; Nancy Baker Jones, "Villegas de Magnón, Leonor," *NHOT,* 6:753–754.

20. Lomas, Introduction to *The Rebel,* pp. xix, xxi, xxii.

21. Ibid., pp. xxiii, xxiv.

22. Jones, "Villegas de Magnón, Leonor," *NHOT,* 6:753–754.

23. Ibid.

24. Juan Gómez-Quiñones, *Sembradores, Ricardo Flores Magón and the Partido Liberal Mexicano: A Eulogy and Critique,* pp. 76–77 n. 60. Gómez-Quiñones cites the statement that women associated with Regeneración made in the publication *Regeneración* on February 25, 1911, in support of women's equality.

25. *San Antonio Light and Gazette,* August 18, 1909.

26. Pérez, *The Decolonial Imaginary,* p. 69.

27. W. Dirk Raat, *Revoltosos: Mexico's Rebels in the United States, 1903–1923,* p. 32. Martha P. Cotera, *Diosa y Hembra: The History and Heritage of Chicanas in the U.S.,* p. 68. Pérez, *The Decolonial Imaginary,* p. 68. Pérez notes that both sisters founded *El Obrero.*

28. Gómez-Quiñones, *Sembradores,* p. 76, n. 60. Gómez-Quiñones notes that Teresa Villarreal was president of Regeneración. Other women served as officers. The last name of Teresa and Andrea is spelled variously by scholars as "Villarreal" and "Villareal." We have used the former.

29. Gómez-Quiñones, *Sembradores,* p. 36.

30. Ibid., pp. 81–82 n. 122.

31. Manuel Gamio, "Sra. Flores de Andrade," in *The Life Story of the Mexican Immigrant,* p. 33.

32. Teresa Palomo Acosta, "Flores de Andrade," *NHOT,* 2:1038.

33. Ibid.

34. See Gamio's interview, "Sra. Flores de Andrade," pp. 29–36; Raat, *Revoltosos,* p. 33; Mirandé and Enríquez, *La Chicana,* p. 205. Mirandé and Enríquez note that Elisa Acuña y Rossetti was a cofounder of the group. They do not note the name of Flores de Andrade or others as cofounders; Raat, *Revoltosos,* p. 33; Acosta, "Flores de Andrade," *NHOT,* 2:1038.

35. Vicki L. Ruíz, *From out of the Shadows: Mexican Women in Twentieth-Century America,* pp. 12–13.

36. Yolanda Chávez Leyva, "I Go to Fight for Social Justice: Children as Revolutionaries in the Mexican Revolution, 1910–1920," *Peace and Change,* October 1998, p. 426.

37. Julie L. Pycior, *LBJ and Mexican Americans: The Paradox of Power,* p. 9.

38. Elizabeth Salas, *Soldaderas in the Mexican Military: Myth and History,* pp. 53, 54.

39. Ibid., pp. 53, 57–58.

40. Ibid., pp. 58–59.

41. José E. Limón, "El Primer Congreso Mexicanista de 1911: A Precursor to Contemporary Chicanismo," *Aztlan* 5 (spring and fall, 1974): 85–106. Women were involved in the Congreso Mexicanista, which addressed several issues of concern: civil rights, education, and culture. The gathering occurred during the Diez y Seis de Septiembre celebration and brought together many organizations. Workshops on social oppression and the poor economic situa-

tion of Texas Mexicans were held. José E. Limón's discussion of the Congreso Mexicanista is one of the in-depth treatments of the meeting. Also see Zamora, "Sara Estela Ramírez," p. 164. Zamora notes that the *congreso* was held in Laredo, a city where Mexican Americans exercised enough political clout to present a show of force against their exploitation by Anglo Texans. Teresa Palomo Acosta, "Congreso Mexicanista," *NHOT,* 2:267; María-Cristina García, "Liga Femenil Mexicanista," *NHOT,* 4:194.

42. See Limón, "El Primer Congreso Mexicanista de 1911"; Zamora, "Sara Estela Ramírez," p. 164; Acosta, "Congreso Mexicanista," *NHOT,* 2:267; García, "Liga Femenil Mexicanista," *NHOT,* 4:194; Jovita López, "Jovita Idar de Juárez," unpublished essay, September 1980, Woman's Collection, Texas Woman's University.

43. López, "Jovita Idar de Juárez." López notes in her essay that Ojuelos was a town in Texas. Nancy Baker Jones, "Idar, Jovita," *NHOT,* 3:814–815.

44. Jones, "Idar, Jovita," *NHOT,* 3:815.

45. López, "Jovita Idar de Juárez."

46. John R. Ross, "Lynching," *NHOT,* 4:347; Don M. Coerver, "Plan of San Diego," *NHOT,* 5:228; Gilberto M. Hinojosa, *A Borderlands Town in Transition: Laredo, 1755–1870,* p. 121. Hinojosa cites the work of Américo Paredes (*With His Pistol in His Hand: A Border Ballad and Its Hero,* p. 26) and Walter Prescott Webb (*The Texas Rangers: A Century of Frontier Defense,* pp. 484–486) in noting the estimated number of Tejanos who were killed during the uprising.

47. Ross, "Lynching," *NHOT,* 4:347.

48. Cynthia E. Orozco, "Cortez Lira, Gregorio," *NHOT,* 2:342–343; also see Américo Paredes's classic *With His Pistol in His Hand: A Border Ballad and Its Hero* for a full account of Cortez.

49. Orozco, " Cortez Lira, Gregorio," *NHOT,* 2:342.

50. Ibid., pp. 342–343.

51. Ruíz, *From out of the Shadows,* p. 13.

52. Julie L. Pycior, "Mexican-American Organizations," *NHOT,* 4:660–662. Also refer to Pycior's "Sociedades Mutualistas," *NHOT,* 5:1132–1133, and Pycior's "La Raza Organizes: Mexican American Life in San Antonio, 1915–1930, as Reflected in Mutualista Activities."

53. Pycior, "Mexican-American Organizations," *NHOT,* 4:660.

54. Ibid; Teresa Palomo Acosta, "Alianza Hispano-Americana," *NHOT,* 1:104.

55. Cynthia E. Orozco, "Hernández, María L. de," *NHOT,* 3:572.

56. Ibid.

57. Ibid., pp. 572–573.

58. Cynthia E. Orozco, "League of United Latin American Citizens," *NHOT,* 4:129–131.

59. Cynthia E. Orozco, "Ladies LULAC," *NHOT,* 4:1–2.

60. Ibid.

61. Alice Dickerson Montemayor, "Son muy hombres(?)," *LULAC News,* March 1938, p. 13.

62. Cynthia E. Orozco, "Montemayor, Alice Dickerson," *NHOT,* 4:798; Cynthia E. Orozco, "Bernardo F. Garza," *NHOT,* 3:105; Montemayor, "Son muy hombres(?)," pp. 11–13.

63. Orozco, "Montemayor, Alice Dickerson," *NHOT,* 4:798.

64. Cynthia E. Orozco, "Machuca, Esther Nieto," *NHOT,* 4:410.

65. Ibid.

66. Jovita González, "America Invades the Border Towns," *Southwest Review* 15, no. 4 (summer 1930): 477.

67. Ibid.

68. Jovita González, "Jovita González: Early Life and Education," in *Dew on the Thorn,* ed. José E. Limón, pp. ix–xiii. Jovita González received her master's degree on that date, according to information provided on November 19, 2001, by the Office of the Registrar, Student Records, University of Texas at Austin.

69. Leticia Garza-Falcón, *Gente Decente: A Borderlands Response to the Rhetoric of Dominance,* pp. 77–78; Guadalupe San Miguel Jr., *"Let All of Them Take Heed": Mexican Americans and the Campaign for Educational Equality in Texas, 1910–1981,* pp. 78–81.

CHAPTER FIVE

1. Douglas E. Foley et al., *From Peones to Politicos: Class and Ethnicity in a South Texas Town, 1900–1987,* p. 56.

2. Ibid., p. 54.

3. Ibid., p. 55.

4. Ibid.

5. Ibid., p. 59.

6. Julie L. Pycior, *LBJ and Mexican Americans: The Paradox of Power,* p. 8. Pycior quotes the editor of *La Crónica,* the important Spanish language newspaper owned by the Idar family of Laredo. David Montejano, *Anglos and Mexicans in the Making of Texas: 1836–1986,* p. 114; Arnoldo De León, "Mexican Americans," *New Handbook of Texas,* 4:666 (hereafter *NHOT*).

7. Sabina Palomo Acosta, interview by Teresa Palomo Acosta, tape recording, McGregor, Texas, November 14, 1999; Juanita Palomo Campos, interview by Teresa Palomo Acosta, tape recording, Moody, Texas, March 18, 2000; Arnoldo De León, *Mexican Americans in Texas: A Brief History,* pp. 65–66.

8. Sabina Palomo Acosta, interview, November 14, 1999; De León, *Mexican Americans in Texas,* p. 69; J. B. Smith, "Hispanics' Local Clout May Grow," *Waco Tribune-Herald,* March 18, 2001, pp. 1A, 6A. The newspaper reported that since 1990 the numbers of Hispanics in McLennan County had

grown by 62 percent. The figures the newspaper cited were based on the 2000 U.S. Census.

9. Montejano, *Anglos and Mexicans,* p. 114.

10. Pycior, *LBJ and Mexican Americans,* p. 9.

11. David M. Vigness and Mark Odintz, "Rio Grande Valley," *NHOT,* 5:588–589.

12. Rebecca Sharpless, *Fertile Ground, Narrow Choices: Women on Texas Cotton Farms, 1900–1940,* p. 183.

13. Sabina Palomo Acosta, interview, November 14, 1999.

14. De León, *Mexican Americans in Texas,* p. 79. Sharpless, *Fertile Ground, Narrow Choices,* p. 15. Sharpless notes that Mexican immigrants gradually moved into Central Texas counties from the Rio Grande Valley. By 1920 they were 4.1 percent of the permanent residents of Williamson County.

15. Andrés A. Tijerina, *History of Mexican Americans in Lubbock County, Texas,* pp. 21, 38. Tijerina quotes the *Lubbock Evening Journal,* July 29, 1939, p. 2, in reporting on the percentage of women working in Lubbock County's cotton fields. Also refer to Yolanda García Romero, "From Rebels to Immigrants to Chicanas: Hispanic Women in Lubbock County," pp. 67–68, 70–71, 73. Romero discusses the experiences of Tejanas who settled in Lubbock County. She also includes information on their reliance on home remedies similar to those used by Tejanas in Central Texas, whose lives are discussed in this chapter.

16. Sabina Palomo Acosta, interview, November 14, 1999; Ruth Alice Allen, *The Labor of Women in the Production of Cotton,* p. 235. Allen includes two photographs of Mexican field workers en route to work in the agricultural fields. Allen notes about one of the photographs: "A group of Mexican casuals are cooking breakfast on the highway."

17. Pycior, *LBJ and Mexican Americans,* pp. 8–9; Neil Foley, *The White Scourge: Mexicans, Blacks, and Poor Whites in Texas Cotton Culture,* pp. 36, 118. Foley states that Sabina Palomo Acosta and her family once worked on the Taft Ranch.

18. Roberto R. Calderón and Emilio Zamora, "Manuela Solis Sager and Emma Tenayuca: A Tribute," in *Chicana Voices: Intersections of Class, Race, and Gender,* ed. Teresa Córdova et al., p. 32; John W. Stanford, "In Memoriam: Manuela S. Sager, 1912–1996," *La Voz de Esperanza,* June 1996, p. 3.

19. Pycior, *LBJ and Mexican Americans,* pp. 9–10.

20. Ibid., *LBJ and Mexican Americans,* p. 10.

21. Lewis Gould, "Progressive Era," *NHOT,* 5:347–354. Gould notes the growing importance of cotton to the state's economy; also refer to the work of Neil Foley in *The White Scourge.* Pycior, *LBJ and Mexican Americans,* p. 10.

22. Pycior, *LBJ and Mexican Americans,* p. 16.

23. Foley, *The White Scourge,* pp. 42–43.

24. Ben H. Procter, "Great Depression," *NHOT,* 3:301–303.

25. Pycior, *LBJ and Mexican Americans,* p. 30.

26. Ibid., pp. 31–32.

27. Sabina Palomo Acosta, interview, November 20, 1999.

28. Allen, *The Labor of Women,* pp. 20, 30. Allen's study also included black and white women. For our purposes, we have focused solely on Mexican origin women.

29. Allen, *The Labor of Women,* pp. 274–275. See Foley, *The White Scourge,* photograph no. 3, following p. 96. Foley states that owning a vehicle provided Mexicans the opportunity to find work "at competitive wages."

30. Allen, *The Labor of Women,* p. 234.

31. Ibid., p. 275. Lucia Alderete Anaya, interviews by Teresa Palomo Acosta, tape recordings, McGregor, Texas, October 1, October 8, October 15, 1999; Sabina Palomo Acosta, interviews, November 14, November 20, November 25, 1999; María Quiroz de León, interview by Teresa Palomo Acosta, tape recording, McGregor, Texas, March 8, 2000; Campos, interview; Sharpless, *Fertile Ground, Narrow Choices,* p. 202.

32. Sabina Palomo Acosta, interview, November 14, 1999; Allen, *The Labor of Women,* p. 230.

33. Sabina Palomo Acosta, interview, November 14, 1999. Sharpless, *Fertile Ground, Narrow Choices,* p. 27. Sharpless notes that some Tejanas arrived in Central Texas as the brides of men who had previously migrated to Central Texas and found work.

34. Anaya, interview, October 1, 1999.

35. Ibid. Acosta interview, November 14, 1999.

36. Anaya, interviews, October 1, October 8, 1999.

37. Campos, interview; Allen, *The Labor of Women,* p. 233. Allen states that the "modal group" of Mexican women she interviewed picked in the range of 100 to 150 pounds of cotton per day.

38. Anaya, interview, October 1, 1999; Sabina Palomo Acosta, interview, November 14, 1999; Sabina Palomo Acosta, in conversation with Teresa Palomo Acosta, McGregor, Texas, July 2000.

39. Sabina Palomo Acosta, interview, November 14, 1999; Sharpless, *Fertile Ground, Narrow Choices,* p. 93. Sharpless notes that in the southern blacklands, nearly one-third of Mexican families had to draw all of their water, for drinking and cleaning alike, from tanks used by "mules, cows, and chickens."

40. Anaya, interview, October 8, 1999.

41. Sabina Palomo Acosta, interviews, November 14, November 20, 1999; Foley, *The White Scourge,* p. 147.

42. Anaya, interviews, October 1, October 8, 1999.

43. Ibid.

44. Quiroz de León, interview.

45. Sabina Palomo Acosta, conversation with Teresa Palomo Acosta, McGregor, Texas, July 2000.

46. Anaya, interview, October 8, 1999.

47. Cynthia E. Orozco, "Mexican-American Women," *NHOT,* 4:680.

48. Anaya, interview, October 1, 1999; Sabina Palomo Acosta, interview, November 14, 1999.

49. Anaya, interview, October 8, 1999; Quiroz de León, interview; Campos, interview.

50. Anaya, interview, October 8, 1999; Sabina Palomo Acosta, interview, November 14, 1999; Quiroz de León, interview.

51. Anaya, interview, October 8, 1999. Anaya demonstrated her ability on the harmonica to the interviewer.

52. Ibid.

53. Anaya, interview, October 8, 1999; Sabina Palomo Acosta, interview, November 14, 1999.

54. Sabina Palomo Acosta, interview, November 20, 1999.

55. Anaya, interview, October 8, 1999; Sabina Palomo Acosta, interview, November 14, 1999.

56. Sabina Palomo Acosta, interview, November 14, 1999.

57. Ibid.

58. Anaya, interview, October 8, 1999.

59. Ibid.

60. Ibid.

61. Ibid. Sharpless, *Fertile Ground, Narrow Choices,* p. 53. Sharpless points out that Mexican women often grew *hierba buena* (mint), *hierba anís* (anise), and *ruda* (rue) in their gardens.

62. Anaya, interview, October 8, 1999. Also, for a good overview of home remedies, see Joe S. Graham, "Folk Medicine," *NHOT,* 2:1061–1063.

63. Sabina Palomo Acosta, interview, November 20, 1999. Acosta recalled that some women she knew had no one assist them in childbirth. Quiroz de León, interview; Sharpless, *Fertile Ground, Narrow Choices,* pp. 44–45. Sharpless writes, "While three-quarters of Anglo women used physicians to attend their births by the late 1920s, more than half of the African American and Mexican women employed midwives, and numerous women from each group had no professional assistance with their births."

64. Anaya, interview, October 8, 1999; Graham, "Folk Medicine," *NHOT,* 2:1061–1063.

65. Anaya, interview, October 1, 1999; Sabina Palomo Acosta, interview, November 14, 1999; Quiroz de León, interview; Sharpless, *Fertile Ground, Narrow Choices,* pp. 122–124.

66. Anaya, interview, October 1, 1999; family history of Juanita Palomo Campos and Sabina Palomo Acosta provided by Teresa Palomo Acosta.

67. Campos, interview.

68. Quiroz de León, interview.

69. Sharpless, *Fertile Ground, Narrow Choices,* p. 193; Anaya, interview, October 1, 1999.

70. Anaya, interview, October 1, 1999.

71. Ibid.; Palomo and Acosta family history provided by Teresa Palomo Acosta.

72. Sabina Palomo Acosta, interview, November 14, 1999; Quiroz de León, interview; Campos, interview.

73. Anaya, interview, October 1, 1999; Allen, *The Labor of Women,* p. 223. Allen wrote that among the Mexican farm women she interviewed, a small number reported reading *La Prensa.*

74. Anaya, interview, October 1, 1999.

75. Campos, interview; Allen, *The Labor of Women,* p. 238.

76. Quiroz de León, interview.

77. Ibid.

78. Campos, interview.

79. Anaya, interview, October 15, 1999; Sabina Palomo Acosta, interview, November 25, 1999; Quiroz de León, interview. Two of Lucía's daughters attained a postsecondary education. Sabina's two daughters did likewise; they also acquired master's degrees. Her two sons served in the military and have had long careers in the postal service and at a local cement plant; both men later pursued technical and community college training. María's children attained professional employment, with at least one of her children acquiring a community college education. Juanita Palomo Campos did not speak directly of her children's education in her interview. Her two daughters both attained their licenses as vocational nurses and her son served in the military and later as an official with a local paper company.

80. Anaya, interviews, October 1, October 8, 1999.

81. Anaya, interview, October 8, 1999; Sabina Palomo Acosta, interview, November 20, 1999; Quiroz de León, interview.

82. Anaya, interview, October 15, 1999; Sabina Palomo Acosta, interviews, November 20, November 25, 1999; Quiroz de León, interview; Campos, interview.

CHAPTER SIX

1. Nancy Baker Jones, "Idar, Jovita," *New Handbook of Texas,* 3:814–815 (hereafter *NHOT*); Pamela A. Smith and Elizabeth E. Ramírez, "Escalona Pérez, Beatriz," *NHOT,* 2:888–889; Debbie Mauldin Cottrell, "Martínez, Faustina Porras," *NHOT,* 4:534–535. For important discussions of Mexican origin women in this period, see Julia Blackwelder, *Women of the Depression: Caste and Culture in San Antonio, 1929–1939;* Mario T. García, *Desert Immigrants: The Mexicans of El Paso, 1880–1920;* and Irene Ledesma, "Unlikely Strikers: Mexican-American Women in Strike Activity in Texas, 1919–1974." Ledesma's work focuses specifically on unionizing and covers labor activism among Tejanas through 1974.

2. Arnoldo De León, *The Tejano Community: 1836–1900,* pp. 94–95.

3. Thomas Kreneck, *Del Pueblo: A Pictorial History of Houston's Hispanic Community,* pp. 36, 44. J. Montiel Oldera, *Primer anuario de los habitantes hispano-americanos de Texas,* p. 63; Cottrell, "Martínez, Faustina Porras," *NHOT,* 4:534–535.

4. Vivian Castleberry, *Daughters of Dallas,* pp. 445, 449; Cottrell, "Martínez, Faustina Porras," *NHOT,* 4:535.

5. Gerald D. Saxon, "Cuellar, Adelaida," *NHOT,* 2:432.

6. Jane Bock Guzmán, "Dallas Barrio Women of Power," pp. 35–43; Jane Bock Guzmán, "María Luna," *Legacies: A History Journal for Dallas and North Central Texas,* fall 2001, pp. 17–18; Kate Singleton, "Landmarks: Fourteen Significant Sites in Dallas County," *Legacies: A History Journal for Dallas and North Central Texas* 8, no. 2 (fall 1996): 50.

7. Arnoldo De León, *Mexican Americans in Texas: A Brief History,* pp. 95–96; Oldera, *Primer anuario,* pp. 28–29; Cynthia E. Orozco, "Rodríguez, Herlinda Morales," *NHOT,* 5:653.

8. Castleberry, *Daughters of Dallas,* pp. 246–247.

9. Oldera, *Primer anuario,* p. 30; Guzmán, "Dallas Women," pp. 44–47.

10. Emma Pérez, *The Decolonial Imaginary: Writing Chicanas into History,* p. 87. Pérez notes that another name for Stella Quintenella was Estela Gómez.

11. Arnoldo De León, *Ethnicity in the Sunbelt: A History of Mexican Americans in Houston,* p. 82; Julia Blackwelder, *Women of the Depression: Caste and Culture in San Antonio, 1929–1939,* p. 8; Gwendolyn Rice, "Little Mexico and the Barrios of Dallas," in *Dallas Reconsidered: Essays in Local History,* ed. Michael V. Hazel, pp. 158–168.

12. García, *Desert Immigrants,* pp. 5, 42–43, 94.

13. Kreneck, *Del Pueblo,* pp. 27, 42.

14. De León, *Mexican Americans in Texas,* pp. 82–83; Kreneck, *Del Pueblo,* p. 43.

15. Blackwelder, *Women of the Depression,* p. 82.

16. Kreneck, *Del Pueblo,* p. 48; Teresa Palomo Acosta, "La Mujer Moderna," *NHOT,* 4:52; Teresa Palomo Acosta, "Chapa, Francisco A.," *NHOT,* 2:42; Nora E. Ríos McMillan, "La Prensa," *NHOT,* 4:73–74; Cynthia E. Orozco, "Lozano, Alicia Guadalupe Elizondo de," *NHOT,* 4:318; Nora E. Ríos McMillan, "Lozano, Ignacio E.," *NHOT,* 4:318.

17. Pérez, *The Decolonial Imaginary,* pp. 84–85; De León, *Ethnicity in the Sunbelt,* p. 70.

18. Pérez, *The Decolonial Imaginary,* pp. 86–91; De León, *Ethnicity in the Sunbelt,* pp. 70–71; Cynthia E. Orozco, "Beyond Machismo, La Familia, and Ladies Auxiliaries: A Historiography of Mexican-Origin Women's Participation in Voluntary Associations and Politics in the United States: 1870–1990," in *Renato Rosaldo Lecture Series Monograph,* ed. Thomas Gelsinon, vol. 10, p. 59.

19. Cynthia E. Orozco, "Hernández, María L. de," *NHOT,* 3:572–573; Cynthia E. Orozco, "Munguía, Carolina Malpica," *NHOT,* 4:887; Gabriela

González, "Cultural Redemption and Female Benevolence: The Class and Gender Ideologies of Carolina Malpica de Munguía," pp. 12–14.

20. Vicki Ruiz, *From out of the Shadows: Mexican Women in Twentieth-Century America,* p. 47.

21. Teresa Palomo Acosta, María-Cristina García, and Cynthia E. Orozco, "Settlement Houses," *NHOT,* 5:977–979; María-Cristina García, "Agents of Americanization: Rusk Settlement and the Houston Mexicano Community, 1907–1950," in *Mexican Americans in Texas History,* ed. Emilio Zamora et al., pp. 121–122.

22. George J. Sánchez, "Go after the Women," in *Unequal Sisters: A Multicultural Reader in U.S. Women's History,* ed. Ellen Carol DuBois and Vicki L. Ruiz, pp. 254–255.

23. Ibid., p. 257.

24. García, "Agents of Americanization," pp. 123–124.

25. Ibid., pp. 129–130, 132.

26. Ruiz, *From out of the Shadows,* pp. 33, 35, 46, 48.

27. García, *Desert Immigrants,* p. 94.

28. Sánchez, "Go after the Women," p. 260.

29. Ruiz, *From out of the Shadows,* p. 50; Guzmán, "Dallas Barrio Women of Power," p. 10.

30. Cynthia E. Orozco, "Mexican-American Women," *NHOT,* 4:681; Blackwelder, *Women of the Depression,* pp. 71–72, 229: table 30.

31. Emilio Zamora, *The World of the Mexican Worker in Texas,* p. 26; Ledesma, "Unlikely Strikers," p. 37.

32. Blackwelder, *Women of the Depression,* pp. 72, 83, 96, 99.

33. Zamora, *The World of the Mexican Worker,* p. 26; Blackwelder, *Women of the Depression,* p. 91.

34. Zamora, *The World of the Mexican Worker,* pp. 27–28.

35. García, *Desert Immigrants,* pp. 74–76, 78, 87.

36. Ibid., pp. 76–77.

37. Ibid., pp. 77–94.

38. Ibid., p. 95.

39. Ibid., p. 78.

40. Ibid., pp. 95–96.

41. Ledesma, "Unlikely Strikers," pp. 34–35.

42. Ibid., pp. 37–38.

43. Ibid., pp. 38–39.

44. Ibid., p. 39.

45. Ibid., pp. 40–41.

46. Ibid., pp. 46–48.

47. Melissa Hield, "Union-Minded: Women in the Texas ILGWU, 1933–1950," in *Women in the Texas Workforce: Yesterday and Today,* ed. Richard Croxdale and Melissa Hield, p. 5; Blackwelder, *Women of the Depression,* p. 98.

48. Blackwelder, *Women of the Depression,* p. 93.
49. Hield, "Union-Minded," pp. 7–8.
50. Blackwelder, *Women of the Depression,* p. 136.
51. Ledesma, "Unlikely Strikers," pp. 60–62.
52. Ibid., pp. 62–64.
53. Ibid., pp. 68–70; Blackwelder, *Women of the Depression,* p. 95.
54. Selden C. Menefee and Orin C. Cassmore, *The Pecan Shellers of San Antonio: The Problem of Underpaid and Unemployed Mexican Labor,* pp. 7–8.
55. Ledesma, "Unlikely Strikers," pp. 69–70; Blackwelder, *Women of the Depression,* p. 105.
56. Ledesma, "Unlikely Strikers," p. 70.
57. Ibid., p. 71.
58. *Labor Advocate,* October 31, 1919, p. 1.
59. Ledesma, "Unlikely Strikers," pp. 83–84.
60. *Labor Advocate,* October 31, 1919, p. 1.
61. Ledesma, "Unlikely Strikers," pp. 82, 85–88; *Labor Advocate,* November 7, 1919, p. 1; Cynthia E. Orozco, "Idar, Clemente Nicasio," *NHOT,* 3:813–814.
62. Ledesma, "Unlikely Strikers," p. 84.
63. *Labor Advocate,* November 7, 1919, p. 1.
64. Ledesma, "Unlikely Strikers," pp. 87, 89–90.
65. Ibid., pp. 91–92.
66. Ibid., p. 95.
67. Zaragoza Vargas, "Tejana Radical: Emma Tenayuca and the San Antonio Labor Movement during the Great Depression," *Pacific Historical Review* 66 (1997): 558–559.
68. Ledesma, "Unlikely Strikers," pp. 92–93.
69. Ibid., pp. 93–94; Blackwelder, *Women of the Depression,* pp. 132–133.
70. Ledesma, "Unlikely Strikers," pp. 96–99; Blackwelder, *Women of the Depression,* pp. 133–135.
71. Blackwelder, *Women of the Depression,* p. 135.
72. Teresa Palomo Acosta, excerpt from poem "About Emma Tenayuca and the Pecan Shellers," in *Passing Time,* pp. 5–6.
73. Richard Croxdale, "The 1938 San Antonio Pecan Shellers' Strike," in *Women in the Texas Workforce,* ed. Richard Croxdale and Melissa Hield, p. 24; Vargas, "Tejana Radical," p. 565; Blackwelder, *Women of the Depression,* p. 7. Some estimates put the number of strikers at 8,000–10,000.
74. Croxdale, "The 1938 San Antonio Pecan Shellers' Strike," p. 26; Ledesma, "Unlikely Strikers," pp. 103–104.
75. Richard Croxdale, "Pecan Shellers' Strike," *NHOT,* 5:117–118; Vargas, "Tejana Radical," p. 566; Ledesma, "Unlikely Strikers," pp. 105–106; Blackwelder, *Women of the Depression,* p. 141. The term *La Pasionaria,* which was used to portray Emma Tenayuca, was taken from the description of Do-

lores Ibarruri, the leader of the Loyalists during the Spanish Civil War. Ibarruri was a defender of the Republic during the 1930s.

76. Ledesma, "Unlikely Strikers," p. 106.

77. Vargas, "Tejana Radical," pp. 556–557, 561. Vargas also notes on pages 568–569 that the League of United Latin American Citizens "professed sympathy for the pecan shellers' deplorable working conditions and dismal wages, but it condemned the strike because of its communist leadership." Vargas notes that the Catholic archdiocese was also opposed to the supposed "communist control of the strike."

78. Blackwelder, *Women of the Depression,* pp. 144–145; Ledesma, "Unlikely Strikers," pp. 108–110; Vargas, "Tejana Radical," pp. 567, 573.

79. Blackwelder, *Women of the Depression,* p. 143; Ledesma, "Unlikely Strikers," pp. 110–113.

80. Ledesma, "Unlikely Strikers," pp. 113–114.

81. Croxdale, "The 1938 San Antonio Pecan Shellers' Strike," p. 31; Vargas, "Tejana Radical," p. 579.

82. Laurie Coyle, Gail Hershatter, and Emily Honig, "Farah Strike," *NHOT,* 2:950. Fuerza Unida, Women and Workers United in Social Action, "Actions," www.fuerza-unida.org (May 4, 2002). The web site summarizes the current work of Fuerza Unida. A recent story on Fuerza Unida is Aïssatou Sidimé's "Women Activists Head to S. Africa," *San Antonio Express-News,* August 25, 2001, pp. 2B, 4B. Also, information on Fuerza Unida's history and activities is available at American Friends Service Committee online, www .afsc.org/tao/112k03.htm. For an in-depth discussion of the women involved in Fuerza Unida, see Raquel Marquez, "Chicana Labor Activists: The Case of Fuerza Unida."

CHAPTER SEVEN

1. Guadalupe San Miguel Jr. "Mexican Americans and Education," *New Handbook of Texas,* 4:671, (hereafter *NHOT*).

2. Ibid. Arnoldo De León, *San Angeleños: Mexican Americans in San Angelo, Texas,* p. 40.

3. Cynthia E. Orozco, "*Del Rio ISD v. Salvatierra,*" *NHOT,* 2:578–579; V. Carl Allsup, "*Cisneros v. Corpus Christi ISD,*" *NHOT,* 2:113; Teresa Palomo Acosta, *Edgewood ISD v. Kirby, NHOT,* 2:784–785. For an in-depth examination of lawsuits that Mexican Americans have filed, refer to Guadalupe San Miguel Jr., *"Let All of Them Take Heed": Mexican Americans and the Campaign for Educational Equality in Texas, 1910–1981,* pp. 77–81.

4. Douglas E. Foley et al., *From Peones to Politicos: Class and Ethnicity in a South Texas Town, 1900–1987,* p. 40.

5. Foley et al., pp. 33–40. Foley presents an insightful discussion of the experiences of Mexicans at the ranch schools in South Texas. John H. McNeely, "Holding Institute," *NHOT,* 3:660–661; R. Douglas Brackenridge,

"Rio Grande Female Institute," *NHOT,* 5:586–587; Keith Guthrie, "Presbyterian School for Mexican Girls," *NHOT,* 5:329; Sister Ignatius Miller, O.S.U., "Ursuline Academy, San Antonio," *NHOT,* 6:680–681; Cynthia E. Orozco, "Mexican-American Women," *NHOT,* 4:681.

6. Brackenridge, "Rio Grande Female Institute," pp. 586–587; Guthrie, "Presbyterian School for Mexican Girls," *NHOT,* 5:329; McNeely, "Holding Institute," *NHOT,* 3:660; Miller, O.S.U., "Ursuline Academy, San Antonio," *NHOT,* 6:680.

7. Jovita Idar, "The Best Education," *El Heraldo Cristiano* (San Antonio), no. 247, October 1940. Translated by Carolyn Galerstein, in Jovita Idar biographical file, Special Collections, Texas Woman's University.

8. Arnoldo De León, *The Tejano Community, 1836–1900,* pp. 188, 190–192.

9. L. Robert Ables, "Zavala, Adina Emilia De," *NHOT,* 6:1146; Mrs. Don Redmon, "Élida García de Falcón," *Worthy Mothers of Texas,* p. 54; Teresa Palomo Acosta, "García de Falcón, Élida," *NHOT,* 3:88; Cynthia E. Orozco, "Rodríguez de Gonzáles, Elvira," *NHOT,* 5:657–658; Teresa Palomo Acosta, "López de Ximenes, Josefina," *NHOT,* 4:290; De León, *San Angeleños,* p. 31.

10. Cynthia E. Orozco, "Mexican-American Women," *NHOT,* 4:681; Anita Torres Smith, in telephone conversation with Ruthe Winegarten, September 30, 2001; Anita Torres Smith, "Praxedis Mata Torres: The First Mexican-American Teacher in the Public Schools in Uvalde County, Texas," *Journal of Big Bend Studies* 3 (January 1991): 161, 164, 169, 176.

11. Cynthia E. Orozco and Teresa Palomo Acosta, "González de Mireles, Jovita," *NHOT,* 3:236–237; González obtained her master's degree on August 29, 1930, according to information provided on November 19, 2001, by the Office of the Registrar, Student Records, University of Texas at Austin; Jovita González de Mireles, "Jovita González: Early Life and Education," in *Dew on the Thorn,* ed. José E. Limón, pp. xi–xiii.

12. Jovita González de Mireles, "Jovita González: Early Life and Education," in *Dew on the Thorn,* ed. José E. Limón, pp. xi–xiii.

13. Cynthia E. Orozco, "Ramírez, Emilia Wilhelmina Schunior," *NHOT,* 5:423.

14. *La Crónica,* September 7, 1911. The translation of the advertisement is in the "Escuelitas" file, Texas Women's History Project Collection, Woman's Collection, Texas Woman's University.

15. Beatriz Vásquez, in conversation with Melissa Hield, July 8, 1980, "Escuelitas" file, Texas Women's History Project Collection, Woman's Collection, Texas Woman's University; Diana J. Kleiner, "Colegio Altamirano," *NHOT,* 2:198; Aida Barrera, *Looking for Carrascolendas: From a Child's World to Award-Winning Television,* pp. 32–33. Barrera notes that Colegio Altimirano had a high reputation among the Texas Mexicans in Hogg and Starr Counties. Some of her relatives founded and taught at the institution.

16. María-Cristina García, "Liga Femenil Mexicanista," *NHOT,* 4:194.

17. Emilio Zamora, "Las Escuelitas: A Texas Mexican Search for Educational Excellence," p. 72, "Escuelitas" file, Woman's Collection, Texas Woman's University. Zamora notes that the *escuelitas* may have been the product of a "feminist" organization formed in Laredo. The known feminist organization in Laredo was the Liga Femenil Mexicanista, which sought to provide Mexican children with an education.

18. Juanita Wells, in telephone conversation with Sherry A. Smith, August 7, 1980, "Escuelitas" file, Woman's Collection, Texas Woman's University; Zamora, "Las Escuelitas," pp. 71–72.

19. *La Crónica,* September 7, 1911. This translated version is in the "Escuelitas" file, Woman's Collection, Texas Woman's University.

20. Advertisement in *La Crónica,* October 19, 1911. The translated version is in the "Escuelitas" file, Woman's Collection, Texas Woman's University.

21. Zamora, "Las Escuelitas," pp. 82–84; Vásquez, in telephone conversation with Melissa Hield, July 8, 1980.

22. Julie L. Pycior, *LBJ and Mexican Americans: The Paradox of Power,* pp. 14, 17.

23. Ibid., p. 17.

24. Sabina Palomo Acosta, interview by Teresa Palomo Acosta, tape recording, McGregor, Texas, November 14, 1999; also, for information on the community of Loma Vista, see Rubén E. Ochoa, "Loma Vista," *NHOT,* 4:266. Ochoa reports that Loma Vista was primarily a ranching area located twelve miles south of Batesville in the southeastern part of Zavala County. He also notes that Loma Vista's schools consolidated with the Crystal City, Texas, schools in 1939.

25. Elia Martínez Gómez, in telephone conversation with Ruthe Winegarten, September 24, 1980.

26. Pycior, *LBJ and Mexican Americans,* pp. xiii, 13, 136, 158.

27. Cynthia E. Orozco, "Mendez, Consuelo Herrera," *NHOT,* 4:618; María de los Angeles Olvera and José Juan Bartolo Hernández, "AISD Hails 1st Hispanic Teacher," *Austin American-Statesman,* May 12, 1986, p. D18.

28. Debbie Graves, "Austin's Innovator of Bilingual Teaching Will Retire in June," *Austin American-Statesman,* May 13, 1984, p. B12.

29. Thomas H. Kreneck, "Little School of the 400," *NHOT,* 4:237.

30. Ibid.

31. Ibid.

32. Pycior, *LBJ and Mexican Americans,* pp. 159–160, 173, 199.

33. Texas Education Agency web site, http://www.tea.state.tx.us/perf report/pocked/2000.

34. A. Phillips Brooks, "District: Vouchers are hurting our schools," *Austin American-Statesman,* February 4, 1999, p. B1.

35. Rich Oppel, "Can Good News Grow to Touch More Children?" *Austin American-Statesman,* October 3, 1999, p. J3.

36. Steve Ray, "Literacy, Equality Are Rangel Aims," *Corpus Christi Caller-Times,* April 6, 1993, p. B1.

37. María-Cristina García, "Mexía de Reygades, Ynés," *NHOT,* 4:652.

38. García, "Mexía de Reygades, Ynés," *NHOT,* 4:653.

39. W. Page Keeton, *"Sweatt v. Painter," NHOT,* 6:168–169.

40. *University of Texas Bulletin: Directory of The University of Texas for the Long Session of 1917–1918,* p. 37; biographical information data card on Rachel Garza, Office of the Executive Vice President and Provost, University of Texas at Austin.

41. Freddie Milam Sanders, "Elena Farías Barrera," *One Hundred Women of the Rio Grande Valley of Texas,* pp. 3–5; Orozco and Acosta, "González de Mireles, Jovita," *NHOT,* 3:236. The Office of the Registrar at the University of Texas at Austin provided information on November 19, 2001, attesting to the fact that González received her master's degree on August 29, 1930.

42. Texas Higher Education Coordinating Board, *Degrees Awarded by Ethnic Origin, Gender: Texas Public Universities, FY 1997.*

43. Ibid.

44. Teresa Palomo Acosta, "In Memoriam: Eva Ruissy García Currie," a biographical sketch prepared for the Faculty Council web site, University of Texas at Austin; biographical data information card in 1940s–1970s personnel records of Eva García Currie, Office of the Executive Vice President and Provost, University of Texas at Austin; Orozco, "Ramírez, Emilia Wilhelmina Schunior," *NHOT,* 5:423.

45. Vita of Norma E. Cantú, Acosta-Winegarten Collection (hereafter AWC).

46. Vita of Cynthia E. Orozco, AWC.

47. Vita of Leticia Magda Garza-Falcón, AWC.

48. "Valenzuela: New Associate Director," *Noticias de CMAS,* p. 3, Center for Mexican American Studies, University of Texas at Austin, summer 2000; "Notas Breves," *Noticias de CMAS,* p. 11, Center for Mexican American Studies, University of Texas at Austin, spring 2001.

49. Texas Higher Education Coordinating Board, *Tenured Faculty Headcount by Ethnic Origin, Gender: Texas Public Universities, Fall 1997.* The University of Texas at Dallas did not have any tenured or tenure-track Hispanic females, according to the report.

50. Bárbara J. Robles, "Latinas in the Academy: Profiling Current and Future Scholars," in *Reflexiones: New Directions in Mexican American Studies* (University of Texas at Austin) 1998: 100.

51. José Roberto Juárez, "Texas Association of Chicanos in Higher Education," *NHOT,* 6:289.

52. Description of "Brindis a la mujer," a conference planned for 2000, e-mail letter from Frieda Werden (Wings@igc.org), December 5, 1999.

53. Texas Higher Education Coordinating Board, *Final Report: The Advi-*

sory Committee on Women and Minority Faculty and Professional Staff, January 1997, p. 21; Teresa Palomo Acosta's knowledge from a four-year tenure at the Coordinating Board, from 1984 to 1988. Similar goals were discussed at least thirteen years prior to the 1997 report as part of the federally mandated Texas Plan for Equal Educational Opportunity that was in place in the state's public postsecondary institutions.

54. Claudia Feldman, "The Woman She Came to Be," Texas supplement, *Houston Chronicle,* January 16, 2000, pp. 8, 11.

55. Vita of Juliet V. García, AWC; vita of Vickie Gómez, AWC.

56. Information on university and community college presidents from a list provided by the Texas Higher Education Coordinating Board, undated; "Nora Garza Elected AAUW-Texas President," *LareDOS,* June 2000, p. 24.

57. Undated document on university and community college governing boards provided by the Texas Higher Education Coordinating Board; it covers the 1990s and possibly 2000. Ray, "Literacy, Equality Are Rangel Aims," p. B1; "Bush Appoints Regents, Judge," p. B3, *Austin American-Statesman,* March 9, 1999.

58. Nancy Baker Jones and Ruthe Winegarten, *Capitol Women: Texas Female Legislators, 1923–1990,* p. 205; Rachel Yates, "UT Ends Pursuit of Hopwood Appeal," *Daily Texan,* November 28, 2001, pp. 1–2.

59. Remi Bello, "Education Officials Mull over Minority Admissions," *Daily Texan,* September 25, 2000, pp. 1–2.

60. University of Texas System, *Annual Report 2000,* pp. 22, 24, 32.

61. Ángela Valenzuela, *Subtractive Schooling: U.S.-Mexican Youth and the Politics of Caring,* pp. 286, 288, 289.

62. Ethan Bronner, "Study: U.S. Schools Resegregating," *Austin American-Statesman,* June 14, 1999, A3.

63. Reynaldo F. Macías, Raymond E. Castro, and Yolanda Rodríguez-Ingle, "Looking for Needles in a Haystack: Hispanics in the Teaching Profession," in *Education of Hispanics in the United States: Politics, Policies, and Outcomes,* ed. Abbas Tashakkori and Salvador Hector Ochoa, vol. 16, pp. 50 (table 4), 51, 59. The authors present an in-depth examination of the need to increase the numbers of Hispanic teachers.

CHAPTER EIGHT

1. *Woman's News* (Dallas), May 1985, p. 1.

2. Ibid., pp. 1, 7; "Influential Women of Texas," *Texas Hispanic,* March 1994, pp. 22–36.

3. "LNB, STNB Honor Women Bankers," *LareDOS,* April 2000, p. 33.

4. *TWU Update,* April 10, 2000, p. 4; Eunice Moscoso and Renae Merle, "Hispanic Companies Growing Rapidly," *Austin American-Statesman,* July 11, 1996, p. C1; Las Manitas is a well-known restaurant in Austin.

5. Katy Vine, "Elisa Jiménez," *Texas Monthly,* March 1999, p. 30; "Women on the Move to Recognize 10 Leaders," *Houston Chronicle,* November 6, 2000, p. D6; Daniel Pérez, "1st Woman Earns Job of City Captain," *El Paso Times,* August 4, 1999, pp. B1, 4; Denise Gamino, "A Pattern to Live By," *Austin American-Statesman,* December 26, 2000, pp. E1, 8; Ray and Yolanda López Gómez, in conversation with Ruthe Winegarten, Austin, September 25, 2000; "KLRU Profiles," *KLRU Program Guide* (Austin), December 1999, p. 4.

6. Arnold García Jr., "Building Hispanic Business Leaders," *Austin American-Statesman,* October 2, 2000, p. A9.

7. Acción Texas web site: http://www.acciontexas.org; "Q & A: Business and Social Change," *Austin American-Statesman,* April 26, 1999, A-8.

8. Teresa Palomo Acosta, "National Women's Employment and Education," *New Handbook of Texas,* 4:949 (hereafter *NHOT*).

9. Irene Ledesma, "Unlikely Strikers: Mexican-American Women in Strike Activity in Texas, 1919–1974," p. 29; also, for a good summary of Mexican American workers in urban Texas since the 1930s, refer to Barbara J. Rozek, "The Entry of Mexican Women into Urban Based Industries: Experiences in Texas during the Twentieth Century," in *Women and Texas History: Selected Essays,* ed. Fane Downs and Nancy Baker Jones, pp. 15–33.

10. Women's Bureau, U.S. Department of Labor, *Women Workers in Texas,* 1970, p. 6.

11. Roger Langley, "Hispanic Women 'at Bottom,'" *San Antonio Light,* August 9, 1981, unnumbered page, Woman's Collection, Texas Woman's University; U.S. Bureau of the Census (http://www.census.gov/income), table P-2: "Race and Hispanic Origin of People by Median Income and Gender: 1947–1997." Data for Hispanic and White women are drawn from the Hispanic and the White columns provided on page 4 of the document. Bill Bishop, "White Men's Wages Grow Faster Than Other Groups'," *Austin American-Statesman,* March 4, 2001, p. A12.

12. Janet Y. Brockmoller, "An Interview with Mrs. Enriquita Rubio López," *Password* 27, no. 1 (spring 1982): 34–40.

13. Biography of Debra López Fix in program notes for Hispanic Heritage Month Dinner Dance at the United States Military Academy at West Point, October 1998, Acosta-Winegarten Collection (hereafter AWC); personal biography provided by Lieutenant Colonel Fix, AWC.

14. Biography of Debra López Fix in program notes for Hispanic Heritage Month Dinner Dance at West Point, October 1998, AWC; personal biography provided by Lieutenant Colonel Fix, AWC; e-mail dated September 25, 2001, from Pauline López, mother of Lieutenant Colonel Fix, citing *Washington Times* news article on her daughter's heroism. On September 11, 2001, four airplanes were hijacked, presumably by members of Al-Queda, a terrorist network headed by Osama bin Laden. Two of the airplanes were deliberately crashed into the World Trade Center in New York City and one into the Pen-

tagon. The fourth airplane, whose intended target remained unknown as this book was being completed, crashed in a field outside Pittsburgh, Pennsylvania. Both towers of the World Trade Center were completely destroyed and the Pentagon was damaged. According to the morning news on *Good Morning, America,* ABC network, as of November 20, 2001, 3,900 or fewer individuals (from many different countries) lost their lives as a result of these events.

15. "Clotilde P. García," Texas Women's Hall of Fame program notes, Austin, September 12–13, 2000, Woman's Collection, Texas Woman's University (photocopy, AWC).

16. María de la Luz Rodríguez Cárdenas, "Jovita Pérez, 1897–1970: A Remarkable Pathfinder, Pioneer in the Licensed Customs House Brokerage World, 1928–1970," photocopy, May 3, 1991, p. 8, AWC.

17. Ibid., pp. 4–8.

18. Ibid., pp. 2, 3.

19. Ibid., pp. 1, 14.

20. Barbara Robedeau, "Goodman, Petronila María Pereida," *NHOT,* 3:239–240; Cynthia E. Orozco, "Mexican-American Women," *NHOT,* 4:681.

21. María Quiroz de León, interview by Teresa Palomo Acosta, tape recording, McGregor, Texas, March 8, 2000.

22. Sammye Munson, *Our Tejano Heroes: Outstanding Mexican-Americans in Texas,* pp. 56–58; 1988 Texas Women's Hall of Fame program; Associated Press, "Bush Family Enjoyed 'Mama' Ninfa's Food," *Austin American-Statesman,* June 19, 2001, pp. B1, B6; Patricia Sharpe, "Ninfa Laurenzo," *Texas Monthly,* August 2001, p. 40.

23. Commission on the Status of Women, "Austin Women: 150 Years of Trial and Triumph," exhibit flyer, 1986, AWC.

24. Ronnie Rubio, in conversation with Ruthe Winegarten, Victoria, October 28, 2000. "Cinco de Mayo Fiesta to Get Underway Friday," *Texan Express* (Goliad), 2000; "Class of '48 Celebrates 50 Years," *Texan Express* (Goliad), October 21, 1998, p. 8, collection of Ronnie Rubio.

25. Cheryl Smith, "A Veteran's True Advocate," *Narratives: Stories of U.S. Latinos and Latinas and World War II* (University of Texas at Austin) 1, no. 1 (fall 1999): 3–4.

26. Sherri Fauver, "Hardship, Pride, and Success," *Narratives: Stories of U.S. Latinos and Latinas and World War II* (University of Texas at Austin) 1, no. 2, (spring 2000): 5–6; Anita Torres Smith, "Praxedis Mata Torres: The First Mexican-American Teacher in the Public Schools in Uvalde County, Texas," *Journal of Big Bend Studies* 3 (January 1991): 174; "Gloria Yzaguirre Stephen," obituary, *Austin American-Statesman,* July 11, 2001, p. B4.

27. "Yolanda Garza Boozer," obituary, *Austin American-Statesman,* May 19, 1998, p. B4; "Ex-Johnson Secretary Boozer Dies," *Austin American-Statesman,* May 18, 1998, p. B4.

28. Bob Dart, "Staffer Brings Diversity to Job at White House," *Austin American-Statesman,* June 5, 1999, pp. A25, 26.

29. Aurora Sánchez, in telephone conversation with Ruthe Winegarten, January 18, 2001.

30. Ruthe Winegarten, *Black Texas Women: 150 Years of Trial and Triumph,* pp. 282–283.

31. "Dr. Mary Headley Edgerton," unnumbered page in Heritage Style Show program notes, Rio Grande City, Woman's Collection, Texas Woman's University.

32. Biographical sketch of Clotilde P. García, in Ruthe Winegarten, *Finder's Guide to the "Texas Women: A Celebration of History" Exhibit Archives;* program notes for Dr. Clotilde García's induction into the Texas Women's Hall of Fame in 1984 (photocopy, AWC); Munson, *Our Tejano Heroes,* pp. 40–44.

33. Program notes for Dr. Clotilde García's induction into the Texas Women's Hall of Fame in 1984 (photocopy, AWC); Munson, *Our Tejano Heroes,* pp. 40–44.

34. Julie L. Pycior, *LBJ and Mexican Americans: The Paradox of Power,* p. 61.

35. Pycior, *LBJ and Mexican Americans,* p. 159.

36. Elena Farías Barrera, "Eva Dolores Carrizales, M.D.," in *One Hundred Women of the Rio Grande Valley of Texas,* ed. the Rio Writers, pp. 23–25; Munson, "Linda Sagarnaga Magill," *Today's Tejano Heroes,* pp. 35–38.

37. Texas Higher Education Coordinating Board, *Medical Degrees Conferred by Ethnicity and Gender, Selected Texas Medical Schools, Fiscal Year 1998–99.* The ethnic breakdown of the data lists Hispanics, not Mexican Americans. Tejanas would fall into the Hispanic category.

38. "Three A&M International Students, Friends, Accepted to Medical School," *LareDOS,* March 2001, p. 31.

39. Cynthia E. Orozco, "García, Eva Carrillo de," *NHOT,* 3:83; Jeanette Flachmeier, *Pioneer Austin Notables,* vol. 2, p. 26; Vicki L. Ruiz, *From out of the Shadows: Mexican Women in Twentieth-Century America,* photo caption for fig. 14 following p. 50; Carmen Zacarías, "Biographical Sketch of Ester Díaz," typescript, AWC; Munson, "Irma Aguilar," *Today's Tejano Heroes,* pp. 2–4.

40. Max J. Castro, "¿Habla Español? The Nursing Profession Needs You," *Vista,* October 2000, p. 40.

41. Melinda Smith, "Minority Women Attorneys Share Their Thoughts and Experiences," *Texas Bar Journal,* October 1990, p. 1053.

42. Ibid.

43. Information from 1994 Texas Women's Hall of Fame records; Irma Rangel, videotape interview by Nancy Baker Jones, Austin, May 25, 1995.

44. "Influential Women of Texas," *Texas Hispanic,* March 1994, pp. 28–30, 32; vita of Sylvia R. García, AWC; Norma Martínez, in telephone conversation with Teresa Palomo Acosta, January 30, 2001; see *United States Reports* for an account of *Lyng* v. *Castillo, et al.,* 477:635–647; Smith, "Minority Women

Attorneys," p. 1051; Munson, "Hilda Tagle," *Today's Tejano Heroes,* p. 60; "Of Note," *On Campus,* University of Texas at Austin, March 5–11, 1990; Carlos Guerra, "Beauty Shop to Bench," *Austin American-Statesman,* April 4, 1998, p. A13.

45. Margo Gutiérrez and Matt S. Meier, "Vilma Socorro Martínez," *An Encyclopedia of the Mexican American Civil Rights Movement,* pp. 141–142. Bonnie Eisenberg, "Vilma Martínez," biographical sketch in Santa Clara, California, National Women's History Project, n.d., pp. 1–4, AWC.

46. Smith, "Minority Women Attorneys," October 1990, p. 1051; information provided by the staff of the State Bar of Texas, February 13, 2001.

47. "Law School Minority Enrollment Increases for Fall Semester," *Daily Texan,* September 1, 2000, p. 6; Texas Higher Education Coordinating Board, *Degrees Awarded by Ethnic Origin, Gender, Texas Public Universities, FY 1997;* information provided by Shelli Soto, assistant dean for admissions, University of Texas School of Law, September 5, 2000.

48. Information provided by Marie Hoepken, Office of the Dean, University of Texas School of Law, September 5, 2000; Rachel Stone, "Former Clinton Staffer Joins UT Faculty," *Daily Texan,* August 17, 2001, pp. 1–2.

49. Cynthia E. Orozco, "Hernández, María L. de," *NHOT,* 3:572–573; Cynthia E. Orozco, "Munguía, Carolina Malpica," *NHOT,* 4:887; María-Cristina García, "Morales, Felix Hessbrook," *NHOT,* 4:828–829.

50. Vita of Aida Barrera, AWC; Aida Barrera, *Looking for Carrascolendas: From a Child's World to Award-Winning Television,* p. 4.

51. Joyce Peterson, "Pressing Concerns," *Austin American-Statesman,* August 19, 1990, p. A1; Karen Olsson, "The Border According to Guerra," *Texas Observer,* February 18, 2000, pp. 12–14, 27.

52. See the *Dallas Morning News* for Mercedes Olivera's regular column on Mexican Americans and other Latinos; Marina Pisano, "Roles for Hispanic Women Changing," *San Antonio Express-News,* September 18, 1983, p. F10; vita of Evangelina (Vangie) Vigil-Piñon, AWC.

53. Clifford Pugh, "Latina Like Me, Latina Como Yo," *Houston Chronicle,* May 29, 1996, pp. D1, D4.

54. Ibid; information on the circulation of *Latina* provided by magazine staff member Elizabeth Carroll, February 6, 2001.

55. "UT 'Tejas' Magazine Places in Nation's Top 3," *Daily Texan,* June 7, 1994; Jim Phillips, "Three UT Students Get Kennedy Awards for Migrant Stories," *Austin American-Statesman,* May 3, 1996, p. B3.

56. Teresa Palomo Acosta, "Mexican American Business and Professional Women's Association," *NHOT,* 4:653–654.

57. Ibid.

58. Ibid.

59. Cynthia E. Orozco, "Hispanic Women's Network of Texas," *NHOT,* 3:631.

60. *Hispanic Women's Network of Texas Directory,* 1994.

61. Bárbara J. Robles, "Latina Entrepreneurial Activity in the 1990s: Lessons for the Twenty-First Century," draft of paper, 2000, provided by the author, p. 10.

62. Robles, "Latina Entrepreneurial Activity," pp. 12, 13.

63. Ibid., p. 23.

64. Andy Alford, "For 20 Million People and Growing, Texas Is Where They Hang Their Hat," *Austin American-Statesman,* December 29, 1999, p. A8.

65. Michael A. Fletcher, "Report: More Latinos Mired in Low Wages," *Austin American-Statesman,* July 5, 2000, pp. A1, A8; Alford, "For 20 Million People and Growing, Texas Is Where They Hang Their Hat," p. A8; College Board, *Projected Social Context for Education of Children: 1990–2015,* p. 28.

66. A. Philips Brooks, "Hispanics Wield New Clout at Capitol," *Austin American-Statesman,* January 31, 1999, p. A1.

67. Ibid., pp. A1, A10.

CHAPTER NINE

1. Kay Frances Turner, "Mexican American Women's Home Altars: The Art of Relationship," p. 212.

2. Virgilio Elizondo, foreword in Jeanette Rodríguez, *Our Lady of Guadalupe: Faith and Empowerment among Mexican-American Women,* pp. x, xi.

3. For an insightful and in-depth discussion of Mexican origin women's work in organizing their community around political, social, and cultural issues, see Cynthia E. Orozco, "Beyond Machismo, La Familia, and Ladies Auxiliaries: A Historiography of Mexican-Origin Women's Participation in Voluntary Associations and Politics in the United States, 1870–1900," in *Renato Rosaldo Lecture Series Monograph,* ed. Thomas Gelsinon, vol. 10, pp. 37–77.

4. Jeanette Rodríguez, *Our Lady of Guadalupe,* p. 129.

5. Rodríguez, *Our Lady of Guadalupe,* pp. 31, 38–39; Teresa Palomo Acosta, "Nuestra Señora de Guadalupe," *New Handbook of Texas,* 4:1064 (hereafter *NHOT*).

6. Rodríguez, *Our Lady of Guadalupe,* pp. 64, 114–142. Rodríguez provides a thorough discussion of the many ways that Mexican American women view the significance of Nuestra Señora de Guadalupe in their lives.

7. Acosta, "Nuestra Señora de Guadalupe," *NHOT,* 4:1065; Timothy Matovina, "New Frontiers of Guadalupanismo," *Journal of Hispanic/Latino Theology* 5, no. 1 (August 1997): 28. Matovina refers to the work of Jesús F. de la Teja in noting the time period during which the celebration of Nuestra Señora de Guadalupe occurred in the Tejano community in and around San Antonio.

8. Timothy M. Matovina, "Our Lady of Guadalupe Celebrations in San

Antonio, Texas, 1840–41," *Journal of Hispanic/Latino Theology* 1, no. 1 (November 1993): 92.

9. Teresa Palomo Acosta, "Home Altars," *NHOT,* 3:677–678.

10. Ibid.; Amalia Mesa-Bains, "Chicano Chronicle and Cosmology: The Works of Carmen Lomas Garza," in Carmen Lomas Garza, *Pedacito de Mi Corazón,* p. 31.

11. Program for "La Vela Prendida: Mexican-American Women's Home Altars," University of Texas at Austin, 1980, Acosta-Winegarten Collection of Tejana History (hereafter AWC). Each year Mexic-Arte Museum sponsors an altar-making exhibition to coincide with Día de los Muertos (All Souls' Day).

12. See Turner, "Mexican American Women's Home Altars," for a comprehensive discussion of home altars.

13. Teresa Palomo Acosta, "Sociedades Guadalupanas," *NHOT,* 5:1131.

14. Ibid., pp. 1131–1132.

15. Ibid.

16. Roberto R. Treviño, "Mexican Americans and Religion," *NHOT,* 4:673–674; Helen Osman, "End of an Order: Last Members of Missionary Order Are Still Going Strong in Taylor," *Catholic Spirit,* June 2000, p. 23.

17. María Eva Flores, "Las Hermanas," *NHOT,* 4:89–90.

18. Raúl García, "Mexican American Cultural Center," *NHOT,* 4:654; Flores, "Las Hermanas," p. 90.

19. Treviño, "Mexican Americans and Religion," *NHOT,* 4:675–676.

20. Ibid., p. 676.

21. Cynthia E. Orozco, "García, Eva Carrillo de," *NHOT,* 3:83; Nancy Baker Jones, "Idar, Jovita," *NHOT,* 3:815; Teresa Palomo Acosta, "García de Falcón, Élida," *NHOT,* 3:88; Treviño, "Mexican Americans and Religion," *NHOT,* 4:676.

22. María-Cristina García, "Liga Femenil Mexicanista," *NHOT,* 4:194; Orozco, "Beyond Machismo, La Familia, and Ladies Auxiliaries," p. 52.

23. Orozco, "Beyond Machismo, La Familia, and Ladies Auxiliaries," p. 46.

24. María-Cristina García, "Comité Patriótico Mexicano," *NHOT,* 2:249; Julie L. Pycior, "Hijos de Texas," *NHOT,* 3:608–609; Teresa Palomo Acosta, "Cruz Azul Mexicana," *NHOT,* 2:429.

25. Acosta, "Cruz Azul Mexicana," *NHOT,* 2:429.

26. Cynthia E. Orozco, "Comisión Honorífica Mexicana," *NHOT,* 2:248–249; Orozco, "Beyond Machismo, La Familia, and Ladies Auxiliaries," p. 61.

27. Acosta, "Cruz Azul Mexicana," *NHOT,* 2:429.

28. Ibid.

29. Orozco, "Comisión Honorífica Mexicana," *NHOT,* 2:248–249; Orozco, "Beyond Machismo, La Familia, and Ladies Auxiliaries," p. 61.

30. Teresa Palomo Acosta, "Confederación de Organizaciones Mexicanas y Latino Americanas," *NHOT,* 2:263–264.

31. Arnoldo De León and Robert A. Calvert, "Segregation," *NHOT,* 5:965; Rodolfo Rodríguez, "Bilingual Education," *NHOT,* 1:542–544.

32. Cynthia E. Orozco, "Spanish-Speaking PTA," *NHOT,* 6:13.

33. Ibid., p. 14; Cynthia E. Orozco, "Rodríguez de Gonzáles, Elvira," *NHOT,* 5:657–658.

34. Orozco, "Spanish-Speaking PTA," *NHOT,* 6:14.

35. Ibid.; Rodríguez, "Bilingual Education," *NHOT,* 1:542.

36. Cynthia E. Orozco, "Lozano, Alicia Guadalupe Elizondo de," *NHOT,* 4:318; Marcy Meffert, "Genoveva González Helped Poor," *San Antonio Light,* May 3, 1981, unnumbered page, in Woman's Collection, Texas Woman's University; Cynthia E. Orozco, "Clínica de la Beneficencia Mexicana," *NHOT,* 2:162–163.

37. Orozco, "Clínica de la Beneficencia Mexicana," *NHOT,* 2:163.

38. Ibid., pp. 162–163; Orozco, "Lozano, Alicia Guadalupe Elizondo de," *NHOT,* 4:318.

39. Carolina Malpica de Munguía to the members of the Círculo Cultural Isabela, la Católica, San Antonio, January 8, 1938, Munguía Family Papers, as noted in Gabriela González, "Cultural Redemption and Female Benevolence: The Class and Gender Ideologies of Carolina Malpica de Munguía," p. 14 (photocopy, AWC).

40. Thomas H. Kreneck, *Del Pueblo: A Pictorial History of Houston's Hispanic Community,* p. 82; María-Cristina García, "Club Terpsicore," *NHOT,* 2:168.

41. González, "Cultural Redemption and Female Benevolence." González provides a lengthy discussion of Carolina Malpica Munguía's views of women's roles within the Mexican origin community. Cynthia E. Orozco, "Círculo Cultural Isabel la Católica," *NHOT,* 2:111–112.

42. V. Carl Allsup, "American G.I. Forum of Texas," *NHOT,* 1:147; Orozco, "Beyond Machismo, La Familia, and Ladies Auxiliaries," p. 56; Teresa Palomo Acosta, "American G.I. Forum Women's Auxiliary," *NHOT,* 1:148; Teresa Palomo Acosta, "Pérez, Beatriz Tagle," *NHOT,* 5:149; program for recognition banquet on Saturday, July 16, 1988, Corpus Christi, for Beatrice Pérez (photocopy, AWC).

43. Teresa Palomo Acosta, "American G.I. Forum Women's Auxiliary," *NHOT,* 1:148.

44. Ibid; Orozco, "Beyond Machismo, La Familia, and Ladies Auxiliaries," p. 56.

45. Cynthia E. Orozco, "Ladies LULAC," *NHOT,* 4:1–2; "Scholarships Awarded," *Laredo Morning Times,* September 14, 1986, p. c10.

46. Cynthia E. Orozco, "League of United Latin American Citizens," *NHOT,* 4:130; Ramón Rentería, "El Pasoan Wins LULAC Presidency," *El Paso Times,* July 3, 1994, pp. A1–A2; Ken Flynn, "Ex-LULAC Boss Shuns Politics," *El Paso Times,* February 1, 1999, pp. 1A–2A; "LULAC Latinas Meet in San Antonio," *Arriba,* March 29–April 5, 2001, p. 1.

47. "LULAC Latinas Meet in San Antonio," p. 1.

48. Mary Beth Rogers, *Cold Anger: A Story of Faith and Power Politics*, p. 112.

49. Rogers, *Cold Anger*, pp. 105–126. Rogers presents numerous examples of how COPS forced improvements on the neglected west side. "San Antonio COPS Presidents," in *25th Anniversary of San Antonio Communities Organized for Public Service, 1974–1999*, pamphlet provided by COPS, AWC.

50. Rogers, *Cold Anger*, pp. 107–108.

51. Ibid., pp. 105–126. In one chapter ("Leave Them Alone. They're Mexicans"), Rogers describes the way that COPS members in San Antonio fought for changes in their neighborhoods and states that women were the principal researchers for projects the organization championed.

52. Rogers, *Cold Anger*, pp. 110–118.

53. Ibid., pp. 113–114, 117, 122–123.

54. Ibid., pp. 110, 112–113.

55. Ibid., pp. 115, 119, 121, 123; "Becoming a Power Organization," *25th Anniversary of San Antonio Communities Organized for Public Service*, p. 5, pamphlet provided by COPS, AWC.

56. Geoff Rips, "A Quiet Revolution," *Texas Observer*, April 14, 2000, pp. 15–19.

57. Teresa Palomo Acosta, "Losoya Taylor, Paula," *NHOT*, 4:297; L. Robert Ables, "Zavala, Adina Emilia De," *NHOT*, 6:1146–1147; María-Cristina García, "Reyna, María Torres," *NHOT*, 5:554–555; Rosalía Solórzano, "Valdes Villalva, María Guillermina," *NHOT*, 6:688.

58. Barbara Williams Prabhu, Katie Sherrod, and Reed K. Bilz, *Outstanding Women of Fort Worth: Hall of Fame, 1987–1995*, pp. 25, 29, 30, 36, 44, 57, 66, 73, 97.

59. Biographical sketch of Gloria G. Rodríguez, program notes for her induction into the Texas Women's Hall of Fame in 1993, Woman's Collection, Texas Woman's University (photocopy, AWC); Holly Ocasio Rizzo, "Latinas of Influence," *VISTA*, January/February 2001, p. 29.

60. Biographical sketch of Gloria G. Rodríguez, program notes for her induction into the Texas Women's Hall of Fame in 1993, Woman's Collection, Texas Woman's University (photocopy, AWC); Holly Ocasio Rizzo, "Latinas of Influence," *VISTA*, January/February 2001, p. 29; Rebecca Thatcher, "Families Learning Life's Lessons," *Austin American-Statesman*, May 28, 1999, pp. B1, B8.

61. "Environmental Activist Is Honored," *Austin American-Statesman*, November 26, 1998, p. B10.

62. Yolanda Chávez Leyva, "Por La Raza y Para La Raza: A Look at Tejana Activists, 1900–1998," *La Voz de Esperanza*, October 1998, pp. 8, 11. "Arts Suit in San Antonio Settled," *Austin American-Statesman*, October 22, 2001, p. B3. According to an Associated Press article, in 2001 the Esperanza Peace and Justice Center was awarded a $500,000 court settlement. United States District Judge Orlando García found that the San Antonio City Council had

violated laws pertaining to free speech, equal protection, and open meetings in 1997 when it cut $62,000 in taxpayer support because the center sponsored a film festival featuring films about gays.

CHAPTER TEN

1. Evey Chapa and Armando Gutierrez, "Chicanas in Politics: An Overview and a Case Study," in *Perspectivas en Chicano Studies I: Papers Presented at the Third Annual Meeting of the National Association of Chicano Social Studies,* ed. Reynaldo Flores Macias, p. 144.

2. Vicki Ruiz, *From out of the Shadows: Mexican Women in Twentieth-Century America,* p. 100.

3. Martha Cotera, *The Chicana Feminist,* pp. 1–6. Cotera wrote the first contemporary books regarding Mexican origin women's quest for liberty and political rights, beginning with indigenous predecessors. Her works, some privately printed, are important documents attesting to Tejana feminists' knowledge of their history. Also see her *Diosa y Hembra: The History and Heritage of Chicanas in the U.S.*

4. Cotera, *The Chicana Feminist,* pp. 17–20. Cotera notes the differences between Anglo and Chicana feminists in the chapter "Feminism as We See It." Also see the Martha P. Cotera Papers at the Benson Latin American Collection, University of Texas at Austin. Cotera has written and spoken extensively about the differences between Chicana and Anglo feminism.

5. Arnoldo De León and Robert A. Calvert, "Civil-Rights Movement," *New Handbook of Texas,* 2:119 (hereafter *NHOT*).

6. Ibid.

7. Matt S. Meier and Margo Gutiérrez, "*Hernandez v. Driscoll Consolidated Independent School District, 1957,*" *Encyclopedia of the Mexican American Civil Rights Movement,* p. 106.

8. Roberto R. Calderón, "Tejano Politics," *NHOT,* 6:241. Calderón discusses Tejano political life, beginning prior to the settlement of Anglos in the state through the early 1990s.

9. Cynthia E. Orozco, "Hernández, Maria L. de," *NHOT,* 3:572. Cynthia E. Orozco, "League of United Latin American Citizens," *NHOT,* 4:129, 131.

10. Calderón, "Tejano Politics," *NHOT,* 6:239–242.

11. V. Carl Allsup, "Felix Longoria Affair," *NHOT,* 2:975–976; Julie L. Pycior, *LBJ and Mexican Americans: The Paradox of Power,* p. 95.

12. Mario T. García, *The Making of a Mexican American Mayor: Raymond L. Telles of El Paso,* p. 48.

13. Ibid., p. 60.

14. Pycior, *LBJ and Mexican Americans,* pp. 95, 118; Meier and Gutiérrez, "Crystal City, Texas," *Encyclopedia of the Mexican American Civil Rights Move-*

ment, p. 69; Ignacio M. García, *Viva Kennedy: Mexican Americans in Search of Camelot,* pp. 51, 100; Teresa Palomo Acosta, "Political Association of Spanish-Speaking Organizations," *NHOT,* 5:256.

15. Alma M. García, "The Development of Chicana Feminist Discourse, 1970–1980," in *Unequal Sisters: A Multicultural Reader in U.S. Women's History,* ed. Ellen Carol DuBois and Vicki L. Ruiz, p. 418; García notes that various groups, including agricultural workers, the youth, and the Raza Unida Party, comprised the Chicano movement throughout the nation. Ignacio M. García, *Chicanismo: The Forging of a Militant Ethos among Mexican Americans,* pp. 68–69, 72–75, 114–115. See Guadalupe San Miguel Jr.'s *Brown, Not White: School Integration and the Chicano Movement in Houston* for an in-depth discussion of the roles that middle-class leaders played in the Tejano community in school integration during the Chicano movement. Moderate leaders—"novice activists," according to San Miguel—included Leonel Castillo, Ben Canales, Mrs. Marcelina Díaz, Mrs. Elvia Quiñones, Abe Ramírez, Bill Gutiérrez, and Gregory Salazar. Salazar, a member of the Mexican American Youth Organization, was apparently the only "militant voice in the group" in challenging the Houston Independent School District's discriminatory practices against Mexican American students. See pages 59–65, 89, 105, 206 in particular. San Miguel considers the actions of these middle-class members "activist" in nature. He also notes that the members of the Mexican-American Education Council, a group organized to fight school discrimination in Houston, supported a "reformist" agenda. Activists, he states, differed with moderates on the pace at which reforms should be pushed. Many of the moderates belonged to the Mexican American Generation.

16. Arnoldo De León, "Chicano," *NHOT,* 2:69; Ruiz, *From out of the Shadows,* p. 98.

17. Richard Bailey, "Starr County Strike," *NHOT,* 6:69; Calderón, "Tejano Politics," *NHOT,* 6:241.

18. Bailey, "Starr County Strike," *NHOT,* 6:69; Henry A. J. Ramos, *The American G.I. Forum: In Pursuit of the Dream, 1948–1983,* p. 42; Teresa Palomo Acosta, "United Farm Workers Union," *NHOT,* 6:629.

19. Acosta, "United Farm Workers Union," *NHOT,* 6:629.

20. García, "The Development of Chicana Feminist Discourse," pp. 418–419.

21. Ibid., p. 420.

22. Ibid., pp. 422–423.

23. Ibid., pp. 422, 424.

24. Ibid., pp. 423–424.

25. See Cotera, *The Chicana Feminist.* The essays in the collection were likely written in the years between 1970 and 1977. Also see Cotera, *Diosa y Hembra.*

26. Cotera, *The Chicana Feminist,* pp. 1–7. Cotera notes a wide variety of Mexican American feminist activities predating the Chicano movement.

27. References to these women's roles appear in the following books: Armando Navarro, *Mexican American Youth Organization: Avant-Garde of the Chicano Movement in Texas;* Ignacio Garcia, *United We Win: The Rise and Fall of La Raza Unida Party;* and José Ángel Gutiérrez, *The Making of a Chicano Militant: Lessons from Cristal.* Also see Orozco, "Hernández, María L. de," *NHOT,* 3:572–573, and Teresa Palomo Acosta, "Conferencia de Mujeres por la Raza," *NHOT,* 2:266.

28. Ruiz, *From out of the Shadows,* p. 116.

29. Cynthia E. Orozco, "Mujeres Por La Raza," *NHOT,* 4:878.

30. Ibid., pp. 878–879; Cotera, *The Chicana Feminist,* p. 51. The "Reading List for Chicanas" is noted in the bibliography of *The Chicana Feminist* and refers to its use by Mujeres Por La Raza at their meeting in San Antonio on August 4, 1973.

31. Orozco, "Mujeres Por La Raza," *NHOT,* 4:878–879.

32. Ibid., p. 879; "Colegio Jacinto Treviño," *El Despertador de Tejas,* December 1970 (vol. 1), p. 1. *El Despertador* was a publication of the Mexican American Youth Organization at the University of Texas at Austin. The newspaper reported that Colegio Jacinto Treviño opened in September 1970 in Mercedes. The college was part of the Antioch College system. Also see Aurelio M. Montemayor, "Colegio Jacinto Treviño," *NHOT,* 3:198. Montemayor notes that the institution closed in the mid-1970s.

33. Orozco, "Mujeres Por La Raza," *NHOT,* 4:878–879.

34. Acosta, "Conferencia de Mujeres por la Raza," *NHOT,* 2:266.

35. Ibid.

36. Cotera, *Diosa y Hembra,* pp. 183–184.

37. Ibid., pp. 185–186.

38. Ibid., pp. 186–188.

39. Ibid., pp. 183–188.

40. Teresa Palomo Acosta, "Mexican American Youth Organization," *NHOT,* 4:682; Navarro, *Mexican American Youth Organization,* p. 179.

41. Navarro, *Mexican American Youth Organization,* p. 212.

42. Ibid., pp. 212, 236.

43. Acosta, "Mexican American Youth Organization," *NHOT,* 4:682–683.

44. Navarro, *Mexican American Youth Organization,* pp. 110–112; Ruiz, *From out of the Shadows,* p. 100; San Miguel Jr., *Brown, Not White,* pp. 105, 123, 125, 126. San Miguel notes the involvement of Yolanda Birdwell in the fight over discrimination in the Houston Independent School District and the general lack of attention by Anglo authorities to the needs of the Mexican American community.

45. Acosta, "Mexican American Youth Organization," *NHOT,* 4:682. Mike Fresques, "MAYO, Administration Map Additional Talks on Demands," *Daily Texan,* February 8, 1972, p. 1; women are listed as editors, writers, and MAYO leaders in the following mid-1970s issues of the UT Austin MAYO chapter newspaper, *El Despertador de Tejas:* March 1975 (vol. 4, no. 1), p. 2;

November 1975 (vol. 5, no. 1), p. 3. The "Chicana Comments" column appears in a couple of issues, including April 1976 (vol. 5, no. 3), p. 6, and July 1976 (vol. 5, no. 5), p. 7; also, Teresa Palomo Acosta's personal observations and knowledge, as a member of MAYO from 1972–1974 at the University of Texas at Austin and as editor of *El Despertador de Tejas* in 1973–1974.

46. This demand was hoisted on a sign by youth commemorating the tenth anniversary of the Crystal City 1969 walkout. Gutiérrez, *The Making of a Chicano Militant,* p. 264.

47. Navarro, *Mexican American Youth Organization,* pp. 133–134.

48. Ibid., pp. 134–135; also see Carol Brochin, "The History I Never Learned in School: Diana Palacios Recounts Crystal City in 1969," *LareDOS,* October 2001, pp. 34–35. In an October 2001 interview with *LareDOS,* Diana Palacios recounts her version of the Crystal City walkout. Palacios notes that after school officials decided to equalize the cheering squad to three Anglos and three Mexican Americans, she tried out for the squad again and became a cheerleader at Crystal City High School. She ultimately also served as head cheerleader.

49. García, *United We Win,* p. 45. Navarro, *Mexican American Youth Organization,* pp. 135–136, 139–140; see appendix 3, pp. 251–252, for a list of the Crystal City walkout demands.

50. Navarro, *Mexican American Youth Organization,* pp. 141–145; Severita Lara, in conversation with Teresa Palomo Acosta, March 2, 2001; information on Severita Lara's term as mayor provided by the city clerk of Crystal City on November 26, 2001.

51. Teresa Palomo Acosta, "Mexican American Legal Defense and Educational Fund," *NHOT,* 4:659. Meier and Gutiérrez, "MALDEF," *Encyclopedia of the Mexican American Civil Rights Movement,* pp. 146–147.

52. Cynthia E. Orozco, "Chicana Rights Project," *NHOT,* 2:69.

53. Ibid.

54. Ibid.

55. Ibid.

56. Evey Chapa, ed., *La Mujer Chicana: An Annotated Bibliography,* p. xi.

57. Evey Chapa, *Chicana Research and Learning Center: A Progress Report, April 1973 to August 1975.* Teresa Palomo Acosta, "Chicana Research and Learning Center," *NHOT,* 2:68.

58. Acosta, "Chicana Research and Learning Center," *NHOT,* 2:68.

59. Ibid.

60. San Francisco Bay Area Farah Strike Support Committee, *Chicanas Strike at Farah* (pamphlet), 1974, unnumbered page.

61. Acosta, "Chicana Research and Learning Center," *NHOT,* 2:68.

62. Ibid.; Chapa, *La Mujer Chicana,* pp. xi–xiv. In her introduction to the publication, Evey Chapa points out how the bibliography was organized and the logic that guided the organizing process.

63. Acosta, "Chicana Research and Learning Center," *NHOT,* 2:68.

64. Various Mexican American women, including a number of graduate students, have taught the course. Harriet Romo, a non–Mexican American sociologist, offered the course for numerous years as well.

65. Acosta, "Chicana Research and Learning Center," *NHOT,* 2:68.

66. Ibid. Flyer announcing the panel "Las Fundadoras: Heritage of Mexican American Women in the U.S." The panel was apparently part of the Semana de la Mujer activities that the Mexican American Business and Professional Women's Association sponsored.

67. Orozco, "Mexican American Republicans of Texas," *NHOT,* 4:663–664.

68. Ibid.

69. Cynthia E. Orozco, "Mexican American Democrats," *NHOT,* 4:654.

CHAPTER ELEVEN

1. José Ángel Gutiérrez, *The Making of a Chicano Militant: Lessons from Cristal,* p. 76.

2. María de los Angeles Olvera and José Juan Bartolo Hernández, "AISD Hails 1st Hispanic Teacher," *Austin American-Statesman,* May 12, 1986, p. D18; Cynthia E. Orozco, "Mendez, Consuelo Herrera," *New Handbook of Texas,* 4:618 (hereafter *NHOT*).

3. Information on Josefina Dodier's attainment of a place on the school board provided by María de la Luz Rodríguez Cárdenas in correspondence, January 31, 2001.

4. Cárdenas, "Laredo Women in Politics," p. 4.

5. Ibid.

6. Information on Josefina Dodier and Norma Zúñiga Benavides was provided to the authors by Lucy Cárdenas in a telephone conversation, January 31, 2001; Cárdenas, "Laredo Women in Politics," p. 2, and abstract of paper for 2002 Texas State Historical Association annual meeting, "Norma Lucila Zúñiga Benavides: Radiant Light against Dark Politics." Additional information on Benavides is in the vertical file "Norma Zuniga Benavides—Laredo Women—Second Half of 20th Century," Webb County Heritage Foundation. This source notes that Benavides was the first woman to hold elected office in Webb County.

7. Cárdenas, "Laredo Women in Politics," p. 3; "Women on the Verge: Latinas in the Democrats' Sights," *Texas Monthly,* July 2000, p. 15; Megan K. Stack, "A Quiet Revolution in Laredo: Betty Flores Hurdled Personal and Cultural Obstacles to Become the City's First Female Mayor," *Austin American-Statesman,* November 23, 2000, p. B25.

8. Martha P. Cotera, *The Chicana Feminist,* p. 20.

9. Gutiérrez, *The Making of a Chicano Militant,* p. 76.

10. Ibid., p. 77.

11. Ibid., p. 230.

12. Ibid., pp. 242, 246.

13. Teresa Palomo Acosta, "Raza Unida Party," *NHOT,* 5:462; Cynthia E. Orozco, "Mujeres Por La Raza," *NHOT,* 4:879.

14. Orozco, "Mujeres Por La Raza," *NHOT,* 4:878–879.

15. "What I See Ahead for Women," panel presentation by Anita Nañez Martínez at Southern Methodist University, April 17, 1970, Woman's Collection, Texas Woman's University. Vivian Castleberry, *Daughters of Dallas,* pp. 450, 452–453.

16. Castleberry, *Daughters of Dallas,* p. 453.

17. Arnoldo De León, *San Angeleños: Mexican Americans in San Angelo, Texas,* pp. 107, 117.

18. National Association of Latino Elected and Appointed Officials (NALEO) Educational Fund, *The National Roster of Hispanic Elected Officials;* data compiled from 1984 roster, pp. vi, vii, viii, xii.

19. Ibid., with data compiled from rosters for various years, including 1984, 1985, 1986, 1988.

20. Ibid.; Thomas H. Kreneck, *Del Pueblo: A Pictorial History of Houston's Hispanic Community,* p. 205; Austin Community College Public Information Office.

21. Biography of Mary Helen Berlanga, updated January 28, 1999, provided by the Texas Education Agency, Acosta-Winegarten Collection (hereafter AWC).

22. National Association of Latino Elected and Appointed Officials Educational Fund, *National Roster of Latino Elected Officials;* data from various years, including 1984, 1986.

23. Ibid., vol. for 1993. National Association of Latino Elected and Appointed Officials Educational Fund, *National Directory of Latino Elected Officials,* vols. for 1996, 1997, 2000.

24. Julie Fernández, "Constable Changing Image, Gomez Takes Aim at Paperwork Backlog, Not Gunslingers," *Austin American-Statesman,* July 23, 1981, neighborhood section, p. 2; "Gomez Feels at Home in New College," *Opportunities for Adult Living,* Saint Edward's University, spring 1981; "County Commissioner, Precinct 4," *Austin American-Statesman,* October 25, 1998, p. D7.

25. Teresa Palomo Acosta, "Mexican American Business and Professional Women's Association," *NHOT,* 4:653–654. Rodolfo Rosales, *The Illusion of Inclusion: The Untold Political Story of San Antonio,* p. 163.

26. Rosales, *The Illusion of Inclusion,* pp. 164–165.

27. Ibid., pp. 166–167.

28. Vita of Alicia R. Chacón, AWC.

29. Ibid.

30. "Women on the Verge," p. 15.

31. Melinda Smith, "Minority Women Attorneys Share Their Thoughts and Experiences," *Texas Bar Journal,* October 1990, p. 1052.

32. "Salinas-Ender Announces Re-Election Bid," *LareDOS,* January 2000, p. 32. Edna McGaffey, "A Close-up of the Women Who Have Made the Bench," *San Antonio Express-News,* October 21, 1990, p. G2.

33. Sammye Munson, *Today's Tejano Heroes,* p. 60. Carlos Guerra, "Beauty Shop to Bench," *Austin American-Statesman,* April 4, 1998, p. A13.

34. McGaffey, "A Close-up of the Women Who Have Made the Bench," p. G2.

35. Campaign materials for Linda Reyna Yañez, undated, AWC. Dave Mc-Neely, "Hispanics Make Gains in Elected Courts," *Austin American-Statesman,* August 14, 1999, p. A11.

36. Nancy Baker Jones and Ruthe Winegarten, *Capitol Women: Texas Female Legislators, 1923–1999,* p. 234.

37. Ibid., p. 204.

38. Ibid., pp. 204–205.

39. Ibid., p. 205.

40. Ibid., p. 227; "Lena Guerrero Biographical Sketch," Office of State Representative Lena Guerrero, ca. 1985.

41. Jones and Winegarten, *Capitol Women,* pp. 228–229.

42. Ibid.

43. Ibid., p. 229.

44. Ibid., p. 233.

45. Ibid., pp. 233–234.

46. Ibid., p. 234.

47. Ibid., pp. 234–235. "Profile of Senator Judith Zaffirini," Office of Texas State Senator Zaffirini, AWC.

48. Jones and Winegarten, *Capitol Women,* pp. 254–255.

49. Ibid., p. 255.

50. Ibid., pp. 10, 205–206.

51. Ibid., p. 262. Ken Herman, "Greenberg to Give Up House Seat," *Austin American-Statesman,* November 5, 1999, p. B1. Program of the Texas Women's Political Caucus honoring State Senator Leticia Van de Putte, Austin, March 5, 2001, AWC.

52. Jones and Winegarten, *Capitol Women,* pp. 250–251, 261–267, 273; Jessica Farrar, videotape interview by Nancy Baker Jones, Austin, May 26, 1995.

53. Diana Dávila, videotape interview by Nancy Baker Jones, Austin, May 29, 1995.

54. Jones and Winegarten, *Capitol Women,* pp. 285–286.

55. Ibid., pp. 234–235.

56. "Run María Run," campaign materials, 1997; "County, District Clerk

Endorsements," editorial, *Austin American-Statesman,* October 16, 1998, p. A14; Jason Spencer, "Official Finds Her Paycheck Is Illegal," *Austin American-Statesman,* February 12, 1999, p. B8; Todd J. Gilman, "Kirk Vows to Address Complaints," *Dallas Morning News,* May 3, 1999, p. A1.

57. Dave McNeely, "A Challenge in Dallas," *Austin American-Statesman,* July 13, 2000, p. A19. Mark Wrolstand, "Candidates Far Apart in Tough House Race," *Dallas Morning News,* October 19, 2000, p. A23; Mark Wrolstad, "Sessions Wins Costly Battle: Montoya Coggins' Challenge of Republican Comes Up Short," *Dallas Morning News,* November 8, 2000, p. A33.

58. Scott S. Greenberger, "Democrat Puts Texas Face on National Convention," *Austin American-Statesman,* September 29, 1999, pp. B1, B6. "Texan to Lead Democratic Convention," *Austin American-Statesman,* September 22, 1999, p. A2.

59. Suzanne Gamboa, "Foundation Seeks to Aid Latinas in Public Service," *Austin American-Statesman,* August 30, 1998, p. B2; Amalia Rodríguez-Mendoza and Lena Guerrero, in conversation with Ruthe Winegarten, January 1999.

CHAPTER TWELVE

1. Lydia Mendoza, *Lydia Mendoza: A Family Autobiography,* comp. Chris Strachwitz with James Nicolopulos, p. 327.

2. Teresa Palomo Acosta, "Chicano Literary Renaissance," *New Handbook of Texas,* 2:71 (hereafter *NHOT*); Russell H. Goodyear, "Caracol," *NHOT,* 1:970.

3. Acosta, "Chicano Literary Renaissance," *NHOT,* 2: 71; for information on Tejana poets participating in literary festivals, see Leonard Carrillo et al., eds., *Canto al Pueblo: An Anthology of Experiences;* Flor y Canto Committee, eds., *Flor y Canto IV and V;* Justo S. Alarcón, Juan Pérez Aldape, and Lupe Cárdenas, eds., *Canto al Pueblo Anthology.*

4. Bryce Milligan, "Ever Radical: A Survey of Tejana Writers," in *Texas Women Writers: A Tradition of Their Own,* ed. Sylvia Ann Grider and Lou Halsell Rodenberger, pp. 237–238.

5. Jovita González and Eve Raleigh, *Caballero: A Historical Novel,* ed. José E. Limón and María Cotera, p. 212.

6. Teresa Palomo Acosta, "Ramírez, Sara Estela," *NHOT,* 5:424; also see Emilio Zamora's "Sara Estela Ramírez," in *Mexican Women in the United States: Struggles Past and Present,* ed. Magdalena Mora and Adelaida R. Castillo, pp. 163–169. Emilio Zamora was one of the first Chicano historians to take note of the political and literary work of Sara Estela Ramírez. Also see Inés Hernández Tovar's doctoral dissertation, "Sara Estela Ramirez: The Early Twentieth Century Texas–Mexican Poet." Also see chap. 2 of Louis Gerard Mendoza's *Historia: The Literary Making of Chicana & Chicano History* for an insightful analysis of Sara Estela Ramírez's political and literary contributions.

7. Acosta, "Ramírez, Sara Estela," *NHOT,* 5:424.

8. Clara Lomas, preface and introduction to Leonor Villegas de Magnón, *The Rebel: Leonor Villegas de Magnón,* pp. viii, ix, xxv, and xxxv.

9. Alicia Arrizón, "Niggli, Josefina Maria," *NHOT,* 4:1013–1014.

10. Juanita Luna Lawhn, "Blanco, Beatriz," *NHOT,* 1:581. Juanita Luna Lawhn, introduction to Olga Beatriz Torres's *Memorias de mi viaje/Recollections of My Trip,* pp. 5, 6.

11. L. Robert Ables, "Zavala, Adina Emilia De," *NHOT,* 6:1146–1147. A new version of *History and Legends of the Alamo and Other Missions in and around San Antonio,* edited and introduced by Richard R. Flores, was published by Arte Público in 1996.

12. Bruce-Novoa, preface to Torres's *Memorias de mi viaje/Recollections of My Trip,* p. x; also refer to Juanita Luna Lawhn's introduction to the book, p. 8.

13. Cynthia E. Orozco, "O'Shea, María Elena Zamora," *NHOT,* 4:1176–1177.

14. Ibid., *NHOT,* 4:1177; also see Texas A&M Press web site link to O'Shea (www.tamu.edu/upress/BOOKS/2000/oshea.htm); Cynthia E. Orozco, "Ramírez, Emilia Wilhelmina Schunior," *NHOT,* 5:423.

15. Cynthia E. Orozco, "Escajeda, Josefina," *NHOT,* 2:887; Cynthia E. Orozco and Teresa Palomo Acosta, "González de Mireles, Jovita," *NHOT,* 3:236; the date of Fermina Guerra's master's thesis (1941) is from the University of Texas Library.

16. Orozco and Acosta, "González de Mireles, Jovita," *NHOT,* 3:236–237.

17. See Jovita González and Eve Raleigh, *Caballero: A Historical Novel;* also see Jovita González, *Dew on the Thorn,* ed. José E. Limón.

18. Ramón Saldívar, "Texas-Mexican Fiction," *NHOT,* 6:361; Bruce-Novoa, *Chicano Authors: Inquiry by Interview,* p. 163.

19. Inés Hernández Tovar, ed. *Hembra: Hermanas en movimiento brotando raíces de Aztlán,* pp. 2, 3, 9, 12.

20. Vita of Evangelina Vigil-Piñon, Acosta-Winegarten Collection (hereafter AWC). Milligan, "Ever Radical"; Milligan discusses poets Evangelina Vigil-Piñon and Carmen Tafolla, pp. 228–236.

21. Milligan, "Ever Radical," p. 223. Teresa Palomo Acosta is less known than her Chicana generation colleagues. For an in-depth examination of some of Acosta's poetry, see Mendoza's *Historia;* Mendoza uses Acosta's work throughout his book to explore the creation of a counter and critical female voice in the literary telling of Chicana and Chicano history. Also see Sheila Marie Contreras's afterword in *Nile & Other Poems* for a discussion of Acosta's work. Gloria Anzaldúa, *Borderlands: La Frontera = The New Mestiza,* p. 3.

22. Milligan, "Ever Radical," p. 243; see Tina Juárez, *Call No Man Master* and *South Wind Come;* Anne Morris, "A Migrant Worker's Labor of Love: IBM Professional Recalls Life in Beet Fields of Minnesota," *Austin American-Statesman,* July 25, 1999, pp. K6–K7.

23. Bryce Milligan, Mary Guerrero Milligan, and Ángela De Hoyos, eds., *¡Floricanto Sí! A Collection of Latina Poetry,* pp. 132–134, 139–142, 171–173, 188–191; Bárbara Renaud González, "To My Unborn Daughter: Tejana Poetry," *La Voz de Esperanza,* March 1999, pp. 7, 9.

24. Biographical sketch of Tammy Gómez, AWC; program of "Palabras: A Latino Literary Festival," Austin, March 30–31, 2001, p. 5; program for "Inculcated Con Fusion," Dallas, April 27–28, 2001; Kamala Platt, "Social Justice Theories in Performance Poetry: Tammy Gómez, Literary Artist with an Attitude," *(sub) TEX* 1, no. 4 (December 1994), unnumbered pages, AWC. See *Texas Observer,* December 4, 1998, p. 24, which features a selection of Sarah Cortez's work. *Arte Público Press 2000 Complete Catalog,* p. 20, AWC.

25. Teresa Palomo Acosta, "Hauschild Music Company," *NHOT,* 3:507; Leonora Rives-Díaz was one of the composers Hauschild published. A reference to her in the original manuscript of the *NHOT* article on Hauschild was deleted in the editing process. Information and sheet music of Rives-Díaz's works provided by Henry J. Hauschild (photocopies, AWC).

26. Henry J. Hauschild, *A Musical Chronicle from the Historical Scrapbooks of Henry J. Hauschild,* unnumbered pages. Rives-Díaz is noted as a composer in various places in the *Musical Chronicle.* Also, handbill from Hauschild Music Company describing early composers, provided by Henry Hauschild, AWC. None of the major orchestras with whom Luis Díaz played are noted.

27. Vivian Castleberry, *Daughters of Dallas,* pp. 455, 456, 458, 459, 460, 461.

28. Teresa Palomo Acosta, "Tejana Singers," *NHOT,* 6:237; Teresa Palomo Acosta, "Mendoza, Leonora," *NHOT,* 4:619.

29. Acosta, "Tejana Singers," *NHOT,* 6:237; also see Yolanda Broyles-González, *Lydia Mendoza's Life in Music/La historia de Lydia Mendoza: Norteño Tejano Legacies,* published in 2001 by Oxford University Press.

30. Acosta, "Tejana Singers," *NHOT,* 6:237.

31. Ibid., p. 238. Ramiro Burr, *The Billboard Guide to Tejano and Regional Mexican Music,* p. 190.

32. Acosta, "Tejana Singers," *NHOT,* 6:238.

33. Betty Trapp Chapman, *Houston Women: Invisible Threads in the Tapestry,* p. 14.

34. Acosta, "Tejana Singers," *NHOT,* 6:238.

35. Ibid.

36. Chris Strachowitz, "The Soulful Women Duets of South Texas," *Arriba* (Austin), November 3–16, 2000, pp. 2–3. Carmen Marroquín, in conversation with Teresa Palomo Acosta, June 1991, during which Marroquín related that Arhoolie Records had acquired the Falcón catalog and planned to release some of the recordings in the future. Also refer to the Arhoolie web site (www.arhoolie.com), which notes the existence of two CDs of Tejana singers in its catalog; program for "First Ladies: Texas Women in Music," a symposium held in Austin on July 16, 2000; "Texas Women in Music at Dougherty Center," *Arriba,* July 14–27, 2000, p. 3.

37. Burr, *The Billboard Guide,* p. 73.

38. Ibid., pp. 71–72.

39. Ibid., p. 137.

40. Las Super Tejanas concert was sponsored on January 29, 2000, by Texas Folklife Resources at the Paramount Theatre in Austin, Texas, undated post-card announcing concert, AWC.

41. Ibid. Burr, *The Billboard Guide,* pp. 108, 128. Katy Vine, "In Concert," *Texas Monthly,* January 2000, p. 38.

42. John T. Davis, "Las Super Tejanas," *Austin American-Statesman,* January 27, 2000, XLent supplement, pp. 6, 8. Vine, "In Concert," p. 38. Program for Las Super Tejanas concert, Austin, January 29, 2000, AWC.

43. Burr, p. 188; Cynthia E. Orozco, "Pérez, Selena Quintanilla," *NHOT,* 5:392–393.

44. John Morthland, "Elida Reyna," *Texas Monthly,* September 2000, pp. 152–153; Burr, *The Billboard Guide,* pp. 51, 195; Madeline Baro Díaz, "Singer Moves beyond Label of 'Next Selena,'" *Austin American-Statesman,* August 10, 1999, pp. E1, E2; Chris Riemenschneider, "Awards Show Reflects Tejano's Ups and Downs," *Austin American-Statesman,* April 10, 2001, p. E2.

45. Elizabeth C. Ramírez, "Mexican-American Theater," *NHOT,* 4:679.

46. Ibid., p. 680.

47. Elizabeth C. Ramírez, "Hernández, Concepción," *NHOT,* 3:572.

48. Elizabeth C. Ramírez, "Carlos Villalongín Dramatic Company," *NHOT,* 1:978.

49. Ramírez, "Hernández, Concepción," *NHOT,* 3:572.

50. Elizabeth C. Ramírez, "Solsona Dramatic Company," *NHOT,* 5:1143.

51. Teresa Palomo Acosta, "Mexican Circuses," *NHOT,* 4:683–684. Nicolás Kanellos, *A History of Hispanic Theatre in the United States: Origins to 1940,* p. 101.

52. Pamela S. Smith and Elizabeth C. Ramírez, "Escalona Pérez, Beatriz," *NHOT,* 2:888. Ramírez, "Mexican-American Theater," *NHOT,* 4:680.

53. Smith and Ramírez, "Escalona Pérez, Beatriz," *NHOT,* 2:888.

54. Ibid.

55. Ramírez, "Mexican-American Theater," *NHOT,* 4:680.

56. Ibid.

57. Organizational history provided by Teatro Dallas, 2000, AWC; resume of Cora Cardona provided by Teatro Dallas, AWC.

58. Shermakaye Bass, "Latinos at Center Stage," *Austin American-Statesman,* June 20, 1997, p. F8; "Amparo García-Crow," *Noticias de CMAS,* fall 2000, p. 4.

59. Publicity materials for *Rosita's Day of the Dead,* AWC. At her November 11, 2000, performance in Austin, Texas, of *Rosita's Day of the Dead,* Ruby Nelda Pérez noted that she provided ideas for the creation of the character of Rosita to the playwright. She also stated that a third play may be written to round out a trilogy; Belinda Acosta, "Something's Cooking: Doña Rosita's

One-Woman Show Whips up an Arts Feast for Students," *Austin American-Statesman,* November 13, 1999, p. 59.

60. Acosta, "Something's Cooking," p. 59; materials on theatrical productions provided by the Guadalupe Cultural Arts Center, San Antonio, Texas; Shermakaye Bass, "Latinos at Center Stage," p. F1.

61. Teresa Palomo Acosta, excerpt from "My Mother Pieced Quilts," *Passing Time,* p. 21.

62. Teresa Palomo Acosta, "Mexican-American Folk Arts and Crafts," *NHOT,* 4:655; for a discussion of Mexican American women's quilting tradition, see Norma Cantú and Ofelia Zapata Vela, "The Mexican-American Quilting Traditions of Laredo, San Ygnacio, and Zapata," in *Hecho en Tejas: Texas-Mexican Folk Arts and Crafts,* ed. Joe S. Graham, pp. 77–83.

63. See Suzanne Yabsley, *Texas Quilts, Texas Women;* also see Pat Jasper and Kay Turner, ed., *Art among Us/Arte entre nosotros: Mexican American Folk Art of San Antonio,* p. 20 (fig. 9), p. 56 (fig. 38).

64. María-Cristina García, "González Amezcua, Consuelo," *NHOT,* 3:235; Cynthia E. Orozco, "Montemayor, Alice Dickerson," *NHOT,* 4:798; Kendall Curlee, "Ximénes, Beatrice Valdez," *NHOT,* 6:1103.

65. García, "González Amezcua, Consuelo," *NHOT,* 3:235–236. Jacinto Quirarte included a discussion of González Amezcua's work in *Mexican American Artists.*

66. Orozco, "Montemayor, Alice Dickerson," *NHOT,* 4:798.

67. Curlee, "Ximénez, Beatrice Valdez," *NHOT,* 6:1103–1104.

68. Carmen Lomas Garza, *Pedacito de Mi Corazón,* p. 13.

69. "Santa Barraza: A MexicTejana from Nepantla," program notes for an exhibition at Mexic-Arte Museum, Austin, Texas, from January 28–April 15, 2000, AWC; holiday card from the Office of the President, the University of Texas at San Antonio, undated, AWC.

70. Jim Davis, "Memories of Home: Art by Kingsville Native Reflects Chicano Life in South Texas," *Corpus Christi Caller Times,* November 8, 1991, p. E6; also refer to the exhibition catalog *Pedacito de Mi Corazón.*

71. See pages 11–13 of *Pedacito de Mi Corazón* for an insightful autobiographical sketch by Garza in which she depicts her artistic values and her struggles to ensure their representation.

72. Megan K. Stack, "Artist Presents Haunting Reality of Juarez Killings: Women's Clothes Laced with Dried Grass, Mesh Fence Are Part of Ghostly Exhibit," *Austin American-Statesman,* September 8, 1999, p. B6.

73. Jeanne Claire Van Ryzin, "Artful Endings: Lyons, Matrix, Galeria Sin Fronteras to Close After Noteworthy Exhibits," *Austin American-Statesman,* November 11, 1999, p. 44; information on the artist in *Gemini Ink,* summer 1999, p. 10; also see *Kathy Vargas: Photographs, 1971–2000,* the catalog of the artist's first retrospective exhibition at the McNay Museum.

74. Mike Kelley and Rebecca Thatcher, "Son Charged with Death of

Mother Near Volente," *Austin American-Statesman,* October 1, 1998, p. B4; Mary Jane Garza, "In Memoriam: Marsha A. Gómez, September 24, 1951– September 29, 1998," *Arriba,* October 9–October 22, 1998, p. 1; Marsha Gómez, "Woman of the Earth: Art and Activism on Sacred Lands," *La Voz de Esperanza,* November 1998, pp. 5–6; "Marsha Gómez: In Memorial," *La Voz de Esperanza,* October 1998, p. 3.

75. Teresa Palomo Acosta, "Chicano Mural Movement," *NHOT,* 2:72–73.

76. Ibid.

77. Associated Press, "San Angelo Teen Paints History on School Walls," *Austin American-Statesman,* November 4, 1998, p. B2.

78. María-Cristina García, "Mujeres Artistas del Suroeste," *NHOT,* 4:878.

79. Ibid.; Teresa Palomo Acosta, "Conferencia Plástica Chicana," *NHOT,* 2:266.

80. García, "Mujeres Artistas del Suroeste," *NHOT,* 4:878.

81. María-Cristina García, "Comité Patriótico Mexicano," *NHOT,* 2:249; Cynthia E. Orozco, "Círculo Cultural Isabel la Católica," *NHOT,* 2:111–112; Teresa Palomo Acosta, "Cruz Azul Mexicana," *NHOT,* 2:429.

82. Kendall Curlee, "Xochil Art and Culture Center," *NHOT,* 6:1104–1105.

83. Kendall Curlee, "La Peña," *NHOT,* 4:72.

84. Kendall Curlee, "Mexic-Arte," *NHOT,* 4:698–699.

85. Ibid.; Leah Quinn, "Mexic-Arte to Keep Site Downtown," *Austin American-Statesman,* October 6, 2000, pp. B1, B3.

86. Vita of Rosa Ramírez Guerrero, AWC; 1994 Texas Women's Hall of Fame biographical sketch of Rosa Ramírez Guerrero, AWC.

87. Materials describing the Casa de Colores Resource Center provided by the Foundation for a Compassionate Society in draft of "Herstory Report," ca. 1997, pp. 24–25, AWC. The Casa de Colores was sponsored by the Foundation for a Compassionate Society and funded by Genevieve Vaughn. Joe Simnacher, "Dolores G. Barzune, Arts Patron, Wins Linz," *Dallas Morning News,* March 11, 2001, pp. A37, A42; program for "Women of Spirit Awards Celebration," sponsored by the American Jewish Congress, Southwest Region, Dallas, September 13, 2001; vita and biography of Lupita Norma Barrera, AWC.

Bibliography

The Acosta-Winegarten Collection (provisional title) is located at the Benson Latin American Collection, the University of Texas at Austin. The collection (hereafter referred to as the AWC) consists of materials on Mexican-origin women living in present-day Texas from approximately 1700 to 2000. The materials were collected during a period of more than twenty years, from 1979 to 2002. Biographical and subject files, as well as excerpts from articles and books, are included in the AWC.

ARCHIVAL AND PRIMARY SOURCES

Acosta, Sabina Palomo. Three interviews by Teresa Palomo Acosta. Tape recordings. McGregor, Texas, November 14, November 20, November 25, 1999. Institute of Oral History, Baylor University, Waco, Texas.

Anaya, Lucia Alderete. Three interviews by Teresa Palomo Acosta. Tape recordings. McGregor, Texas, October 1, October 8, October 15, 1999. Institute of Oral History, Baylor University, Waco, Texas.

Bexar Archives, 1731–1836. Center for American History, University of Texas at Austin.

Campos, Juanita Palomo. Interview by Teresa Palomo Acosta. Tape recording. Moody, Texas, March 18, 2000. Institute of Oral History, Baylor University, Waco, Texas.

Canary Islanders Papers. Center for American History, University of Texas at Austin.

Dávila, Diana. Interview by Nancy Baker Jones. Videotape. Austin, May 29, 1995. Archives for Research on Women and Gender, University of Texas at San Antonio.

Farrar, Jessica Cristina. Interview by Nancy Baker Jones. Videotape. Austin, May 26, 1995. Archives for Research on Women and Gender, University of Texas at San Antonio.

González de Mireles, Jovita. "Memoirs." Updated. E. E. Mireles and Jovita González de Mireles Papers, Special Collections and Archives, Bell Library, Texas A&M University–Corpus Christi.

Quiroz de León, María. Interview by Teresa Palomo Acosta. Tape recording. McGregor, Texas, March 8, 2000. Institute of Oral History, Baylor University, Waco, Texas.

Rangel, Irma. Interview by Nancy Baker Jones. Videotape. Austin, May 25, 1995. Archives for Research on Women and Gender, University of Texas at San Antonio.

Texas General Land Office. Archives and Records Division, Austin.

Texas Woman's University Library, Denton. Woman's Collection, Archives of "Texas Women: A Celebration of History" exhibit; Emma Tenayuca Collection; Hilda Tagle Collection.

University of Texas at Austin. Benson Latin American Collection. AWC.

University of Texas Institute of Texan Cultures at San Antonio. Biographical and subject files and photographs.

"Women in the Texas Legislature" oral interviews, 1995. Archives for the Study of Women and Gender, University of Texas at San Antonio.

SECONDARY SOURCES

Abernethy, Francis C., ed. *The Folklore of Texan Cultures.* Austin: Encino Press, 1974.

Ables, L. Robert. "The Second Battle for the Alamo." *Southwestern Historical Quarterly* 70, no. 3 (January 1967): 372–413.

———. "Zavala, Adina Emilia De." *New Handbook of Texas,* 6:1146–1147.

Acción Texas. "Our Clients." http://www.acciontexas.org (January 22, 2001).

Acosta, Teresa Palomo. "Alianza Hispano-Americana." *New Handbook of Texas,* 1:104.

———. "American G.I. Forum Women's Auxiliary." *New Handbook of Texas,* 1:148.

———. "Cassiano, María Gertrudis Pérez." *New Handbook of Texas,* 1:1016.

———. "Chapa, Francisco." *New Handbook of Texas,* 2:42.

———. "Chicana Research and Learning Center." *New Handbook of Texas,* 2:68.

———. "Chicano Literary Renaissance." *New Handbook of Texas,* 2:71–72.

———. "Chicano Mural Movement." *New Handbook of Texas*, 2:72–73.

———. "Confederación de Organizaciones Mexicanas y Latino Americanas." *New Handbook of Texas*, 2:263–264.

———. "Conferencia de Mujeres por la Raza." *New Handbook of Texas*, 2:266.

———. "Conferencia Plástica Chicana." *New Handbook of Texas*, 2:266.

———. "Congreso Mexicanista." *New Handbook of Texas*, 2:267.

———. "Cruz Azul Mexicana." *New Handbook of Texas*, 2:429–430.

———. "*Edgewood ISD* v. *Kirby*." *New Handbook of Texas*, 2:784–785.

———. "Flores de Andrade." *New Handbook of Texas*, 2:1038.

———. "Flores de Barker, Josefa Augustina." *New Handbook of Texas*, 2:1038.

———. "García de Falcón, Élida." *New Handbook of Texas*, 3:88.

———. "Hauschild Music Company." *New Handbook of Texas*, 3:507.

———. "Home Altars." *New Handbook of Texas*, 3:677–678.

———. "*In re Ricardo Rodríguez*." *New Handbook of Texas*, 3:856.

———. "López de Ximenes, Josefina." *New Handbook of Texas*, 4:290.

———. "Losoya Taylor, Paula." *New Handbook of Texas*, 4:297.

———. "Mendoza, Leonora." *New Handbook of Texas*, 4:619.

———. "Mexican American Business and Professional Women's Association." *New Handbook of Texas*, 4:653–654.

———. "Mexican-American Folk Arts and Crafts." *New Handbook of Texas*, 4:655.

———. "Mexican American Legal Defense and Educational Fund." *New Handbook of Texas*, 4:659.

———. "Mexican American Youth Organization." *New Handbook of Texas*, 4:682.

———. "Mexican Circuses." *New Handbook of Texas*, 4:683–684.

———. "*La Mujer Moderna*." *New Handbook of Texas*, 4:52.

———. "National Women's Employment and Education." *New Handbook of Texas*, 4:949.

———. *Nile & Other Poems*. Austin: Red Salmon Press, 1999.

———. "Nuestra Señora de Guadalupe." *New Handbook of Texas*, 4:1064–1065.

———. "Partido Liberal Mexicano." *New Handbook of Texas*, 5:77–78.

———. *Passing Time*. Austin: privately printed, 1984.

———. "Pérez, Beatriz Tagle." *New Handbook of Texas*, 5:149.

———. "Political Association of Spanish-Speaking Organizations." *New Handbook of Texas*, 5:256.

———. "Ramírez, Sara Estela." *New Handbook of Texas*, 5:424.

———. "Raza Unida Party." *New Handbook of Texas*, 5:462–463.

———. "Rebecca Flores Harrington." Program notes for symposium "César Chávez: Historical and Current Dimensions of His Leadership," April 24, 1994, pp. 4–5.

————. "Rodríguez, Thomas A." *New Handbook of Texas,* 5:656–657.

————. "Sociedades Guadalupanas." *New Handbook of Texas,* 5:1131–1132.

————. "Tejana Singers." *New Handbook of Texas,* 6:237–238.

————. "United Farm Workers Union." *New Handbook of Texas,* 6:629.

Acosta, Teresa Palomo, and Kendall Curlee. "Chicano Art Networks." *New Handbook of Texas,* 2:69–71.

Acosta, Teresa Palomo, María-Cristina García, and Cynthia E. Orozco. "Settlement Houses." *New Handbook of Texas,* 5:977–979.

Adams, William L., and Anthony K. Knapp. *Portrait of a Border City: Brownsville, Texas.* Austin: Eakin Press, 1997.

¡Adelante, mujeres! Video. Windsor, Calif.: National Women's History Project, 1992.

Alarcón, Justo S., Juan Pérez Aldape, and Lupe Cárdenas, eds. *Canto al Pueblo Anthology.* Mesa, Ariz.: Arizona Canto al Pueblo, ca. 1980.

Allen, Ruth Alice. *The Labor of Women in the Production of Cotton.* Reprint, New York: Arno Press, 1975.

Allsup, V. Carl. "American G.I. Forum of Texas." *New Handbook of Texas,* 1:147–148.

————. "*Cisneros* v. *Corpus Christi ISD.*" *New Handbook of Texas,* 2:113.

————. "Felix Longoria Affair." *New Handbook of Texas,* 2:975–976.

Almaráz Jr., Félix D. "Castañeda, Carlos Eduardo." *New Handbook of Texas,* 1:1016–1017.

Alonzo, Armando C. "Mexican-American Land Grant Adjudication." *New Handbook of Texas,* 4:656–659.

————. *Tejano Legacy: Rancheros and Settlers in South Texas, 1734–1900.* Albuquerque: University of New Mexico Press, 1998.

American Friends Service Committee. "Fuerza Unida." http://www.afsc .org/tao/112k03/htm (March 3, 2001).

Anderson, Adrian N., and Ralph A. Wooster. *Texas and Texans.* Rev. ed., Austin: Steck-Vaughn Co., 1978; new ed., New York: Glencoe/Macmillan/McGraw-Hill, 1993.

Anderson, H. Allen. "Pastores." *New Handbook of Texas,* 5:84–86.

————. "Romero, Casimero." *New Handbook of Texas,* 5:671–672.

Andrus, Pearl. *Juana, A Spanish Girl in Central Texas.* Burnet: Eakin Press, 1982.

Anzaldúa, Gloria. *Borderlands: La Frontera = The New Mestiza.* San Francisco: Spinsters/Aunt Lute, 1987; 2d ed., Aunt Lute Books, 1999.

Arrizón, Alicia. "Niggli, Josefina María." *New Handbook of Texas,* 4:1013–1014.

"Arts Suit in San Antonio Settled." *Austin American-Statesman,* October 22, 2001.

Ashton, John, and Edgar P. Sneed. "King Ranch." *New Handbook of Texas,* 3:1111–1112.

Austin, Mattie Alice. "The Municipal Government of San Fernando de Bexar, 1730–1800." *Quarterly of the Texas State Historical Association* 8, no. 4 (April 1905): 336.

"Austin Women: 150 Years of Trial and Triumph." Exhibit information sheet. Austin: Commission on the Status of Women, 1986.

Bailey, Richard. "Starr County Strike." *New Handbook of Texas,* 6:69–70.

Barrera, Aida. *Looking for Carrascolendas: From a Child's World to Award-Winning Television.* Austin: University of Texas Press, 2001.

Barrera, Elena Farías. "Estella Minerva Cuellar." In *One Hundred Women of the Rio Grande Valley of Texas,* edited by the Rio Writers, pp. 29–30. Austin: Eakin Press, 1983.

———. "Eva Dolores Carrizales, M.D." In *One Hundred Women of the Rio Grande Valley of Texas,* edited by the Rio Writers, pp. 23–25. Austin: Eakin Press, 1983.

Baulch, Joe R. "Garza War." *New Handbook of Texas,* 3:113.

Bazán, Evangelina Ximénez. "Ximénez, Fernando." *New Handbook of Texas,* 6:1104.

Benavides, Adán, Jr., comp. and ed. *Béxar Archives, 1717–1836: A Name Guide.* Austin: University of Texas Press for the University of Texas Institute of Texan Cultures at San Antonio, 1989.

Blackwelder, Julia Kirk. *Women of the Depression: Caste and Culture in San Antonio, 1929–1939.* College Station: Texas A&M University Press, 1984.

Blake, Robert Bruce. "Leal, Antonio." *New Handbook of Texas,* 4:133.

Boatright, Mody, ed. *From Hell to Breakfast.* Dallas: Southern Methodist University Press for the Texas Folklore Society, 1944.

Brackenridge, R. Douglas. "Rio Grande Female Institute." *New Handbook of Texas,* 5:586–587.

Brochin, Carol. "The History I Never Learned in School: Diana Palacios Recounts Crystal City in 1969." *LareDOS,* October 2001.

Bruce-Novoa, Juan. *Chicano Authors: Inquiry by Interview.* Austin: University of Texas Press, 1980.

Burr, Ramiro. *The Billboard Guide to Tejano and Regional Mexican Music.* New York: Billboard Books, 1999.

Calderón, Roberto R. "Tejano Politics." *New Handbook of Texas,* 6:239–242.

Calderón, Roberto R., and Emilio Zamora Jr. "Manuela Solis Sager and Emma Tenayuca, A Tribute." In *Chicana Voices: Intersection of Class, Race, and Gender,* edited by Teresa Cordova et al., pp. 30–41. Austin: Center for Mexican American Studies, University of Texas at Austin, 1986.

Callcott, Wilfred H. "Santa Anna, Antonio López de." *New Handbook of Texas,* 5:881–882.

Callihan, Jeanne, *Our Mexican Ancestors.* Vol. 1 of *Stories for Young Readers.* San Antonio: University of Texas Institute of Texan Cultures at San Antonio, 1981.

Calvert, Robert, and Arnoldo De León. *The History of Texas.* 1990. 2d ed., Arlington Heights, Ill.: Harlan Davidson, 1996.

Campbell, Camilla. "Navarro, José Ángel." *New Handbook of Texas,* 4:953–954.

Campbell, Thomas N. "Muruam Indians." *New Handbook of Texas,* 4:897–898.

Cantú, Norma, and Ofelia Zapata Vela. "The Mexican American Quilting Traditions of Laredo, San Ygnacio, and Zapata." In *Hecho en Tejas: Texas-Mexican Folk Arts and Crafts,* edited by Joe S. Graham, pp. 77–83. Denton: University of North Texas Press, 1991.

Cárdenas, María de la Luz Rodríguez. "Laredo Women in Politics: Fearless Voices in a Common Struggle." 1998. Photocopy. AWC.

Carrillo, Leonard, et al., eds. *Canto al Pueblo: An Anthology of Experiences.* San Antonio: Penca Books, 1978.

Carrington, Evelyn M., ed. *Women in Early Texas.* Sponsored by American Association of University Women, Austin branch. Austin: Pemberton Press, 1975; reprint, Austin: Texas State Historical Association, 1994.

Castañeda, Antonia I. "The Political Economy of Nineteenth Century Stereotypes of Californianas." In *Regions of La Raza,* edited by Antonio Rios-Bustamante. Encino, Calif.: Floricanto Press, 1993.

Castañeda, Carlos. *Our Catholic Heritage in Texas.* 7 vols. Austin: Von Boeckman-Jones, 1936–1958; reprint, New York: Arno, 1976.

Castleberry, Vivian. *Daughters of Dallas.* Dallas: Odenwald Press, 1994.

Castro, Max J. "¿Habla Español? The Nursing Profession Needs You." *Vista,* October 2000, p. 40.

Cazneau, Jane (McManus). *Eagle Pass; or Life on the Border by Cora Montgomery.* New York: Putman, 1852.

Chabot, Frederick C. *With the Makers of San Antonio.* San Antonio: privately printed, 1937.

Chapa, Evey. *Chicana Research and Learning Center: A Progress Report, April 1973 to August 1975.* Austin: Chicana Research and Learning Center, 1975.

Chapa, Evey, ed. *La Mujer Chicana: An Annotated Bibliography.* Austin: Chicana Research and Learning Center, 1976.

Chapa, Evey, and Armando Gutiérrez. "Chicanas in Politics: An Overview and a Case Study." In *Perspectivas en Chicana Studies I: Papers Presented at the Third Annual Meeting of the National Association of Chicano Social Studies, 1975,* edited by Reynaldo Flores Macias, pp. 137–155. n.p.: The National Association of Chicano Studies, 1977.

Chapman, Betty Trapp. *Houston Women: Invisible Threads in the Tapestry.* Houston: B. T. Chapman, ca. 2000.

Chávez, John R., *The Lost Land: The Chicano Image of the Southwest.* Albuquerque: University of New Mexico Press, 1984.

Chipman, Donald E. "Agreda, María de Jesús de." *New Handbook of Texas,* 1:56.

————. "Rábago y Terán, Felipe de." *New Handbook of Texas,* 5:399–400.

————. *Spanish Texas, 1519–1821.* Austin: University of Texas Press, 1992.

Chipman, Donald E., and Harriett Denise Joseph. *Notable Men and Women of Spanish Texas.* Austin: University of Texas Press, 1999.

Chipman, Donald E., and Patricia R. Lemée. "St. Denis, Louis Juchereau de." *New Handbook of Texas,* 5:755–756.

"Coahuiltecan Indians." *New Handbook of Texas,* 2:171–174.

Coalson, George O. "Alavez, Francita." *New Handbook of Texas,* 1:91.

————. "Villanueva, Andrea Castañón." *New Handbook of Texas,* 6:752.

Coerver, Don M. "Plan of San Diego." *New Handbook of Texas,* 5:228.

College Board. *Projected Social Context for Education of Children: 1990–2015.* New York: College Board, 1999.

Connor, Seymour V. "Rankin, Melinda." *New Handbook of Texas,* 5:445.

Corbin, Diane H. "Angelina." In *Legendary Ladies of Texas,* edited by Francis E. Abernethy, pp. 15–19. Denton: University of North Texas Press, 1994.

Cotera, Martha P. *The Chicana Feminist.* Austin: Information Systems Development, 1977.

————. *Diosa y Hembra: The History and Heritage of Chicanas in the U.S.* Austin: Information Systems Development, 1976.

Cottrell, Debbie Mauldin. "Martínez, Faustina Porras." *New Handbook of Texas,* 4:534–535.

Cox, I. Waynne, "Calvillo, María del Carmen." *New Handbook of Texas,* 1:912.

Cox, J. J. "Educational Efforts in San Fernando." *Texas State Historical Association Quarterly* 6 (July 1902): 36–49.

Coyle, Laurie, Gail Hershatter, and Emily Honig. "Farah Strike." *New Handbook of Texas,* 2:950.

Crimm, A. Carolina Castillo. "The Economic Impact of Hispanic Family Structure: The Families of Petra Vela de Vidal Kenedy and Patricia de la Garza de León." Paper presented at the eighth forum of the Daughters of the Republic of Texas, San Antonio, Texas, October 27, 2000. Photocopy. AWC.

Crimm, Caroline Castillo. Work in progress (untitled). Photocopy of partial manuscript. AWC.

Croxdale, Richard. "Pecan Shellers' Strike." *New Handbook of Texas,* 5:117–118.

Croxdale, Richard, and Melissa Hield, eds. *Women in the Texas Workforce: Yesterday and Today.* Austin: People's History in Texas, 1979.

Curlee, Kendall. "La Peña." *New Handbook of Texas,* 4:72.

————. "Mexic-Arte." *New Handbook of Texas,* 4:698–699.

————. "Ximénez, Beatrice Valdez." *New Handbook of Texas,* 6:1103–1104.

————. "Xochil Art and Culture Center." *New Handbook of Texas,* 6:1104–1105.

De Aguayo, Marqués de San Migúel. Printed Petition to the King of Spain, n.p., ca. 1718, notation in rare book catalogue of Dorothy Sloan, title and date unknown.

de Ballí, Rosa María de Hinojosa. Typed copy of the certified copy of her will, executed in the year 1798, Reynosa, Tamaulipas, Mexico. Cameron County. "Deed Record Book X," p. 113.

de la Teja, Jesús F. "Seguín, Juan Nepomuceno." *New Handbook of Texas,* 5:966–967.

————. "Veramendi, Fernando." *New Handbook of Texas,* 6:722.

de la Teja, Jesús F., and John Wheat. "Bexar: Profile of a Tejano Community, 1820–1832." *Southwestern Historical Quarterly* 89, no. 1 (July 1985): 7–34.

De León, Arnoldo. *Apuntes tejanos.* 2 vols. Ann Arbor: University Microfiles International for Texas State Historical Association, 1978.

————. "Chicano." *New Handbook of Texas,* 2:69.

————. *Ethnicity in the Sunbelt: A History of Mexican Americans in Houston.* Houston: Mexican American Studies Program, University of Houston, 1989.

————. "Mexican Americans." *New Handbook of Texas,* 4:666.

————. *Mexican Americans in Texas: A Brief History.* Wheeling, Ill.: Harlan Davidson, 1993.

————. *San Angeleños: Mexican Americans in San Angelo, Texas.* San Angelo: Fort Concho Museum Press, 1985.

————. *The Tejano Community, 1836–1900.* 1982; rev. ed., Dallas: Southern Methodist University Press, 1997.

————. *The Tejano Yearbook, 1519–1978.* San Antonio: Caravel, 1978.

————. *They Called Them Greasers: Anglo Attitudes toward Mexicans in Texas, 1821–1900.* Austin: University of Texas Press, 1983.

De León, Arnoldo, and Robert A. Calvert. "Civil-Rights Movement." *New Handbook of Texas,* 2:118–121.

————. "Segregation." *New Handbook of Texas,* 5:965.

El Despertador de Tejas (University of Texas at Austin). March 1975 (vol. 4, no. 1); November 1975 (vol. 5, no. 1); April 1976 (vol. 5, no. 3); November 1976 (vol. 6, no. 1); July 1976 (vol. 5, no. 5).

De Zavala, Adina. *History and Legends of the Alamo and Other Missions in and around San Antonio.* Edited by Richard Flores. Houston: Arte Público Press, 1996.

Directory of the University of Texas for the Long Session. Vols. for 1917–1918, 1924–1925, 1925–1926. Austin: University of Texas at Austin.

DuBois, Ellen Carol, and Vicki L. Ruiz, eds. *Unequal Sisters: A Multicultural Reader in U.S. Women's History.* New York: Routledge, 1990.

Dysart, Jane. "Mexican Women in San Antonio, 1830–1860: The Assimilation Process." *Western Historical Quarterly* 7 (October 1976): 365–375.

Eisenberg, Bonnie. "Vilma Martínez." Information sheet. National Women's History Project, n.d. AWC.

Esparza, Reynaldo J. "Esparza, Enrique." *New Handbook of Texas,* 2:893.

Everett, Donald. *San Antonio: The Flavor of Its Past.* San Antonio: Trinity University Press, 1975.

Fauver, Sherri. "Hardship, Pride, and Success." *Narratives: Stories of U.S. Latinos and Latinas and World War II* (University of Texas at Austin) 1, no. 2 (spring 2000): 5–6.

"First Ladies: Texas Women in Music." Program from the symposium "Texas Women in Music at Dougherty Center," held July 16, 2000. *Arriba,* July 14–27, 2000, p. 3. AWC.

Flachmeier, Jeanette. *Pioneer Austin Notables.* Vol. 2. Austin: privately printed, 1980.

Flores, María Eva. "Las Hermanas." *New Handbook of Texas,* 4:89–90.

Flores, Richard R. "Mexicans, Modernity, and Martyrs of the Alamo." *Reflexiones: New Directions in Mexican American Studies* (University of Texas at Austin) 1998: 3–4.

Flor y Canto Committee, ed. *Flor y Canto IV and V.* Albuquerque: Pajarito Publications and Flor y Canto Committee, 1980.

Foley, Douglas Earl, et al. *From Peones to Politicos: Class and Ethnicity in a South Texas Town, 1900 to 1987.* Austin: University of Texas Press, 1988.

Foley, Neil. *The White Scourge: Mexicans, Blacks, and Poor Whites in Texas Cotton Culture.* Berkeley: University of California Press, 1997.

Foster, William C. *Spanish Expeditions into Texas, 1689–1768.* Austin: University of Texas Press, 1995.

Fuerza Unida, Women and Workers United in Social Action. "Actions." www.fuerzaunida.org.actions/htm (May 4, 2002).

Gamio, Manuel. "Sra. Flores de Andrade." In *The Life Story of the Mexican Immigrant.* 1931. Reprint, New York: Dover Publications, 1971.

García, Alma M. "The Development of Chicana Feminist Discourse, 1970–1980." In *Unequal Sisters: A Multicultural Reader in U.S. Women's History,* edited by Ellen C. DuBois and Vicki L. Ruiz, pp. 418–431. New York: Routledge, 1990.

———, ed. *Chicana Feminist Thought: The Basic Historical Writings.* New York: Routledge, 1997.

García, Clotilde P. "Garza Falcón, María Gertrudis de la." *New Handbook of Texas,* 3:111.

———. "Hinojosa de Ballí, Rosa María." *New Handbook of Texas,* 3:629.

García, Ignacio M. *Chicanismo: The Forging of a Militant Ethos among Mexican Americans.* Tucson: University of Arizona Press, 1997.

————. *United We Win: The Rise and Fall of La Raza Unida Party*. Tucson: Mexican American Studies and Research Center, University of Arizona, 1989.

————. *Viva Kennedy: Mexican Americans in Search of Camelot*. College Station: Texas A&M University Press, 2000.

García, María-Cristina. "Agents of Americanization: Rusk Settlement and the Houston Mexicano Community, 1907–1950." In *Mexican Americans in Texas History*, edited by Emilio Zamora et al., pp. 121–137. Austin: Texas State Historical Association, 2000.

————. "Club Terpsicore." *New Handbook of Texas*, 2:168.

————. "Comité Patriótico Mexicano." *New Handbook of Texas*, 2:249.

————. "González Amezcua, Consuelo." *New Handbook of Texas*, 3:235–236.

————. "Liga Femenil Mexicanista." *New Handbook of Texas*, 4:194.

————. "Mexía de Reygades, Ynés." *New Handbook of Texas*, 4:652–653.

————. "Morales, Felix Hessbrook." *New Handbook of Texas*, 4:828–829.

————. "Mujeres Artistas del Suroeste." *New Handbook of Texas*, 4:878.

————. "Reyna, María Torres." *New Handbook of Texas*, 5:554–555.

García, Mario T. *Desert Immigrants: The Mexicans of El Paso, 1880–1920*. New Haven: Yale University Press, 1981.

————. *The Making of a Mexican-American Mayor: Raymond L. Telles of El Paso*. El Paso: Texas Western Press, 1998.

García, Raúl. "Mexican American Cultural Center." *New Handbook of Texas*, 4:654.

Garza, Alicia A. "Convent of the Incarnate Word and Blessed Sacrament." *New Handbook of Texas*, 2:296.

————. "Treviño Circle T Ranch." *New Handbook of Texas*, 6:562–563.

————. "Young, Salomé Ballí." *New Handbook of Texas*, 6:1128.

Garza, Carmen Lomas. *Pedacito de mi corazón*. Austin: Laguna Gloria Art Museum, 1991.

Garza, Hedda. *Latinas: Hispanic Women in the United States*. Chicago: Franklin Watts, 1994.

Garza-Falcón, Leticia M. *Gente Decente: A Borderlands Response to the Rhetoric of Dominance*. Austin: University of Texas Press, 1998.

Gibson, Charles. *The Aztecs under Spanish Rule*. Stanford, Calif.: Stanford University Press, 1964.

Gilbert, Minnie. "Texas's First Cattle Queen." In *Roots by the River*, by Valley By-Liners. Book 2 of Valley By-Liners trilogy. Mission, Tex.: Border Kingdom Press, 1978, pp. 15–24.

Glasscock, Martin Bryan. "Rancho Santa María." *New Handbook of Texas*, 5:435.

"Gloria Yzaguirre Stephen." Obituary. *Austin American-Statesman*, July 11, 2001.

Gómez, Marsha. "Woman of the Earth: Art and Activism on Sacred Lands." *La Voz de Esperanza,* November 1998, pp. 5−6.

Gómez-Quiñones, Juan. *Sembradores, Ricardo Flores Magón y El Partido Liberal Mexicano: A Eulogy and Critique.* Los Angeles: Aztlan Publications, 1973.

Gonzáles, Jovita. "America Invades the Border Towns." *Southwest Review* 15 (summer 1930): 469−477.

———. *Dew on the Thorn.* Edited by José E. Limón. Houston: Arte Público Press, 1997.

———. "Social Life in Cameron, Starr, and Zapata Counties." Master's thesis, University of Texas at Austin, 1930.

Gonzáles, Jovita, and Eve Raleigh. *Caballero: A Historical Novel.* Edited by José Limón and María Cotera. College Station: Texas A&M University Press, 1996.

González, Gabriela. "Cultural Redemption and Female Benevolence: The Class and Gender Ideologies of Carolina Malpica de Munguía." Paper presented at Berkshire Conference of Women Historians, Rochester, N.Y., June 1999. AWC.

González, Gilbert G. *Mexican Consuls and Labor Organizing: Imperial Politics in the American Southwest.* Austin: University of Texas Press, 1999.

Goodyear, Russell H. "Caracol." *New Handbook of Texas,* 1:970.

Gould, Florence C., and Patricia N. Pando. *Claiming Their Land: Women Homesteaders in Texas.* El Paso: Texas Western Press, 1991.

Gould, Lewis. "Progressive Era." *New Handbook of Texas,* 5:347−355.

Graham, Joe. "Curanderismo." *New Handbook of Texas,* 2:452.

———. *El Rancho in South Texas: Continuity and Change from 1750.* Kingsville: John E. Conner Museum and University of North Texas Press, 1994.

———. "Folk Medicine." *New Handbook of Texas,* 2:1061−1063.

———. *Hecho en Tejas: Texas-Mexican Folk Arts and Crafts.* Denton: University of North Texas Press, 1991.

Green, Rena Maverick, ed. *Memoirs of Mary A. Maverick.* San Antonio: Alamo Press, 1921.

Grider, Sylvia Ann, and Lou Halsell Rodenberger, eds. *Texas Women Writers: A Tradition of Their Own.* College Station: Texas A&M University Press, 1997.

Grimm, Agnes G. "Pérez, Pablo." *New Handbook of Texas,* 5:150.

Guerra, Manuel. "Alberca de Arriba Ranch." *New Handbook of Texas,* 1:93−94.

Guide to Spanish and Mexican Land Grants in South Texas. Austin: Texas General Land Office, 1999.

Guthrie, Keith. "Presbyterian School for Mexican Girls." *New Handbook of Texas,* 5:329.

Gutiérrez, José Ángel. *The Making of a Chicano Militant: Lessons from Cristal.* Madison: University of Wisconsin Press, 1998.

Gutiérrez, Margo, and Matt S. Meier. "Vilma Socorro Martínez." In *Encyclopedia of the Mexican American Civil Rights Movement,* edited by Matt S. Meier and Margo Gutiérrez. Westport, Conn.: Greenwood Press, 2000.

———, eds. *Encyclopedia of the Mexican American Civil Rights Movement.* Westport, Conn.: Greenwood Press, 2000.

Guzmán, Jane Bock. "Dallas Barrio Women of Power." Master's thesis, University of North Texas, 1992.

———. "María Luna." *Legacies: A History Journal for Dallas and North Central Texas,* fall 2001, pp. 17–18.

Hammett, A. B. J. *The Empresario Don Martín de León: The Richest Man in Texas.* Reprint, Waco: Texian Press, 1973.

Hauschild, Henry J. *A Musical Chronicle from the Historical Scrapbooks of Henry J. Hauschild.* Victoria: privately printed, 1999.

Hebert, Rachel Bluntzer. *The Forgotten Colony: San Patricio de Hibernia.* Burnet: Eakin Press, 1981.

———. *Shadows on the Nueces: The Saga of Chipita Rodríguez.* Atlanta, Ga.: Emory University, Banner Press, 1942.

Henson, Margaret Swett. "Hispanic Texas, 1519–1836." In *Texas: A Sesquicentennial Celebration,* edited by Donald W. Whisenhunt. Austin: Eakin Press, 1984.

Hickerson, Nancy P. "Jumano Indians." *New Handbook of Texas,* 3:1016–1018.

Hinojosa, Gilberto M. *A Borderlands Town in Transition: Laredo, 1755–1870.* College Station: Texas A&M University Press, 1983.

Hispanic Women's Network of Texas Directory. Austin: Hispanic Women's Network of Texas, 1994.

Holden, Frances Mayhugh. "Urrea, Teresa." *New Handbook of Texas,* 6:678–679.

Hughes, Diane L. "Angelina." *New Handbook of Texas,* 1:179–180.

Jackson, Jack. *Los Mesteños: Spanish Ranching in Texas, 1721–1821.* College Station: Texas A&M University Press, 1986.

Jasper, Pat, and Kay Turner. *Art among Us/Arte entre nosotros: Mexican American Folk Art of San Antonio, San Antonio Museum of Art, 27 April–15 June 1986.* Catalog. Project of the San Antonio Museum of Art and the Guadalupe Cultural Arts Center in cooperation with Texas Folklife Resources. San Antonio: San Antonio Museum of Art, 1986.

John, Elizabeth A. H. *Storms Brewed in Other Men's Worlds: The Confrontation of Indians, Spanish, and French in the Southwest, 1540–1795.* College Station: Texas A&M University Press, 1975.

Jones, Nancy Baker. "Idar, Jovita." *New Handbook of Texas,* 3:814–815.

———. "Villegas de Magnón, Leonor." *New Handbook of Texas,* 6:753–754.

Jones, Nancy Baker, and Debbie Mauldin Cottrell. *Women and Texas History: An Archival Bibliography.* Austin: Texas State Historical Association, 1990.

Jones, Nancy Baker, and Ruthe Winegarten. *Capitol Women: Texas Female Legislators, 1923–1999.* Austin: University of Texas Press, 2000.

———. *"Getting Where We've Got to Be": Women in the Texas Legislature, 1923–1999.* Video. Produced by the Center for the Study of Women and Gender, University of Texas at San Antonio. Distributed by University of Texas Press, 2000.

Juárez, José Roberto. "Texas Association of Chicanos in Higher Education." *New Handbook of Texas,* 6:289.

Juárez, Tina. *Call No Man Master.* Houston: Arte Público Press, 1995.

———. *South Wind Come.* Houston: Arte Público Press, 1998.

Kanellos, Nicolas. *A History of Hispanic Theatre in the United States: Origins to 1940.* Austin: University of Texas Press, 1990.

Keeton, W. Page. *"Sweatt v. Painter." New Handbook of Texas,* 6:168–169.

Kennelly, Sister Josephine, C.C.V.I. "Sisters of Charity of the Incarnate Word, San Antonio." *New Handbook of Texas,* 5:1065.

Kleiner, Diana J. "Colegio Altamirano." *New Handbook of Texas,* 2:198.

———. "Magnolia Park." *New Handbook of Texas,* 4:461–462.

Kreneck, Thomas H. *Del Pueblo: A Pictorial History of Houston's Hispanic Community.* Houston: Houston International University, 1989.

———. "Little School of the 400." *New Handbook of Texas,* 4:237–238.

Lack, Paul. *The Texas Revolutionary Experience: A Political and Social History, 1835–1836.* College Station: Texas A&M University Press, 1992.

Larralde, Carlos M. "Esparza, Francisca Reyes." *New Handbook of Texas,* 2:893.

"La Vela Prendida, Mexican-American Women's Altars: The Art of Relationship." Program for exhibition at Texas Memorial Museum, the University of Texas at Austin, November 15–December 22, 1980.

La Vere, David. *Life among the Texas Indians: The WPA Narratives.* College Station: Texas A&M University Press, 1998.

Lawhn, Juanita Luna. "Blanco, Beatriz." *New Handbook of Texas,* 1:581.

Lea, Tom. *The King Ranch.* 2 vols. Boston: Little, Brown, 1957.

Ledesma, Irene. "Unlikely Strikers: Mexican-American Women in Strike Activity in Texas, 1919–1974." Ph.D. diss., Ohio State University, 1992.

Lemée, Patricia R. "St. Denis, Manuela Sánchez Navarro de." *New Handbook of Texas,* 5:756.

Letter to Louise Langardner, Texas Women's History Project, from Matilda Rosales-McLemore, Spanish archivist, Texas General Land Office, August 7, 1980. Special Collections, Texas Woman's University.

Leutenegger, Benedict, O.F.M., trans. and ed. *Inventory of the Mission San Antonio de Valero: 1772.* Austin: Texas Historical Commission, 1977.

Leyva, Yolanda Chávez. "I Go to Fight for Social Justice: Children as Revolutionaries in the Mexican Revolution, 1910–1920." *Peace and Change,* October 1998, pp. 423–439.

Limón, José E. "El Primer Congreso Mexicanista de 1911, A Precursor to

Contemporary Chicanismo." *Aztlan: A Chicano Journal of the Social Sciences and the Arts* 5, nos. 1, 2 (1974): 85–117.

Lipscomb, Carol A. "Comanche Indians." *New Handbook of Texas,* 2:242–245.

———. "Karankawa Indians." *New Handbook of Texas,* 3:1031–1033.

López, Jovita. "Jovita Idar de Juárez." Typescript. Emma Tenayuca Papers, Woman's Collection, Texas Woman's University.

McDaniel, Ruel. "The Day They Hanged Chipita [Rodríguez]." *Texas Parade,* September 1962.

McIlvain, Myra Hargrave. *Shadows on the Land: An Anthology of Texas Historical Marker Stories.* Austin: Texas Historical Commission, 1984.

McKnight, Joseph W. "Community Property Law." *New Handbook of Texas,* 2:252.

McLean, Malcolm D. *Papers Concerning Robertson's Colony in Texas.* Vols. 4–12. Arlington: University of Texas at Arlington Press, 1977–1986.

McMillan, Nora E. Ríos. "La Prensa." *New Handbook of Texas,* 4:73–74.

———. "Lozano, Ignacio E." *New Handbook of Texas,* 4:318.

McNeeley, John E. "Holding Institute." *New Handbook of Texas,* 3:660–661.

Macías, Reynaldo F., Raymond E. Castro, and Yolanda Rodríguez-Ingle. "Looking for Needles in a Haystack: Hispanics in the Teaching Profession." In *Education of Hispanics in the United States: Politics, Policies, and Outcomes,* vol. 16, edited by Abbas Tashakkori and Salvador Hector Ochoa. New York: AMS Press, 1999.

"'Mama' Ninfa Introduced Fajitas outside the Southwest." *Austin American-Statesman,* June 19, 2001.

Marquez, Raquel. "Chicana Labor Activists: The Case of Fuerza Unida." Master's thesis, University of Texas at Austin, 1995.

Marsh, Gloria Candelaria. "Moya, Juan." *New Handbook of Texas,* 4:873–874.

Matovina, Timothy M. "New Frontiers of Guadalupanismo." *Journal of Hispanic/Latino Theology* 5, no. 1 (August 1997): 20–36.

———. "Our Lady of Guadalupe Celebrations in San Antonio, Texas, 1840–41." *Journal of Hispanic/Latino Theology* 1, no. 1 (November 1993): 77–96.

———. *Tejano Religion and Ethnicity: San Antonio, 1821–1860.* Austin: University of Texas Press, 1995.

Menafree, Seldon, and Orin C. Cassmore. *The Pecan Shellers of San Antonio: The Problems of Underpaid and Unemployed Mexican Labor.* Federal Works Agency, Works Projects Administration. Washington, D.C.: U.S. Government Printing Office, 1941.

Mendoza, Louis Gerard. *Historia: The Literary Making of Chicana & Chicano History.* College Station: Texas A&M University Press, 2001.

Mendoza, Lydia. *Lydia Mendoza: A Family Autobiography.* Compiled and introduced by Chris Strachwitz with James Nicolopulos. Houston: Arte Público Press, 1993.

Mesa-Bains, Amalia. "Chicano Chronicle and Cosmology: The Works of Carmen Lomas Garza." In Carmen Lomas Garza, *Pedacito de Mi Corazón.* Austin: Laguna Gloria Art Museum, 1991.

Milligan, Bryce. "Ever Radical: A Survey of Tejana Writers." In *Texas Women Writers: A Tradition of Their Own,* edited by Sylvia Ann Grider and Lou Halsell Rodenberger, pp. 207–246. College Station: Texas A&M University Press, 1997.

Milligan, Bryce, Mary Guerrero Milligan, and Ángela de Hoyos, eds. *¡Floricanto Sí! A Collection of Latina Poetry.* New York: Penguin Books, 1998.

Mirandé, Alfredo, and Evangelina Enríquez. *La Chicana: The Mexican-American Woman.* Chicago: University of Chicago Press, 1979.

Monday, Jane Clements, and Betty Bailey Colley. *Voices from the Wild Horse Desert: The Vaquero Families of the King and Kenedy Ranches.* Austin: University of Texas Press, 1997.

Montejano, David. *Anglos and Mexicans in the Making of Texas, 1836–1986.* Austin: University of Texas Press, 1987.

Montemayor, Aurelio M. "Colegio Jacinto Trevino." *New Handbook of Texas,* 3:198.

Mora, Magdalena, and Adelaida R. Del Castillo, eds. *Mexican Women in the United States: Struggles Past and Present.* Los Angeles: Chicano Studies Research Center Publications, University of California, 1980.

Morthland, John. "Elida Reyna." *Texas Monthly,* September 2000, pp. 152–153.

Munson, Sammye. *Our Tejano Heroes: Outstanding Mexican-Americans in Texas.* Austin: Panda Books, 1989.

———. *Today's Tejano Heroes.* Austin: Eakin Press, 2000.

National Association of Latino Elected and Appointed Officials Educational Fund. *National Directory of Latino Elected Officials.* Vols. for 1996, 1997, 1999, 2000. Washington, D.C.: NALEO Educational Fund.

———. *National Roster of Hispanic Elected Officials.* 1984–1994. Washington, D.C.: NALEO Educational Fund.

Navarro, Armando. *Mexican American Youth Organization: Avant-Garde of the Chicano Movement in Texas.* Austin: University of Texas Press, 1995.

Newcomb, W. W., Jr. *The Indians of Texas.* Austin: University of Texas Press, 1961.

Newton, Lewis W. "Aguayo, Marqués de San Miguel de." *New Handbook of Texas,* 1:71.

Ochoa, Rubén E. "Loma Vista." *New Handbook of Texas,* 4:266.

Oldera, J. Montiel. *Primer anuario de los habitantes hispano-americanos de Texas (First Yearbook of the Latin American Population of Texas).* N.p., 1939.

Olmsted, Frederick Law. *Journey through Texas.* Austin: Von Boeckmann-Jones Press, 1962.

Olsson, Karen. "The Border According to Guerra." *Texas Observer,* February 18, 2000, pp. 12–14, 27.

Orozco, Cynthia E. "Barnard, Juana Josefina Cavasos." *New Handbook of Texas,* 1:385.

———. "Beyond Machismo, La Familia, and Ladies Auxiliaries: A Historiography of Mexican-Origin Women's Participation in Voluntary Associations and Politics in the United States." In *Renato Rosaldo Lecture Series Monograph,* ed. Thomas Gelsinon, vol. 10, pp. 37–77. Tucson: Mexican American Studies and Research Center, University of Arizona, 1994.

———. "Chicana Rights Project." *New Handbook of Texas,* 2:69.

———. "Círculo Cultural Isabel la Católica." *New Handbook of Texas,* 2:111–112.

———. "Clínica de la Beneficencia Mexicana." *New Handbook of Texas,* 2:162–163.

———. "Comisión Honorífica Mexicana." *New Handbook of Texas,* 2:248–249.

———. "Cortez Lira, Gregorio." *New Handbook of Texas,* 2:342–343.

———. "*Del Rio ISD* v. *Salvatierra.*" *New Handbook of Texas,* 2:578–579.

———. "Escajeda, Josefina." *New Handbook of Texas,* 2:887.

———. "García, Eva Carrillo de." *New Handbook of Texas,* 3:83–84.

———. "Garza, Bernardo F." *New Handbook of Texas,* 3:105.

———. "Garza, José Antonio de la." *New Handbook of Texas,* 3:107.

———. "Guerra, Fermina." *New Handbook of Texas,* 3:368.

———. "Hernández, María L. de." *New Handbook of Texas,* 3:572–573.

———. "Hispanic Women's Network of Texas." *New Handbook of Texas,* 3:631.

———. "Idar, Clemente Nicasio." *New Handbook of Texas,* 3:813–814.

———. "Kenedy, Petra Vela de Vidal." *New Handbook of Texas,* 3:1065.

———. "Ladies LULAC." *New Handbook of Texas,* 4:1–2.

———. "League of United Latin American Citizens." *New Handbook of Texas,* 4:129–131.

———. "Lozano, Alicia Guadalupe Elizondo de." *New Handbook of Texas,* 4:318.

———. "Machuca, Esther Nieto." *New Handbook of Texas,* 4:410.

———. "Mendez, Consuelo Herrera." *New Handbook of Texas,* 4:618.

———. "Mexican American Democrats." *New Handbook of Texas,* 4:654–655.

———. "Mexican American Republicans of Texas." *New Handbook of Texas,* 4:663–664.

———. "Mexican-American Women." *New Handbook of Texas,* 4:680–682.

———. "Montemayor, Alice Dickerson." *New Handbook of Texas,* 4:798.

———. "Mujeres Por La Raza." *New Handbook of Texas,* 4:878–879.

———. "Munguía, Carolina Malpica." *New Handbook of Texas,* 4:887.

———. "O'Shea, María Elena Zamora." *New Handbook of Texas,* 4:1176–1177.

————. "Quintanilla Pérez, Selena." *New Handbook of Texas,* 5:392–393.

————. "Ramírez, Emilia Wilhelmina Schunior." *New Handbook of Texas,* 5:423–424.

————. "Rodríguez de Gonzáles, Elvira." *New Handbook of Texas,* 5:657–658.

————. "Sada, María G." *New Handbook of Texas,* 5:750–751.

————. "Salazar de Esparza, Ana." *New Handbook of Texas,* 5:774–775.

————. "Spanish-Speaking PTA." *New Handbook of Texas,* 6:13–14.

Orozco, Cynthia E., and Teresa Palomo Acosta. "González de Mireles, Jovita." *New Handbook of Texas,* 3:236–237.

Ortego y Gasca, Philip, and Arnoldo De León, eds. *The Tejano Yearbook: 1519–1978.* San Antonio: Caravel Press, 1978.

Paredes, Américo. *With His Pistol in His Hand: A Border Ballad and Its Hero.* Austin: University of Texas Press, 1958.

Parker, Edith Olbrich. "Cassiano, María Gertrudis Pérez Cordero." In *Women in Early Texas,* edited by Evelyn M. Carrington. Austin: Jenkins, 1975.

Pérez, Emma. *The Decolonial Imaginary: Writing Chicanas into History.* Bloomington: Indiana University Press, 1999.

Perlin, Doris E. *Eight Bright Candles: Courageous Women of Mexico.* Plano, Tex.: Woodware Publishing, Republic of Texas Press, 1995.

Perttula, Timothy K. *The Caddo Nation: Archaeological and Ethnohistoric Perspectives.* Austin: University of Texas Press, 1992.

Petty Jr., J. W., ed. *Victor Rose's "History of Victoria."* Rev. ed. Victoria, Tex.: Book Mart, 1961.

Pletcher, David M. "Treaty of Guadalupe Hidalgo." *New Handbook of Texas,* 6:558–559.

Poyo, Gerald E., ed. *Tejano Journey, 1770–1850.* Austin: University of Texas Press, 1996.

Poyo, Gerald E., and Gilberto M. Hinojosa, eds. *Tejano Origins in Eighteenth-Century San Antonio.* Austin: University of Texas Press, 1991.

Prabhu, Barbara Williams, Katie Sherrod, and Reed K. Bilz. *Outstanding Women of Fort Worth: Hall of Fame, 1987–1995.* Fort Worth: Fort Worth Commission on Women, 1995.

Procter, Ben H. "Great Depression." *New Handbook of Texas,* 3:301–303.

Pycior, Julie Leininger. "Hijos de Texas." *New Handbook of Texas,* 3:608–609.

————. "La Raza Organizes: Mexican American Life in San Antonio, 1915–1930, as Reflected in Mutualista Activities." Ph.D. dissertation, University of Notre Dame, 1979.

————. *LBJ and Mexican Americans: The Paradox of Power.* Austin: University of Texas Press, 1997.

————. "Mexican-American Organizations." *New Handbook of Texas,* 4:660–662.

————. *"Sociedades Mutualistas." New Handbook of Texas,* 5:1132–1133.

Quién es cada cual en la población hispano-americana del estado de Texas (Who's Who in the Latin American Population of Texas). N.p., 1939. Tenayuca Collection, Texas Woman's University.

Quirarte, Jacinto. *Mexican American Artists.* Austin: University of Texas Press, 1973.

Quiroga, Miguel González. "Mexicanos in Texas during the Civil War." In *Mexican Americans in Texas History,* edited by Emilio Zamora Jr., Cynthia Orozco, and Rodolfo Rocha, pp. 51–62. Austin: Texas State Historical Association, 2000.

Raat, W. Dirk. *Revoltosos: Mexico's Rebels in the United States, 1903–1923.* College Station: Texas A&M University Press, 1981.

Ragsdale, Crystal Sasse. "Alsbury, Juana Gertrudis Navarro." *New Handbook of Texas,* 1:131–132.

———. "Mathilda Doebbler Gruen Wagner." *The Golden Free Land.* Austin: Landmark Press, 1976.

———. *Women and Children of the Alamo.* Austin: State House Press, 1994.

Ramírez, Elizabeth C. "Carlos Villalongín Dramatic Company." *New Handbook of Texas,* 1:978.

———. *Footlights across the Border: A History of Spanish-Language Professional Theatre on the Texas Stage.* New York: Peter Lang Publishing, 1990.

———. "Hernández, Concepción." *New Handbook of Texas,* 3:572.

———. "Mexican-American Theater." *New Handbook of Texas,* 4:679–680.

———. "Solsona Dramatic Company." *New Handbook of Texas,* 5:1143.

Ramírez, Sara Estela. "Surge." In Inés Hernández, "Sara Estela Ramírez: Sembradora." *Legacy* 6:1 (1989):22.

Ramos, Henry A. J. *The American GI Forum: In Pursuit of the Dream, 1948–1983.* Houston: Arte Público Press, 1998.

Ramsdell, Charles. *San Antonio: A Historical and Pictorial Guide.* Revised by Carmen Perry. Austin: University of Texas Press, 1956; rev. ed., 1976.

Red, Mrs. George Plunkett. *The Medicine Man in Texas.* Houston: Standard Printing, 1930.

Rhor, Monica. "Lydia Camarillo." *Latina,* September 2000, p. 106.

Rice, Gwendolyn. "Little Mexico and the Barrios of Dallas." In *Dallas Reconsidered: Essays in Local History,* edited by Michael V. Hazel, pp. 158–168. Dallas: Three Forks Press, 1995.

Ricklis, Robert A. *The Karankawa Indians of Texas: An Ecological Study of Cultural Tradition and Change.* Austin: University of Texas Press, 1996.

Robedeau, Barbara. "Goodman, Petronila María Pereida." *New Handbook of Texas,* 3:239–240.

Robles, Bárbara J. "Latina Entrepreneurial Activity in the 1990s: Lessons for the Twenty-First Century." Photocopy. AWC.

————. "Latinas in the Academy: Profiling Current and Future Scholars." *Reflexiones: New Directions in Mexican American Studies* (University of Texas at Austin) 1999: 91–113. Richard R. Flores, issue ed.

Rodríguez, Jeanette. *Our Lady of Guadalupe: Faith and Empowerment among Mexican-American Women.* Austin: University of Texas Press, 1995.

Rodríguez, Rodolfo. "Bilingual Education." *New Handbook of Texas,* 1:542–543.

Roell, Craig H. "Benavides, Plácido." *New Handbook of Texas,* 1:484.

————. "De León, Martín." *New Handbook of Texas,* 2:571.

————. "De León's Colony." *New Handbook of Texas,* 2:573–574.

Rogers, Lisa Waller. *Angel of the Alamo: A True Story of Texas.* Austin: W. S. Benson, ca. 2000.

Rogers, Mary Beth. *Cold Anger: A Story of Faith and Power Politics.* Denton: University of North Texas Press, 1990.

Romero, Yolanda García. "From Rebels to Immigrants to Chicanas: Hispanic Women in Lubbock County." Master's thesis, Texas Tech University, 1986.

Rosales, Rodolfo. *The Illusion of Inclusion: The Untold Political Story of San Antonio.* Austin: University of Texas Press, 2000.

Rose, Victor. *History of Victoria.* Laredo, 1883; reprint, Victoria, Tex.: Book Mart, 1961.

Ross, John R. "Lynching." *New Handbook of Texas,* 4:347.

Rubio, Abel. *Stolen Heritage: A Mexican-American's Rediscovery of His Family's Lost Land Grant.* Austin: Eakin Press, 1986; paperback ed., 1998.

Ruiz, Vicki. *From out of the Shadows: Mexican Women in Twentieth-Century America.* New York: Oxford University Press, 1998.

Salas, Elizabeth. *Soldaderas in the Mexican Military: Myth and History.* Austin: University of Texas Press, 1990.

Saldívar, Ramón. "Texas-Mexican Fiction." *New Handbook of Texas,* 6:361.

San Antonio Bicentennial Heritage Committee. *San Antonio in the Eighteenth Century.* San Antonio: The Committee, 1976.

"San Antonio COPS Presidents." In *25th Anniversary of San Antonio Communities Organized for Public Service, 1974–1999.* Pamphlet. San Antonio: COPS, 1999. AWC.

Sánchez, George. "Go after the Women." In *Unequal Sisters: A Multicultural Reader in U.S. Women's History,* edited by Ellen C. DuBois and Vicki L. Ruiz, pp. 250–263. New York: Routledge, 1990.

Sanders, Freddie Milam. "Elena Farías Barrera." In Rio Writers (Texas), *One Hundred Women of the Rio Grande Valley of Texas,* p. 4. Austin: Eakin Press, 1983.

San Francisco Bay Area Farah Strike Support Committee. *Chicanas Strike at Farah.* Pamphlet. N.p.: San Francisco Bay Area Farah Strike Support Committee, 1972.

San Miguel Jr., Guadalupe. *Brown, Not White: School Integration and the Chicano Movement in Houston.* College Station: Texas A&M University Press, 2001.

———. *Let All of Them Take Heed: Mexican Americans and the Campaign for Educational Equality in Texas, 1910–1981.* Mexican American Monographs, no. 11. Austin: University of Texas Press, 1987.

———. "Mexican Americans and Education." *New Handbook of Texas,* 4:671–672.

"Santa Barraza: A MexicTejana from Nepantla." Program notes for exhibition at Mexic-Arte Museum, Austin, Texas, January 28–April 15, 2000.

Saxon, Gerald D. "Cuellar, Adelaida." *New Handbook of Texas,* 2:432.

Schilz, Thomas F. "Battle of Palo Duro Canyon." *New Handbook of Texas,* 5:28.

Schoen, Harold. "The Free Negro in the Republic of Texas." Part 1. *Southwestern Historical Quarterly* 39, no. 4 (April 1936); 40, nos. 1–4 (July, October 1936, January, April 1937, 26–34, 85–113, 169–199, 267–289).

Scott, Janelle. "Patricia de la Garza de León." January 8, 1982. Photocopy. Special Collections, Texas Woman's University Library.

Seaholm, Meagan. "Midwifery." *New Handbook of Texas,* 4:714.

Sears, Edward S. "The Low Down on Jim Bowie." In *From Hell to Breakfast,* edited by Mody Boatright, p. 176. Dallas: Southern Methodist University Press for the Texas Folklore Society, 1934.

Sharpe, Patricia. "Ninfa Laurenzo." *Texas Monthly,* August 2001, p. 40.

Sharpless, Rebecca. *Fertile Ground, Narrow Choices: Women on Texas Cotton Farms, 1900–1940.* Chapel Hill: University of North Carolina Press, 1999.

Sidimé, Aïssatou. "Women Activists Head to S. Africa." *San Antonio Express-News,* August 25, 2001.

Simons, Helen, and Cathryn A. Hoyt, eds. *A Guide to Hispanic Texas.* Austin: University of Texas Press, 1996.

Singleton, Kate. "Landmarks: Fourteen Significant Sites in Dallas County." *Legacies: A History Journal for Dallas and North Central Texas* 8, no. 2 (fall 1996): 50.

Smith, Anita Torres. "Praxedis Mata Torres: The First Mexican-American Teacher in the Public Schools in Uvalde County, Texas." *Journal of Big Bend Studies* 3 (January 1991): 157–179.

Smith, Cheryl. "A Veteran's True Advocate." *Narrative Stories of U.S. Latinos and Latinas and World War II* 1, no. 1 (fall 1999): 3–4. Department of Journalism, University of Texas at Austin.

Smith, Melinda. "Minority Women Attorneys Share Their Thoughts and Experiences." *Texas Bar Journal,* October 1990, pp. 1051–1053.

Smith, Pamela S., and Elizabeth C. Ramírez. "Escalona Pérez, Beatriz." *New Handbook of Texas,* 2:888.

Smylie, Vernon. *A Noose for Chipita [Rodríguez].* Corpus Christi: Texas Syndicate Press, 1970.

Solórzano, Rosalía. "Valdes Villalva, María Guillermina." *New Handbook of Texas,* 6:688.

Sonnichsen, C. I. "Salt War of San Elizario." *New Handbook of Texas,* 5:783.

Stewart, Paula. "De León, Patricia de la Garza." *New Handbook of Texas,* 2:571–572.

Stone, Rachel. "Former Clinton Staffer Joins UT Faculty." *Daily Texan,* August 17, 2001, pp. 1–2.

Stott, Kelly M. "The Intent and Effect of the [1848] Texas Married Women's Separate Property Law." Paper presented at Texas State Historical Association annual meeting, Dallas, March 4, 1999. AWC.

Stuntz, Jean A. "The Persistence of Castillian Law in Frontier Texas." Master's thesis, University of North Texas, 1996.

———. "Spanish Laws for Texas Women: The Development of Marital Property Laws to 1850." *Southwestern Historical Quarterly* 104, no. 4 (April 2001): 543–559.

Sullivan, Mary L., and Bertha Blair. *Women in Texas Industries: Hours, Wages, Working Conditions, and Home Work. Bulletin of the Women's Bureau.* No. 126. Washington, D.C.: U.S. Government Printing Office, 1936.

Supplee, Joan E. "San Xavier Missions." *New Handbook of Texas,* 5:893–894.

Tarín, Randell G. "Leal Goraz, Juan." *New Handbook of Texas,* 4:133–134.

Tejano Roots: The Women (1946–1964). El Cerrito, Calif.: Arhoolie Records, 1991.

Texas A&M University Press. "Description of *El Mesquite: A Story of the Early Spanish Settlements between the Nueces and the Rio Grande.*" http://www.tamu.edu/upress/BOOKS/2000/oshea.htm (March 8, 2001).

Texas Education Agency. "Teacher Profiles by Gender, Ethnicity, and Highest Degree Attained." http://www.tea.state.us/perfreport/pocked/2000/panel8.html (February 15, 2001).

Texas General Land Office. *Guide to Spanish and Mexican Land Grants in South Texas.* Austin: Texas General Land Office, 1988.

Texas Higher Education Coordinating Board. *Degrees Awarded by Ethnic Origin, Gender: Texas Public Universities, FY 1997.* Austin, 1997.

———. *Final Report: The Advisory Committee on Women and Minority Faculty and Professional Staff.* Austin, January 1997.

———. *Medical Degrees Conferred by Ethnicity and Gender, Selected Texas Medical Schools, Fiscal Year 1998–99.* Austin, 1999.

———. *Tenured Faculty Headcount by Ethnic Origin, Gender: Texas Public Universities, Fall 1997.* Austin, 1997.

Texas Mother Committee. *Worthy Mothers of Texas, 1776–1976.* Belton, Texas: Stillhouse, Hollow Publishers, 1976.

Thompson, Jerry. "Benavides, Santos." *New Handbook of Texas,* 1:485.

———. "Cortina, Juan Nepomuceno." *New Handbook of Texas,* 2:343–344.

———. *Juan Cortina and the Texas-Mexico Frontier, 1858–1877.* El Paso: Texas Western Press, 1994.

———. *A Wild and Vivid Land: An Illustrated History of the South Texas Border.* Austin: Texas State Historical Association, 1999.

Thonhoff, Robert H. "Arredondo, Joaquín de." *New Handbook of Texas,* 1:255.

Tijerina, Andrés. *History of Mexican Americans in Lubbock County, Texas.* Lubbock: Texas Tech University Press, 1979.

———. *Tejano Empire: Life on the South Texas Ranchos.* College Station: Texas A&M University Press, 1998.

———. *Tejanos and Texas under the Mexican Flag, 1821–1836.* College Station: Texas A&M University Press, 1994.

Torres, Olga Beatriz. *Memorias de mi viaje/Recollections of My Trip.* Translated by Juanita Luna Lawhn. Albuquerque: University of New Mexico Press, 1994.

Tovar, Inés Hernández. "Sara Estela Ramirez: The Early Twentieth Century Texas-Mexican Poet." Ph.D. dissertation, University of Houston, 1984.

———, ed. *Hembra: Hermanas en movimiento brotando raíces de Aztlán.* Austin: Center for Mexican American Studies, University of Texas at Austin, 1976.

Treviño, Roberto R. "Mexican Americans and Religion." *New Handbook of Texas,* 4:672–676.

Trinidad, David. "Rebecca Flores Harrington: Life under the Hot Texas Sun." *Tejas,* spring 1995, p. 37.

Turner, Kay Frances. "Mexican American Women's Home Altars: The Art of Relationship." Ph.D. dissertation, University of Texas at Austin, 1990.

Underwood, Marylyn. "The Ghost of Chipita." In *Legendary Ladies of Texas,* 2d ed., edited by Francis Edward Abernethy. Denton: University of North Texas Press, 1994.

———. "Rodríguez, Josefa." *New Handbook of Texas,* 5:654–655.

University of Texas System. *Annual Report 2000.* Austin: The System, 2000.

U.S. Bureau of the Census. Table P-2: "Race and Hispanic Origin of People by Median Income and Gender, 1947-1997." http://www.census.gov/income (June 20, 2000).

U.S. Department of Labor. Women's Bureau. *Women Workers in Texas.* Washington, D.C.: U.S. Government Printing Office, 1970.

Valenzuela, Ángela. *Subtractive Schooling: U.S.-Mexican Youth and the Politics of Caring.* Albany: State University of New York Press, 1999.

Valley By-Liners. *Roots by the River: A Story of Texas Tropical Borderlands.* Book 2 of Valley By-Liners trilogy. Mission, Tex.: Border Kingdom Press, 1978.

Vargas, Kathy. *Kathy Vargas: Photographs, 1971–2000.* San Antonio: Marion Koogler McNay Art Museum, 2000.

Vargas, Zaragosa. "Tejana Radical: Emma Tenayuca and the San Antonio Labor Movement during the Great Depression." *Pacific Historical Review* 66 (1997): 553–580.

"Veramendi, Juan Martín de." *New Handbook of Texas,* 6:722.

Victoria Sesquicentennial Scrapbook, 1824–1974. Victoria, Tex.: Victoria Sesquicentennial, Inc., 1974.

Vielé, Teresa Griffin. *Following the Drum: A Glimpse of Frontier Life.* Lincoln: University of Nebraska Press, 1984.

Villegas de Magnón, Leonor. *The Rebel: Leonor Villegas de Magnón.* Edited by Clara Lomas. Houston: Arte Público Press, 1994.

Ward, Hortense Warner. "Ear Marks." In *From Hell to Breakfast,* edited by Mody Boatright, 106–116. Dallas: Southern Methodist University Press for the Texas Folklore Society, 1944.

Webb, Walter Prescott. *The Texas Rangers: A Century of Frontier Defense.* 2d ed. Austin: University of Texas Press, 1965.

Weber, David J. "Cart War." *New Handbook of Texas,* 1:1003.

———. *La frontera norte de Mexico, 1821–1846: El sudoeste norteamericano en su época mexicana.* Mexico: Fondo de Cultura Económica, 1988.

———. *The Spanish Frontier in North America.* New Haven: Yale University Press, 1992.

Weddle, Robert S. *San Juan Bautista: Gateway to Spanish Texas.* Austin: University of Texas Press, 1991.

West, Richard. "Our Lady of the Taco (Tula Borunda Gutiérrez)." *Texas Monthly,* January 1986, p. 198.

Wheeler, Kenneth. *To Wear a City's Crown: The Beginnings of Urban Growth in Texas, 1836–1865.* Cambridge: Harvard University Press, 1968.

Winegarten, Ruthe. *Black Texas Women: 150 Years of Trial and Triumph.* Austin: University of Texas Press, 1995.

———. *Finder's Guide to the "Texas Women: A Celebration of History" Exhibit Archives.* Denton: Texas Woman's University Press, 1984.

———. *Governor Ann Richards & Other Texas Women: From Indians to Astronauts.* 2d ed. Austin: Eakin Press, 1993.

———. *Texas Women's History Project Bibliography.* Austin: Texas Foundation for Women's Resources, 1980.

Women in Texas History 1976 Calendar. Austin: People's History in Texas, 1976.

Wright, Robert E., O.M.I. "Spanish Missions." *New Handbook of Texas,* 6: 10–13.

Yabsley, Suzanne. *Texas Quilts, Texas Women.* College Station: Texas A&M University Press, 1984.

Yates, Rachel. "UT Ends Pursuit of Hopwood Appeal." *Daily Texan,* November 28, 2001.

Zacarías, Carmen. "Biographical Sketch of Esther Díaz." Typescript, 2001. AWC.

Zamora, Emilio. Cynthia Orozco, and Rodolfo Rocha, eds. *Mexican Americans in Texas History.* Austin: Texas State Historical Association, 2000.

———. "Las Escuelitas: A Texas Mexican Search for Educational Excellence." Photocopy. Escuelitas file, Woman's Collection, Texas Woman's University.

———. "Sara Estela Ramírez: Una rosa roja en el movimiento." In *Mexican Women in the United States: Struggles Past and Present,* edited by Magdalena Mora and Adelaida del Castillo, pp. 163–169. Los Angeles: Chicano Studies Research Center Publications, University of California, 1980.

———. *The World of the Mexican Worker in Texas.* College Station: Texas A&M University Press, 1993.

Zirkel, Ray. "Zambrano, Juan José Manuel Vicente." *New Handbook of Texas,* 6:1141.

EXHIBITS

Los tejanos: Sus huellas en esta tierra (The Texas Mexicans: Their Footprints on the Land). Lupita Barrera, curator. Lyndon Baines Johnson Library and Museum, Austin, October 12, 1997 to September 8, 1998.

Texas Women: A Celebration of History. Touring exhibition, 1981–1983. Austin: Foundation for Women's Resources. On permanent display at Blagg-Huey Library, Texas Woman's University, Denton.

Index

(Note: Page numbers in italics refer to photographs and other illustrations, as well as the captions of illustrations. To find information about a specific geographic location, see the name of both the city or town and the corresponding county. All cities, towns and counties are in Texas unless otherwise indicated.)